VOLUME 579 JANUARY 2002

THE ANNALS

of The American Academy *of* Political
and Social Science

ALAN W. HESTON, *Editor*
NEIL A. WEINER, *Assistant Editor*

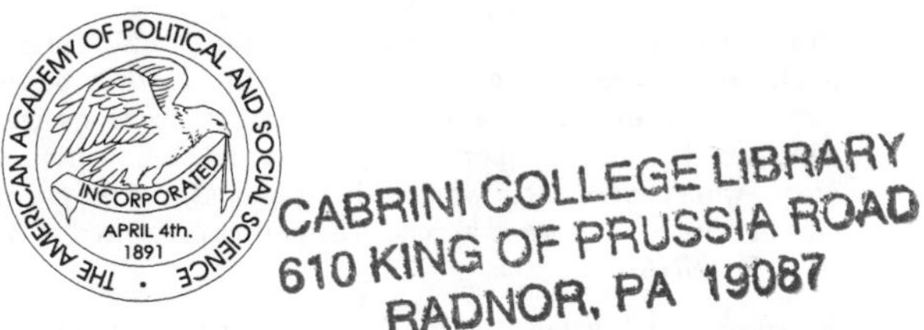

EXCHANGE-RATE REGIMES AND CAPITAL FLOWS

Special Editors of this Volume

GEORGE S. TAVLAS
Bank of Greece
MICHAEL K. ULAN
U.S. Department of State

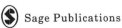

Sage Publications *THOUSAND OAKS LONDON NEW DELHI*

The American Academy of Political and Social Science
c/o Fels Center of Government, University of Pennsylvania, 3814 Walnut Street,
Philadelphia, PA 19104; (215) 746-6500; (215) 898-1202 (fax); www.1891.org

---

Origin and Purpose. The Academy was organized December 14, 1889, to promote the progress of political and social science, especially through publications and meetings. The Academy does not take sides in controverted questions, but seeks to gather and present reliable information to assist the public in forming an intelligent and accurate judgment.

Meetings. The Academy occasionally holds a meeting in the spring extending over two days.

Publications. THE ANNALS of the American Academy of Political and Social Science is the bimonthly publication of The Academy. Each issue contains articles on some prominent social or political problem, written at the invitation of the editors. Also, monographs are published from time to time, numbers of which are distributed to pertinent professional organizations. These volumes constitute important reference works on the topics with which they deal, and they are extensively cited by authorities throughout the United States and abroad. The papers presented at the meetings of The Academy are included in THE ANNALS.

Membership. Each member of The Academy receives THE ANNALS and may attend the meetings of The Academy. Membership is open only to individuals. Annual dues: $65.00 for the regular paperbound edition (clothbound, $100.00). For members outside the U.S.A., add $24.00 for shipping of your subscription. Members may also purchase single issues of THE ANNALS for $20.00 each (clothbound, $28.00).

Subscriptions. THE ANNALS of the American Academy of Political and Social Science (ISSN 0002-7162) is published six times annually—in January, March, May, July, September, and November—by Sage Publications, 2455 Teller Road, Thousand Oaks, CA 91320. Telephone: (800) 818-SAGE (7243) and (805) 499-9774; FAX/Order line: (805) 375-1700. Institutions may subscribe to THE ANNALS at the annual rate: $420.00 (clothbound, $475.00). Add $24.00 per year for subscriptions outside the U.S.A. Institutional rates for single issues: $81.00 each (clothbound, $91.00).

Periodicals postage paid at Thousand Oaks, California, and at additional mailing offices.

Single issues of THE ANNALS may be obtained by individuals who are not members of The Academy for $32.00 each (clothbound, $42.00). Single issues of THE ANNALS have proven to be excellent supplementary texts for classroom use. Direct inquiries regarding adoptions to THE ANNALS c/o Sage Publications (address below).

All correspondence concerning membership in The Academy, dues renewals, inquiries about membership status, and/or purchase of single issues of THE ANNALS should be sent to THE ANNALS c/o Sage Publications, 2455 Teller Road, Thousand Oaks, CA 91320. Telephone: (800) 818-SAGE (7243) and (805) 499-9774; FAX/Order line: (805) 375-1700. *Please note that orders under $30 must be prepaid.* Sage affiliates in London and India will assist institutional subscribers abroad with regard to orders, claims, and inquiries for both subscriptions and single issues.

Printed on recycled, acid-free paper

THE ANNALS

Editorial Office: Fels Center of Government, University of Pennsylvania, 3814 Walnut Street, Philadelphia, PA 19104-6197.

For information about membership (individuals only) and subscriptions (institutions), address:*

SAGE PUBLICATIONS
2455 Teller Road
Thousand Oaks, CA 91320

Sage Production Staff: BARBARA CORRIGAN, SCOTT SPRINGER, and ROSE TYLAK

From India and South Asia, write to:
SAGE PUBLICATIONS INDIA Pvt. Ltd
P.O. Box 4215
New Delhi 110 048
INDIA

From Europe, the Middle East, and Africa, write to:
SAGE PUBLICATIONS LTD
6 Bonhill Street
London EC2A 4PU
UNITED KINGDOM

**Please note that members of The Academy receive THE ANNALS with their membership.*

International Standard Serial Number ISSN 0002-7162
International Standard Book Number ISBN 0-7619-2601-1 (Vol. 579, 2002 paper)
International Standard Book Number ISBN 0-7619-2600-3 (Vol. 579, 2002 cloth)

Manufactured in the United States of America. First printing, January 2002.

The articles appearing in THE ANNALS are abstracted or indexed in *Academic Abstracts, Academic Search, America: History and Life, Asia Pacific Database, Book Review Index, CAB Abstracts Database, Central Asia: Abstracts & Index, Communication Abstracts, Corporate ResourceNET, Criminal Justice Abstracts, Current Citations Express, Current Contents: Social & Behavioral Sciences, e-JEL, EconLit, Expanded Academic Index, Guide to Social Science & Religion in Periodical Literature, Health Business FullTEXT, HealthSTAR FullTEXT, Historical Abstracts, International Bibliography of the Social Sciences, International Political Science Abstracts, ISI Basic Social Sciences Index, Journal of Economic Literature on CD, LEXIS-NEXIS, MasterFILE FullTEXT, Middle East: Abstracts & Index, North Africa: Abstracts & Index, PAIS International, Periodical Abstracts, Political Science Abstracts, Sage Public Administration Abstracts, Social Science Source, Social Sciences Citation Index, Social Sciences Index Full Text, Social Services Abstracts, Social Work Abstracts, Sociological Abstracts, Southeast Asia: Abstracts & Index, Standard Periodical Directory (SPD), TOPICsearch, Wilson OmniFile V,* and *Wilson Social Sciences Index/Abstracts*, and are available on microfilm from University Microfilms, Ann Arbor, Michigan.

Information about membership rates, institutional subscriptions, and back issue prices may be found on the facing page.

Advertising. Current rates and specifications may be obtained by writing to THE ANNALS Advertising and Promotion Manager at the Thousand Oaks office (address above).

Claims. Claims for undelivered copies must be made no later than six months following month of publication. The publisher will supply missing copies when losses have been sustained in transit and when the reserve stock will permit.

Change of Address. Six weeks' advance notice must be given when notifying of change of address to ensure proper identification. Please specify name of journal. **POSTMASTER:** Send address changes to: THE ANNALS of the American Academy of Political and Social Science, c/o Sage Publications, 2455 Teller Road, Thousand Oaks, CA 91320.

THE ANNALS

of The American Academy *of* Political
and Social Science

FORTHCOMING

TRANSITION TO ADULTHOOD
Special Editor: Frank Furstenburg
Volume 580 March 2002

GLOBAL DEMOCRACY
Special Editor: Roberto Munck
Volume 581 May 2002

ALTERNATIVE MEDICINE
Special Editors: Helen Scheehan
and Barry Brenton
Volume 582 July 2002

See page 2 for information on Academy membership and purchase of single volumes of **The Annals.**

CONTENTS

BOOK DEPARTMENT CONTENTS

INTERNATIONAL RELATIONS AND POLITICS

AFRICA, ASIA, AND LATIN AMERICA

EUROPE

UNITED STATES

SOCIOLOGY

ECONOMICS

The American Academy of Political and Social Science

EXECUTIVE OFFICES ♦ FELS CENTER OF GOVERNMENT ♦ UNIVERSITY OF PENNSYLVANIA
3814 WALNUT STREET ♦ PHILADELPHIA, PA 19104-6197 ♦ TELEPHONE: (215) 746-6500
FAX: (215) 898-1202 ♦ HTTP://WWW.1891.ORG

The American Academy of Political and Social Science invites you to attend the

2002 Annual Meeting

Monday, April 15, 2002
9:30-12:30 AM
National Press Club
Washington, D.C.

Stephen B. Burbank, David Berger Professor for the Administration of Justice at the University of Pennsylvania Law School and Barry Friedman, Professor of Law at New York University will present the new Academy Monograph,

Judicial Independence at the Crossroads: An Interdisciplinary Approach

Including chapters by:

- *Stephen B. Burbank & Barry Friedman*
- *Charles M. Cameron*
- *Lee Epstein, Jack Knight & Olga Shvetsova*
- *Charles H. Franklin*
- *Charles Gardner Geyh*
- *Lewis A. Kornhauser*
- *Terri Jennings Peretti*
- *Edward Rubin*
- *Kim Lane Scheppele*

Authors' Symposium to follow

For more information, please contact Jennifer A. Warren at (215) 746-5709 or jawarren@sas.upenn.edu

PREFACE

The exchange rate and financial crises of the 1990s and early twenty-first century have moved the debate about how to reform the international monetary system to center stage in international fora and the front pages of newspapers. Beginning with the speculative attacks against the currencies in the European Monetary System in 1992-1993 and continuing with the attacks against the Mexican peso in 1994-1995, the Thai baht in 1997, the Russian ruble in 1998, the Brazilian real in 1999, and the Turkish lira in 2001, increasing concern with the operation of the international financial system has emerged. Scores of articles and books have been published addressing the issue of how to, and whether to, "fix" the international monetary system. The culmination of this concern occurred following the outbreak of the Mexican crisis when the G7 industrial countries launched an effort to reform the international financial architecture, an effort that was accelerated in the aftermath of the Asian crisis.

The point of departure of the architecture exercise has been the view that the present international monetary system has worked fairly well, though much can be done to strengthen the system to help keep crises from occurring and to resolve crises should they occur. The following specific areas have been at the center of the debate about the architecture: reform of the exchange rate arrangements, particularly whether intermediate regimes between floating rates and hard pegs are viable in a world of highly mobile capital; the role of the International Monetary Fund and other international institutions in crisis resolution; the role of capital controls in preventing or delaying (so that the authorities can buy time to implement necessary policies) crises; and the role of the private sector in crisis resolution.

Where, then, do we stand in the international monetary reform debate? What are the viable exchange rate arrangements at the beginning of the twenty-first century? This issue of *The Annals* takes stock. It brings together both leading proponents of reform and leading proponents of the existing regime. The articles address the issue of why recent exchange rate and financial crises occurred, the lessons learned from those crises, and the implications of those lessons for international monetary reform. By bringing together an eminent group of contributors, we hope that a wider group of the populace can make more informed judgments about a critical issue.

Barry Eichengreen argues that emerging economies can control inflation by targeting it directly rather than using the exchange rate as an anchor for their monetary regimes. W. Max Corden asserts that the effects of the 1997-1998 Asian financial crisis would have been less severe if the economies concerned had rigidly fixed or freely floating exchange rates rather than adjustable pegs. Martin Wolf agrees that the middle ground cannot hold and says that the Eurozone countries should consider a ceiling for the value of the euro against the dollar in the longer term. Harris Dellas, P.A.V.B. Swamy, and

George S. Tavlas describe the regime-specific characteristics of an international monetary system comprising both floating rates and pegged rates, the operating domain of a nominal anchor peg that produce externalities relative to a pure float or a fixed-rate regime and the way those externalities can lead to instability for small countries that peg to the currency of a large country. John Williamson argues that "intermediate" regimes, or "soft pegs," are feasible and advantageous. Steve Hanke makes the case that currency boards facilitate both domestic and international economic balance for the economies that have adopted them. George von Furstenberg predicts that the costs of maintaining small independent currencies will be seen as overly expensive, leading to an increase in the number of economies in currency blocs. Robert Mundell examines the questions of sovereignty involved in the adoption of the euro and traces the emergence of the various types of sovereignty through history. Dominick Salvatore examines the implications of the emergence of the euro for participating countries and the role and effect of the European Central Bank on the international financial system. Eduard Hochreiter and Helmut Wagner discuss the route that ten candidate countries are taking to EU and euroland membership and the implications of such membership for both the candidate countries and the existing EU states. Michele Fratianni and John Pattison propose that the United States and the United Kingdom, the world's principal financial markets, set the standard for prudential regulation of financial markets. Ronald I. McKinnon asserts that in emerging markets on the periphery of the industrial world, a "good" fixed-exchange-rate regime is better than a floating-rate regime, which in turn is better than a "bad" fixed-rate regime. Even the "good" fixed-rate regime must be complemented by sound regulation of financial markets, however. Joseph Stiglitz maintains that the International Monetary Fund/U.S. Treasury–led push to liberalize developing economies' capital accounts is not well founded in economic theory and has had disastrous effects. Michael Ulan discusses the justifications for and the perceived costs and benefits of Chile's capital-control regime and concludes that prudential regulation of its financial system—rather than its capital controls—was responsible for the performance of that country's economy during the 1990s. While Sebastian Edwards recognizes that liberalized international capital movements deepen financial crises, he also concludes that the solution to that problem is prudential regulation of economies' financial systems—not controls on the capital movements. He points out that the much-vaunted Chilean unremunerated reserve requirement did not protect Chile from the effects of the financial crisis of the late 1990s.

GEORGE S. TAVLAS
MICHAEL K. ULAN

ANNALS, *AAPSS*, **579**, January 2002

International Monetary Options for the Twenty-First Century

By BARRY EICHENGREEN

ABSTRACT: The crises of the 1990s convinced many observers that intermediate exchange rate arrangements are fragile and crisis prone. But calling for emerging markets to abandon the exchange rate as an anchor for policy compels those issuing the call to offer an alternative. In this article, the author assesses whether inflation targeting is a viable alternative for emerging markets. He focuses on distinctive characteristics of the policy environment that bear on its feasibility: these include the speed of pass-through, the difficulty of forecasting inflation, imperfect credibility, and liability dollarization. The author concludes that none of these complications renders inflation targeting infeasible, although a number render it more complex.

Barry Eichengreen is the George C. Pardee and Helen N. Pardee Professor of Economics and Political Science at the University of California, Berkeley; a research associate of the National Bureau of Research; and a research fellow of the Centre for Economic Policy Research.

THE crises of the 1990s, including Asia's in 1997-1998, made it impossible to dispute that intermediate exchange rate arrangements—those lying between very hard pegs and relatively free floats—are fragile and crisis prone. These crises provided compelling evidence, at no little discomfort to the participants in the experiment, of the costs when pegged rates collapse. The decline in the value of the currency, when it comes, is "larger, more rapid and more unanticipated than when a depreciation occurs under a floating exchange-rate regime" (Mishkin 2001, 36). The distress suffered by banks and firms with unhedged foreign currency exposures is greater. There is at least impressionistic evidence that the associated output losses are larger.

These effects can be understood as consequences of the buildup of unhedged foreign exposures among banks and corporations led to believe that they are insured against currency fluctuations by the authorities' commitment to peg the rate, resulting in serious balance sheet damage when the pegged exchange rate is unpegged under duress, and of the shock to confidence when the anchor for monetary policy, namely the one and same exchange rate peg, is withdrawn abruptly. A more prudent arrangement, the conclusion follows, would be to move to a more flexible rate, voluntarily rather than under duress. Currency fluctuations would then remind borrowers of the need to limit their borrowing and to hedge their exposures, and the central bank and government would have to build up independent sources of credibility. Alternatively, the country could adopt a hard peg to a foreign currency or make that foreign currency the exclusive circulating medium and legal tender, eliminating currency risk and allowing policy credibility to be imported from abroad rather than laboriously grown at home.

Statements of this increasingly conventional wisdom became commonplace following the Asian crisis. In the February 1998 speech that introduced "international financial architecture" to the policy lexicon, then–U.S. treasury secretary Robert Rubin declared that the International Monetary Fund (IMF) should no longer provide financial assistance to support overvalued currency pegs. His successor, Lawrence Summers (2000), stated that

> the choice of appropriate exchange rate regime . . . for economies with access to international capital markets, increasingly means a move away from the middle ground of pegged but adjustable fixed exchange rates towards the two corner solutions of either flexible exchange rates or a fixed exchange rate supported, if necessary, by a commitment to give up altogether an independent monetary policy. (P. 8)

Stanley Fischer (2001), drawing on IMF staff's assessment of the de facto exchange rate regime in IMF member countries, showed that the proportion with intermediate arrangements (neither hard pegs nor floats) was significantly lower in 1999 than in 1991 (34 percent vs. 62 percent for all countries, 42 percent vs. 64 percent for emerging markets) (Fischer 2001, fig. 1).[1] Fischer's testimony to the Meltzer Commission forecasted that more countries would move to the corners. IMF staff's recent paper for the executive board on exchange rate arrangements (Mussa et al. 2000) similarly concluded that

> for developing countries with important linkages to modern global capital markets . . . the requirements for sustaining pegged exchange rates have become significantly more demanding. For many emerging market economies, therefore, regimes that allow substantial exchange rate flexibility are probably desirable. Some emerging market countries, of course, may go in the other direction—toward hard currency pegs (such as currency boards), supported by the requisite policy discipline and institutional structures. (P. 31)

Thus, an international system of hard pegs and relatively free floats is increasingly seen as the monetary component of the new international financial architecture.[2] For members of the "missing middle school," this consensus, together with the observed movement away from intermediate arrangements, is one area of real progress in rationalizing the international financial system.

RESERVATIONS

Less heartening is the fact that many countries—most recently Turkey—have moved away from intermediate arrangements not in a measured manner but as the result of a crisis. Also disturbing is the observation that a not insignificant number of emerging markets that claim to operate floating rates intervene heavily to damp currency fluctuations, in practice operating what amounts to a soft ("noncredible") peg (the term and the observation are from Calvo and Reinhart 2000). Insofar as the authorities have changed the name but not the reality of the exchange rate regime, firms and banks, still confident that they are protected from large currency fluctuations by the authorities' implicit commitment to stabilize the rate, may fail to hedge their exposures, while the authorities, for their part, will fail to invest in the development of a new monetary anchor and a source of credibility independent of the exchange rate. The crisis problem has been disguised, in other words, but it has not been solved.

It is not hard to understand why countries are reluctant to abandon intermediate exchange rate arrangements. Abandoning the national currency for the dollar (or the euro) is a symbolic sacrifice, as acknowledged even by those who believe that dollarization (used henceforth as a generic term) has more benefits than costs. Abandoning a peg for greater flexibility will be a shock to the balance sheets of both the public and private sectors. It will undermine confidence if the exchange rate had previously served as the anchor for monetary policy and if the commitment to peg it had been the main source of policy credibility for the government and the central bank. Knowing that exiting from the peg will be a shock to confidence and that it may precipitate a recession, governments are understandably inclined to put off the decision to another day.[3]

It follows that if countries are going to exit from soft pegs voluntarily, the IMF needs to counter this status quo bias. The Council on Foreign Relations Task Force on Strengthening the International Financial Architecture (Council on Foreign Relations 1999) argued that the Fund should provide the appropriate incentives by committing not to provide large-scale financial assistance to governments intent on defending overvalued currency pegs. But, the qualification that the Fund should not support overvalued currency pegs provides a convenient pretext for exceptions, and the pressure to make exceptions on political grounds will remain great. In other words, the Council on Foreign Relations did not explain how such a commitment could be made credible. The Meltzer Commission (International Financial Institution 2000), while urging the more active use of Article IV consultations to remind countries of the risks associated with pegged rates, did not propose that their abandonment should be a precondition for IMF assistance.

The reality is that the IMF is an institution of many members. Reflecting their diverse structures, histories, and circumstances, they have achieved no consensus about the appropriate exchange rate arrangement, forcing the Fund to qualify its recommendations. Nor is it clear that the IMF is any better placed than governments to trade off the political and economic costs of recession now for the benefits of a more robust exchange rate regime later. The Fund's own status quo bias is clear in the recent cases of Argentina and Turkey. The institution is now a strong supporter of Argentine convertibility, in contrast to its lukewarm attitude at the time of adoption, reflecting fears that abandoning that regime would impart a sharp shock to confidence. And in the case of Turkey, the January 2000 IMF program sought to sustain the lira's crawling peg for eighteen months rather than moving immediately to a more flexible rate.

This last case is revealing of the underlying dilemmas. Diagnoses of Turkey's problems were informed by the Asian crisis. The banks had received implicit guarantees as the price of being used as instruments of the government's industrial and agricultural policies. The combination of a pegged exchange rate and an open capital account encouraged them to lever up their bets. A more flexible exchange rate could solve this problem by encouraging the banks to more prudently manage their exposures, but a sudden change in the rate would disturb balance sheets and confidence. Hence, the IMF program sought to move gradually in the direction of greater flexibility over a period of eighteen months, at the end of which the banks would have limited their exposures sufficiently that neither they nor the Turkish economy would be destabilized.

The Turkish crisis showed that this program was shaped by wishful thinking. The preconditions for holding the exchange rate stable are formidable when the political commitment is tenuous and the banks are weak. The knowledge that the authorities plan to move to greater flexibility creates the perception of a one-way bet. And, hopes that the banks will hedge their exposures today in response to the knowledge that the exchange rate will be allowed to float more freely tomorrow will surely be dashed if those banks are public or well connected politically and if tomorrow is not scheduled to come for eighteen months. In the end, Turkey's case is just another example of the difficulties of operating an intermediate arrangement for even a limited period of time.

Early post–Asia crisis statements by the U.S. treasury recommended that emerging markets move toward more flexible rates. This reflected worries that widespread dollarization might create political and diplomatic complications if the Fed did not adjust U.S. monetary policy to accommodate the needs of the newly dollarized economies, together with skepticism of the workability of monetary union. Europeans have always been more sympathetic to pegs (reflecting the lessons drawn from the currency turbulence of the 1930s) and more optimistic about the prospects for monetary union. And, now that a European monetary union exists, joining it provides an obvious solution for Eastern European countries seeking to eliminate the exchange rate problem.

The IMF, for its part, has overcome its initial skepticism regarding currency boards, dollarization, and monetary unification, having been influenced by the successes of these arrangements in the 1990s. IMF economists on their way to the staff cafeteria traverse a corridor lined with cases displaying the currency notes of the institution's members; in the 1990s, they regularly referred to this fact, proclaiming that the rule of "one country, one currency" was one of the most robust regularities in all of monetary economics. Europe's success in launching the euro would have appeared to have rendered this conviction less firm. (See, e.g., Asante and Masson 2001, where two Fund economists provide a sympathetic discussion of the case for a monetary union for the Economic Community of West African States). And, while not exactly an enthusiast of dollarization, the Fund did not resist Ecuador's decision to adopt the U.S. currency. Evidently, both corners are increasingly regarded as viable options within the corridors of the Fund.[4]

ALTERNATIVES

But, who should move to which corner? In Europe, where there is a commitment to political as well as economic integration, monetary union is the best option available. Each country enjoys currency stability vis-à-vis its principal trade and financial partners but flexibility useful for facilitating adjustment against the rest of the world. The commitment to political integration allows the creation of institutions of shared governance, in turn enabling each member to have a voice in the common monetary policy. This is a luxury not enjoyed by an El Salvador that unilaterally adopts the dollar or a Hong Kong that pegs to it via a currency board. Absent a comparable commitment to political integration in Latin America and Asia, there are reasons to question whether there exist realistic prospects for monetary union on those continents in coming decades.

A hard peg is the obvious solution for small countries with ties to larger neighbors and/or weak institutions. Small countries that trade heavily with a single larger partner and rely on it for external finance satisfy the classic optimum currency area criteria for pegging. It makes eminent sense from this point of view for El Salvador to adopt the U.S. dollar and for Estonia to peg to the deutsche mark.[5] Similar arguments can be made for countries with underdeveloped financial markets that leave firms and banks unable to hedge against currency fluctuations and with weak institutions, chronic budget deficits, and banking-sector problems that prevent the authorities from credibly committing to policies of low inflation. Advocates of dollarization will argue that we have just described the universe of emerging markets. In other words, since all emerging markets are characterized by these conditions, the world is destined to move toward three currency blocs centered on the dollar, the euro, and the yen, unilaterally in the short run (via dollarization and its equivalent) or in a more concerted fashion in the long run (via a proliferation of monetary unions).

Even leaving the politics aside, there are reasons to doubt this forecast. While the peso is pegged to the dollar by Argentina's currency board, the United States is not that country's most important trading partner; Brazil is. Foreign investment flows to Argentina not just from the United States but from Spanish banks and European bond markets. Hence, the single-currency peg creates serious difficulties when the euro or the real shift against the dollar. Argentine economy minister Cavallo's proposal for a basket peg against the dollar and the euro (still under consideration by the Argentine congress at the time of writing) promises to ameliorate the problems caused by shifts in G3 currencies, but it does not address the difficulties created by fluctuations in the Brazilian real. Asia faces a similar dilemma, as evidenced by the near-fatal consequences in 1997 of the combination of dollar pegs and dollar-yen fluctuations. There, too, this is not a problem that can be solved by unilaterally adopting basket pegs against the G3 currencies, given the growing importance of intraregional trade in Asia.

Thus, there remains a case for independent floating by countries with the capacity to operate such a system, assuming—contrary to the assertions of the advocates of dollarization—that such countries exist. These countries will presumably be relatively large and have relatively diversified trade and financial linkages. They will have independent central banks, well-regulated financial systems, efficient fiscal institutions, and stable political institutions. These preconditions should enable monetary policy makers to acquire credibility and follow sound and stable policies without orienting monetary policy around a particular value for the exchange rate. As their commitment to do so gains credibility, the volatility of the exchange rate (which reflects uncertainty about future policy) will diminish accordingly.

IS INFLATION TARGETING A VIABLE OPTION?

Acquiring credibility following the abandonment or collapse of an exchange rate peg requires the authorities to articulate and implement an alternative monetary policy operating strategy.[6] The leading candidate is inflation targeting. Inflation targeting entails an institutionalized commitment to price stability as the primary goal of monetary policy, mechanisms rendering the central bank accountable for attaining its monetary policy goals, the public announcement of targets for inflation, and a policy of communicating to the public the rationale for the decisions made by the central bank.[7] Central bank independence is needed to give the monetary authorities the leeway necessary to commit to price stability. And, a sound and stable fiscal policy and banking system are needed to avoid problems of fiscal dominance that would otherwise prevent the central bank from subordinating other goals to the objective of price stability or cause its independence to be undermined.

The multidimensional nature of this definition explains why there is no consensus about which emerging markets practice inflation targeting. Brazil, Chile, the Czech Republic, Israel, South Africa, Poland, Colombia, Thailand, Mexico, the Philippines, and South Korea are all cited in this connection. While the length of this list would appear to pose a challenge to those who argue that floating, backed by inflation targeting, is not viable in emerging markets, there is the question of whether these countries are actually practicing inflation targeting or they are really just covertly pegging their currencies. That some, such as Israel, also maintain bands for their exchange rates while others, including South Korea, intervene to limit or offset exchange rate fluctuations has been pointed to as evidence that they are really covert peggers. And, since a soft commitment to peg the exchange rate is the worst of all arrangements, it follows according to this view that these countries would be better off dollarizing.

But, the fact that their central banks alter monetary policy when the exchange rate moves may not in fact mean that they are not really inflation targeting. Insofar as depreciation is a leading indicator of inflation, the standard inflation-targeting framework suggests tightening monetary policy when the exchange rate weakens. This is the prescribed response when there is a change in the direction or availability of capital flows due to, say, a rise in foreign interest rates or a deterioration in foreign investor sentiment toward the country. A higher foreign interest rate implies less capital inflow for a given domestic interest rate and therefore a weaker currency. As the exchange rate weakens, higher import prices are passed through into inflation. The appropriate response is thus to raise interest rates. This is not because the central bank cares about the exchange rate in and of itself but because it cares about inflation.

If the disturbance is to the foreign component of aggregate demand (to the terms of trade or export demand), again the exchange rate will weaken, since export revenues will have declined while nothing else affecting the foreign exchange market will have changed in the first instance. In addition, demand will decline since foreigners are demanding fewer of the country's exports. Now there are two offsetting effects on inflation: while higher import prices will be passed through into inflation, weaker aggregate demand will be deflationary. If the second effect dominates, then inflation will decline with the growth in the gap between potential and current output, and the appropriate response for an inflation-targeting central bank will be to cut interest rates regardless of the weight it attaches to output variability. The more policy-relevant case is probably the one in which this shock, by depreciating the exchange rate, is inflationary on balance. If the central bank attaches a high weight to output variability, it still may want to cut interest rates. If on the other hand it attaches a high weight to deviations of inflation from target, it may instead raise interest rates to limit currency depreciation and inflation in the short run while still allowing the exchange rate to adjust eventually to its new long-run equilibrium level. In other words, it will acknowledge that the weakness of demand requires a weaker exchange rate, but it will still smooth the downward adjustment of the currency by leaning against the wind to prevent a sharp spike in inflation.

This framework suggests a test of whether countries such as Korea have really begun to practice inflation targeting. Find instances where the shock is to commodity rather than capital markets, since these are the cases where the weakness of output creates a case for interest rate cuts and for allowing the exchange rate to adjust. Consider not just the tendency for the central bank to lean against the wind in the short run but also its willingness to allow the exchange rate to adjust subsequently. The year 2001 will be a useful data point insofar as the shock to the Korean economy is mainly from commodity markets (reflecting the U.S. recession, continuing Japanese difficulties, and the high-tech slump). While the won has weakened considerably, fanning inflation, there are also worries of rising unemployment. An inflation-targeting central bank will tighten as inflation heats up, but it should also allow the exchange rate to adjust if the slump persists. My reading of the Korean experience is that the central bank has done just that: while it is concerned with inflation, which is running just below the official 3 percent target at the time of writing, it has nonetheless allowed the won to fall (by fully 10 percent against the dollar in the six months from late November 2000) as the economy has weakened. This behavior does not obviously resemble fear of floating. Of course, more time and more data will be needed before we can make a definitive assessment.

INFLATION TARGETING IN THE PRESENCE OF LIABILITY DOLLARIZATION

A key characteristic of emerging markets that may affect their ability to target inflation is liability dollarization. In many emerging markets, the obligations of banks, corporations, and governments are denominated in foreign currency, while the bulk of their revenues are domestic-currency denominated.[8] When the exchange rate depreciates, their balance sheet positions weaken, and this "financial accelerator" depresses output and employment.

The simplest way of thinking about liability dollarization is as reducing the response of output to currency depreciation.[9] While depreciation renders domestic goods more competitive, as before, now it also weakens the balance sheets of banks, firms, households, and governments, depressing consumption and investment. Consider the response to a negative shock to capital markets. Weaker consumption and investment due to adverse balance sheet effects now imply less inflation in the intermediate run. An inflation-targeting central bank will therefore feel less compelled to raise interest rates to push up the exchange rate and damp down the increase in import prices. If the shock to the exchange rate instead emanates from commodity markets, higher import prices will still be passed through into inflation, but now aggregate demand will be even weaker than before because of adverse balance sheet effects. Since output is lower and inflation is no higher than in the absence of liability dollarization, again there will be less pressure to hike interest rates to stabilize the currency and damp down inflation and more incentive to cut interest rates to stimulate production. This suggests, regardless of the source of shocks, that reluctance to let the exchange rate adjust will be less in the presence of liability dollarization.

While this may seem counter-intuitive, it is just a specific illustration of the general point that when the central bank worries more about variables other than inflation, either because of a heavier weight on those variables in its objective function or because the parameters of the model cause those other variables to be displaced further from their equilibrium levels (where the latter is the case presently under discussion), it will move more gradually to eliminate discrepancies between actual and target inflation. Because the exchange rate must move more to increase output and employment, and because measures that would limit its fluctuation and thereby reduce imported inflation tend to destabilize the real economy, the now weaker tendency for depreciation to stimulate activity means that the central bank will do even less to limit depreciation.[10]

Clearly, those who argue that liability dollarization creates fear of floating have something else in mind, presumably that the balance sheet effects of currency depreciation are so strong that a cut in interest rates that weakens the exchange rate depresses output on balance. In this case, a negative shock to capital markets still fuels inflation through higher import prices, encouraging the authorities to raise rates. But now, in addition, it lowers output through the adverse balance sheet effect. The appropriate response, which damps down inflation and stabilizes output by limiting balance sheet damage, is to raise interest rates and push the exchange rate back up toward its preshock level. Fear of floating-type behavior results. If the disturbance is instead to commodity markets, the weaker exchange rate again means more imported inflation and lower levels of output.[11] Again, interest rate hikes are the appropriate response to both problems since a higher interest rate that strengthens the exchange rate not only damps down inflation but also strengthens balance sheets. Again, the central bank will not hesitate to raise interest rates. Again, its response will resemble fear of floating.

This formulation has some peculiar implications. For one, a negative commodity market shock that reduces export demand and depresses output must be offset in the new equilibrium by an appreciated exchange rate, not a depreciated one. This is a world where overvaluation is good for output because its favorable financial effects dominate its adverse competitiveness effects, even in the long run, which hardly seems realistic.

A possible reconciliation is that when the exchange rate depreciates by a large amount, the adverse balance sheet effects dominate, but when it depreciates by a small amount, the favorable competitiveness effects dominate. Large depreciations cause severe financial distress because they confront banks and firms with asset prices for which they are unprepared while doing little to enhance competitiveness because of the speed with which they are passed through into inflation. For small depreciations, the balance of effects is the opposite; small depreciations are more likely therefore to satisfy the conditions for an expansionary devaluation.[12]

If the exchange rate falls sufficiently to enter the first range, then an inflation-targeting central bank will raise interest rates sharply with the goal of pushing up the currency and minimizing the financial damage to banks, firms, and households. But, if the depreciation is modest, so too will be the rise in interest rates; the central bank will allow the currency to fall to a new lower level as long as the competitiveness effects continue to dominate the balance sheet effects.[13]

Thus, whether emerging markets can implement an inflation-targeting regime that allows the exchange rate to fluctuate more freely depends on the precise extent and effects of their liability dollarization. If even a small depreciation of the exchange rate threatens to destabilize balance sheets and the macroeconomy (i.e., the country immediately enters the zone where depreciation and lower interest rates are contractionary), then the central bank will not be willing to let the exchange rate move. While the preceding propositions for how the central bank should respond flow directly from the standard inflation-targeting framework, inflation targeting and a hard peg are basically indistinguishable under these conditions. If the perceived advantage of inflation targeting is that it permits greater exchange rate flexibility, then the advantages of inflation targeting are correspondingly less in highly dollarized economies. Under these circumstances, inflation targeting has no obvious advantages over a hard peg, which has the merits of simplicity, transparency, and credibility.

For countries where the adverse balance sheet effects dominate only when exchange rate movements exceed a critical threshold, inflation targeting will be viable as long as shocks and exchange rate fluctuations are small, while the desire to intervene and stabilize the exchange rate will dominate when they grow large. The additional exchange rate flexibility promised by inflation targeting will be feasible, but the central bank's appetite for indulging in it will have limits. When those limits are reached, intervention to stabilize the exchange rate will become the overriding objective of policy.[14]

This discussion suggests that exchange rate arrangements consistent with the new architecture will vary not by region but with the characteristics of individual countries. Small countries heavily dependent on trade and financial transactions with a single larger partner will prefer to peg rigidly or perhaps even adopt the latter's currency. Larger countries where the extent of liability dollarization is limited, fiscal institutions are strong, and the political commitment to price stability is firm will prefer to practice inflation targeting and allow the exchange rate to vary. There are examples of both kinds of arrangements in Latin America (contrast El Salvador and Brazil) and Asia (contrast Hong Kong and Korea). The present perspective does not suggest that exchange rate arrangements will be uniform within regions or that they will vary in some systemic way across them.

CONCLUSION

Financial integration has many implications, among the most prominent of which are the constraints it imposes on monetary and exchange rate policies. It makes intermediate exchange rate arrangements (soft pegs, as they are colloquially known) fragile and difficult to maintain. It forces governments to choose between credibly and unconditionally subordinating monetary policy to the exchange rate (hardening the peg), something that can be accomplished by institutional changes that entail abolishing the central bank or even the domestic currency itself (in favor of a currency board in the first instance and in favor of dollarization or its equivalent in the second) versus subordinating the exchange rate to domestic monetary policy (abandoning the peg), a policy that can be lent credibility by articulating and implementing a coherent alternative monetary policy operating strategy such as inflation targeting. Both responses are consistent and sustainable, but the same is not true of intermediate arrangements that attempt to split the difference. Countries have to choose.

This conclusion is challenged on two grounds. First, many countries remain reluctant to evacuate the middle. They continue to intervene heavily to limit the variability of the exchange rate. They continue to operate something resembling an intermediate exchange rate arrangement de facto if not de jure. Second, an inflation-targeting regime that permits a significant increase in the actual variability of the exchange rate is not likely to be viable in economies where the liabilities of the public and private sectors are heavily dollarized, in which case exchange rate fluctuations may be seriously destabilizing of balance sheets and the macroeconomy.

The first objection is factual, but its extent is a matter of dispute.[15] It does not change the fact that monetary policy strategies that are designed to limit the variability of the exchange rate but do not also subordinate monetary policy to that objective and involve the support of credibility-enhancing institutional changes are fragile and crisis prone. Central banks and governments that pursue these policies continue to set themselves up as targets for speculators. Sooner or later, market pressures will force them to choose between hardening the peg and allowing the currency to float more freely.

The second objection suggests that emerging markets have good reasons to prefer harder pegs to freer floats. The corresponding forecast is that dollarization and euroization will become increasingly popular, leading to a world of two or three regionally based currency blocs organized around the dollar, the euro, and possibly the yen. In this article, I have sought to challenge this forecast. Inflation targeting, I suggest, is not obviously infeasible or undesirable for emerging markets with geographically diversified trade and financial links, reasonably strong financial systems, and limited levels of liability dollarization. Brazil and South Korea are examples of the kind of countries I have in mind. For these countries, an independent monetary policy remains feasible and attractive. The implication is that the international financial architecture is likely to remain less homogeneous than suggested by the currency-bloc school and that it is likely to remain so for some time to come.

Notes

1. Some would dispute that these numbers are informative, arguing that a nonnegligible share of emerging markets that claim to float independently or to operate a managed float in fact intervene heavily to limit the variability of the rate (Calvo and Reinhart 2000). Since Fischer's tabulations are based on IMF economists' assessments of the de facto regime, and not the regime announced by the authorities, it is necessary to argue that they are subject to capture in the context of Article IV and program negotiations. I return to this argument below.

2. In fairness, I should note that there remain defenders of intermediate arrangements. Frankel (1999) argued that "intermediate solutions are more likely to be appropriate for many countries than are corner solutions" (p. 30). Williamson (2000), while acknowledging the fragility of intermediate arrangements, argued that these can be redesigned so as to limit their vulnerability to speculative pressures. Leaving aside countries that are not yet able to access international capital markets, which is a species that will presumably grow increasingly endangered over time, this is not an argument for which I have much sympathy. In my view, the evidence of movement away from the middle is incontrovertible. As Goldstein (2001) observed, the list of countries that have been able to maintain a fixed rate for five years or longer is now very short; at the time of writing, it is composed of just two: Argentina and Hong Kong.

3. Eichengreen and Masson (1998) showed that exits from pegs have typically been associated with significant recessions. Eichengreen and Rose (2001) provided supporting evidence, generalizing the sample to include de facto as well as de jure pegs and focusing on exits that take place in response to speculative pressure.

4. But here, it and the other multilaterals have followed rather than led. It is not some international monetary architecture lowered down from the rafters but rather decisions of national governments that are reshaping the exchange rate system.

5. Similar arguments can be made for small Caribbean island economies, some Pacific Island economies, and the members of the CFA franc zone.

6. This means more than simply moving to a floating exchange rate. Floating, as Calvo (2000) has put it, is not a monetary strategy; it is the absence of a monetary strategy.

7. This definition and the subsequent discussion follow Eichengreen (2001). The policy-relevant case is flexible inflation targeting, when there is also a positive weight on other variables besides inflation—output, for example—in the central bank's reaction function. Strict inflation targeting, in contrast, is when only inflation enters the objective function. Since few central banks and polities are prepared to disregard all other variables under all circumstances, flexible inflation targeting is the policy-relevant case.

8. Insofar as banks and other intermediaries close their open foreign-currency positions by issuing dollar-denominated loans, the liability dollarization of their customers will be greater still.

9. As it turns out, this is not precisely what those concerned with the perverse effect of exchange rate changes in the presence of liability dollarization have in mind, as I explain momentarily.

10. The same is true when the problem in the financial system is maturity mismatches rather than currency mismatches. Again, the more the central bank fears that an interest rate hike designed to damp down inflation will cause financial distress (because the maturity of banks' liabilities is shorter than their assets or because higher interest rates will increase default rates among bank borrowers), the less sharply it will raise interest rates in the intermediate run to strengthen the exchange rate and limit inflation.

11. The decline in output is even larger than before because the direct effect of the decline in foreign demand is reinforced by the indirect effect of exchange rate depreciation via its adverse impact on balance sheets.

12. This nonlinearity in the effect of the exchange rate on output might seem arbitrary, but it is precisely the way authors like Aghion, Bacchetta, and Banerjee (1999) and Krugman (2001) model the interplay of competitiveness and balance sheet effects: the latter dominates for small depreciations, but the former dominate for large ones, producing a nonlinear aggregate-demand equation of precisely the sort being assumed here.

13. In fact, heavy intervention when the exchange rate drops precipitously and light intervention when it fluctuates around normal levels is not unlike the observed behavior of many central banks.

14. Observe that this commitment to prevent the exchange rate from moving further when it reaches the edge of the band should be credible since the central bank will not be sacrificing something else to stabilize the rate. In conventional models (without liability dollarization), stabilizing the currency by raising interest rates sacrifices output and employment. In the present model, in contrast, raising rates at this point will be good for output and employment as well as the exchange rate. All this assumes that liability dollarization is an immutable fact. If, on the other hand, it is something that countries can grow out of by strengthening their institutions and policy credibility and therefore cultivating the ability to borrow in their own currency, then the range of emerging markets for which floating and inflation targeting is a viable option will increase further with time.

15. For example, Hernandez and Montiel (2001) reported evidence that Asian countries have moved in the direction of greater exchange rate flexibility in the wake of their crisis, while Calvo and Reinhart (2000) remained impressed by the extent of fear of floating.

References

Aghion, Philippe, Philippe Bacchetta, and Abijit Banerjee. 1999. Capital markets and instability in open economies. Unpublished manuscript, Study Center Gerzensee.

Asante, R. D., and Paul Robert Masson (with Jacqueline Irvine). 2001. The pros and cons of expanded monetary union in West Africa. In *Finance and Development* 38 (March). Retrieved from http://www.imf.org/external/pubs/ft/fandd/2001/03/index.htm.

Calvo, Guillermo. 2000. Capital markets and the exchange rate, with special reference to the dollarization debate in Latin America. Unpublished manuscript, University of Maryland at College Park.

Calvo, Guillermo, and Carmen Reinhart. 2000. Fear of floating. NBER working paper no. 7993.

Council on Foreign Relations. 1999. *Safeguarding prosperity in a global financial system: The future international financial architecture*. New York: Council on Foreign Relations.

Eichengreen, Barry. 1994. *International monetary arrangements for the 21st century*. Washington, DC: Brookings Institution.

———. 2001. Can emerging markets float? Should they inflation target? Unpublished manuscript, University of California, Berkeley. Retrieved from http://emlab.berkeley.edu/users/eichengr/website.htm.

Eichengreen, Barry, and Paul Masson (with Hugh Bredenkamp, Barry Johnston, Javier Hamann, Esteban Jadresic, and Inci Otker). 1998. *Exit strategies: Policy options for countries seeking greater exchange rate flexibility*. Occasional paper no. 168. Washington, DC: International Monetary Fund.

Eichengreen, Barry, and Andrew Rose. In press. Does it pay to defend against a speculative attack? In *Currency crises in emerging markets*, edited by Michael Dooley and Jeffrey Frankel. Chicago: University of Chicago Press.

Fischer, Stanley. 2001. Exchange rate regimes: Is the bipolar view correct? Distinguished lecture on economics in government delivered at the meetings of the American Economic Association, New Orleans, LA, January.

Frankel, Jeffrey A. 1999. No single currency regime is right for all countries or at all times. In *Essays in international finance*. No. 215. Princeton, NJ: International Finance Section, Department of Economics, Princeton University.

Goldstein, Morris. 2001. An evaluation of proposals to reform the international financial architecture. Paper presented at the NBER Conference on the Management of Financial Crises, Monterey, CA, 28-30 March.

Hernandez, Leonardo, and Peter J. Montiel. 2001. Post-crisis exchange rate policy in five Asian countries: Filling in the "Hollow Middle"? Unpublished manuscript, International Monetary Fund.

International Financial Institution Advisory Commission. 2000. *Report*. Washington, DC: Government Printing Office.

Krugman, Paul. 2001. Crises: The next generation. Unpublished manuscript, Princeton University.

Mishkin, Frederic. 2001. Financial policies and the prevention of financial crises in emerging market countries. NBER working paper no. 8087.

Mussa, Michael, Paul Masson, Alexander Swoboda, Esteban Jadresic, Paulo Mauro, and Andrew Berg. 2000. *Exchange rate regimes in an increasingly integrated world economy*. Occasional paper 193. Washington, DC: International Monetary Fund.

Summers, Lawrence H. 2000. International financial crises: Causes, prevention, and cures. *American Economic*

Review Papers and Proceedings 90 (May): 1-16.

Williamson, John. 2000. Exchange rate regimes for emerging markets: Reviving the intermediate option. No. 60. In *Policy Analyses in International Economics*. Washington, DC: Institute for International Economics.

ANNALS, *AAPSS*, **579**, January 2002

Exchange Rate Regimes for Emerging Market Economies: Lessons from Asia

By W. MAX CORDEN

ABSTRACT: This article discusses the role of the exchange rate regime in the 1997 East Asian crisis. Most of the countries had, more or less, fixed-but-adjustable exchange rate regimes before the crisis. The article outlines special problems of this regime when there is high capital mobility, including the loss of political credibility that results when governments cannot maintain fixed exchange rates to which they have committed. The article discusses how the crisis would have played out under alternative exchange rate regimes, namely floating rates and currency boards. There would still have been a boom followed by a crisis, though in the short run, the recessions might have been less deep. The article also discusses Hong Kong's currency board regime; the reasons the Indonesian crisis was especially severe; the reasons some Asian countries, notably India, avoided a crisis; and the role of capital controls, especially in Malaysia.

W. Max Corden is the Chung Ju Yung Distinguished Professor of International Economics at the Paul H. Nitze School of Advanced International Studies of the Johns Hopkins University. He is a graduate of the University of Melbourne and the London School of Economics. He has held positions at Oxford University and the Australian National University, and for two years, he was a senior adviser at the International Monetary Fund. He is the author of many books and articles on international economics.

NOTE: This article draws on material in my forthcoming book *On the Choice of Exchange Rate Regimes*, to be published by MIT Press in spring 2002. The book contains further references.

THE 1997 EAST ASIAN CRISIS

A prolonged private-sector investment-spending boom ends in a banking and then a currency crisis. The exchange rate depreciates severely, followed by some rebound. There is a deep recession, and recovery takes a long time. The financial sector is in ruins. Until the currency crisis, the country had, more or less, a fixed-but-adjustable exchange rate (henceforth FBAR, for short) regime, with the value of the currency fixed to the U.S. dollar. Essentially, the FBAR was the exchange rate regime that operated worldwide under the Bretton Woods system that ended in 1973. As a result of the crisis, the exchange rate floats. That, roughly, is the story of the five-country East Asian crisis that began in 1997.

The question is, Would the story have been different with a different exchange rate regime initially and during the crisis? Does the fact that this boom-and-bust episode happened under an FBAR regime condemn that kind of regime? It is a common, almost conventional, view that this is indeed so. But, it could also be argued that there were fundamental factors causing the excessive boom and the inevitable crisis that followed it, which would have operated under any of the alternative regimes.

The five Asian-crisis countries were Thailand—where the 1997 currency crisis started—Indonesia, Malaysia, the Philippines, and Korea. In all cases, though relatively less in the Philippines, there was massive foreign capital inflow in the boom, turning into outflow when market expectations changed and so causing a currency crisis. In all cases, the financial sector was in difficulty well before this crisis, essentially because there had been excessive borrowing to finance unwise or unlucky investments, much of them in real estate in the cases of Thailand and Malaysia.

There were other factors leading to the turnaround. In 1996, the countries' terms of trade deteriorated, and Japanese banking problems slowed capital inflow. The details of the several causes of the boom and the subsequent slump go beyond the discussion here. The main point here is that there were fundamental factors independent of the exchange rate regime that turned euphoria into panic and, in the case of some of the countries, long periods of high growth into a sudden and severe recession.

The suddenness of the transformation from boom to crisis is usually explained by the fact that a large part of the foreign borrowing, whether by banks, by nonbank financial institutions, or by corporations, was short term and debt creating, rather than foreign direct investment. But here, it is interesting to note that this was not true in the case of Malaysia where debt-creating foreign borrowing had been restricted by the central bank. The large current account deficit was financed by portfolio flows into the booming domestic stock market and by foreign direct investment. But, portfolio flows into Malaysia turned out to be as volatile as debt-creating flows into the other countries.

THE EAST ASIAN EXCHANGE RATE REGIMES BEFORE THE CRISIS

It is actually not quite accurate to describe the exchange rate regimes that existed before the crisis as FBAR regimes. Usually, they were officially described as managed floating regimes or, in the case of Indonesia, as a crawling peg regime with a band. But in practice, intervention in the foreign exchange market had kept the value of the currency almost fixed to the U.S. dollar, with occasional adjustments. So the exchange rates were almost fixed. The precise details, and how they differed among the countries, hardly matter. To say that the exchange rate was adjustable meant that the countries maintained independent exchange rate and monetary policies, and a significant exchange rate change was always possible, even though it had been infrequent.

Given these policies, capital inflows did not lead to appreciations of nominal exchange rates in terms of the dollar, as would have happened if exchange rates had floated. But in real terms, the exchange rates did actually appreciate first because the dollar itself was appreciating relative to the yen and second because domestic prices rose faster than U.S. prices. When capital inflows declined and eventually turned into outflows, the central banks in all cases at first tried to maintain the exchange rate by running down their foreign exchange reserves. Hence, any exchange rate adjustment was reluctant. This is a characteristic of FBARs, with the result that market forces eventually forced an end to the regime.

The fundamentals that led to the decline in foreign exchange reserves, and that I have already discussed, made a devaluation within the FBAR system, or a depreciation of the currency as a result of a shift to a floating rate regime, inevitable. Eventually, the foreign exchange reserves combined with emergency support from the International Monetary Fund would have run out. But speculation on an inevitable depreciation triggered the crisis and made it temporarily more severe—forcing more initial depreciation than the fundamentals actually required.

THE CLASSIC ARGUMENTS AGAINST FBAR REGIMES

The classic argument against this regime in an environment with high capital mobility goes back to the Bretton Woods era. Exchange rates were firmly fixed but were occasionally, reluctantly, adjusted. As international capital movements were liberalized and opportunities for speculation increased, there were several crises, including the crises of sterling and the French franc, and finally the crises of the dollar in 1971 and 1973 that led to the breakdown of the system. Speculation against a currency would lead to increases in interest rates designed to make speculation less attractive. But, such interest rate increases are deflationary for demand, damage the financial system, and raise the public debt. Hence they often cannot be sustained.

This and later experiences led to the "impossible trinity" proposition that independent monetary policies, high capital mobility, and fixed exchange rates were not compatible. FBAR regimes are excessively vulnerable to speculation even when the fundamentals do not justify devaluation. In the Asian-crisis case, the fundamentals did clearly require some devaluation or depreciation, though surely not to the extent that initially took place.

Attempts to maintain unsustainable exchange rates by central banks create three big problems. First, there are the adverse effects of temporary high interest rates. Second, there are the big losses that central banks make to the benefit of speculators when finally the exchange rate does depreciate. And third, there is the loss of political credibility that results when the government or central bank finally is unable to fulfil its promise that the exchange rate would not be altered. FBAR regimes cannot be recommended to ministers of finance, who usually lose their jobs after a crisis. All this is familiar and was evident in the European Monetary System crisis of 1992 and then the various emerging markets crises, noticeably the Mexican crisis of 1994 and the Asian crisis of 1997.

UNHEDGED FOREIGN-CURRENCY-DENOMINATED BORROWING

One particular feature of the Asian borrowing boom turned out to have particularly bad effects once the currencies depreciated. During the borrowing boom, debt-creating borrowing by banks, other financial intermediaries, and corporations was usually dollar denominated and not hedged against the possibility of a devaluation or of a depreciation of the currency as a result of the currency's being allowed to float. It was unhedged foreign-currency-denominated borrowing. When the currencies actually depreciated severely—by 50 percent or so in the case of Thailand, Korea, and Malaysia and to an incredible degree in the case of Indonesia—the domestic currency values of these debts and of interest payments due on them vastly increased. The value of the Indonesian rupiah declined from 2,500 rupiah to the dollar to a peak of more than 15,000 rupiah. Banks and corporations were bankrupted, domestic lending ceased, and so the recession that was in any case under way because of the sudden ending of the spending boom was intensified.

The effect was particularly serious in the case of Indonesia because of the extent of the exchange rate depreciation. The huge depreciation was explained by a complete loss of confidence in the economic and political management of the Soeharto regime and the future of the country. Indonesia was really a special case and by 2001 had not recovered.

Before the crisis, the fundamentals, as indicated by the extent of borrowing and current accounts and the efficiency of use of the resources obtained by borrowing, were probably no worse, and possibly in some respects even better, than those of the other crisis countries. But, a potential problem did exist. It resulted from the decline in the quality of the Soeharto regime (which had earlier achieved more than twenty-five years of high growth) and from the doubts about the succession to an aging president. A moderate economic crisis touched off a political and social crisis, which has not yet ended, and which rebounded disastrously on the economy. The excessive depreciation, both in nominal and in real terms, was a crucial element in this process.

Coming back to unhedged foreign borrowing, the question arises whether the problems caused by it were uniquely associated with the particular exchange rate regime and its ending in crisis. Is there a way of averting this problem in the future?

One view is that developing countries, unlike developed countries, cannot borrow other than in the short term and in the form of unhedged foreign currency–denominated (usually dollar-denominated) form, nor is there a market where they can hedge. They either borrow internationally, running the risk of devaluation, or they do not borrow. They have no choice. In this view, the only solution is to establish a regime where devaluation or depreciation is impossible or at least firmly avoided by institutions that constrain domestic monetary policy.

The usual policy recommendation is then for the country to dollarize (giving up its own currency completely), to join a monetary union with the country in whose currency most foreign debts are denominated, or to establish a currency board regime. The first is patently unreal for Asian countries, and the second is a remedy available only in Europe, but the third is conceivable for some Asian countries. There is an important example in Hong Kong.

The alternative view, to which I subscribe, is that opportunities for hedging and markets for domestic-currency-denominated bonds would develop if there were a demand. Borrowing was dollar denominated in the Asian case because dollar interest rates were lower than domestic-currency interest rates for the same borrower. When it is said that borrowing in domestic-currency form was not possible, it is really meant that such borrowing would be excessively expensive. The interest rate differential indicated the market's belief that there was some chance, possibly a slight chance, of devaluation of the domestic currency. But, exchange rates had actually been relatively stable, so that borrowers gambled that they would stay that way. Indeed, it was reasonable to believe that large devaluations were highly improbable.

Private borrowers, especially banks, may also have assumed that they would be rescued by the government or central bank in case of devaluation. As it happened, they gambled and lost, and even when they were rescued, the crisis was rarely costless to them.

One could argue that this was a learning experience, and even if there were a return to an FBAR regime, it is not a risk they would run again. Unhedged foreign borrowing has not been common in countries with floating rate regimes. Therefore, it has also been argued that the true lesson is that only the actual experience of exchange rate instability would lead to adequate hedging.

THE FLOATING RATE ALTERNATIVE

Once the crisis came, the five Asian-crisis countries really had little alternative but to float their exchange rates, at least temporarily. The interesting question is how the boom-and-bust story would have played out if exchange rates had started to float much earlier, perhaps when the boom began. Floating may have been managed to some extent, with some degree of intervention by the central bank in the foreign exchange market, but there would not have been any formal or informal commitment to exchange rate stability.

It is reasonable to assume that the fundamentals would have been the same: a borrowing boom followed by its ending for various reasons. But, the special crisis problems of the FBAR regime listed above would have been avoided. During the capital inflow period, the nominal exchange rate would have appreciated, rather than the money supply rising because of the accumulation of foreign exchange reserves. There would have been the same sort of real appreciation, though it would have happened more quickly than under the FBAR regime.

The exchange rates would certainly have depreciated earlier, once the economic situation (the fundamentals) turned around. Exchange rates would not have been kept up by deliberate interventions. Such earlier depreciations would have been preferable to the depreciations that took place in crisis conditions in 1997. The beneficial effects of depreciation on competitiveness would have set in earlier. Probably depreciation would have been smoother and less traumatic. The experience of floating might have induced borrowers who acquired dollar-denominated (or yen-denominated) debt to hedge against the possibility of depreciation. Such hedging might have been costly but would have avoided the unhedged foreign borrowing problem. It would also have been some discouragement to borrowing, and given that it had become excessive, this would have been desirable.

These are the undoubted positives. But, there is a negative aspect that is sufficiently important to discourage most developing countries (and some developed countries as well) from pure or near-pure floating. During the boom, the nominal exchange rate, while generally appreciating, would have been unstable, as is usual with floating rate regimes, and such instability would have had the usual adverse effects on investment (notably foreign direct investment), capital inflows, trade, and domestic income distribution. Such instability is particularly likely when foreign exchange markets are thin, with a shortage of stabilizing speculation, as in many developing countries. The central banks would have felt obliged to intervene in the market or to manage interest rates, so as to achieve some stability.

In practice, after the crisis, all the countries except Malaysia moved to managed floating regimes. In these regimes, the exchange rate is certainly less stable than it was before the crisis, but very short-term instability tends to be avoided by foreign exchange intervention by the central bank. There are no formal or informal exchange rate commitments. The exchange rates depreciated sharply when the crisis began, and then they partially recovered. In all cases, there was a net real depreciation, which improved competitiveness and, after a lag, helped to increase exports and thus contributed to the necessary improvement in the current account. The exception is Malaysia, which returned to an FBAR. In that case, the exchange rate is formally fixed, though there is no long-term commitment to the rate.

THE CURRENCY BOARD ALTERNATIVE

With a currency board regime, there is a very strong commitment to a fixed exchange rate and, in addition, a rule that requires the money base to be fully backed by foreign exchange reserves. In its strictest form, there can be no independent monetary policy whether to finance a budget deficit, rescue banks, or boost demand so as to increase employment. I shall assume here that the currency board regime is completely credible, with no doubt about its continuance, and that it was established before the boom began.

During the boom, the story would have been much the same as with the FBAR. Foreign banks would have lent and domestic banks and others would have borrowed short term, and the funds would have been on loan to various enterprises. Owing to capital inflow, the foreign exchange reserves, and hence the money supply, would have increased, and there would have been real appreciation, leading to rising prices. But, when the boom came to an end, the story would have been different.

First, there could not have been rescues of troubled financial institutions by the currency board. Conceivably, the government might have financed such rescues directly, if it were able to borrow; otherwise, there would have been more and earlier defaults. A banking crisis and recession might then have come earlier. Second, if the regimes had really been credible, there would not have been any speculation on the exchange rate, and thus there would not have been an actual currency crisis involving financial losses by the central bank and loss of credibility by the government and central bank. This is the main respect in which the currency board regime would have been preferable to the FBAR. Third, since there would not have been any devaluation or depreciation, there would not have been any unhedged foreign borrowing problem, and for this reason, the depth of the recession initially might have been less.

The main negatives are two. First, a decline in capital inflow and in export income—leading inevitably to a decline in foreign exchange reserves—would have automatically led to a decline in the money supply and hence to a rise in interest rates that might have been greater than actually took place. For this reason, the recession might actually have been deeper and the effects on the financial system more severe. There would have been no flexibility for monetary policy at all. Second—and I regard this as the overwhelming argument against currency boards for most countries—the recession would not have been offset or modified eventually by the stimulating effect of depreciation on exports. There would have been no favorable effect on competitiveness, an effect that has been clearly apparent in all the Asian crisis countries, notably Korea and Thailand.

At the peak of the Indonesian crisis in early 1998, when the rupiah had depreciated drastically, a switch to a currency board regime was under discussion in Indonesia. The basic argument was that the establishment of a currency board would restore confidence and that the regime would be credible. The currency board would be established at an exchange rate that was significantly depreciated relative to the original value of the rupiah but would reverse the extreme movement of the exchange rate that had actually taken place but that was not justified by fundamentals.

One might doubt that in the long run, Indonesia is an appropriate candidate for a currency board regime, but the immediate criticism was that everything would hinge on the successful establishment of credibility. The market would have to be convinced that the exchange rate chosen was justified by fundamentals. But, great political uncertainty and lack of confidence would throw doubt on any concept of fundamentals in Indonesia at that time. Could monetary discipline as required by a currency board regime actually have been maintained? It is more likely that a currency board regime would have crashed and turned out to be another FBAR case, leading to losses by the central bank to the benefit of successful speculators or inside traders.

HONG KONG'S CURRENCY BOARD REGIME

Hong Kong has had a currency board regime, with a fixed rate to the dollar, since 1983. It is the major example of this kind of regime in Asia. The system is not a pure currency board case because there has been some modest degree of sterilization of the domestic monetary effects of changes in foreign exchange reserves. In addition, the monetary authority has acted, again to a modest extent, as a lender of last resort to commercial banks. But basically, there has been a very strong fixed exchange rate commitment maintained since 1983 and throughout the Asian crisis, and active monetary policy has been foregone.

In spite of the strong commitment and the very high level of foreign exchange reserves, and in addition, the backing of the vast reserves of the People's Republic of China, there was speculation against the Hong Kong dollar during the Asian crisis. But, such speculation did not last long. Hong Kong was adversely affected by the Asian crisis, but its recession lasted only one year.

There are three reasons for the success of the regime. First, the system and specifically the exchange rate commitment have been very credible, apart from the brief Asian crisis episode when there was speculation against the exchange rate. The credibility has rested on a high level of reserves, on the length of the period during which the rate has stayed fixed, and on the strong support of the Hong Kong public for the system. The fact that China's currency, the renminbi, was fixed to the dollar must also have played a role. If the dollar peg of the renminbi is given up one day—as is likely—Hong Kong's policy makers may have to reconsider their regime.

Second, pragmatic fiscal sterilization and lender-of-last-resort policies of the Hong Kong government have moderated recessions. High fiscal surpluses accumulated during the good times allowed the government to engage in countercyclical fiscal policy during the Asian crisis.

Third, the downward flexibility of wages and prices has greatly moderated recessions. Indeed, such flexibility is crucial to the maintenance of such a regime and cannot be found to that extent in the various Asian-crisis countries. During the Asian crisis, there was absolute price deflation, so that competitiveness improved in spite of the fixed nominal exchange rate.

ASIAN COUNTRIES THAT AVOIDED A CRISIS

The East Asian economies that had more or less FBAR regimes but avoided a currency crisis were China (the People's Republic), Hong Kong, Singapore, and Taiwan. They did not avoid some overspill from the crisis in the form of reduced demand and some speculative pressures, but what they all had in common was a high level of foreign exchange reserves relative to short-term debt. They had current account surpluses and had borrowed very little in short-term form. In China, capital controls had discouraged short-term foreign borrowing, and there were strict controls on capital outflows.

Finally, the crisis of the Philippines was less severe and shorter than that of the other five Asian-crisis countries because its boom was smaller and briefer, and that in turn reflected its earlier Latin American–style troubles that had led to high fiscal and current account deficits and a series of International Monetary Fund programs. In 1997, it was still subject to an International Monetary Fund program.

It is worth saying something about India as a counterexample. Its exchange rate regime since 1993 has been not so different from those of most of the other countries I have discussed. While it was officially described as a market-determined exchange rate regime, actually, intervention in the market kept the exchange rate pegged, or almost pegged, to the dollar, with occasional bouts of depreciation. Essentially, it was another FBAR regime. From 1993, capital inflows surged, just as in the case of the Asian-crisis countries. The fundamentals, as reflected in the budget deficit; the poor quality of its financial system, including politically influenced lending by banks; and its current account deficit relative to the gross national product were no better than in the crisis countries.

Comprehensive capital controls on both inflows and outflows played a key role in averting a crisis. Inflows consisted primarily of potentially volatile portfolio flows into the stock market, not short-term debt-creating flows. While such portfolio flows had been liberalized, inflows into India were more recent and had not reached euphoria levels. By contrast with Malaysia, where portfolio flows had also been important, there was no stock market boom and hence also no bust.

THE ROLE OF CAPITAL CONTROLS

The FBAR regime, whether of the formal Bretton Woods type or the more informal, close-to-managed-floating type—that all the economies that I have discussed, other than Hong Kong, had before the crisis—has several advantages. Provided adjustments are made in good time on the basis of fundamentals, such a regime yields the benefits of exchange rate stability and a nominal anchor. In addition, it allows adjustments to be made to capital market, terms of trade, and other shocks and to restore competitiveness after periods of real appreciation. It works well when governments choose to make timely adjustments and, most important, when governments rather than speculative markets are free to choose the time. The problem with open capital markets is that governments lose that freedom.

Speculation may anticipate devaluations or, when speculation is self-fulfilling, may force devaluations or abandonment of the regime even when devaluation was not needed on the basis of the fundamentals alone. Restrictions on capital outflows are designed to avoid this situation. They allow FBAR regimes to be maintained. Such restrictions cannot change the fundamentals that might make devaluation inevitable, but they give governments some freedom in policy making. They take away a short-term constraint on monetary policy. That, at least, is the theory. In practice, there are many forms of evasion possible so that the effectiveness of controls may be limited and, perhaps, short lived. Furthermore, controls have various well-known distorting effects and can be costly to enforce, increasing the scope for corruption.

Considering the Asian countries I have discussed here, India did have strict comprehensive controls on outflows, but speculative pressure, in any case, was not strong. China also had such controls, and there were speculative pressures based on market perception that there was a significant probability of devaluation. In both cases, capital controls, as many other controls, were comprehensive. In the case of India, the whole structure of controls and interventions in the domestic economy, as well as in trade and international capital movements, had notoriously adverse effects on economic efficiency and growth. In both countries, there were opportunities for evasion, but the net result was that the exchange rate regime was not under any threat.

When Malaysia was in deep recession in 1998, capital controls were introduced, designed to slow speculation against the currency and specifically to allow interest rates to be reduced. These measures, though limited in scope, shocked the financial community, being imposed in a country that had been a favorite of the international capital market and had been exceptionally open.

The Malaysian controls did succeed in insulating the domestic capital market from the world market with respect to short-term flows and thus made possible some fiscal and monetary expansion that otherwise might quickly have been inhibited by capital outflows and further depreciation. Thus, the controls sustained an exchange rate fixed at a new, more depreciated level. But, they were limited in scope, and eventually a crucial element was converted into a graduated tax on the repatriation of portfolio capital. Hence, a very transparent market-based discouragement of capital outflow replaced quantitative control. As an example for other countries, it has to be remembered that Malaysia had both a disciplined banking system and a competent central bank. Not all countries are so blessed.

I have discussed only controls or taxes on capital outflows. The absence of adequate controls or taxes on short-term capital inflows, and of regulations that limited bank borrowing, clearly played a role in the extent of the initial boom, the ending of which gave rise to the crisis. It is widely agreed that liberalization of capital inflows, especially short-term debt-creating borrowing, played a major role in the crises of Thailand and Korea. This is a large subject of its own and does not bear directly on the choice of exchange rate regime. Excessive foreign borrowing, especially in the form of short-term borrowing and of volatile portfolio flows, has been highly destabilizing but presents a problem irrespective of the exchange rate regime.

With a floating rate regime, such excessive foreign borrowing leads to large appreciations of the exchange rate followed by depreciations; with a currency board regime, it would lead to inflation and real appreciations, followed by deep recessions. And, with an FBAR regime, it leads to real appreciations followed by a currency crisis with all the problems I have discussed.

CONCLUSION: WHAT LESSONS FOR THE CHOICE OF REGIME?

Let me draw together some of the lessons that seem to emerge from a rather complex story.

First, the Asian crisis was not caused by the FBAR regimes (or near-FBAR regimes) that existed before the crisis. Because of excessive international borrowing and other factors during the boom, there would eventually have been a crisis even with floating rates, managed floating rate regimes, or currency boards. Other factors were more important, notably the extent of short-term private debts accumulated relative to the level of foreign exchange reserves.

Second, the financial crisis and the recessions that resulted were greater because of the unhedged foreign borrowing problem, and that, in turn, may have been caused by the

FBAR regime. Furthermore, with a floating rate regime, the boom might have ended earlier. Pegging to the U.S. dollar was one cause of the real appreciations that took place during the boom periods, and possibly pegging to a basket that included at least the yen might have been better.

Third, the efforts on the part of some central banks, notably those of Thailand and Korea, to maintain their pegged rates once speculation against the currencies intensified created a typical FBAR problem, leading eventually to losses by the central banks and to a loss of political credibility. With a floating rate regime, the necessary depreciations would have come earlier and more gradually. Four of the five crisis countries now have managed floating regimes, with some intervention designed to moderate exchange rate instability. That is currently the general trend among emerging market economies and seems to me the right policy. Malaysia went back to an FBAR regime, though there is no long-term commitment to it.

Fourth, the currency board regime in Hong Kong has been successful, but Hong Kong is very much a special case. A currency board would be inappropriate for any of the Asian-crisis countries, principally because the benefits of real depreciation in increasing exports after a crisis would not be available.

Finally, exchange controls on capital outflows were effective in Malaysia, with a favorable outcome. It is a policy that cannot be ruled out in crisis situations for other countries, but Malaysia has a less corrupt financial system and a more competent civil service compared with many or most other developing countries. But, there is no doubt that the ability to sustain an FBAR regime can be strengthened, as in China, by effective controls. More important for avoiding a crisis in the first place are adequate regulation of foreign borrowing by banks and taxes or controls on short-term capital inflows when these reach exceptional levels. But, these are all matters of dispute where recommendations must differ country by country.

ANNALS, *AAPSS*, **579**, January 2002

Exchange Rates in a World of Capital Mobility

By MARTIN WOLF

ABSTRACT: All exchange rate regimes create difficulties. But, painful experience has now reinforced the theoretical presumption against adjustable pegs in a world of capital account convertibility. Liberalization of the capital account has forced countries away from the middle ground toward the polar option of free-floating exchange rates, with monetary autonomy, or hard pegs, without it.

Martin Wolf is the associate editor and chief economics commentator of the Financial Times, *London. He was awarded the Commander of the British Empire in 2000 for services to financial journalism. He is a visiting fellow of Nuffield College, Oxford University, and a special professor at the University of Nottingham. Mr. Wolf was joint winner of the Wincott Foundation senior prize for excellence in financial journalism for 1989 and 1997, and he won the RTZ David Watt memorial prize for 1994, a prize granted annually "to a writer judged to have made an outstanding contribution in the English language towards the clarification of national, international and political issues and the promotion of their greater understanding." Mr. Wolf obtained the master of philosophy in economics from Oxford University in 1971. He joined the World Bank as a young professional in 1971. In 1981, he joined the Trade Policy Research Centre, London, as director of studies. He joined the* Financial Times *as chief economics leader writer in 1987. He was promoted to associate editor in 1990 and to chief economics commentator in 1996.*

NOTE: This article is based on columns written for the *Financial Times*. These are, in particular, "Argentina's Riches to Rags Tale" (21 March 2001), "Turkey Trips on Its Weak Peg" (28 February 2001), "Capital Punishment" (5 May 1999), "Off Target" (3 February 1999), and an earlier "Capital Punishment" (17 March 1998).

TURKEY'S recent experience illustrates the difficulty of using an exchange rate anchor for disinflation in the absence of tight exchange controls. Such a regime has worked in other countries in the past, but those successes needed luck, discipline, and timing. Turkey lacked all three. As a result, its peg collapsed in February 2001. While damaging, that need not be a disaster, provided counterinflationary credibility is preserved and the balance sheet losses consequent on both the devaluation and the high interest rates needed to control inflation are manageable. In both respects, Turkey has reached the limits of what is tolerable and may be forced back to very high inflation or default.

An alternative way of gaining credibility is a very hard currency peg, notably a currency board. Argentina adopted such a regime in the early 1990s. For a long time, this regime worked rather well. But, a series of adverse external events has caused a prolonged recession. That, in turn, has put Argentina in a vicious downward spiral of weak credibility, high real interest rates, and back to economic contraction. As a result, credit risk has replaced exchange rate risk, as creditors have increasingly come to question Argentina's ability to service its debt. The resulting debt trap has undermined exchange rate credibility as well. Now Argentina is left with three options, all bad: struggling on, default, and devaluation.

Behind the difficulties of emerging market economies lie the fluctuations in capital flows. In the case of the crisis-hit East Asian countries, the shift in net capital flows between 1996 and 1998 was equal to 12 percent of precrisis GDP. This punishing experience underlines the risks attendant on financing sizeable current account deficits with debt-creating inflows. The central lesson is the importance of strengthening a country's capacity to borrow sensibly and to adjust to financial circumstances swiftly. An important element in this is avoiding unsustainable exchange rate commitments, which encouraged excessive borrowing prior to the crises.

Floating exchange rates are inevitable in relations between the so-called G3—the United States, the eurozone, and Japan. There is no chance of agreeing to a symmetrical target zone among these currencies, because that would require a willingness to implement a joint monetary policy when currencies reached the limits of their bands. However, it would be possible for Japan and the eurozone to implement a ceiling against the dollar unilaterally. In Japan's case, that could be highly desirable. In the eurozone's, it is possible to imagine circumstances in which it would be useful.

All exchange rate regimes create difficulties: floating exchange rates create relatively small problems for much of the time, adjustable pegs create much bigger problems for some of the time, and permanent fixes can create monstrous problems, though only occasionally. A country's monetary history, size and sophistication, openness to trade, principal trading partners, and political destiny will all help determine which of the available regimes it does—and should—choose. But, painful experience has now reinforced the theoretical presumption against adjustable pegs in a world of capital account convertibility. We know beyond question that a country cannot combine an open capital account with monetary autonomy and a fixed exchange rate. Not surprisingly, the liberalization of the capital account by an ever-increasing number of countries, both developed and developing, has forced them away from the middle ground where monetary autonomy meets the adjustable peg toward the polar option of freely floating exchange rates, with monetary autonomy, or hard pegs, without it.

This article will illustrate a few of these issues. It will start by considering the implications of the failure of Turkey's recent attempt to use the exchange rate as an anchor for a disinflationary monetary policy. It will then turn to the potential risks of a currency board, focusing on the case of Argentina. That will lead to a broader discussion of the challenge of managing capital flows for developing countries. Finally, it will turn to exchange rate management among the so-called G3—the United States, the European Union, and Japan.

EXCHANGE RATE–BASED DISINFLATION—THE CASE OF TURKEY

It can be very damaging to make promises one may be unable to keep. Yet, that is exactly what a country does when it employs a weak exchange rate peg as the core of its monetary policy. The costs of a failure can be great, as Turkey learned with the collapse of its exchange rate peg on 19 February 2001.

Stanley Fischer (2001), the International Monetary Fund's (IMF's) first deputy managing director, has pointed out that

> each of the major international capital-market related crises since 1994—Mexico in 1994, Thailand, Indonesia and South Korea in 1997, Russia and Brazil in 1998, and Argentina and Turkey in 2000—has in some way involved a fixed or pegged exchange rate regime.

In all but one of these cases—that of Argentina's currency board—the peg collapsed. Turkey is in good—or bad—company.

Such failures impose big costs. These come in two main forms: loss of monetary credibility and balance sheet deterioration.

In a country with a record of high inflation, the devaluation will be taken as a signal of its imminent return. The resulting behavior will make the prophecy self-fulfilling. The usual IMF-supported solution is to impose high real interest rates, to signal resolve and increase the cost of an inflationary flight from the currency. However, this policy will simultaneously push the economy into recession and worsen the plight of debtors. Under a peg, huge profits can apparently be made by borrowing in foreign currency to buy domestic assets that pay higher interest rates. Once the peg fails, unhedged borrowers—many of them banks—will suffer huge costs. Because banks are explicitly or implicitly guaranteed by the state, these costs fall on taxpayers.

What makes such a failure particularly pernicious is that it is those who trusted the government the most who lose the most. The loss of trust in government further undermines political credibility in countries that used the peg precisely because credibility was so weak in the first place.

For these reasons, the bipolar view seems compelling. Countries open to global capital flows should either have irrevocable long-term fixes—such as currency boards, adoption of another country's currency as their own, or currency unions—or flexible rates—such as free or managed floats (without announced targets or bands) or pegs with very wide bands. What are precluded are systems in which the government is thought to be wedded to a particular exchange rate or narrow range of rates but is not institutionally committed to defending those rates at all costs.

While the failure of a peg almost always imposes significant costs, their extent depends on the circumstances in which the peg was created. The advanced and emerging market economies that employed adjustable pegs in the 1990s fell into three categories:

- Advanced economies with sophisticated financial systems and close to universal use of the domestic currency for domestic transactions, such as the United Kingdom;
- Emerging market economies, such as Thailand, Indonesia, and South Korea, that were heavily dependent on trade and had inefficient and costly financial systems but had enjoyed relatively long histories of monetary and fiscal stability and, in consequence, had high ratios of bank credit to GDP; and
- Emerging market economies with records of monetary instability, such as Mexico, Russia, and Brazil, which wanted a disinflationary anchor.

Exchange rate collapses imposed small costs on advanced countries because monetary credibility had been reasonably good, and unhedged foreign-currency liabilities correspondingly modest. They imposed modest credibility losses on the East Asian economies (except for Indonesia) but big balance sheet losses, largely because the peg had long been credible. Members of the third group tended to suffer smaller balance sheet losses than the second because their pegs had lacked credibility. But, they tended to suffer bigger credibility losses than the other two and needed longer periods of high real interest rates.

Turkey fits into this third category. It has had a very long history of high inflation. It was reasonable to believe that some signal of the change in policy was needed, both to control the politicians and to convince the markets. Several countries have succeeded in using such a disinflationary exchange rate peg and jumping off it in time: Israel and Poland are examples.

Yet, these successes have needed luck, discipline, and timing. Turkey lacked all three: it was subject to significant adverse shocks, not least the rise in energy prices and the high interest rates on emerging market debt; its politicians did not behave themselves (indeed, a row between the president and the prime minister triggered the exchange rate collapse); and its built-in exit from the complex crawling rate regime became what economists call "time inconsistent"—once the rate had come to be considered overvalued, people expected it to fall sharply after floating—but this then guaranteed huge pressure for the immediate fall that has happened.

Turkey thus joins the countries whose disinflationary pegs have collapsed. That may be damaging but need not be a total disaster. Whether it is depends on how far credibility is preserved and how big the balance sheet losses turn out to be. The two are related via the extent of depreciation.

The more the Turkish authorities can convince people that inflation will not be allowed to explode, the smaller will be the exchange rate overshoot (and vice versa). High interest rates will be needed for some time. However, the more credible the commitment to low inflation, the shorter that period needs to be. That is why the move to operational independence of the central bank—part of the IMF program agreed on 15 May 2001—and the planned move to inflation targeting are so important.

The smaller the exchange rate collapse, the more modest will also be the balance sheet losses. To minimize balance sheet losses and hold up the exchange rate, the country will need help in keeping foreign-currency credit lines in place. Fortunately, Turkey is heavily dependent on foreign banks, particularly European ones. It may be possible to persuade these banks to keep lines open, in their own collective interest. But, the country also needs to restructure its own banks swiftly to minimize the chance that insolvent institutions will throw good money after bad. That has become an important part of the new IMF program.

Turkey's case underlines the extreme danger of weak exchange rate pegs. Today, the country suffers from a malign combination of its long-standing lack of monetary credibility with the further loss consequent on an exchange rate collapse. Yet, it has lost only a battle. Experience elsewhere demonstrates that it can still win its war, provided it acts decisively to retain fiscal discipline, institutionalize monetary credibility, and clean up the financial system. At the time of writing, in the summer of 2001, whether Turkey will win its battle to gain credibility and secure stability remains doubtful but not inconceivable.

CURRENCY BOARDS—THE CASE OF ARGENTINA

One alternative to the adjustable peg—or, as in Turkey, a preannounced crawling peg with narrow margins of fluctuation—is a permanently fixed exchange rate in the form of a currency board. In such an arrangement, there is a one-to-one relationship between the supply of the domestic currency and the foreign-currency reserves of the central bank. In the 1990s, Argentina became one of the most significant users of the currency board, with its one-to-one convertibility of the U.S. dollar into the peso. To preclude inflation forever, it tied itself to the mast of its convertibility plan. But by

2001, the economy was in danger of drowning, as the economy foundered on the rocks of recession.

The arguments for tight currency arrangements—such as a currency board, use of another country's currency as one's own, or membership in a currency union—are that they guarantee monetary discipline and eliminate currency risk. But, if policy is insufficiently disciplined elsewhere, particularly fiscal policy, as in Argentina, or regulation of commercial banking, currency and inflation risk can be transformed into credit risk.

The tragedy is that Argentina's performance improved dramatically in the 1990s. It was the world's tenth richest country in 1913. But by 1990, its income per head had fallen to 40 percent of the Western European average. Then, between 1990 and 1998, GDP per head rose by 42 percent. During those years, the economy expanded by 60 percent, against some 25 percent in Mexico and Brazil. Alas, it has not lasted. The economy fell into a prolonged recession. In a desperate throw, president Fernando de la Rua brought back Domingo Cavallo, architect of the initial reforms.

What went wrong? Adverse external events—the emerging market financial crises of 1997 and 1998, a sharp deterioration in the terms of trade, the devaluation of the Brazilian real and the strength of the U.S. dollar—hit the economy. Given the pegged exchange rate, these shocks delivered a big loss of competitiveness: on the basis of relative unit labor costs, the real exchange rate appreciated by about a third between early 1998 and the middle of 1999.

The link with the dollar generated deflation. Between September 1998 and February 2001, U.S. consumer prices rose by 8 percent. During the same period, Argentinean prices fell by 3 percent. Given enough time, the adjustment in relative prices would restore competitiveness. However, the time was long and hard: at the end of 2000, GDP per head was about 8 percent lower than at its peak in the second quarter of 1998.

This lengthy deflation was not caused by loss of competitiveness alone. Just as important were high real interest rates. Real prime interest rates, in pesos, were as high as 10 percent. At the long end, real interest rates in dollars have been still higher. At a spread over U.S. treasuries of 850 basis points, the Argentinean government would be borrowing at a real rate of nearly 15 percent relative to changes in the domestic price level.

Such high real interest rates are not just contractionary; they are unsustainable. Argentina's public and external debt are both just a little more than 50 percent of GDP. This would be perfectly manageable at the rates of interest paid by high-income countries but not at those paid by Argentina. These high interest rates have reflected perceptions of Argentina's political fragility and the likelihood of a default. But, that perception has, in turn, been worsened by recession. Thus, the system that eliminated inflation and exchange rate risk has created a vicious downward spiral of worsening credit risk, deepening recession, and back to worsening credit risk yet again.

In the long run, even exchange rate and inflation risk have reemerged. Not only have spreads on dollar borrowing vis-à-vis U.S. treasuries soared, but so has the gap between rates on borrowing in pesos and dollars. If the exchange rate were certain, these would be the same. But in March 2001, the spread on three-month interbank borrowing was almost 500 basis points, against a usual spread of about 100 points.

Argentina's currency board has itself been solid. The government could also survive without new borrowing for some time. But, if it did not come up with a credible and politically acceptable program, the country was likely to be driven to default, to feel obliged to devalue, or even to do both.

Ricardo Lopez Murphy, economics minister for fifteen days, failed the political test. His proposed fiscal adjustment was not huge, at some 1 percent of GDP. It would have brought the fiscal position into line with the country's agreement with the IMF. But, that would still have left a sizeable consolidated fiscal deficit—forecast by the IMF in December at 3.1 percent of GDP for 2001—and a modest primary fiscal surplus (surplus, before interest payments) of 1.5 percent. That would not even have stabilized the debt ratio. But, even this package did not gain political support and so, inevitably, failed to secure the required improvement in confidence.

Could Mr. Cavallo do better? The answer has to be, "Yes, but with difficulty." Conceptually, Argentina has just three options: to struggle on, to default, or to devalue.

Struggling on would work if a new package restored confidence to the market and growth to the economy. If there were renewed growth, confidence would revive; if there were renewed confidence, growth would improve. But, given the perception that the real exchange rate, albeit improving, is overvalued and that the president, albeit trying, is weak, it would need a miracle to pull this off. Mr. Cavallo's desperate policy expedients—tariffs, export subsidies, and modification of the convertibility plan—have convinced markets that Argentina cannot bear the pain of deflationary adjustment. He has as a result done more to undermine confidence than to restore it.

The second option is default. Debt is unsustainable at current real interest rates and prospective growth rates, without implausible improvements in the fiscal and external balances. While it is reasonable to try to devise a package designed to support growth and make fiscal sustainability credible in the medium term, this may not work. An orderly debt restructuring would then be preferable to chaos.

The third option is devaluation. Most outsiders would consider a floating exchange rate preferable to this peg. But Argentina is so dollarized—and bound to become still more so if confidence weakens further—that it is hard to see how it could get from here to there without wrecking much of the private sector. The government would probably have to enact a law converting dollar debt into peso debt. But, if devaluation seems horribly difficult, the polar opposite—dollarization—is irrelevant. The economy's chief problem has become credit risk, not currency risk. But, dollarization would do little or nothing about the former.

The wider lesson is that very hard exchange rate regimes do not eliminate risks. They are as likely merely to change them. Countries choose such regimes to control politicians and eliminate inflation. However, if politicians remain ill disciplined and economies unstable and inflexible, the risks will reemerge somewhere else. Argentina has been learning this lesson. Mr. Cavallo eliminated inflation with a stroke. Restoring growth to the economy and confidence to markets is far harder.

CAPITAL PUNISHMENT—LESSONS OF THE EAST ASIAN FINANCIAL CRISIS

Behind the difficulties in developing satisfactory exchange rate regimes for emerging market economies lies the volatility of capital flows and the difficulty in winning credibility in financial markets. Robert Rubin (1999b), when U.S. secretary of the treasury, argued that "international capital flows have the potential to provide immense benefits to emerging markets and other developing countries. They also pose some risks." With these remarks, Mr. Rubin showed a remarkable talent for understatement. Some risks indeed! Unfortunately, the objections to his remarks go deeper still. Debt-creating capital inflows are symbiotically linked to the bacillus that causes crises. The more a country enjoys the benefits, the greater is its exposure to the risks.

The scale of the East Asian financial crisis should not be forgotten. According to the Washington-based Institute for International Finance, between 1996 and 1998, the five crisis-hit Asian countries (Indonesia, Malaysia, the Philippines, South Korea, and Thailand) experienced an aggregate swing of $124 billion in their current accounts, from deficits of $55 billion to estimated surpluses of $69 billion. This shift, over two years, was equivalent to 12 percent of 1997 aggregate precrisis GDP. Behind this huge adjustment lay a shift of $130 billion in the net supply of private finance over the two years; 96 percent of this swing was accounted for by debt-creating flows, which moved from an inflow of $84 billion in 1996 to an outflow of $41 billion in 1998. Commercial banks, in particular, shifted from an inflow of $63 billion to an outflow of $36 billion.

This was a devastating turnaround. Worse, the turmoil that followed Thailand's devaluation of the baht in July 1997 came a mere two and a half years after the start of the so-called Tequila Crisis, triggered by Mexico's devaluation in December 1994. To experience one crisis may be a misfortune; to experience two in less than three years looks like carelessness.

This depressing story bears directly on Mr. Rubin's (1999b) claims that the potential gains of private capital flows are "immense" while posing "some" risks.

No sensible person doubts the immense benefits of inflows of foreign direct investment and portfolio equity. The former, in particular, are not just impressively stable; they give countries access to invaluable technology and organizational knowhow. Foreign-currency debt-creating inflows, in general, and short-term flows, in particular, are a different story.

Borrowing and lending allow people to separate the timing of their consumption from that of their earnings. They permit them to invest beyond their ability to save or save beyond their opportunities to invest. They allow people to cope with crises and postpone the benefits of a windfall. Countries can gain exactly the same benefits. Larry Summers (1999), the former U.S. treasury secretary, made the classic case for capital flows when he remarked in April 1999 that "there are few things with as great a potential to raise human welfare as the creation of a safe and sustainable system for the flow of capital from the developed world to the developing one."

If a country is to invest more than it saves (or spend more than it earns, which is the same thing), it must run a current account deficit. These are identically equivalent statements. So the test of whether countries gain an immense benefit from inflows is whether they are able to run sizeable current account deficits. The answer to that question is clear: alas, they cannot do so, at least not for long.

The IMF's *World Economic Outlook* of May 1999 contained a lengthy discussion of financial contagion. Among its conclusions were that "external imbalances" are closely correlated with the risk of crisis. However, the term "imbalance" is merely a pejorative label for a current account deficit. The *World Economic Outlook* also stated that it is essential to avoid a "significant exchange rate overvaluation." This seems absurd. If a country is to accommodate a capital inflow, the real exchange rate normally has to appreciate. That is how a current account deficit appears. In the presence of a strong capital inflow, it is difficult to prevent such an appreciation.

One possible way of avoiding such appreciation and limiting the risk created by the capital inflow is to accumulate foreign exchange reserves. Analytically, this is equivalent to a capital outflow by the public sector offsetting the inflow by the private sector. For the country as a whole, however, this is an expensive proposition. Not only does it forgo the net inflow of resources, but it pays an additional price, because the cost of the private sector's borrowing is always higher than the return on the public sector's investment abroad.

The conclusion is simple: the immense benefits of debt-creating inflows only arise if they are used in ways known to increase the risk of crises. They can be made safer, but only by forgoing the current account deficits that represent their chief advantage.

Indeed, today's best policy advice is probably that countries should pay a price to avoid running a large debt-financed current account deficit. They should accumulate reserves, instead. As the *World Economic Outlook* (IMF 1999) states, the likelihood of an attack on a country's currency and the country's chances of repelling the attack depends on its stock of foreign exchange reserves. It is the ratio of short-term debt to international reserves that matters, rather than simply the level of short-term debt. (84)

The benefits and the risks of debt-creating capital inflows are two sides of the same coin. The more a country attempts to enjoy of the former, the more it is exposed to the latter. It can minimize the risks, but only by minimizing the benefits.

It is important to understand why the risks are associated with debt-creating inflows. Debt is a contract that is supposed to be honored, whatever the circumstances. If the contract is in foreign exchange, the money must be found, whatever its price. If the debt contract is short term, the principal must be found, whenever the lender refuses to roll it over. Foreign-currency debt-creating inflows are unavoidably risky—and the more willing countries are to enjoy the benefits, the riskier they necessarily become. The question to be asked of all efforts at reform of the international financial architecture is how far they can alter this unpleasant logic.

An encouraging but over-optimistic view of the challenge is the one advanced by Alan Greenspan (1998), chairman of the Federal Reserve, in a speech on 3 March 1998: the high-technology capital markets of today are efficient; this "exposes and punishes underlying economic imprudence swiftly and decisively." Among the most important requirements for them to work, he suggested, is more transparency.

What emerges from the Asian crisis is tragically different: when euphoric, markets ignored bad news; when depressed, they underplayed good news. Either way, they overshot wildly, punishing countries with significant current account deficits or foreign-currency liabilities.

This is true, whichever of the two dominant stories about the crisis one is inclined to believe. One—told by Paul Krugman (1998), formerly at the Massachusetts Institute of Technology and now at Princeton University—is of bad policies: overguaranteed and underregulated financial institutions that blew a bubble bound to burst. The second—told by Steven Radelet and Jeffrey Sachs (1998) of the Harvard Institute for International Development—is of panic: financial markets that unnecessarily devastated sound economies.

The first story suggests the Asians deserved their fate, even if the punishment was disproportionate to the crime. If so, capital markets, far from punishing imprudence swiftly and decisively, indulged it for years. In the process, they also ignored all the signs of Asian "crony capitalism" and of unsustainable capital inflows, both of which had long been obvious. Professor Krugman's (1998) explanation for the market's mistakes was that investors thought themselves guaranteed. But, this is not all that convincing: much of the investment went to private companies that nobody can have supposed were safe; moreover, these countries could not have guaranteed foreign-currency liabilities, even if they promised to do so.

Investors were not so stupid, argued Radelet and Sachs (1998). The trouble was that panic, albeit rational for each individual institution, turned a necessary, ideally quite modest, adjustment into a catastrophe. Moreover, the inflows had exacerbated the economies' underlying weaknesses. Large-scale inflows raised the real exchange rate, created current account deficits, lowered domestic interest rates, and exacerbated overheating. In this view, inflows were a response to past Asian triumphs—and transmuted them to disaster.

On these two explanations, markets either got things wrong or made them so. The obvious conclusion is that managing openness to capital flows is a horribly tricky task. If the dominant cause of the crises is the first story, that of domestic policy failures, the answers include strengthening macro-economic fundamentals, eliminating incentives to inflow of the wrong sort of capital, opening the financial system to foreign financial service providers, introducing an improved supervisory and regulatory regime, eliminating inappropriate government guarantees, strengthening financial institutions, increasing transparency, and minimizing bailouts. If countries need to do all of this before they can liberalize safely, it will take decades, not years.

Unfortunately, the second story also has great force. Short-term lending against long-term assets is subject to panic. In domestic finance, the answer has long been a lender of last resort—an institution capable of providing needed liquidity. Yet, if a commercial bank in Thailand borrows dollars, no central bank can provide it with the currency it may need. Similarly, if Thailand as a country borrows dollars, there is no lender of last resort to assist it if creditors suddenly want their money back. The IMF lacks the resources needed to perform this role.

Suppose there will never be such a lender of last resort or the intrusive regulation of national policies the regime would entail. Potential borrowers must then protect themselves on their own. How to do so can be learned from the experience of those Asian countries that avoided the crisis and of successful economies elsewhere, notably Chile.

Here then are seven rules for avoiding the dangers of panic:

- Try to avoid current account deficits that are both large and sustained, even if they can be readily financed.
- Keep foreign-currency reserves, in the central bank or in the commercial banks, equal ideally to the country's short-term foreign-currency liabilities.
- Impose tight prudential regulation of the foreign-currency liabilities and assets of banks.
- Operate either a floating exchange rate or a currency board. Do not make strong commitments to potentially adjustable pegs.
- Consider controlling or taxing short-term foreign-currency borrowing, as has been done relatively successfully by Chile.
- Make the economy flexible enough to cope with sudden changes in the availability of capital.
- Create a bankruptcy regime capable of protecting companies from creditors.

Mr. Summers (1998) likened the capital markets to a jet plane. "We can go where we want much more quickly, we can get there more comfortably, more cheaply and most of the time more safely—but the crashes when they occur are that much more spectacular." It is an arresting simile. However, another obvious comparison is with the oceans. Sometimes, they are completely calm. But, if one is trying to cross them in safety, one needs a sound boat. And even then, it might be overwhelmed if the waves are high enough.

TARGET ZONES—THE CASE OF THE G3

The management of exchange rates is a challenge not only for emerging market economies. Because of the volatility of exchange rates among the G3, some analysts have recommended the adoption of target zones. Policy makers have generally disagreed. Former U.S. treasury secretary Robert Rubin (1999a), for example, argued at the annual meeting of the World Economic Forum in Davos on 30 January 1999 that "target zones and similar measures are no substitute for sound underlying policies and suffer from the defect that they could be pro- rather than counter-cyclical, thereby exacerbating, rather than countering adverse economic developments." This rejection did not preclude ad hoc intervention to deal with extreme volatility or large misalignments. But, Mr. Rubin's restatement of a long-held U.S. position appeared to end the ambitions of a few European and Japanese policy makers for target zones. Nothing has changed under the administration of George W. Bush.

Yet, establishment of partial target zones does not require U.S. agreement. Japanese and European policy makers might find it advantageous to establish targets unilaterally. More precisely, they might wish to set ceilings for the yen and euro against the dollar. The idea is workable. It could even appeal to those European politicians who fear the European Central Bank's (ECB's) orthodoxy.

The difficulty in establishing a reciprocal exchange rate regime among the three currencies is that they would need an agreed anchor for monetary policy. Consider a wide-band target zone regime of the kind recommended by Fred Bergsten (cited in How to target exchange rates 1998) of the Washington-based Institute for International Economics. Most of the time currencies would float freely. When they reached their limits, however, there would need to be an acceptable and agreed basis for deciding whose policy was "too loose" and whose "too tight".

Suppose an economy were in recession, with low interest rates. This would be likely to weaken the currency (though any such statement about exchange rates must be made with great caution). If the currency then reached the floor of its band (suggested by Mr. Bergsten, cited in How to target exchange rates 1998, at 15 percent around a central rate), the country would be required to tighten policy, thereby worsening the recession, unless the strong currency country were persuaded to loosen, instead. This, Mr. Rubin (1999a) rightly complained, could be "pro-cyclical." Since this is not a policy the United States is likely to accept, it is safe to assume such a reciprocal target zone system will never be agreed on.

Yet, even if such a target zone system is out of the question, a more one-sided one is not. It is difficult for a country to keep its currency up when it comes under downward pressure. By contrast, a currency under upward pressures can always be kept down with a sufficiently expansionary monetary policy. For this reason, pegs tend to fail whenever the anchor currency of the system becomes too strong. This is what happened to Europe's exchange rate mechanism in the aftermath of German unification and to dollar pegs worldwide after the currency's post-1995 appreciation.

In the case of the yen and euro, however, the danger can be avoided by the simple expedient of not having explicit lower limits. It is reasonable to assume the U.S. authorities would normally take advantage of any inordinate dollar appreciation to loosen policy. Moreover, neither the ECB nor the Bank of Japan is at all likely to start an inflationary spree. Thus, there seems little need for exchange rate floors.

Ceilings on the appreciation of the yen and euro against the dollar are a different matter. An argument can be made for announcing a permanent ceiling to the yen-dollar rate. Ronald McKinnon of Stanford University and Kenichi Ohno of Faitama University (1997, 1998) argued that convincing the Japanese public there is a ceiling to the yen's rate against the dollar would be the single most effective way of eliminating the specter of deflation. If that ceiling were set at, say, ¥120 to the dollar, it would impose a lower bound on yen inflation in tradable goods and services. Japanese inflation could not then be consistently below that in the United States. This would make it easier for the Japanese authorities to establish negative real rates of interest, when needed.

What about Europe? The position of the ECB is that price stability is the sole goal of policy. The proposition seems to be that monetary policy only affects economic activity via inflation, even in the short run. Unfortunately, when inflation is very low, it can also be very sticky. Price stability can then be consistent with many different paths for nominal and real demand. Look, for example, at Japan in the 1990s. Japan enjoyed close to perfect consumer price stability in the 1990s. Yet, even as orthodox an institution as the IMF has concluded that this achievement coincided with the emergence of a yawning output gap (difference between potential and actual GDP as a percentage of potential output) of 10 percent. Yet, despite this shortfall, Japan has not suffered a deep deflation.

The ECB's price stability objective may similarly prove compatible with stagnation. It is possible to imagine a situation in which a threat by the European finance ministers to impose a ceiling on the euro's rate against the dollar might be a sensible tactic. What is more, the treaty establishing monetary union says that "the council, acting by a qualified majority . . . on a recommendation from the Commission and after consulting the ECB . . . may formulate general orientations for exchange rate policy" (European Union 1999). So let the commission make the recommendation. The ECB will protest furiously. But, the ministers can, it appears, override such objections—or agree to drop the proposal in return for an explicit symmetrical inflation target of, say, 2 percent a year (perfectly consistent with price stability, plausibly measured).

A unilateral exchange rate ceiling can always be revoked. For Europe, this would pose no problem. However, without the fruitless task of negotiating a reciprocal target zone system, the eurozone finance ministers would be removing one of the world's potential threats: ECB complacency in the face of a destabilizing slowdown in aggregate demand. The suggestion of an exchange rate ceiling might persuade central bankers to reconsider their position. It would be a beautiful irony if European finance ministers in the brave new world of the euro threatened partially to subordinate the new currency to the dollar, merely to bring an overcautious (and overindependent) ECB to heel.

CONCLUSION

In a world of capital mobility, adjustable pegged exchange rates have had to be abandoned. Most countries have moved toward more or less managed floats. Some have tried currency boards, adoption of another country's currency as their own, or monetary union, as in the European Union. It is too early to tell which of these alternatives will prove the final destination—a world of many floating currencies or of very few big currencies, with smaller countries tightly attached to the big currency blocs.

Whatever exchange rate regime is chosen, experience of the past two decades underlines the extreme importance of managing capital account liberalization wisely. Too many countries have been devastated by financial crises that have resulted from throwing open poorly regulated financial systems underpinned by comprehensive government guarantees. While liberalization is desirable, it has to be done in the right way.

Floating rates are certainly the only possible way to relate the G3 currencies for the near future. However, it is still possible for the Japanese or European authorities to consider temporary or permanent ceilings on their currencies against the dollar. At present, such a ceiling seems an irrelevance, given the strength of the dollar. But, that is unlikely to last. It may make good sense therefore for the Japanese and Europeans to limit the extent of the dollar's fall.

References

European Union. 1999. Title VII, economic and monetary policy, article 111.2. *Selected instruments taken from the treaties*. Retrieved from http://europa.eu.int/eur-lex/en/treaties/dat/treaties_en.pdf.

Fischer, Stanley. 2001. Exchange rage regimes: Is the bipolar view correct? Available from www.imf.org. January.

Greenspan, Alan. 1998. Implications of recent Asian developments for community banking. Statement by Federal Reserve Board chairman before the Annual Convention of the Independent Bankers Association of America. Retrieved from http://www.federalreserve.gov/boarddocs/speeches/1998/19980303.htm. 3 March.

How to target exchange rates. 1998. *Financial Times*, 20 November.

International Monetary Fund (IMF). 1999. Chronic unemployment in the euro area: Causes and cures. In *World economic outlook*. Washington, DC: International Monetary Fund. May.

Krugman, Paul. 1998. Will Asia bounce back? Retrieved from http://web.mit.edu/krugman. March.

McKinnon, Ronald, and Kenichi Ohno. 1997. *Dollar and yen: Resolving conflict between the United States and Japan*. Cambridge, MA: MIT Press.

McKinnon, Ronald, and Kenichi Ohno. 1998. The real yen worry. *Financial Times*, 26 June.

Radelet, Steven, and Jeffrey Sachs. 1998. The East Asian financial crisis: Diagnosis, remedies, prospects. In *Brookings papers on economic activity*, vol. 1, edited by William C. Brainard and George L. Perry, 1-90. Washington, DC: Brookings Institution.

Rubin, Robert. 1999a. Remarks by Treasury Secretary Robert Rubin before the World Economic Conference, Davos. Retrieved from http://www.treas.gov/press/releases/pr2920.htm. 30 January.

Rubin, Robert. 1999b. Statement by treasury secretary Robert Rubin to the IMF Interim Committee. Retrieved from http://www.treas.gov/press/releases/pr3109.htm. 27 April.

Summers, Larry. 1998. Remarks by deputy treasury secretary before the International Monetary Fund. Retrieved from http://www.treas.gov/press/releases/pr2286.htm. 9 March.

Summers, Lawrence H. 1999. Roots of the Asian crises and the road to a stronger global financial system. Remarks by deputy secretary of the treasury to the Institute of International Finance. Retrieved from http://www.treas.gov/press/releases/pr3102.htm. 25 April.

Wolf, Martin. 1998. Capital punishment. *Financial Times*, 17 March.

———. 1999a. Capital punishment. *Financial Times*, 5 May.

———. 1999b. Off target. *Financial Times*, 3 February.

———. 2001a. Argentina's riches to rags tale. *Financial Times*, 21 March.

———. 2001b. Turkey trips on its weak peg. *Financial Times*, 28 February.

ANNALS, *AAPSS*, **579**, January 2002

The Collapse of Exchange Rate Pegs

By HARRIS DELLAS, P.A.V.B. SWAMY, and GEORGE S. TAVLAS

ABSTRACT: All pegged exchange rate arrangements are subject to predicaments that cast doubt on the ability of the policy makers to maintain the peg. This article organizes the literature dealing with the fragility of exchange rate nominal-anchor regimes around six fundamental and interrelated problems that can undermine the ability of policy makers to maintain their commitment to an exchange rate peg. It describes the regime-specific characteristics of an international monetary system comprising both floating rates and pegged rates—the operating domain of a nominal-anchor peg—that produce externalities relative to a pure float or a fixed-rate regime. Those externalities can lead to instability for small countries that peg to the currency of a large country, magnify the effects of asymmetric shocks on exchange rates against third currencies, and provide an escape mechanism that may help absolve the policy makers of the disciplinary constraint of a pure peg.

Harris Dellas holds a Ph.D. in economics from the University of Rochester. He currently holds the chair of applied macroeconomics at the University of Bern (Switzerland) and is a director of the Institute of Economics. He has been on the faculty of, among other places, Vanderbilt University (United States), the University of Maryland (United States), the Catholic University of Louvain (Belgium), and the University of Bonn (Germany). He is also a research associate of the Center for Economic and Policy Research and the Athens Institute of Economic Policy Studies.

P.A.V.B. Swamy is with the Bureau of Labor Statistics in Washington, D.C. He has previously worked at the Federal Reserve Board and the Office of the Comptroller of the Currency. He received a Ph.D. from the University of Wisconsin–Madison and taught at the State University of New York at Buffalo and the Ohio State University. He also did part-time teaching at three Washington-area universities. He was a visiting scholar at the International Monetary Fund in the month of June 2001. He is the author (or coau-

INTRODUCTION

The progression of attacks against currencies with pegged exchange rates in recent years has led a number of economists to argue that there is little, if any, middle ground between floating exchange rates and the adoption of a common currency. Pegged exchange rates have come to be increasingly viewed as a problematic way to conduct policy, an invitation to the sudden whims of foreign-exchange speculators that can wreak havoc on domestic economic conditions.[1] The fall from standing of pegged exchange rates among economists represents a remarkable turn of events. Just ten years ago—during the early 1990s—a pegged exchange rate arrangement was viewed by many as a viable, if not desirable, alternative between the extremes of floating exchange rates and a single currency. If credible, such an arrangement promised to deliver anti-inflation benefits with low output and employment costs to a country that pegged its exchange rate to the currency of a low-inflation country.

What has happened in the intervening ten years to turn the tide of professional opinion? This article addresses this issue. The article argues that the credibility hypothesis, which was used to support the use of a pegged exchange rate arrangement as a nominal-anchor mechanism, promised considerably more than it could deliver and contained the seeds of its own demise. The article organizes the literature dealing with the fragility of exchange rate nominal-anchor regimes around six fundamental and interrelated problems that can undermine the ability of policy makers to maintain their commitment to an exchange rate peg: (1) the liquidity problem; (2) the credibility problem; (3) the transition problem; (4) the adjustment problem; (5) problems posed by capital flows, contagion, and self-fulfilling attacks; and (6) mixed-regime problems. An inference drawn from the discussion is that exchange rate nominal-anchor regimes contain internal dynamics that make such regimes especially fragile.

---

thor) of one book and ninety-six published research papers. His research interests include foundations of econometrics, econometric theory, estimation of economic relationships and their applications in macroeconomics, banking, and finance.

George S. Tavlas is Director-Advisor, Economics Research Department, Bank of Greece, Athens, Greece. He was previously Chief of the General Resources and SDR Policy Division of the International Monetary Fund. He has also worked at the U.S. Department of State and has been a consultant for the Organization for Economic Cooperation and Development in Paris and a guest scholar with the Brookings Institution. He is a member of the board of directors of the Center for Economics Planning and Research in Athens, an affiliated scholar with the Center for the Study of Central Banks (New York University School of Law), and a research associate of the Athens Institute of Economic Policy Studies.

NOTE: The views expressed are the authors' own and are not necessarily those of their respective institutions.

DISCIPLINE AND CREDIBILITY

The discipline hypothesis

The credibility hypothesis is a close relative of the discipline hypothesis, which has long been used in support of pegged exchange rates. Early advocates of flexible exchange rates (e.g., Sohmen 1963; Harberler 1964) regarded the argument that flexible rates reduce the resolve or discipline to fight inflation as perhaps the most serious objection to a system of flexible exchange rates.

Under pegged exchange rates, a country that inflates at a higher rate than its trading partners will experience a deterioration in its balance of payments. According to the discipline argument, such a country faces the following choices: (1) it can run down its holdings of reserves and, in the process, risk a speculative attack against its currency; (2) it can devalue its currency before a speculative attack materializes; or (3) it can restrain aggregate demand so that its inflation rate is brought into conformity with those of its trading partners. A policy bias toward discipline is fostered for two primary reasons. First, the country's reserves are put on the line, and the quantity of such reserves is limited. Second, the authorities who devalue are often considered to have failed in their macroeconomic management. The need to preserve scarce reserves and the desire to maintain the exchange rate peg to avoid political costs leave the authorities with little choice but to impose restrictive and, perhaps, unpopular macroeconomic policies.

The discipline hypothesis argues that such a self-correcting disciplinary mechanism is absent under floating rates because the only consequences of a relatively high inflation rate are a depreciating currency and a higher price level in the high-inflation country. Since a flexible exchange rate helps equilibrate supply and demand in the foreign exchange market, the balance of payments constraint on domestic policy is said to be eliminated. As Goldstein (1980) put it in his critique of the discipline hypothesis, "external pressures to reduce the inflation rate in the high-inflation country will disappear, and . . . inflation will be higher than under fixed rates" (p. 6).

The discipline hypothesis has been shown to be subject to several limitations, which have diminished its relevance. First, the hypothesis (at least in its earlier versions) is based on the assumption that the supply of reserves is limited (Halm 1969) and an analytic framework in which macroeconomic policies affect the balance of payments primarily through trade flows and, thereby, affect the level of reserves and/or the exchange rate. Under conditions of high capital mobility, however, the relationship between changes in macroeconomic policies and reserves is (in the short run) not clear-cut. An expansionary fiscal policy, for example, can raise domestic interest rates and (with pegged exchange rates) lead to an increase in (gross) reserves. Consequently, changes in reserves are not always accurate indicators of a country's policy stance when exchange rates are pegged and capital is mobile. Second, and related to the first limitation, the replacement of the flow model of exchange rate determination with the asset model has led to the view that under floating rates, expansionary macroeconomic policies can lead to abrupt and undesirable movements in exchange rates. These movements can provide a strong constraint on the use of such policies (Mishkin 1997, 17). Viewed in this light, exchange rate changes under floating rates can themselves provide discipline since they happen immediately and are very visible whereas reserve changes usually become public after some delay.

Importing credibility

Although the above limitations served to diminish the relevance of the discipline hypothesis, during the 1980s and early 1990s, the view that exchange rate pegging can impart discipline was resuscitated in light of developments in rational expectations. The discipline hypothesis argued that an exchange rate commitment would help a high-inflation country attain a low-inflation equilibrium, but there would be a cost to pay. Along the way to lower inflation, the country in question would experience the higher-unemployment and lower-output costs that would derive from any restrictive policies. The credibility hypothesis promised more. It argued that if the exchange rate commitment should be credible, so that it is really believed in the goods, labor, and foreign exchange markets, then the unemployment and output costs of the restrictive policies would be reduced. Whereas the discipline hypothesis stressed the disciplinary effects of pegged exchange rates on the policy makers, the credibility hypothesis emphasized that if credible, the use of the exchange rate as a nominal anchor could discipline both the policy makers and the private agents (Corden 1994, 76-84). By changing the expectations of the latter, the costs of attaining a low-inflation equilibrium would be lessened.

The credibility hypothesis is based on work by Barro and Gordon (1983) on optimal monetary policy design, which seeks to explain how a positive inflation rate can exist, on average, even when long-run real economic performance does not seem to be correlated with expansionary policies. The explanation is that the public views policy making as opportunistic. The next election is never far away, and policy makers are tempted to improve the situation in the short run at the cost of higher inflation in the long run. Thus, policy makers are willing to manufacture an unexpected expansion in macroeconomic policy even in the absence of a long-run trade-off between unemployment and inflation. Assuming that the public has rational expectations (so that inflation cannot come as a surprise on average) and that the government values both price stability and high employment, this explanation yields the following strong policy conclusions: (1) the policy makers do not succeed in surprising the public systematically (and thus do not permanently increase employment), and (2) the actual and expected rates of inflation are higher than the inflation rate that would prevail if the policy makers could credibly precommit.

If the policy makers of a high-inflation country (which we also call the "peripheral" country) could persuade economic agents that they have really changed their preferences, they could move the economy from a high-inflation state to a low-inflation state without incurring as much unemployment as would be incurred in the absence of the credibility of their policies. The policy makers can make credible their intentions by pegging their exchange rate to the currency of the low-inflation country (which we also call the "center" country). By doing so, the high-inflation country announces that the equilibrium inflation rate will be that of the low-inflation country. According to the credibility hypothesis, inflation expectations in the high-inflation country will decline faster than they would have in the absence of the announcement of the exchange rate peg, allowing less unemployment during the adjustment process (Giavazzi and Pagano 1988; Melitz 1998; Giavazzi and Giovannini 1989). It is the view that a high-inflation country can import the credibility of a low-inflation anchor country by pegging—thereby lowering the output and employment costs of moving to a low-inflation equilibrium—that has formed the analytic core of the exchange rate nominal-anchor hypothesis.

WHY DO NOMINAL EXCHANGE RATE ANCHOR REGIMES COLLAPSE?

All pegged exchange rate arrangements are subject to predicaments that cast doubt on the ability to maintain the commitment to the peg. Klein and Marion (1994) studied a sample of sixty-one pegged exchange rate episodes in Latin America during the 1957 to 1991 period and found that they had a mean duration of twenty-nine months, a median duration of ten months, and a standard deviation of forty-four months. Obstfeld and Rogoff (1995) found that since 1973, only a few major countries have been able continuously to maintain tightly fixed exchange rates (generally within ±2 percent bands) for at least five years, and most of those were special cases.[2] The pre-1973 literature, framed in the context of the discipline hypothesis, identified several (interconnected) problems that could undermine the ability to maintain a peg, including the $n - 1$—or liquidity—problem and the adjustment problem.[3] In what follows, it is argued that additional factors relating to (1) the post-1973 predilection to use the exchange rate as a nominal anchor, (2) the post-1973 increase in capital mobility, and (3) the logical implications of an international monetary system that includes both floating and pegged rates have compounded the potential destabilizing properties of the liquidity and adjustment problems and introduced additional problems that can undermine the sustainability of pegged arrangements.

The liquidity problem

The liquidity problem arises because policy makers (in either the center country or a peripheral country) change their preferences. A pegged exchange rate arrangement requires a consensus among the participants about the stance of monetary policy, but in a system of n countries, there are only $n - 1$ independent exchange rates. In the absence of a generally accepted, purely international money such as gold, a mechanism is needed to pin down the stance of monetary policy in the system (Mundell 1968). The members of the system can opt to follow a cooperative (symmetric) arrangement by jointly determining the stance of monetary policy in the system. Alternatively, the system can be asymmetric, whereby one country determines the stance of monetary policy for the system as a whole. A nominal-anchor exchange rate arrangement, whether a formal system or a unilateral peg, is asymmetric since it presupposes that peripheral countries gain credibility by forfeiting the conduct of monetary policy to the center country. As in any asymmetric regime, conflicts can arise between the policy makers of the center country and those of the peripheral countries.

To explain, suppose that a new government has been elected in a peripheral country and the new policy makers attach more weight to reducing unemployment in the short run than the previous policy makers did. An implication of the Barro-Gordon model (1983) is that the new policy makers have an incentive to cheat to gain a more favorable short-term trade-off. Alternatively, the liquidity problem can arise not because of a new government but because the existing government changes its preferences once it has attained its goal of reducing inflation. Suppose the importance that the government attaches to reducing inflation diminishes when inflation has been reduced and the unemployment rate is at its natural (or long-run) level. In this circumstance, the government has an incentive to cheat so as to reduce the unemployment rate in the short run, leading to differences about the stance of monetary policy between the peripheral and center countries. The liquidity problem, therefore, can arise because the preferences of a given set of policy makers are state dependent.

The credibility problem

The credibility problem occurs because economic agents are uncertain about the preferences of the authorities and/or the structure of the economy. To procure credibility, the policy makers of a high-inflation country who peg their currency to that of a low-inflation country will need to prove to the public that they are committed to reducing inflation if they are to reap the credibility gains. The public can get proof of such a change in preferences if the policy makers allow the unemployment rate to increase so as to demonstrate that they care less about increasing employment (in the short run) and more about reducing inflation.[4] Put differently, a high-inflation country will still have to endure a rise in unemployment to prove that the preferences of its policy makers have become the same as those of the low-inflation country (De Grauwe 1996, 69-71).

The following problem arises in implementing this strategy. Suppose an economy has experienced a rise in the unemployment rate. This situation may reflect the willingness of the policy makers to bite the bullet and put up with a temporary increase in unemployment to prove that their preferences have changed. The outcome may also be due, however, to a temporary, negative asymmetric shock that increases unemployment and weakens the policy makers' commitment to the pegged exchange rate. Unless economic agents know the structural characteristics of the economy, they will be uncertain whether the policy makers have changed their preferences, the economy has experienced a negative asymmetric shock, a combination of these influences has occurred, or something else has caused the unemployment rate to rise. Such uncertainty about the underlying source of the increase in unemployment can make it difficult to establish low inflation equilibrium without risking an attack on the peg.[5]

The transition problem

The transition problem occurs because the currency of a peripheral country can become overvalued during the move to a low inflation regime. The resulting increase in the price of nontraded goods relative to traded goods encourages producers to shift production toward the former and consumers to shift demand toward the latter, causing the current account position to worsen. If the transition period is a long one, the current account position may become unsustainable, and the official exchange rate could cease to be an equilibrium rate (assuming it had earlier been an equilibrium rate). The length of the transition period will depend on a number of factors including the slope of the short-run Phillips curve (i.e., the sort-run relationship between the unemployment rate and the inflation rate), the initial discrepancy between the inflation rates in the high-inflation country and the anchor country, and the speed at which expectations adjust to actual inflation. The aim of the peg is primarily to influence the last of these factors by increasing credibility so that the adjustment process is less painful than otherwise. If the inflation process contains inertia—because of, perhaps, indexation or backward-looking expectations—then the adjustment process may entail considerable overvaluation of the currency.

The adjustment problem

The classical adjustment problem originates because asymmetric shocks give rise to disequilibria in the balance of payments that in the absence of nominal exchange rate adjustments can be eliminated only by allowing large domestic disequilibria to occur (De Grauwe 1996, 55). A nominal-anchor regime is more likely to accentuate the effects of shocks at the periphery than other pegged arrangements because of the desire for the policy makers of the center country to reaffirm their toughness, so that their currency can remain the anchor. Consider the case where a peripheral country experiences a negative shock, which reduces output and thus reduces the demand for money. With a given money stock, interest rates will fall (because the demand for money has declined), leading to a flow of capital from the periphery to the center. The center country can allow the capital inflow to increase its monetary base and lower its interest rates so that interest rates become equalized and the capital outflow from the peripheral country ceases. But, as its overriding concern is to keep inflation in check and maintain its anti-inflation credentials, it will probably sterilize the inflows and keep its monetary base and interest rates unchanged (McKinnon 1996, 75). This situation presents a problem for the peripheral country. It can allow its interest rate to remain at the lower level and go on losing reserves, jeopardizing the peg. Alternatively, it can raise interest rates to their preshock levels. To do so, however, requires that it reduce its money supply so that the supply of money moves into equality with the demand for money at the higher interest rate. This policy reaction exacerbates the effects of the asymmetric shock in the peripheral country, resulting in a contractionary policy stance at a time when policy should be eased (Tavlas 1993, 671; De Grauwe 1997, 42). If speculators perceive that the situation is unsustainable, a risk premium could be built into the structure of interest rates, implying a further monetary tightening.

As with the transition problem, the adjustment problem arises because of a conflict between the internal objectives and external objectives of an economy, as reflected in the evolution of the fundamental economic variables. There is, however, a crucial difference between the two situations. Under the transition problem, an economy's equilibrium real exchange rate need not change. With an unchanged equilibrium real exchange rate and a constant nominal exchange rate, an inflation differential with the anchor currency country produces a change in the actual real exchange rate; the actual real rate and the equilibrium real rate diverge because the former has changed while the latter has stayed the same. This divergence can influence the evolution of key variables, such as the current account and the unemployment rate. Under the adjustment problem, fundamental changes in the structural characteristics of an economy cause its equilibrium real exchange rate to change. With an unchanged nominal rate, and sticky domestic wages and prices, the current real rate is also unchanged and diverges from the (changed) equilibrium real rate, accentuating changes in the evolution of fundamental variables. A resolution to each of the problems often involves an adjustment of the nominal exchange rate to bring the real exchange rate into line with its equilibrium real rate.

Capital flows and speculative attacks

The recent currency crises have highlighted the potentially disruptive role of international capital flows. In a number of cases, the crises have occurred in the context of newly liberated capital accounts, suggesting that "the liberalization of the capital account heightens countries' susceptibility to crises" (Eichengreen and Mussa 1998, 41). While differential movements in fundamental economic variables can lead to speculative attacks in the absence of capital mobility, the attacks would be delayed, as economic agents would have to reduce their holdings of currency through current account transactions. With open capital accounts, however, changes in expectations can lead to sudden and massive reversals of capital flows.

Increases in the size and speed of capital movements have proved especially detrimental to the sustainability of nominal exchange rate anchor pegs since a basis of these pegs, at least in their initial stages, is a peripheral country with relatively high inflation. A fundamental problem with pegs is that although economic agents may expect the high-inflation country to devalue at some point in the future, they may attach a low probability of a devaluation in the near future and not hedge their exposure. In the interim, the relatively high interest rates in the peripheral country attract capital inflows and distort market signals for a number of reasons.

1. The inflows (if unsterilized) increase the monetary base and push down nominal interest rates. With a given level of inflation expectations, real interest rates decline. Both the increase in the monetary base and the decline in real interest rates imply an expansionary monetary policy, contrary to the tightening needed to disinflate. An increase in inflows can be used to finance widening current account deficits, reinforcing the unsustainability of the peg.

2. Sterilization of such inflows produces quasi-fiscal costs, which add to the budget deficit (or reduce the surplus). Moreover, to the extent that sterilization causes domestic interest rates to be higher than they would otherwise be, capital inflows will tend to be higher than they would be in the absence of sterilization.

3. In the early stages of the peg, the weak (i.e., high-inflation) currency can be at the bottom of its band (expressed in terms of domestic currency units per unit of foreign currency), having appreciated, and the anchor currency can be at the top, with the implication that the weak currency is a candidate for appreciation (Walters 1992).

4. A "new" European Monetary System (EMS)–type of regime,[6] involving a numeraire anchor currency, relatively narrow bands, wide inflation differentials between some of the members, and a bilateral parity grid, provides a further layer of distortion of market signals. This is because official interventions are governed by attempts to preserve the bilateral parity grids. As Pill (1995) pointed out with regard to the EMS, any country with a low inflation rate (say, France) that wanted to use the deutsche mark as an anchor continuously found itself being bound by its bilateral obligations to member countries other than Germany.[7]

5. The increase in reserves arising in situations in which net capital inflows exceed the current account

deficit makes the use of reserves as a leading indicator of currency crises inappropriate.

6. Some writers have argued that the availability of International Monetary Fund (IMF) bailouts has been an important source of moral hazard, leading to excessive (and volatile) capital flows. In this connection, Friedman (1998, 34) has argued that the IMF rescue of Mexico in 1995 allowed foreign investors to get out whole, encouraging them to make loans to and invest in Asia, fueling the crises that erupted in that region. Friedman also argued that there is no need for an international lender of last resort under a floating exchange rate regime. Fischer (1998), however, stressed the need to balance concerns over moral hazard against the costs for the system by failing to assist countries in need.

Self-fulfilling attacks. Prior to the recent crises, first-generation models of speculative attacks stressed the role of misaligned macroeconomic fundamentals in generating an attack. A speculative attack on a fixed exchange rate was explained in terms of overly expansive macroeconomic policies, declining foreign exchange reserves, and the retention of a pegged exchange rate (Krugman 1979; Flood and Garber 1984). The recent crises, especially the East Asian crisis, have led to a reassessment of the applicability of first-generation models since the crisis involved countries with seemingly sound fundamentals. In response, explanations of speculative attacks have been developed that stress the role of nonfundamental factors and the possibility of multiple equilibria in currency crises. The new models (the so-called second- and third-generation models of speculative attacks) focus explicitly on the costs and benefits of maintaining an exchange rate peg in the event of an attack (Obstfeld 1997).

The main idea in these models is that in the absence of an attack, an exchange rate peg could be sustainable. Should an attack occur, however, it "can itself precipitate a devaluation that would have not occurred in its absence" (Eichengreen 1999, 136). Since governments have multiple objectives, there is a trade-off between a pegged exchange rate and other objectives. The benefits of a peg "take the form of enhancing the credibility of the authorities' policies oriented toward the maintenance of price stability" (Eichengreen 1999, 135). The costs of maintaining the peg in the event of a speculative attack include the effects of high interest rates on a weak banking system, the unemployment rate, and the costs of servicing the debt. Thus, one reason cited for the success of the attacks against the East Asian currencies was the fragility of the banking systems in many of the countries (IMF 1998, 74-97). Maintaining interest rates at high levels to forestall the attacks could have led to defaults by borrowers, aggravating the conditions of the already weak banking systems. In this view, the fundamentals were so poor as to make a successful defense of the fixed regime very costly. A devaluation was justified once a speculative attack had been launched. Nevertheless, it must also be noted that according to this explanation, the fundamentals may not have been so bad as to bring the fixed regime down on their own (i.e., without the attack).[8]

In the case of the crises in South Asia, the main source of vulnerability for the fixed regime may be found in the banking (financial) system. In modern economies, strong linkages have developed between monetary and credit systems, partly as a solution to adverse selection and moral hazard problems. Because the same institutions are involved in both the allocation of credit and the provision of transactions services, this situation creates a connection between exchange rate crises and banking crises (Stockman 1999; Wolf 2002).

To explain, consider that the kind of countries that have been attracted to nominal-anchor exchange rate pegs are typically capital scarce, implying a need for capital inflows, and have usually experienced high and variable inflation rates. The high-inflation experience creates two fundamental problems with respect to borrowing arrangements (Mishkin 1999). First, short-term debt contracts will dominate because they entail less inflation risk than do long-term contracts. Second, because high and variable inflation leads to uncertainty about the future value of the currency, borrowers in these countries find it easier to issue debt if it is denominated in foreign currencies. Also, the relatively high domestic interest rates provide an incentive for domestic firms to borrow in foreign currencies. Often, the pegged exchange rate acts as an implicit guarantee against currency risk and therefore is unhedged.

In these circumstances, capital flows create liquidity risks (because of the need to frequently roll over short-term domestic currency contracts), currency risks, or both, generating currency and financial crises that feed on each other. Assuming banks have a large foreign exchange exposure, an exchange-rate crisis can lead to a banking crisis because a devaluation exposes banks to a sizable currency mismatch and a deterioration in their balance sheets. If prudential regulations force banks to match their foreign currency liabilities with foreign currency assets, the foreign currency loans are typically made to domestic firms.[9] A devaluation, therefore, leads to a deterioration of firms' balance sheets, with the result that borrowers are not able to repay the banks; the banks' foreign currency loans decrease in value as the foreign exchange risk of the firms is converted into credit risk for the banks. The deterioration in banks' balance sheets arising from a currency devaluation is harmful to the economy because of the important role played by banks in the financial system. The result is then a triple crisis: currency, banking, and output.

Aghion, Bacchetta, and Banerjee (2001) developed a "third generation" model of financial and currency crises that can account for this triple crisis. Their approach employs sticky prices and credit constraints and is based on the idea that the crisis is the result of a shock (actual or imagined) that is amplified by a financial accelerator mechanism. A simple story of currency crisis emerges: when nominal goods prices are rigid in the short run, an unanticipated currency devaluation leads to an increase in the debt obligations of domestic firms that have borrowed in foreign currency, lowering profits and net worth. This, in turn, reduces investment and production. The reduction in output lowers the demand for money requiring a currency depreciation (given the rigidity of goods prices). The expectation of a future domestic currency devaluation then puts pressure on the current value of the domestic currency. A currency crisis may occur simply because people expect that the domestic currency will become weaker in the future. This is a situation of multiple equilibria.

The main advantage of this approach over related (i.e., multiple equilibria, self-fulfilling) theories of currency crises is that it captures some important features of actual crises. First, it can account for the triple crises. Second, it explains the finding that countries with less developed financial systems are more likely to experience an output decline during a crisis. Finally, it is consistent (by assumption) with the fact that large exchange rate devaluations are not followed by significant upsurges in the rate of consumer price index inflation.

It must be emphasized, though, that the chain of events described above (from currency to banking crises) is not unique. It is also quite possible that the crisis is due exclusively to fundamentals, and in particular, that it spreads from the banking sector to the foreign exchange rate market even in the absence of multiple equilibria and self-fulfilling expectations (Mishkin 1999; Pesenti and Tille 2000). The initial banking crisis may be due to imprudent bank lending or could be the result of a deterioration in bank balance sheets due to an adverse change in the economic environment. Since the cost of dealing with a banking crisis, including the liquidation of insolvent banks, is typically borne by the public sector, the unexpected worsening of the public sector fiscal balance can lead to expectations of future money creation, triggering a speculative attack on the currency.

Burnside, Eichenbaum, and Rebello (in press) offered an alternative explanation of the East Asian crises based on a modified first-generation model along the lines suggested above. The critical fundamental in their model is the large prospective deficits associated with implicit bailout guarantees to failing banks. The expectation that these deficits would—at least in part—be financed by seigniorage revenues or an inflation tax on outstanding nominal debt led to the collapse of the fixed regimes.

Burnside, Eichenbaum, and Rebello (in press) offered evidence that their theory can account well for the Asian currency crisis. Their evidence suggests that the exchange rate crises were preceded by publicly available signs of imminent banking crises and that governments were either unwilling or unable to raise the resources required to pay for the bank bailouts via fiscal reforms. Finally, their model can, with a simple extension along the lines of Burnstein, Eichenbaum, and Rebello (2001),[10] also explain the limited pass-through of the large exchange rate changes on goods prices even with perfectly flexible prices.

Contagion. An interesting feature of currency crises is that they tend to occur simultaneously in several countries, and in particular, they tend to be clustered. This clustering is often attributed to contagion and can be explained using a combination of first- and third-generation models.

Consider the attacks during the East Asian crisis of 1997-1998. The trigger for the crisis was the attack against the Thai baht in July 1997, an attack that can be explained in terms of first-generation models (Eichengreen 1999). Thailand's fundamentals were misaligned; its exchange rate was considered to be overvalued, and its current account deficit—at 8 percent of GDP in 1996—was unsustainable (Goldstein 1998). Most other East Asian economies, however, did not appear to have fundamentals that were misaligned, but their currencies were nevertheless attacked.[11]

A key feature of the East Asian economies prior to the crisis was a surge in capital inflows. Between 1990 and 1996, net private capital inflows to the five Asian economies hit hardest by the 1997-1998 crisis—Indonesia, Korea, Malaysia, the Philippines, and Thailand—almost tripled, rising from U.S.$24 billion to U.S.$62 billion. One factor underpinning the capital inflows was the pegged exchange rate regimes, which as noted above, served as a form of implicit guarantees. Both the unhedged foreign currency exposure and the short-term duration of the exposure left the East Asian economies susceptible to an attack.[12] As Corden (1999, 7) put it, the "borrowers simply gambled that the slight probability of devaluation would not happen, and the gamblers lost." In 1997, Indonesia, Korea, Malaysia, the Philippines, and Thailand experienced an abrupt reversal of U.S.$80 billion in net capital flows, leaving many banks in a greatly weakened condition (Sneddon-Little and Olivei 1999, 61-62).

The fragile underpinnings of the capital inflows to the East Asian countries were responsible for their sharp reversal. In these circumstances, a number of factors have been cited as having contributed to the contemporaneous nature of the East Asian crisis (Masson 1998).

Country risk. Sudden changes in market expectations or in the market's interpretation of existing information can lead to financial market spillovers from one country to another. The occurrence of a crisis in one country might induce investors to rebalance their portfolios for risk management reasons. For example, when a crisis breaks out in one country, investors who have positions in that country might want to reduce their increased risk exposure and will sell assets whose returns are highly variable and positively correlated with those of the assets in the crisis country (IMF 1999, 69). Country risk is greater the larger the share of short-term obligations in the country's total liabilities, the larger the maturity mismatch between assets and liabilities, and the higher its foreign currency exposure. Moreover, changes in expectations can give rise to herd behavior. For example, if investment fund managers are evaluated on the basis of their performance relative to other managers, they may find it optimal to "follow the herd" (IMF 1999, 69).

Monsoonal effects. Crises often stem from common external causes. The appreciations of the U.S. dollar against the yen and the European currencies between mid-1995 and 1997 and a fall in the terms of trade for electronic goods exporters have been cited as important factors underlying the East Asian crisis (IMF 1998). These shocks brought into question the sustainability of the currency pegs contributing to a sharp reversal of market confidence and a sudden withdrawal of funds.

Trade spillovers. When a country experiences a significant devaluation of its currency, countries in the same region, and sometimes beyond, that have not devalued, experience a deterioration in competitiveness, making their currencies more susceptible to speculative attacks. If a country's exchange rate was in equilibrium before the devaluation in a competitor country, the exchange rate of the former is unlikely to be in equilibrium after the devaluation (Goldstein 1998, 19-20). The competitiveness effect operates not only through bilateral trade linkages but also through competition in third markets.

Monsoonal effects and trade spillovers involve changes in macroeconomic fundamentals that can affect more than one country contemporaneously. Essentially, these are first-generation reasons for contagion. External shocks cause a change in the equilibrium real exchange rate. With an unchanged nominal rate and sticky wages and prices, disequilibria occur between the current real rate and the changed equilibrium rate that precipitates an attack. In contrast, the effects of self-fulfilling expectations and country risk operate through changes in expectations, perhaps because of shifts in market sentiment or changes in the interpretation of existing information, for unchanged values of a country's fundamentals (Masson 1998). The changes in expectations can be self-fulfilling because by altering the trade-off between the costs and benefits of maintaining the peg, they can lead to a devaluation that would not have occurred in the absence of the change in expectations. These are, in effect, second-generation reasons for contagion. With a pegged nominal exchange rate, an otherwise equilibrium exchange rate becomes a disequilibrium exchange rate as a result of a self-fulfilling speculative run (Clarida 1999, 50). Changes in market expectations generate the disequilibrium and provoke the attack.

Regime problems

An international monetary system comprising both floating rates and pegged rates—that is, a mixed regime—can produce externality problems that distinguish such a mixed regime from the extremes of a pure float or a fixed-rate regime.

Small-country instability. Consider the case of a small country that pegs the exchange rate of its currency rigidly against the U.S. dollar. Assume that the U.S. dollar appreciates sharply relative to other major currencies. Other things remaining the same, this means that the dollar prices of many of the small country's imports (and import substitutes) will decline. The prices of exports might also decline—depending on how much leeway there is for the producers in the small country to absorb the exchange-rate change. Since traded goods often account for a relatively large part of small economies, the decline in the prices of such goods could impart deflationary pressures on the economy in question.

Clements (1986) analyzed such a situation when interest rate parity holds. Assuming that the peg is credible, he argued that movements of interest rates in the small country depend on what happens to rates in the United States. For simplicity, suppose that U.S. interest rates are fixed. (Typically, an increase in interest rate differentials in favor of dollar-denominated assets induces an appreciation of the dollar. If so, then the following conclusion is strengthened.) With nominal interest rates in the small country fixed and inflation lower as a result of the appreciation of the dollar, (ex post) real interest rates rise, adding to the deflationary impact of the appreciation. Moreover, because traded goods in the United States most probably account for a smaller fraction of the overall economy than do traded goods in the country that pegs its currency to the dollar, the appreciation of the dollar is not likely to bring down U.S. inflation as much as it reduces inflation in the small economy. Thus, the difference in the relative sizes of the traded goods sectors between the small country and the large country imparts asymmetrical effects of the change in exchange rate on prices.[13]

Magnification effects. A mixed system can magnify the effects of asymmetric shocks on exchange rates compared to those of a pure float or a fixed-rate regime. To demonstrate, consider the implications of the German-reunification shock of 1990 within a portfolio-balance framework.[14] Beginning in 1990, Germany undertook a massive fiscal expansion to finance investment in infrastructure and unemployment benefits to the former East Germany. To keep a lid on inflation, the Bundesbank reacted by progressively tightening monetary policy. The fiscal expansion and monetary tightening put upward pressure on interest rates, causing a net capital inflow and appreciation of the real equilibrium value of the mark. In this framework, the fiscal shift causes a shift in Germany's international net investment position. If it began in a position of current account balance, Germany would run a current account deficit (in the short run) as its net investment position fell. The fiscal expansion increased the relative demand for German goods versus rest-of-world goods and for nontraded goods versus traded goods in Germany, also requiring a real appreciation to restore equilibrium.[15]

In a mixed floating and pegged monetary system, the effects of this kind of an asymmetric shock on the center country can be compounded. This result occurs because the needed current account adjustment operating through the change in the real exchange rate is not allowed to work through usual channels. Since the German-reunification shock was asymmetric, an appreciation of the mark against the currencies of Germany's trading partners was required, but many of Germany's main trading partners pegged their currencies to the mark. Consequently, the necessary relative-price adjustment through the current account initially had to operate primarily through currencies that did not peg to the mark. The implication for the EMS is that the exchange rate pegs against the mark meant that the mark had to appreciate in the short run even more against third currencies than it would have done otherwise.

Escape mechanism. An underlying assumption of both the credibility and discipline arguments is that it is politically more costly to adjust a pegged rate than to allow the nominal exchange rate to move by a corresponding amount in a flexible exchange rate arrangement, because the former is clearly visible (since it involves a discrete change rather than a continuous change) whereas the latter is less of an event and can be attributed to the market. Under a nominal-anchor regime, however, the increased number of options available to policy makers compared with the number available under a Bretton Woods type of system means that it can be difficult for the public to distinguish between exchange rate adjustments that reflect government decisions and those that are precipitated by the market's herd behavior. A devaluation under the Bretton Woods system made newspaper headlines, but an adjustment of a currency pegged to a nominal-anchor currency may not (Collins 1996, 120), and even if it does, it can be ascribed to market behavior that is divorced from the fundamentals. For example, a devaluation under a nominal-anchor arrangement may be attributed to the effects of an appreciation of the anchor currency against third currencies and not to a deterioration of economic fundamentals produced by the policies of the domestic authorities. The political cost of devaluation is reduced further when there is a cluster of devaluations.

CONCLUSIONS

The restrictive analytical underpinnings of the credibility hypothesis have led to a situation where the hypothesis has limited applicability in practice. The hypothesis requires that economic agents know, for example, the values of such parameters of the economy as the natural rate of unemployment (i.e., the location of the long-run Phillips curve) and the slope of the short-run Phillips curve. Lacking full knowledge of these parameters, economic agents will not be able to discern with certainty whether, say, a rise in unemployment is attributable to a commitment by the policy makers to a new policy regime as they bite the bullet to establish their credibility credentials or to a negative asymmetric shock that could presage an easing of policy. If the former, economic agents also need to be convinced that the policy makers' objective function will not change once the initial goal of lower inflation has been achieved. This is the essence of the credibility problem that derives from the credibility hypothesis.

This article has described the regime-specific characteristics of an international monetary system comprising both floating rates and pegged rates—the operating domain of a nominal-anchor peg—that produce externalities relative to a pure float or a fixed-rate regime. Those externalities can lead to instability for small countries that peg to the currency of a large country, magnify the effects of asymmetric shocks on exchange rates against third currencies, and provide an escape mechanism that may help absolve the policy makers of the disciplinary constraint of a pure peg. Changes in fundamentals, or changes in expectations for unchanged fundamentals, can lead to contagion, undermining the sustainability of exchange rate pegs.

Notes

1. The term *pegged exchange rate* is used to refer to any system in which a monetary authority announces buying and selling rates for a currency in terms of a foreign currency and promises to trade unlimited quantities at that rate. The buying and selling rates could be the same, but in most systems they differ, a circumstance that gives rise to (usually narrow) bands within which even a "fixed" exchange rate may fluctuate.

2. The case that most puzzled Obstfeld and Rogoff (1995) was that of the Thai baht, which adhered to a ±2.5 percent band against the U.S. dollar from January 1987. In July 1997, after Obstfeld and Rogoff published their study, Thailand moved from a peg to a managed floating system, which resulted in a de facto devaluation of the baht. The baht subsequently came under further attack.

3. A third problem that received considerable attention was the confidence problem, involving a portfolio shift between dollar holdings and gold holdings. As outstanding dollar liabilities held by the rest of the world's monetary authorities increased relative to the U.S. monetary gold stock, the likelihood of a run on the "bank" increased, leading to a decline in the probability that all dollar holders could convert their dollars into gold at the official fixed price (Triffin 1960).

4. Barro (1986) argued that policy makers would need to "bite the bullet," whereby "the costs from surprisingly low inflation are accepted in order to enhance one's reputation for low inflation" (p. 20).

5. Drazen and Masson (1994) provided evidence showing that in certain circumstances, maintaining the exchange rate peg in the face of an adverse shock can diminish credibility since higher unemployment increases the likelihood that a further shock to unemployment will push the costs of not devaluing above some "threshold" level. Policies that raise unemployment in the future, for example, will lower the threshold level of a random shock at which future policy makers will find it optimal to devalue.

6. The term "new" European Monetary System (EMS) was coined by Giavazzi and Spaventa (1990) to describe the no-realignment strategy adopted in the Exchange Rate Mechanism of the EMS in 1987. Prior to the EMS crisis of 1992-1993, the bands were narrow (mostly ±2 ¼ percent).

7. Pill (1995) cited the example of the peseta/sterling rate as a constraint on the Bank of England's monetary policy in the summer of 1992 because of the (unjustified) strength of the peseta during this period.

8. Another reason an attack can be self-fulfilling is that if economic agents expect that as a result of a speculative run, the government will impose capital controls to maintain a pegged rate, self-fulfilling expectations may cause such an attach to take place (Dellas and Stockman 1993).

9. This situation existed in Thailand in 1997 at the time of the attack on the Thai baht.

10. Burnstein, Eichenbaum, and Rebello (2001) showed that the introduction of distribution and retail costs as well as "inferior" domestic substitutes for traded goods can account for the observed deviations in purchasing power parity.

11. Malaysia, Korea, and the Philippines had current account deficits of more than 4 percent of GDP in 1996, the level some observers consider the upperbound for sustainability (e.g., Sneddon-Little and Olivei 1999).

12. In Thailand, banks were required to hedge their positions by acquiring offsetting assets in foreign currency. They did so, however, by making foreign currency loans to domestic corporations, which became the holders of the unhedged exposure (Eichengreen and Hausmann 1999, 9).

13. Sjaastad (1985) provided evidence showing that in the cases of the Chilean and Uruguayan pesos in the early 1980s, a sharp appreciation of the dollar (against most third currencies) in the face of dollar pegs by Chile and Uruguay resulted in high real interest rates and declines in traded goods' prices in each of these countries and led to attacks against both currencies.

14. Cobham (1996) reviewed the literature dealing with the effects of the German reunification shock.

15. An implication of the portfolio model is that in the long run, the real exchange rate would have to depreciate beyond its initial value to generate the larger net exports required to service its larger foreign debts.

References

Aghion, P., P. Bacchetta, and A. Banerjee. 2001. A corporate balance-sheet approach to currency crisis. Mimeographed.

Barro, R. J. 1986. Reputation in a model of monetary policy with incomplete information. *Journal of Monetary Economics* 17:3-20.

Barro, R. J., and D. Gordon. 1983. Rules, discretion, and reputation in a model of monetary policy. *Journal of Monetary Economics* 12:101-21.

Burnside, C., M. Eichenbaum, and S. Rebello. In press. Prospective deficits and the Asian currency crises. *Journal of Political Economy*.

Burnstein, A., M. Eichenbaum, and S. Rebello. 2001. Why are rates of inflation so low after large devaluations? Mimeographed.

Clarida, R. 1999. G3 exchange rate relationships: A recap of the record and a review of proposals for change. NBER working paper no. 7434. Cambridge, MA: National Bureau of Economic Research.

Clements, K. W. 1986. Perspectives on exchange rate regimes. In *Alternative exchange rate regimes*, edited by C. D. Campbell and W. R. Dougan. Baltimore: Johns Hopkins University Press.

Cobham, D. 1996. Causes and effects of the European monetary crises of 1992-93. *Journal of Common Market Studies* 34:584-604.

Collins, S. 1996. On becoming more flexible: Exchange rate regimes in Latin America and the Carribean. *Journal of Development Economics* 51:117-38.

Corden, W. M. 1994. *Economic policy, exchange rates, and the international system*. Chicago: University of Chicago Press.

———. 1999. Choosing exchange rate regimes: Lessons from Europe and Asia. Unpublished Hinshaw Lecture. (Available from the author at wmcorden@erols.com)

De Grauwe, P. 1996. *International money: Postwar trends and theories*. 2d ed. Oxford, UK: Oxford University Press.

———. 1997. *The economics of monetary integration*. 3d ed. Oxford, UK: Oxford University Press.

Dellas, H., and A. Stockman. 1993. Self-fulfilling expectations, speculative attacks, and capital controls. *Journal of Money, Credit and Banking* 25:721-30.

Drazen, A., and P. Masson. 1994. Credibility of policies versus credibility of policymakers. *Quarterly Journal of Economics* 109:735-54.

Eichengreen, B. 1999. *Toward a new international financial architecture.* Washington, DC: Institute for International Economics.

Eichengreen, B., and Hausmann. 1999. Exchange rate and financial fragility. Working paper no. 7418. Cambridge, MA: National Bureau of Economic Research.

Eichengreen, B., and M. Mussa (with G. Dell' Ariccia, E. Detragiache, G. M. Milesi-Ferretti, and A. Tweedie). 1998. *Capital account liberalization: Theoretical and practical aspects.* IMF occasional paper no. 172. Washington, DC: International Monetary Fund.

Fischer, S. 1998. Lessons from a crisis. *The Economist*, 3 October, 23-30.

Flood, R., and P. Garber. 1984. Collapsing exchange rate regimes: Some linear examples. *Journal of International Economics* 20:1-13.

Friedman, M. 1998. A primer on exchange rates. *Forbes*, 2 November, 33-34.

Giavazzi, F., and A. Giovannini. 1989. *Limiting exchange rate flexibility: The European Monetary System.* Cambridge, MA: MIT Press.

Giavazzi, F., and M. Pagano. 1988. The advantage of tying one's hands: EMS discipline and Central Bank credibility. *European Economic Review* 32:1055-75.

Giavazzi, F., and L. Spaventa. 1990. The "new" EMS. In *The European Monetary System in the 1990s*, edited by P. De Grauwe and L. Papademos, 133-71. New York: Longman.

Goldstein, M. 1980. *Have flexible exchange rates handicapped macroeconomic policy?* Special papers in international economics no. 14. Princeton, NJ: International Financial Section, Princeton University.

———. 1998. *The Asian financial crisis: Causes, cures and systemic implications.* Washington, DC: Institute for International Economics.

Halm, G. N. 1969. *Toward limited exchange-rate flexibility.* Essays in international finance no. 73. Princeton, NJ: International Financial Section, Princeton University.

Harberler, G. von. 1964. Integration of the world economy in historical perspective. *American Economic Review* 54:1-22.

International Monetary Fund (IMF). 1998. Financial crises: Characteristics and indicators of vulnerability. In *World Economic Outlook*, 74-97. Washington, DC: International Monetary Fund. May.

———. 1999. International financial contagion. In *World Economic Outlook*, 66-87. Washington, DC: International Monetary Fund. May.

Klein, M. W., and N. Marion. 1994. Explaining the duration of exchange rate pegs. NBER working paper no. 4651. Cambridge, MA: National Bureau of Economic Research.

Krugman, P. 1979. A model of balance of payments crisis. *Journal of Money, Credit and Banking* 11:311-25.

Masson, P. 1998. Contagion: Monsoonal effects, spillovers, and jumps between multiple equilibria. IMF working paper no. 98/142. Washington, DC: International Monetary Fund.

McKinnon, R. I. 1996. *The rules of the game: International money and exchange rates.* Cambridge, MA: MIT Press.

Melitz, J. 1998. Monetary discipline, Germany, and the European Monetary System. In *The European Monetary System*, edited by F. Giavazzi, S. Micossi, and M. Miller, 51-79. Cambridge, UK: Cambridge University Press.

Mishkin, F. 1997. Strategies for controlling inflation. NBER working paper no. 6122. Cambridge, MA: National Bureau of Economic Research.

———. 1999. Lessons from the Tequila Crisis. *Journal of Banking and Finance* 23:1521-33.

Mundell, R. 1968. The redundancy problem and the world price level. In *International economics*, edited by R. Mundell. New York: Macmillan.

Obstfeld, M. 1997. Destabilizing effects of exchange rate escape clauses. *Journal of International Economics* 43:61-77.

Obstfeld, M., and K. Rogoff. 1995. The mirage of fixed exchange rates. *Journal of Economic Perspectives* 9:73-96.

Pesenti, P., and C. Tille. 2000. The economics of currency crises and contagion: An introduction: Federal Reserve Bank of New York. *Economic Policy Review* 6:3-16.

Pill, H. 1995. Target zones and the European Monetary System: A reconciliation. Unpublished manuscript, Stanford University.

Sjaastad, L. 1985. Exchange rate regimes and the real rate of interest. In *The economies of the Carribean basin*, edited by M. Connolly and J. McDermott. New York: Praeger.

Sneddon-Little, J., and G. Olivei. 1999. Why the interest in reforming the international monetary system? *New England Economic Review* (September/October): 53-84.

Sohmen, E. 1963. *International monetary problems and the foreign exchanges.* Special papers in international economics no. 4. Princeton, NJ: International Finance Section, Princeton University.

Stockman, A. 1999. Choosing an exchange rate regime. *Journal of Banking and Finance* 29:1483-98.

Tavlas, G. S. 1993. The "new" theory of optimum currency areas. *World Economy* 16:663-85.

Triffen, R. 1960. *Gold and the dollar crisis.* New Haven, CT: Yale University Press.

Walters, A. 1992. Walters critique. In *The new Palgrave dictionary of money and finance*, vol. 3, edited by P. Newman, M. Milgate, and J. Eatwell, 781-83. London: Macmillan.

Wolf, M. 2002. Exchange rates in a world of capital mobility. *Annals of the American Academy of Political and Social Science* 579:38-52.

ANNALS, *AAPSS*, **579**, January 2002

The Evolution of Thought on Intermediate Exchange Rate Regimes

By JOHN WILLIAMSON

ABSTRACT: This article traces the origins and evolution of proposals for exchange-rate regimes intermediate between fixed and floating rates. The origins are traced to Keynes's interwar writings. Keynes's ideas were revived in the 1960s literature on the (wide) band proposal and crawling peg and developed in the 1970s by the literatures on the reference rate proposal and optimal peg. The target zone proposals of the 1980s combined the band proposal and the crawling peg. Paul Krugman showed that a credible target zone would make speculation stabilizing. In the 1990s, a number of emerging markets employed such regimes until they were swept away in crises. This spawned the bipolar view, which asserts that in a world of capital mobility, countries have to choose between firmly fixed and freely floating rates. The article concludes by arguing that even the most attenuated form of intermediate regime, the reference rate proposal, would carry advantages over a floating regime.

John Williamson was born in England and educated at LSE and Princeton Universities. He has taught at several universities in Brazil, Britain, and the United States, as well as serving for short spells at the UK Treasury, the IMF, and the World Bank.

NOTE: This article was commissioned for this issue of *The Annals of the American Academy of Political and Social Science* on exchange rate regimes. The author is indebted to George Tavlas for comments on a previous draft.

AS with so many of the ideas in twentieth-century macroeconomics, the basic foundations were laid by Keynes. Specifically, in an article in the *Manchester Guardian* published just before the Genoa conference in 1922 (Moggridge 1980, vol. 18, p. 365), Keynes recommended countries to adopt a band of ±5 percent around a parity that was appropriate to their existing price level. It is difficult to credit it now, but the latter was a novel idea at the time, when many countries were pursuing the goal of restoring their prewar parities despite intervening inflations of tens or even hundreds of percent. As a sop to this desire, Keynes proposed that a country determined to revert to its prewar parity might be allowed to do so via a crawling appreciation provided that it was not more than 20 percent depreciated from its prewar parity (Moggridge 1980, vol. 17, p. 364). So here one had both the ideas that subsequently figured in the debate on limited flexibility (or intermediate regimes): a wide band and a crawling peg.

Keynes periodically reverted to playing with these ideas during the interwar period, and even in some of his early thinking about the design of what became the Bretton Woods system (see the account in Williamson 1983, 94-99). But although an intermediate regime was embodied in early drafts of the Keynes Plan, this was in due course superceded by the adjustable peg. There seems to be no account of how this happened; it may even have been due to Keynes himself, for in replying to Harrod in December 1941, when the draft of the Keynes Plan still allowed regular parity changes cumulating up to 5 percent in any year, Keynes (cited in Moggridge 1980, vol. 25) wrote that "it would often be preferable, if a change were necessary, to make it by a single significant amount rather than by a series of small steps" (p. 97). It has been conjectured that Keynes's appointment as a director of the Bank of England might have led him to absorb some of the bank's traditional attachment to stable rates. In any event, the exchange rate regime endorsed by Bretton Woods, which became the foundation for the postwar monetary order, was the adjustable peg. That is, the exchange rate was to be held constant (within a band of ±1 percent) until further notice, although the level at which it was pegged could be changed, by permission of the International Monetary Fund (IMF), in the event of fundamental disequilibrium.

EARLY LITERATURE ON INTERMEDIATE REGIMES

When the debate on the exchange rate regime was renewed by Milton Friedman (1953) and James Meade (1955), the alternative that was discussed was floating rather than any intermediate regime. It was only at the very end of the 1950s that Maurice Scott (1959) revived the idea of the crawling peg and only in the 1960s that a substantial body of literature on the idea of keeping a parity but allowing it to change gradually over time emerged (see the survey in Williamson 1981, chap. 1). At that time, the intellectual origins of the idea were traced back to Harrod (1933) rather than to Keynes. Much of the discussion concerned which formula, if any, should be used to guide the choice of the rate of crawl. Most proponents saw a crawl as a way of maintaining the spirit of Bretton Woods, in which the exchange rate was a decision variable of government that should be used to help reconcile internal and external balance while ridding the system of the periodic speculative crises that were already occurring as a result of the reemergence of capital mobility. It is a curious fact that this literature was all directed to exchange rate management in the main developed countries, and none of the authors were aware that crawling was already being implemented in Latin America (starting in Chile in 1965, then in Colombia in 1967 and Brazil in 1968). The main purpose for which crawling was there utilized was offsetting the payments impact of rapid inflation, which was a fairly minor theme in the literature that focused on developed countries, even though this was before the Phillips curve had been inflation augmented. Most authors in the developed country literature regarded crawling mainly as a less disruptive way of making a parity adjustment needed to correct a fundamental disequilibrium, that is, as facilitating payments adjustment.

The postwar literature on the other central feature of intermediate regimes, a wide band, was launched by George Halm in 1965. Neither Halm nor the early writers on the crawling peg recognized any complementarity between the two proposals. Despite this, the first major manifestation of interest in limited flexibility was a statement in favor of both the wider band and the crawling peg that was signed by twenty-seven economists in 1966 (Fellner, Machlup, and Triffin 1966, chap. 5). It became increasingly clear as time passed that the economists willing to sign on to such statements fell into two distinct camps. One, which was more common among those who emphasized the wider band, consisted of those who saw limited flexibility as a tactical device for advancing toward what they saw as the real prize, floating rates. The other consisted of those who were suspicious of how floating rates would behave and therefore saw genuine intellectual merit in a system of limited flexibility as offering the possibility of securing constructive interaction between official and private sectors in determining exchange rates.

Another suggested dichotomy saw the crawling peg as reflecting monetarist thinking and a wide band as reflecting a Keynesian view of the world (McKinnon 1971). McKinnnon (1971) argued that a monetarist sees monetary policy as leading to changes in inflation that needed to be offset by a crawling change in the parity, whereas a Keynesian sees monetary policy as determining interest rates to be used for anticyclical purposes in a world of price stability. The price stability obviates any need for a crawl, but in a world of capital mobility, interest rates can be employed in the cause of nation-specific anticyclical policy only if the exchange rate is able to move enough so that the expectation of a subsequent rebound to parity can offset the cumulative interest differential.

McKinnon's identification of crawling with monetarism was paradoxical inasmuch as few monetarists saw any value in accommodating inflation (whereas many Keynesians at that time did), but his diagnosis of the very different functions performed by the two different forms of limited flexibility was important in the subsequent literature.

In 1973, the world stumbled into generalized floating, at least among the industrial countries. New writing on intermediate regimes almost ceased, as even those advocates of such regimes who preferred them to floating assumed that they were no longer on the agenda. There were nonetheless two developments in the 1970s that are significant in light of the later development of the literature.

The first was the development of what was called the "reference rate proposal" by Ethier and Bloomfield (the standard reference is Ethier and Bloomfield 1975, although their paper was widely circulated at least a year before that). This was suggested as a way of disciplining the management of a floating exchange rate. They proposed that any country wishing to intervene (or take other measures intended to influence its exchange rate) should be required to agree to a "reference rate" with the IMF; one may think of a reference rate as a parity, an agreed view of what the exchange rate ought to average in the medium term. A country would then be entitled, but not obliged, to intervene with a view to pushing the rate toward the reference rate, but it would be forbidden from pushing the rate away from that value. This basic idea was actually incorporated in the temporary guidelines for floating that the fund adopted in 1974, which were guided through the fund board by J. Marcus Fleming. The thrust of the guidelines was to prevent or discipline aggressive intervention, meaning policy actions that aimed to push the exchange rate in a direction opposite to that where market forces were taking it. Thus, countries were permitted to intervene to smooth out erratic fluctuations or lean against the wind, but other intervention required a country first to agree with the fund to a target zone of rates lying within the "range of reasonable estimates of the medium-term norm for the exchange rate." This was the first use of the term "target zone" for exchange rates, and it was used without any suggestion that rates had to be held within the target zone. However, these guidelines were swept away by the growing enthusiasm for exclusively market-determined exchange rates when the IMF adopted the second amendment to its articles in 1978, to be replaced by a set of guidelines without substance.

The other academic writing of the 1970s that has some relevance for understanding subsequent developments was the emergence of a literature on the optimal exchange rate peg. This literature was aimed at developing countries, which at that time had not joined the move to float but had discovered that floating among the industrial countries confronted them with a new problem. Specifically, countries with diversified trade found that if they pegged to any single (industrial country) currency, exchange rate variations among the industrial country currencies could alter their effective exchange rates and thereby disrupt their macroeconomic balance. The questions asked in the literature on the optimal peg were, Under what circumstances was it desirable to peg to a basket of currencies rather than a single currency? and, How was the optimal basket composed? I surveyed that literature as it was reaching maturity (Williamson 1982) and argued that one could draw some stylized answers. First, the objective should be to choose a basket that would stabilize the effective exchange rate. Second, although the weights in the basket should in principle be based on trade elasticities, in practice it was likely that trade weights would be the best that would be feasible. In general, therefore, countries should be advised to peg to a trade-weighted basket of the currencies of their principal trading partners.

TARGET ZONES

When the world moved to generalized floating in 1973, some people feared that markets would be quite unable to handle the task of determining exchange rates and there would be a general seizing up of the markets. Most economists thought this was silly, and experience soon sufficed to dismiss those fears. In fact, most economists were at the other extreme and had an unrealistically sanguine view of how floating exchange rates would behave. They would adjust gradually to reflect the evolving fundamentals in such a way as to keep current account imbalances in line with capital flows. Balance of payments problems would vanish.

It was not long after the move to floating that exchange rates started to move to more extreme levels than seemed to make any sense in terms of what economists thought of as the fundamentals. The dollar was weak in 1973-1974, strong in 1975-1976, weak again in the late 1970s, and then extremely strong during the first five years of the Reagan administration. Similarly, the pound was extremely weak in 1975-1976 and then far stronger than could be rationalized by traditional theories in the early 1980s. It was these experiences that motivated the search for some better exchange rate regime in the 1980s.

When Fred Bergsten and I first started thinking in 1982 about what that might imply, we quickly concluded that it would need to involve a combination of both of the forms of limited flexibility that had figured in the debate of the 1960s. We also chose rapidly, perhaps even without thinking about it, “target zones” as the term for what we had in mind. At that time, we were influenced less by any recollection of terms the IMF had used in its ill-fated guidelines of 1974 to 1978 than by the terminology that Robert Roosa had periodically used in his speeches in the late 1970s. But Roosa had never spelled out what might be involved in an attempt to rein in market forces so as to limit exchange rate misalignments, which is what we perceived the essence of the problem to be (Bergsten and Williamson 1983).

In my subsequent work developing the target zone proposal (Williamson 1985), I diagnosed the fundamental problem with floating as being the propensity of floating rates to become misaligned, that is, systematically and substantially overvalued or undervalued for prolonged periods. This can have a number of troubling effects, including inducing distortions in the time path of consumption, creating unnecessary adjustment costs, causing unemployment, limiting investment and therefore growth, ratcheting up the rate of inflation, and nurturing protectionism. The purpose of exchange rate management was therefore conceived as that of combating misalignments. Such an objective made sense only if one could develop reasonable measures of the equilibrium exchange rate, so I endeavored to specify what I termed the "fundamental equilibrium exchange rate," or FEER. This was simply the obverse of the concept of fundamental disequilibrium that had figured as the criterion for a parity change in the Bretton Woods system: it was that (real) exchange rate that would reconcile internal and external balance in the medium term. I tried to measure FEERs and therefore misalignments, with a view to showing how badly wrong the market sometimes got it, and therefore the need for governments to play a role in setting exchange rates.

But of course, the critical question was, How should the government play a role? The argument we developed was that the authorities should try to keep the exchange rate within a broad zone—a target zone—around their estimate of equilibrium. The zone should be as wide as was needed to justify the idea that one could identify "clearly wrong rates" even though no one could reasonably claim to know "the" equilibrium rate; that seemed to point to a zone of something like ±10 percent. The authorities should deploy a variety of tools to encourage the exchange rate to stay in this zone: monetary policy, provided that there was no severe conflict with internal objectives; sterilized intervention; capital controls; and so on. But my own view was that one could not realistically give complete priority to maintaining the exchange rate within the specified band; in the event of strong market pressures pushing the rate outside the zone when monetary actions would have run counter to the needs of domestic stabilization, one might have to allow the rate to go outside the band (soft margins). The assumption was that markets would be unlikely to challenge the authorities given that the latter were defending realistic, constantly updated estimates of equilibrium rates, rather than the disequilibrium rates inherited from the past and outdated by differential inflation or real shocks that parities so often became under the Bretton Woods system. This constant updating of the equilibrium rate would result in the zone's crawling.

The target zone proposal left some issues unresolved. First, there was a question as to how much credibility one could expect the zones to have when the commitment of monetary policy to defending the zones was so weak, effectively being called off in the event of a clash with the needs of domestic economic management. Second, the advice was being dispensed to the principal industrial countries, but it took no account of the fact that these were large countries whose policy actions impacted one another. Recognition of those two weaknesses stimulated a subsequent study by Marcus Miller and me (Williamson and Miller 1987). This offered a blueprint for coordination of macroeconomic policies among the major industrial countries, which would have relied on each of the countries' pursuing two intermediate targets. One was an exchange rate target (with a wide target zone surrounding it), where the targets were calculated to be mutually consistent by virtue of the consistent balance of payments (current account) targets on which they were based. The other was a target for the rate of growth of domestic demand that may be thought of as a somewhat ad hoc antecedent of the Taylor Rule. These two were supposed to be pursued by each of the participating countries choosing monetary and fiscal policies accordingly, directing monetary policy to the external target if the exchange rate was threatening to breach its target zone. The argument was that countries could afford to commit their monetary policies in that way since they also had fiscal policies that could be used to compensate any untoward effects on domestic demand. That would still leave the world level of interest rates undetermined, since exchange rates are determined by interest differentials. This missing degree of freedom would be filled by a rule that strong currency countries should be the ones to change (i.e., lower) their interest rates in defense of the target zones if world demand was growing slower than capacity, while weak currency countries would change (raise) their interest rates if global inflation were threatening to accelerate.

The blueprint attracted a certain amount of attention in academic circles, but politically it never built any momentum at all. The reason is that it was based on the Keynesian supposition that it makes sense to direct fiscal policy to macroeconomic management, an idea that is as dead as the dodo. Politicians are quite convinced that fiscal policy is far too important to be influenced by sound economics. So when the G5 showed momentary interest in policy coordination in 1987 (the Louvre Accord), it was on the basis of target zones rather than anything resembling the blueprint that implied a willingness to coordinate fiscal policy as well.

At the very end of the 1980s, Paul Krugman developed his analysis of target zones in which a "honeymoon effect" results in the exchange rate's being held within a band with merely the promise of intervention at the margin and without the need for any actual intervention to occur (Krugman 1991). This seemed to provide the theoretical underpinning for a target zone system that had previously been lacking, and Krugman's analysis certainly succeeded in stimulating the emergence of a substantial theoretical literature. It provided a rationale for the intuition that as the authorities built up credibility, they would be able to get help from the market in stabilizing the rate in the desired zone. Expectations would become stabilizing. Krugman's analysis was stimulated by the experience of the Exchange Rate Mechanism (ERM) of the European Monetary System, and his model was extensively tested on the data that had been generated by the ERM. First tests were reassuring: it did indeed seem that expectations within the ERM were mean reverting, in contrast to those that held in a floating rate system. But, further tests created doubts: Krugman's model predicted that exchange rates would spend most of their time relatively close to the edges of the target zones, but this did not seem to have happened in the ERM. The two findings could be reconciled by the presence of intramarginal intervention or other policy measures directed to keeping the exchange rate within its target zone, but that cast doubt on whether the target zone was in fact fulfilling its key purpose of making expectations stabilizing.

It was arguable that in its early years, from 1979 to 1987, the ERM operated rather like a target zone of the sort I had advocated. That is, while there were bands that were defended at any time, those bands were periodically realigned in relatively small steps to keep them in line with the fundamentals. But in 1987, a fundamental change in the ERM occurred, when a decision was made to try to avoid future realignments. Since there was still significant differential inflation within the ERM, and since Germany suffered a major real shock as a result of unification in the early 1990s, substantial misalignments emerged, and in consequence the ERM experienced a series of crises in 1992-1993. These were finally resolved by a substantial further widening of the band.

EXPERIENCE WITH CRAWLING BANDS

By the early 1990s, the term "target zones" was being widely used among economists in its Krugmanian sense of a fairly wide but fixed band. When Jacob Frenkel, as governor of the Bank of Israel, put the Israeli shekel's band on a crawl in 1991, he labeled this a "crawling band." That is the term that has most often been used since to describe such regimes among emerging market countries.

By the mid-1990s, the ERM was heading for monetary union, and all other industrial country currencies were floating. The ERM used broad target zones (of ±15 percent) during the transition to monetary union, which was achieved in 1999 with the launch of the euro. It has been succeeded by ERM-II for countries aspiring to euro membership, although ERM-II at present contains only Denmark. Target zones as we had conceived of them, to keep exchange rates roughly where they would be if the models that are supposed to explain exchange rates on the basis of the fundamentals were correct, were no longer on the agenda of relations among the main industrial countries. But, they were thriving among emerging markets: the Israeli shekel was far from alone in using a crawling band. Chile, Colombia, and Israel were the three that operated exchange rate regimes closest to the spirit of my target zones for a substantial period, but in 1994, other countries with a band system included Brazil, Ecuador, Mexico, Poland, and Russia, while Indonesia was gradually widening its band. All of these had movable (and published) parities and wide bands, although some of them used the exchange rate as a nominal anchor rather than making sure that the parity stayed realistic in terms of the fundamentals.

When attention was focused on the main industrial countries, we argued that the bands should be specified in terms of effective exchange rates rather than in terms of bilateral rates against the dollar. As attention switched to emerging markets, it still seemed sensible to keep the focus on the effective exchange rate. As described earlier when outlining the literature on the optimal peg, a small country that pegged to a single currency would be bombarded by repeated shocks as a result of extraneous events, namely changes in third country exchange rates. At least, that would be true for countries with diversified trade relations; a country that traded mainly with a single country or bloc could sensibly peg to the currency of the country in question, or the leader of the bloc. But for others, the natural strategy was to peg to a basket of the currencies of the country's principal trade partners. Thus, another name for the crawling band regime was the "BBC rules," where BBC stands for basket, band, and crawl. (This was Rudi Dornbusch's term.)

For a time, it looked as though these crawling bands were working well, as I argued in a book published in 1996 (Williamson 1996). At that time, I could dismiss the Mexican crisis as a result of the misguided policy of trying to use the exchange rate as a nominal anchor to force inflation down, a policy that has repeatedly led to overvaluation and an ensuing crisis. My policy prescription was instead to use domestic economic policy (meaning fiscal and monetary policy, possibly with the addition of appropriate indexation rules or incomes policies where circumstances suggested these could play a useful role) to reduce inflation gradually over time and to adjust the exchange rate as needed to keep it sufficiently competitive to avoid unsustainable payments imbalances. I argued that it would be possible to defend an exchange rate band by sufficiently determined policy actions as long as it was not overvalued, since the market could be persuaded that the rate being defended was one compatible with a viable payments outcome.

The Asian crisis resulted in a major change in perception. Most of the countries that became victims of the crisis had been defending more or less fixed exchange rates, and in some cases (like Korea and Thailand), it seemed fairly clear that the attempt to mount such a defense had contributed to the run on the currency and that confidence had collapsed as a direct result of abandonment of the currency peg. Some of the countries afflicted by the crisis had crawling bands: Brazil and Russia were overvalued because of the use of the exchange rate as a nominal anchor to wind inflation down, but

Indonesia had conducted its macro policies competently and still fell victim to contagion. Meanwhile, it seemed that some of the emerging market countries that had started to float escaped the crisis largely unscathed: Mexico, South Africa, and Turkey being three instances. It became difficult to argue that speculative pressures could be resisted provided only that the target rate being defended was a sensible one in line with the fundamentals. Experience seemed to indicate that the markets developed strong pressures that were largely independent of anything that economists had been accustomed to think of as fundamentals. (This was formalized in the economics literature in terms of second-generation crisis models, in which self-fulfilling crises could result from the presence of multiple equilibria, in contrast to first-generation crisis models in which crises result from an attempt to defy the fundamentals.)

THE BIPOLAR VIEW

These experiences nurtured what has become known as "the bipolar view" (Fischer 2001). This holds that there are only two things that a country can sensibly do with its exchange rate: either fix it firmly with a currency board to provide an institutional guarantee that it will stay fixed or else stop worrying about what the exchange rate is and let it float. Intermediate regimes should be eschewed: certainly the adjustable peg, but also target zones and crawling bands.[1] All are potentially vulnerable to speculative attack and should therefore be abandoned in favor of one of the poles. And indeed, emerging market countries have been doing just that. Brazil, Indonesia, and Russia all started to float under the pressure of a crisis. Chile and Colombia both abandoned their bands in favor of floating in 1998 without any crisis. Israel and Poland have both broadened their bands to the ±15 percent at which one begins to doubt whether the band is making much difference. Ecuador has dollarized. About the only crawling bands left seem to be those of Hungary and Singapore (and Singapore does not publish the parameters of its band, meaning that its band does not fulfill what I have always regarded as a central reason for having a band, namely to inform the market of the official view of what the equilibrium rate is).

It would be difficult to deny that even a well-managed BBC regime seems to be more vulnerable to speculative crises than floating is. (Currency boards are another matter; neither Argentina nor Hong Kong has exactly enjoyed a crisis-free existence in recent years. The mere fact that a crisis does not end with a devaluation does not mean that it was not a crisis or that it was not costly.) Does that imply that it is time to endorse floating?

That would necessarily follow only if there were no reason to think that an intermediate regime could offer countervailing advantages. Many economists find it difficult to conceive of what those advantages might be. They assume that exchange rates are determined in the way that standard models hypothesize, according to which the exchange rate differs from its long-run purchasing-power-parity equilibrium basically by the integral of the expected interest differential between now and the long run. If that were really so, then it is indeed difficult to see what purpose could be served by exchange rate targeting other than the provision of a nominal anchor, which can also be provided by adopting an inflation target to guide monetary policy. But the evidence is that exchange rates are not in fact determined that way (Meese and Rogoff 1983), but rather that they are often driven by fads and bubbles. Apart from engendering periodic crises, perhaps the most damaging consequence of this is that it makes it unlikely that a country with a floating rate would be able to achieve the long-lasting competitive exchange rates that have in the past provided the basis for fast, export-led growth. It would not be much of a bargain to escape crises if the cost were a permanent deceleration in the growth rate.

Hence, I have tried to ask whether there may be a form of intermediate regime that would still be capable of helping to avoid misalignments while minimizing the danger of provoking speculative crises (Williamson 2000). I suggested three possibilities. The first was to go back to the 1985 version of the target zone proposal, in which target zones had soft margins that could be suspended in the event of strong speculative pressures, a feature that was largely suppressed when the blueprint added fiscal policy to the toolkit so as to permit monetary policy to be dedicated primarily to exchange rate management. The second was to go back even further to the reference rate proposal of 1974 vintage, that is, to abandon the margins without abandoning the parity. The third proposal originated from the report of the Tarapore Committee (1997), which was asked to report on how India should approach capital account convertibility but also suggested a strategy for the exchange rate policy that should accompany capital account liberalization. It proposed that the authorities should announce a relatively narrow (±5 percent) "monitoring band" within which they would commit to not intervene. This might once again serve to focus market expectations on where the exchange rate might be expected to be in the longer term. The authorities would be able, but not obliged, to intervene to steer the rate toward the monitoring band when it deviated outside. Thus, this regime would once again involve a basically floating rate, but with an obligation on the authorities to think about where the exchange rate ought to be in the interest of macroeconomic balance, and would give notice to the market that it should be prepared for the possibility of intervention to back that judgment up.

Why should any of these regimes be preferable to a system of unstructured floating in which the authorities stand prepared to intervene to discourage the rate's floating to misaligned levels without explaining what they are doing? There are three potential advantages. The first is greater transparency: because governments are expected to explain the basis for their actions, there is a better chance that they will think carefully about what they are doing. The second is that public knowledge of the authorities' estimates of where equilibrium rates lie may encourage stabilizing speculation a la Krugman. Perhaps this is unlikely with the present low level of government credibility on exchange rate issues, but it is a pity to abandon the possibility of working back to a situation in which governments and markets interact constructively in setting rates, for neither seems to do much of a job left on its own. The third potential advantage lies in providing a basis for regional monetary collaboration, which seems unlikely to amount to anything substantive without some form of agreed exchange rate target.

Is there any chance that some form of zone or band system will one day supercede the floating that has now become so widespread? I would answer that there is some chance, especially where there are regional ambitions for monetary coordination, but I am not holding my breath for any wider agreement. Two factors weigh against it. The first is that the authorities have accumulated such an appalling record of defending disequilibrium exchange rates that an announcement of exchange rate targets would now command almost no credibility. That in turn makes it extremely costly to defend any rates that are announced, and indeed vitiates the main potential benefit of such announcements. Doubtless, credibility could be reestablished over time given a decision to invest effort in calculating targets seriously and a willingness to alter policies in pursuit of those targets, but the question is whether it will seem worth making such investments. The second factor weighing against a future intermediate regime is that typically major structural reforms are adopted only under the spur of a crisis, and the one thing that has to be said for floating is that it has so far proved to be relatively crisis proof. Perhaps that will change when the dollar falls below, say, 1.60 euros and 75 yen, but at the moment, most Americans are convinced that this will not happen and that if it did, the foreigners would step in and prevent Americans' experiencing any hardships.

Perhaps the least unlikely development toward an intermediate regime would be universal adoption of the reference rate proposal. This is somewhat less unlikely because rates would still unambiguously float: there would still be no margins, which is what has scared officials because they have encountered so many crises in the course of trying to defend margins. The purpose would be to discipline the behavior of governments with floating rates so as to prevent their saying things that are unhelpful to global stability, such as being in favor of a strong dollar. A strong dollar must mean a weak euro and/or yen, if it means anything at all; and if a strong dollar is good for the United States, then presumably a strong euro is good for Europe (although admittedly a good case can be made for thinking that a weak yen is good for Japan in its current situation). Certainly one can argue that a stronger euro would have resulted in lower inflationary pressures in Europe and thus given the European

Central Bank latitude to cut interest rates. So if the declarations of fidelity to a strong dollar that have emanated regularly from Washington in recent years have been more than empty rhetoric, one can hold them responsible for the high interest rates in Europe.

Of course, it is nonsense to claim that it is, in general, in a country's interest to have a strong currency. Certainly it is not usually in a country's interest to have a weak currency, but at some point, a currency becomes too strong for a country's long-run good. Payments deficits balloon and build up a dangerous overhang of foreign debt. In fact, the U.S. treasury secretaries who have proclaimed their love for a strong dollar have de facto recognized that since they have occasionally sanctioned intervention designed to weaken the dollar on the exchanges. It would be thoroughly healthy if they were required to think ex ante about how strong a dollar makes this appropriate, agree their estimate with the IMF, and then publish it for the markets to be able to factor it into their decision making. This is what the reference rate proposal would achieve.

Note

1. Fischer (2001) seemed a little uncertain as to whether a system with a sufficiently wide band might not be vulnerable to his critique.

References

Bergsten, C. Fred, and John Williamson. 1983. Exchange rates and trade policy. In *Trade policy in the 1980s*, edited by W. R. Cline, 99-120. Washington, DC: Institute for International Economics.

Ethier, Wilfred, and Arthur I. Bloomfield. 1975. *Managing the managed float*. Princeton essays in international finance no. 112. Princeton, NJ: Princeton University Press.

Fellner, William, Fritz Machlup, and Robert Triffin. 1966. *Maintaining and restoring balance in international payments*. Princeton, NJ: Princeton University Press.

Fischer, Stanley. 2001. Exchange rate regimes: Is the bipolar view correct? Distinguished lecture on economics in government presented at the meetings of the American Economic Association in New Orleans, January.

Friedman, Milton. 1953. The case for floating exchange rates. In *Essays in positive economics*. Chicago: University of Chicago Press.

Halm, George N. 1965. The "band" proposal: The limits of permissible exchange rate variations. Princeton special papers in international economics no. 6. Princeton, NJ: Princeton University Press.

Harrod, Roy. 1933. *International economics*. London: Macmillan.

Krugman, Paul. 1991. Target zones and exchange rate dynamics. *Quarterly Journal of Economics* 106 (3): 669-82.

McKinnon, Ronald I. 1971. Monetary theory and controlled flexibility in the foreign exchanges. Princeton essays in international finance no. 84. Princeton, NJ: Princeton University Press.

Meade, James. 1955. The case for variable exchange rates. *Three Banks Review* (September): 3-27.

Meese, Richard, and Kenneth Rogoff. 1983. Empirical exchange rate models of the 1970s: Do they fit out of sample? *Journal of International Economics* 14:67-105.

Moggridge, Donald, ed. 1980. *The collected writings of John Maynard Keynes*. London: Macmillan.

Scott, Maurice F. G. 1959. What should be done about the sterling area? *Bulletin of the Oxford University Institute of Statistics* 21 (November): 213-51, 373-75.

Tarapore Committee. 1997. *Report of the committee on capital account convertibility.* Mumbai: Reserve Bank of India.

Williamson, John. 1982. A survey of the emergent literature on the optimal peg. *Journal of Development Economics* 11 (August): 39-61.

———. 1983. Keynes and the international economic order. In *Keynes and the modern world*, edited by David Worswick and James Trevithick, 87-113. Cambridge, UK: Cambridge University Press.

———. 1985. *The exchange rate system.* Washington, DC: Institute for International Economics.

———. 1996. *The crawling band as an exchange rate regime.* Washington, DC: Institute for International Economics.

———. 2000. *Exchange rate regimes for emerging markets: Reviving the intermediate option.* Washington, DC: Institute for International Economics.

———, ed. 1981. *Exchange rate rules: The theory, performance and prospects of the crawling peg.* London: Macmillan.

Williamson, John, and Marcus Miller. 1987. *Targets and indicators: A blueprint for the international coordination of economic policy.* Washington, DC: Institute for International Economics.

ANNALS, *AAPSS*, **579**, January 2002

Currency Boards

By STEVE H. HANKE

ABSTRACT: In contrast to central banks, currency boards are rule-bound monetary institutions without discretionary monetary policies. Currency boards first appeared in the mid-nineteenth century, were widespread prior to World War II, were replaced by central banks after the war, and have made something of a resurgence in the 1990s. This article discusses the distinguishing features of currency boards and central banks. Data that compare the performance of currency boards to that of central banks are presented. The arguments against currency boards are itemized and evaluated. The article concludes that the opposition to currency boards ignores the empirical evidence and is, at best, half baked. In developing countries, currency boards are superior to central banks. By applying a remediableness criterion, the article concludes that there are more than sixty countries that should replace their central banks with currency boards.

Steve H. Hanke is a professor of applied economics at the Johns Hopkins University in Baltimore and chairman of the Friedberg Mercantile Group, Inc., in New York. He has played a role in the design and establishment of the currency board systems established in the 1990s (Hanke and Schuler 1991a, 1991b; Hanke, Jonung, and Schuler 1992; Hanke and Schuler 1994b; and Hanke 1996/1997).

NOTE: The author thanks Matt Sekerke for his assistance in preparing this article.

In the beginning God created
sterling and the franc.
On the second day He created the
currency board and, Lo, money
was well managed.
On the third day God decided
that man should have free will
and so He created the budget
deficit.
On the fourth day, however, God
looked upon His work and was
dissatisfied. It was not enough.
So, on the fifth day God created
the central bank to validate
the sins of man.
On the sixth day God completed
His work by creating man and
giving him dominion over all
God's creatures.
Then, while God rested on the
seventh day, man created
inflation and the balance-of-
payments problem.

—Peter B. Kenen (1978, 13)

Central banks issue currency and exercise wide discretion over the conduct of monetary policy. Although widespread today, central banks are relatively new institutional arrangements. In 1900, there were only 18 central banks in the world. By 1940, forty countries had them, and today there are 174. Of those, 6 are bound by currency board rules that do not permit discretionary monetary policies. In addition, there are seven monetary authorities that operate as stand-alone currency boards (see Table 1).

An orthodox currency board issues notes and coins convertible on demand into a foreign anchor currency at a fixed rate of exchange. As reserves, it holds low-risk, interest-bearing bonds denominated in the anchor currency and typically some gold. The reserve levels are set by law and are equal to 100 percent, or slightly more, of its monetary liabilities (notes, coins, and if permitted, deposits). A currency board's convertibility and foreign reserve cover requirements do not extend to deposits at commercial banks or to any other financial assets. A currency board generates profits (seigniorage) from the difference between the interest it earns on its reserve assets and the expense of maintaining its liabilities. By design, a currency board has no discretionary monetary powers and cannot engage in the fiduciary issue of money. Its operations are passive and automatic. The sole function of a currency board is to exchange the domestic currency it issues for an anchor currency at a fixed rate. Consequently, the quantity of domestic currency in circulation is determined solely by market forces, namely the demand for domestic currency (Walters and Hanke 1992).

The currency board idea originated in Britain in the early 1800s. A notable proponent was David Ricardo. Sir John Hicks (1967) made this perfectly clear when he wrote, "On strict Ricardian principles, there should have been no need for Central Banks. A Currency Board, working on a rule, should have been enough" (pp. 167-78).

Currency boards have existed in about seventy countries. The first one was installed in the British Indian Ocean colony of Mauritius in

TABLE 1

CURRENCY BOARDS AND CURRENCY BOARD–LIKE SYSTEMS TODAY

Country	System Began	Exchange Rate	Population	GDP (in U.S.$)[a]
Argentina[b]	1991	1 peso = U.S.$1	37 million	$374 billion
Bermuda	1915	Bermuda$1 = U.S.$1	62,000	$1.9 billion
Brunei[b]	1952	Brunei$1 = Singapore$1	320,000	$5.4 billion
Bosnia[b]	1997	1 convertible mark = DM 1	3.5 million	$5.8 billion
Bulgaria[b]	1997	1 lev = DM 1	8.2 million	$34 billion
Cayman Islands	1972	Cayman$1 = U.S.$1.20	39,000	$930 million
Djibouti[b]	1949	177.72 Djibouti francs = U.S.$1	450,000	$530 million
Estonia[b]	1992	8 kroons = DM 1	1.4 million	$7.8 billion
Falkland Islands	1899	Falklands£1 = U.K.£1	2,800	unavailable
Faroe Islands	1940	1 Faroese krone = 1 Danish krone	41,000	$700 million
Gibraltar	1927	£1 = U.K.£1	29,000	$500 million
Hong Kong[b]	1983	Hong Kong$7.80 = U.S.$1	6.8 million	$168 billion
Lithuania[b]	1994	4 litai = U.S.$1	3.6 million	$18 billion

SOURCES: Hanke, Jonung, and Schuler (1993); Central Intelligence Agency (1999).

a. Expressed in terms of purchasing power parity, not at current exchange rates.

b. Currency board–like system.

1849. By the 1930s, they were widespread in British colonies in Africa, Asia, the Caribbean, and the Pacific islands. Currency boards have also existed in a number of independent countries and city-states, such as Danzig and Singapore. One of the more interesting currency boards was installed in North Russia on 11 November 1918, during the civil war. Its architect was John Maynard Keynes, who was a British Treasury official responsible for war finance at the time (Hanke, Jonung, and Schuler 1993).

DISTINGUISHING FEATURES OF CURRENCY BOARDS AND CENTRAL BANKS

The features that distinguish typical currency boards and central banks are itemized in Table 2 and are generally self-explanatory. Several merit further comment, however. One concerns balance sheets. Unfortunately, most economists are incapable of performing basic balance sheet diagnostics and ignore these important documents. This was not always the case. Sir John Hicks—a high priest of economic theory and 1972 Nobelist—thought there was nothing more important than a balance sheet (Klamer 1989). I agree, particularly when it comes to understanding monetary institutions.

A balance sheet reveals a monetary authority's liabilities (high-powered base money). It also shows the make-up of those liabilities, or the split between net domestic assets (the domestic component of base money) and net foreign reserves (the foreign component of base money).

The asset side of a central bank's balance sheet contains both net domestic assets and net foreign reserves. This means that a central bank can engage in discretionary

TABLE 2

A TYPICAL CURRENCY BOARD VERSUS A TYPICAL CENTRAL BANK

Typical Currency Board	Typical Central Bank
Usually supplies notes and coins only	Supplies notes, coins, and deposits
Fixed exchange rate with reserve currency	Pegged or floating exchange rate
No conflicts between exchange rate policies and monetary policies	Frequent conflicts between exchange rate policies and monetary policies
No balance of payments crises	Frequent balance of payments crises
Foreign reserves of 100 percent	Variable foreign reserves
Cannot become insolvent	Can become insolvent
Does not hold domestic assets	Does hold domestic assets
Full convertibility	Limited convertibility
Rule-bound monetary policy	Discretionary monetary policy
Not a lender of last resort	Lender of last resort
Does not regulate commercial banks	Often regulates commercial banks
Transparent	Opaque
Immune from corruption scandals	Prone to corruption scandals
Protected from political pressure	Politicized
High credibility	Low credibility
Earns seigniorage only from interest	Earns seigniorage from interest and inflation
Cannot create inflation	Can create inflation
Cannot finance spending by domestic government	Can finance spending by domestic government
Requires no preconditions for monetary reform	Requires preconditions for monetary reform
Rapid monetary reform	Slow monetary reform
Small staff	Large staff

monetary policy—or fine-tuning—by buying and selling domestic assets (bonds and bills). This results in changes in the fiduciary issue of money, with the domestic component of the monetary base increasing when a central bank buys bonds and bills and contracting when a central bank sells bonds and bills.

Net foreign reserves are the only asset on a currency board's balance sheet because it cannot buy and sell domestic assets. Consequently, a currency board cannot engage in fine-tuning, and its monetary liabilities (base money) are exclusively made up of a foreign component. Changes in base money in a currency board system are, therefore, exclusively driven by changes in the balance of payments and net foreign reserves.

A quick glance at a monetary authority's balance sheet will show whether it is engaging in discretionary monetary policy and whether it is operating as a currency board or a central bank. Since currency boards conduct no monetary policy and have nothing to hide, they post their current balance sheets on the Web and are transparent. This is not the case for central banks. Of the 174 central banks, only 124 have Web sites. And, only 82 post some form of balance sheet. Of those, only 14 display current balance sheets (Hanke 2001). This lack of central bank transparency causes no end of problems for those who wish to conduct balance sheet diagnostics and determine what central banks are actually doing.

A second feature that distinguishes currency boards and central banks is the exchange rate regimes they employ. With currency board rules, a monetary authority sets the exchange rate—it is fixed—but it has no monetary policy. The quantity of base money in the system is solely determined by the demand for it in the market. Consequently, there can be no conflicts between exchange rate policies and monetary policies in a currency board system. Balance-of-payments problems cannot rear their ugly heads because market forces automatically act to rebalance financial flows. This explains why speculative attacks against currencies issued by currency boards have always ended in failure, with no devaluations. Argentina in 1995 and 2001 is but one example.

Central banks in developing countries simultaneously manage exchange rate policies and monetary policies. They operate with pegged exchange rate systems that are variously referred to as pegged, pegged but adjustable, bands, or managed floating systems. With pegged rates, the monetary base contains both domestic and foreign components because both net domestic assets and foreign reserves on the monetary authority's balance sheet can change, and these changes cause its monetary liabilities to fluctuate.

Pegged rates invariably result in conflicts between exchange rate policies and monetary policies. For example, when capital inflows become excessive under a pegged system, a monetary authority often attempts to sterilize the effect by reducing the domestic component of the monetary base through the sale of government bonds. And, when outflows become excessive, the authority attempts to offset the changes with an increase in the domestic component of the monetary base by purchasing government bonds. Balance-of-payments crises erupt as a monetary authority increasingly offsets the reduction in the foreign component of the monetary base with domestically created base money. When this occurs, it is only a matter of time before currency speculators spot the contradiction. This is exactly what happened in Turkey during February of 2001.

A third feature that merits attention concerns the issuance of credit by a monetary authority. Central banks can act as a lender of last resort and extend credit to the banking system. They can also make loans to the fiscal authorities and state-owned enterprises. Consequently, central banks can go bankrupt. The Bank of Indonesia is the most recent example of an insolvent central bank (Hanke 2000a).

A problem in many developing countries is that the rule of law is weak and so are the institutions of government. Consequently, a principal-agent problem exists because the voters (principals) have very little effective control over their agents (politicians) (Williamson 1996). Currency boards remedy the principal-agent problem, in part, because they cannot extend credit to the fiscal authorities or state-owned enterprises. In addition, currency boards cannot engage

TABLE 3
CURRENCY BOARD VERSUS CENTRAL BANK PERFORMANCES (NINETY-EIGHT DEVELOPING COUNTRIES, 1950-1993)

System	GDP Growth Rate (%)	Annual Average Inflation (%)	Fiscal Deficit (% of GDP)
Currency board	2.6 (535)	7.0 (523)	2.2 (338)
Central bank	1.7 (2,694)	33.8 (2,663)	3.7 (1,769)

SOURCE: Based on Hanke (1999).
NOTE: Number of observations in parentheses.

TABLE 4
CURRENCY BOARD VERSUS CENTRAL BANK PERFORMANCES (MEMBERS OF THE INTERNATIONAL MONETARY FUND, 1970-1996)

System	Number of Observations	GDP Growth Rate (%)	Annual Average Inflation (%)	Fiscal Deficit (% of GDP)
Currency board	115	3.2	5.6	2.8
Central bank	695	1.6	48.3	4.4

SOURCE: Based on Ghosh, Gulde, and Wolf (1998).

in lender of last resort activities. The fiscal regime, therefore, is subordinated to the monetary regime, and a hard budget constraint is imposed on the politicians.

Much as the gold standard was adopted to control the fiscal authorities (James 2001), I can attest to the fact that every currency board in the 1990s was adopted primarily to impose a hard budget constraint. With few exceptions, this key currency board feature has been overlooked by economists (Horváth and Székely 2001).

PERFORMANCE OF CURRENCY BOARDS AND CENTRAL BANKS

All currency boards have performed well, when compared to central banks (Hanke, Jonung, and Schuler 1993). Countries with currency boards have realized price stability, respectable growth rates, and fiscal discipline (for the first detailed quantitative study that compares currency boards and central banks in 155 countries, see Schuler 1996).

Tables 3 and 4 present pooled time-series, cross-section data for a large number of countries spanning nearly fifty years. The data speak for themselves. The currency boards' performance is unambiguously superior to the central banks'. Currency boards, therefore, satisfy Karl Schiller's (cited in Marsh 1992) test of a sound monetary system: "stability might not be everything, but without stability, everything is nothing" (p. 30).

Karl Schiller's test is particularly relevant when judging the performance of the five currency boards installed in the 1990s. All were installed in countries that were politically and/or economically very unstable. Furthermore, prior to the installation of currency boards, all countries had soft budget constraints and faced the prospect of continued instability. Argentina was attempting to cope with repeated bouts of hyperinflation. Estonia had just gained independence from the U.S.S.R and was still using the hyperinflating Russian ruble. Lithuania was in the grip of a collapsing real economy and very high inflation. To make matters worse, its new political institutions could not effectively control what threatened to be a runaway fiscal deficit. Bulgaria had defaulted on its international debt, narrowly escaped a revolution in late 1996, and was battling hyperinflation that had virtually wiped out its banking system and sent the real economy into a free fall. Finally, the newly independent Bosnia and Herzegovina had just come out of a bloody civil war, one that had disrupted and displaced most of the population, destroyed 18 percent and damaged 60 percent of the housing stock, and covered much of the territory with land mines. Its economy was in shambles, declining to about 20 percent of the 1990 level. With the exception of the deutsche mark, the other three currencies in circulation—the Bosnia and Herzegovina dinar, the Croatian kuna, and the Yugoslav dinar—were either unstable or very unstable.

Tables 5 through 9 constitute event studies, with the events being the installation of a currency board. Economic and financial data are presented before and after the event. Although these basic data speak for themselves, several points merit attention. For each of the five countries, the foreign reserves increased dramatically after the currency board was introduced. Given that the monetary liabilities of the boards are solely a function of the demand for those liabilities and given that they must be backed by a minimum of 100 percent foreign reserves, the demand for the domestic currency, as indicated by foreign reserve levels, increased dramatically after the introduction of the currency board.

The currency boards' imposition of a hard budget constraint is not fully revealed by the fiscal balance data. These data show fiscal balances on a standard cash basis, which excludes revenues from privatization. Also, in the years prior to the introduction of the currency boards, the fiscal authorities were all running up large arrears. This practice stopped after boards were installed. Consequently, the fiscal deficits prior to their introduction would have been larger if bills had been paid on time. In addition, in the years following their introduction, privatizations increased significantly. If these were included in the fiscal data, the deficits after the installation of the currency boards would have been much smaller. Therefore, the fiscal effects of currency boards are, in reality, much more impressive than those implied by the standard data presented in Tables 5 through 9.

For the four countries in which data were available (see Tables 5-8), foreign direct investment and portfolio flows registered healthy increases after currency boards were installed.

TABLE 5

ARGENTINA BEFORE AND AFTER SETTING UP A CURRENCY BOARD (1 APRIL 1991)

	1989	1990	1991	1992	1993	1994	1995	1996	1997	1998	1999	2000
Annual inflation (year-end %)	4,928.6	1,344.5	84.0	17.5	7.4	3.9	1.6	0.0	0.3	0.7	–1.8	–0.5
Change in real GDP (%)	–6.9	–1.8	10.6	9.6	5.7	5.8	–2.8	5.5	8.1	3.9	–3.1	–0.2
Interest rates (money market rate, % per annum, at year-end)	1,387,179	9,695,422	71.33	15.11	6.31	7.66	9.46	6.23	6.63	6.81	6.99	8.15
Fiscal balance (% of GDP)	–7.6	0.1	–0.1	–0.2	0.9	–0.3	–1.0	–2.2	–1.5	–1.4	–2.5	–2.4
Foreign reserves (in U.S.$ billions)	3	6	7	12	15	16	16	20	22	25	26.4	22.9
Foreign direct investment (in U.S.$ millions)	1,028	1,836	2,439	4,045	2,555	3,635	5,610	6,949	9,161	7,280	24,148	11,154
Portfolio assets (investment abroad by Argentines, in U.S.$ millions)	NA	–241	–8,261	–80	–2,037	–1,485	–2,882	–2,380	–1,449	–2,065	–2,037	–1,456
Portfolio liabilities (investment by foreigners in Argentina, in U.S.$ millions)	–1,098	–1,105	8,227	1,060	22,345	9,853	4,752	12,209	11,753	10,829	–4,418	–94
Exports (% of GDP)	13.0	10.4	7.8	6.7	7.0	7.6	9.7	10.5	10.6	10.4	9.8	10.8
Seigniorage (% of GDP)			0.24	0.30	0.33	0.38	0.35	0.42	0.48	0.43	0.52	0.52

SOURCES: International Monetary Fund, Argentine Ministry of Economy, Banco Central de la Republica Argentina, Lehman Brothers.

NOTES: (1) The fiscal balance is calculated on a cash basis and excludes privatization revenues. The arrears were very high in 1990, suggesting that the cash deficit as a percentage of GDP would have been quite high in 1990 if the government had been paying its bills on time. (2) For portfolio assets, a negative number indicates an increase in holdings of foreign assets by Argentines (a net outflow of capital), while a positive number reflects a decrease in holdings. Conversely, for portfolio liabilities, a positive number indicates an increase in holdings of Argentine assets by foreigners (a net inflow of capital), and a negative number reflects a decrease in Argentine assets held by foreigners. (3) Seigniorage is calculated by multiplying foreign reserves less gold, special drawing rights, and the country's net International Monetary Fund position by the long bond yield in the reserve currency.

TABLE 6

ESTONIA BEFORE AND AFTER SETTING UP A CURRENCY BOARD (20-24 JUNE 1992)

	1990	1991	1992	1993	1994	1995	1996	1997	1998	1999	2000
Annual inflation (annual average %)	23.1	210.5	1,076	89.0	47.7	29.0	23.1	11.2	8.1	3.3	4.0
Change in real GDP (%)	–6.5	–13.6	–14.2	–9.0	–2.0	4.3	4.0	10.4	5.0	–0.7	6.9
Commercial banks average lending rates (short-term, 1-3 months, %)	NA	NA	59.2	36.6	24.6	19.0	14.8	11.9	15.1	11.1	7.4
Fiscal balance (% of GDP)	2.9	4.7	–0.3	–0.7	1.3	–1.2	–1.5	2.2	–0.3	–4.6	–0.3
Foreign reserves (in U.S.$ millions)	NA	NA	196	389	447	583	640	760	813	906	935
Foreign direct investment (in U.S.$ millions)	NA	NA	82.3	162.2	214.4	201.5	150.2	266.2	580.5	305.2	386.9
Portfolio assets (investment abroad by Estonians, in U.S.$ millions)	NA	NA	NA	–0.4	–22.5	–33.2	–52.7	–165.0	–10.9	–132.3	39.9
Portfolio liabilities (investments by foreigners in Estonia, in U.S.$ millions)	NA	NA	NA	0.2	8.4	11.1	198.1	427.5	1.1	153.3	76.2
Exports (% of GDP)	NA	31.9	60.0	70.3	76.0	72.4	67.1	78.1	79.8	77.4	96.2
Seigniorage (% of GDP)			1.25	1.26	1.29	1.06	0.82	0.83	0.68	0.71	0.97

SOURCES: International Monetary Fund, Estonian Central Bank, European Bank for Reconstruction and Development, Lehman Brothers.

NOTES: (1) Reliable data for interest rates and foreign reserves are not available for 1990 and 1991 because Estonia was still part of the U.S.S.R. during most of that period. A referendum was held in March 1991, and 77.8 percent of the votes cast favored Estonian independence. Estonia declared independence on 20 August 1991, and an independent status was conceded by the U.S.S.R. State Council on 6 September 1991. (2) When the currency board was established in June 1992 and the kroon replaced the Russian ruble, foreign reserves were $98.1 million. (3) For portfolio assets, a negative number indicates an increase in holdings of foreign assets by Estonians (a net outflow of capital), while a positive number reflects a decrease in holdings. Conversely, for portfolio liabilities, a positive number indicates an increase in holdings of Estonian assets by foreigners (a net inflow of capital), and a negative number reflects a decrease in Estonian assets held by foreigners. (4) Seigniorage is calculated by multiplying foreign reserves less gold, special drawing rights, and the country's net International Monetary Fund position by the long bond yield in the reserve currency.

TABLE 7

LITHUANIA BEFORE AND AFTER SETTING UP A CURRENCY BOARD (1 APRIL 1994)

	1992	1993	1994	1995	1996	1997	1998	1999	2000
Annual inflation (year-end %)	1,175	188.8	72.2	35.5	13.1	8.4	2.4	0.3	1.5
Change in real GDP (%)	–21.3	–16.2	–9.8	3.3	4.7	7.3	5.1	–4.2	2.7
Commercial banks' average lending rates (short-term, 1-3 months, %)	135.2	91.6	33.0	29.5	20.0	13.3	13.3	14.5	13.4
Fiscal balance (% of GDP)	0.5	–5.3	–4.8	–4.5	–4.5	–1.8	–5.9	–8.5	–2.8
Foreign reserves (in U.S.$ millions)	107	412	587	819	834	1,063	1,460	1,242	1,356
Foreign direct investment (in U.S.$ millions)	NA	30.2	31.3	72.6	152.4	354.5	925.5	486.5	378.9
Portfolio assets (investment abroad by Lithuanians, in U.S.$ millions)	NA	–0.9	–0.2	–10.5	–26.9	7.7	–10.1	–1.9	–141.4
Portfolio liabilities (investment by foreigners in Lithuania, in U.S.$ millions)	NA	0.6	4.6	26.6	89.6	180.5	–42.7	507.5	405.9
Exports (% of GDP)	23.3	82.5	55.4	53.0	53.4	54.5	47.2	39.7	45.5
Seigniorage (% of GDP)			0.85	0.81	0.62	0.66	0.68	0.63	0.70

SOURCES: International Monetary Fund, European Bank for Reconstruction and Development, Lehman Brothers.

NOTES: (1) For portfolio assets, a negative number indicates an increase in holdings of foreign assets by Lithuanians (a net outflow of capital), while a positive number reflects a decrease in holdings. Conversely, for portfolio liabilities, a positive number indicates an increase in holdings of Lithuanian assets by foreigners (a net inflow of capital), and a negative number reflects a decrease in Lithuanian assets held by foreigners. (2) Seigniorage is calculated by multiplying foreign reserves less gold, special drawing rights, and the country's net International Monetary Fund position by the long bond yield in the reserve currency.

This, in part, can be attributed to the fixed exchange rate regimes and the marked reduction in exchange rate risks that accompany a currency board system.

The story of Hong Kong provides another event study. The authorities allowed the Hong Kong dollar to float in November 1974. The floating Hong Kong dollar became wildly volatile and steadily lost value against the U.S. dollar. The volatility reached epic proportions in late September 1983, after the fourth round of Sino-British talks on Hong Kong's future. Financial markets and the Hong Kong dollar went into tailspins.

At the end of July 1983, the Hong Kong dollar was trading at Hong Kong$7.31 to U.S.$1. By Black

TABLE 8

BULGARIA BEFORE AND AFTER SETTING UP A CURRENCY BOARD (1 JULY 1997)

	1991	1992	1993	1994	1995	1996	1997	1998	1999	2000
Annual inflation (year-end %)	338.9	79.4	63.8	121.9	32.9	310.8	549.2	1.7	7.0	11.4
Change in real GDP (%)	–11.7	–7.3	–1.5	1.8	2.1	–10.1	–6.9	3.5	2.4	5.3
Interest rates (money market rate, % per annum)	69.6	49.7	66.4	101.2	39.8	435.0	7.0	5.2	4.6	4.7
Fiscal balance (% of GDP)	–3.7	–5.2	–10.9	–5.8	–5.6	–12.7	–2.5	1.0	–1.0	–1.0
Foreign reserves (in U.S.$ millions)	616	1,207	960	1,311	1,545	793	2,474	3,056	3,222	3,460
Foreign direct investment (in U.S.$ millions)	56	42	40	105	90.4	109.0	504.8	537.2	806.1	1001.5
Portfolio assets (investment abroad by Bulgarians, in U.S.$ millions)	NA	NA	NA	–222	9.7	–7.1	–13.7	–129.5	–207.5	–62.0
Portfolio liabilities (investment by foreigners in Bulgaria, in U.S.$ millions)	NA	NA	NA	–10	–75.4	–122.2	146.5	–112.0	8.0	–114.9
Exports (% of GDP)	43.4	47.3	38.1	45.1	44.7	62.9	61.4	45.2	44.1	NA
Seigniorage (% of GDP)							1.10	0.99	1.02	NA

SOURCES: International Monetary Fund, Lehman Brothers, European Bank for Reconstruction and Development.

NOTES: (1) For portfolio assets, a negative number indicates an increase in holdings of foreign assets by Bulgarians (a net outflow of capital), while a positive number reflects a decrease in holdings. Conversely, for portfolio liabilities, a positive number indicates an increase in holdings of Bulgarian assets by foreigners (a net inflow of capital), and a negative number reflects a decrease in Bulgarian assets held by foreigners. (2) Seigniorage is calculated by multiplying foreign reserves less gold, special drawing rights, and the country's net International Monetary Fund position by the long bond yield in the reserve currency.

TABLE 9

BOSNIA AND HERZEGOVINA BEFORE AND AFTER SETTING UP A CURRENCY BOARD (11 AUGUST 1997)

	1995	1996	1997	1998	1999	2000
Annual inflation (annual average %)	–4	–25	14	5	0	2
Change in real GDP (%)	21	86	40	13	9	10
Commercial banks' median lending rates to households (short-term, 1-3 months, %)	146.7	55.6	29.6	26.0	28.0	24.0
Fiscal balance (% of GDP)	0	–3	–1	–2	–1	–3
Foreign reserves (in U.S.$ millions)	207	235	80	175	455	488

SOURCES: Central Bank of Bosnia and Herzegovina, International Monetary Fund.

NOTES: (1) Interest rate data for 1996 are for April. All interest rates are for the federation only. (2) Between 1995 and 10 August 1997, the National Bank of Bosnia and Herzegovina (NBBiH) operated and issued a Bosnia-Herzegovina dinar (BHD). That currency was pegged to the German mark at BHD = DM 100. During that period, the NBBiH operated as a pseudo-currency board. However, there were some deviations in which credits were issued to the government. Moreover, those credits were not fully backed by DM assets. On 11 August 1997, the Central Bank of Bosnia and Herzegovina (CBBiH) was established, and the convertible marka (KM) became the unit of account. The CBBiH operates under currency board–like rules. On 22 June 1998, the KM notes were put into circulation, and on 9 December 1998, KM coins were put into circulation. On 7 July 1998, the BHD ceased to be legal tender. (3) The last cease-fire agreement in the civil war was signed on 10 October 1995; the Dayton/Paris Treaty that ended the war was initialed in Dayton on 21 November 1995 and signed in Paris on 14 December 1995.

Saturday, 24 September, it had fallen to Hong Kong$9.55 to U.S.$1, with dealer spreads reported as large as ten thousand basis points. Hong Kong was in a state of panic, with people hoarding toilet paper, rice, and cooking oil. The chaos ended abruptly on 15 October, when Hong Kong reinstated its currency board.

In the seventeen years since the currency board, Hong Kong's GDP growth has been positive and strong in all but one year, 1998, the year after the Asian crisis engulfed the region. Annual inflation has come down from 9.2 percent during the floating period to an average of 3.7 percent during the currency board period. And, the fiscal authorities have generated budget surpluses in fourteen out of the seventeen years.

THE DEMISE AND RESURGENCE OF CURRENCY BOARDS

Given the superior performance of currency boards, the obvious question is, What led to their demise and replacement by central banks after World War II?

The demise of currency boards resulted from a confluence of three factors. A choir of influential economists was singing the praises of central banking's flexibility and fine-tuning capacities. In addition to changing intellectual fashions, newly independent states were trying to shake off their ties with former imperial powers, which sometimes included chasing away foreign investment. And, the International Monetary Fund (IMF) and World

Bank, anxious to obtain new clients and "jobs for the boys," lent their weight and money to the establishment of new central banks. In the end, the Bank of England provided the only institutional voice that favored currency boards. That was obviously not enough (Tignor 1998).

Why, then, did currency boards begin to make something of a resurgence in the 1990s? As someone who observed these developments at close range, I can attest that it had very little to do with the usual things economists write about currency boards. Instead, the resurgence was largely motivated by the desire to install a monetary regime to which the fiscal regime would be subordinated. By putting the monetary authorities in a straitjacket, currency boards were viewed as a means to impose fiscal discipline. And, as Tables 5 through 9 indicate, they have satisfied that expectation, a fact acknowledged in the IMF's (2001f) most recent edition of the *World Economic Outlook*: "a currency board tends to discourage persistently large fiscal deficits and the use of the inflation tax" (p. 131).

The resurgence has not gone unchallenged, however. Indeed, a cottage industry housing passionate opponents of currency boards has developed over the past decade. The works they produce, much like those in development economics, have been promoted by "the disregard for contrary opinions" (Bauer 1976, 231). Indeed, they suffer from parasitic citation loops in which opponents exclusively cite other opponents. As for the empirical evidence, it is swept away like flies. Indeed, the opponents use as their method "nirvana economics" in which the ideal of central banking is compared to the actual operation of currency boards.

But, why all this opposition? The most charitable answer to this phenomenon was given by Michael Polanyi (1958). He wrote that it is "the normal practice of scientists to ignore evidence which appears incompatible with the accepted system of scientific knowledge" (p. 138).

Be that as it may, there are a number of objections that were anticipated and refuted in a chapter devoted to that task (Hanke and Schuler 1994a). Unfortunately, these objections have become little more than clichés (Williamson 1995) and merit comment, once again.

The most common cliché that has been propagated by the opponents of currency boards is the notion that certain preconditions must be satisfied before currency boards can be adopted. It was embraced by the Council of Economic Advisers (1999), which wrote, "A currency board is unlikely to be successful without the solid fundamentals of adequate reserves, fiscal discipline and a strong and well-managed financial system, in addition to the rule of law" (p. 289).

This statement is literally fantastic and demonstrates how far off base professional economists can get when they fail to carefully study the history, workings, and results of alternative real-world institutions. After all, none of the successful currency boards of the 1990s was installed in a country that came close to satisfying even one of the alleged preconditions.

The second oft-cited criticism of currency boards asserts that they are rule bound and rigid. Consequently, countries that employ them are more subject to external shocks than are countries with central banks. If this were true, the variability of growth measured by the standard deviations in growth rates in currency board countries would be larger than in central banking countries. The facts do not support this thesis (Hanke 1999). Indeed, the variability of growth rates between the two sets of countries is almost identical. This suggests that while currency board countries are subject to external shocks, central banking countries are subject to internal shocks, and their magnitudes are almost the same. The currency board shock argument is, therefore, little more than a straw man.

The inability of a currency board to extend credit to the banking system, or what is referred to as the lack of a lender of last resort, constitutes a third criticism. As the United Nations Conference on Trade and Development (2001) put it, "a currency board regime makes payments crises less likely only by making bank crises more likely" (p. 117). This is another straw man argument. The major banking crises in the world have all occurred in central banking countries in which the lender of last resort function was practiced with reckless abandon (Frydl 1999). In contrast, currency board countries have not only avoided banking crises, but their banking systems—knowing they would not be bailed out by a lender of last resort—have tended to strengthen over time. Bulgaria is but one example. The 1999 Organization for Economic Cooperation and Development (OECD) Economic Survey of Bulgaria stated, "By mid-1996, the Bulgarian banking system was devastated, with highly negative net worth and extremely low liquidity, and the government no longer had any resources to keep it afloat" (p. 60). However, the OECD also observed, "By the beginning of 1998, the situation in the commercial banking sector had essentially stabilized, with operating banks, on aggregate, appearing solvent and well-capitalized" (p. 59).

A fourth cliché states that competitiveness cannot be maintained after the adoption of a currency board. Hong Kong contradicts this conventional wisdom. Since its currency board was installed in 1983, it has retained its rank as the most competitive economy in the world (Gwartney and Lawson 2001). Moreover, countries that adopted currency boards in the 1990s have maintained their competitiveness measured by exports as a percent of GDP (see Tables 5-8). Argentina is of particular interest because virtually every report about the current problems in Argentina contains an assertion about how the currency board–like system has made Argentina uncompetitive. What nonsense. Exports are the only bright spot in Argentina's economy. Indeed, the value of exports in the first half of 2001 grew by 3.2 percent compared to the first six months of 2000 (Dow Jones Newswires 2001).

A fifth assertion made by opponents of currency boards is that they are desirable only in small, if not tiny, economies. It is true that most currency boards today are in relatively small economies (see Table 1). However, Argentina and Hong Kong are not small. Indeed, Argentina and Hong Kong rank as the seventeenth and twenty-fourth largest economies in the world, respectively (World Bank 2001). If the size of Argentina's economy is the standard, then 115 countries—including every one in Africa—would qualify for currency boards because their economies are smaller than Argentina's (World Bank 2001).

A sixth concern expressed by economists is that currency boards are not suitable for most countries because the prospective currency board country is not in an optimum currency area with the anchor currency country. An optimum currency area is an artificial construct within which exchange rates should be fixed and between which exchange rates should be flexible. The problem is that the facts on the ground contradict the economists' notion of an optimal currency area. For example, Argentines have voluntarily chosen to hold most bank deposits and make most bank loans in dollars, and the value of the dollar notes (paper money) held in Argentina exceeds the value of the peso notes held. Therefore, Argentines have themselves determined that the dollar is the best currency, no matter what the optimal currency area theorists have concluded.

A seventh argument designed to stir populist ire concerns sovereignty. It is argued that monetary sovereignty is lost by the adoption of a currency board. An independent monetary policy is given up. True. After all, a currency board has no monetary policy. However, national sovereignty over a country's monetary regime is retained. Indeed, history has shown that many countries that once had currency boards have unilaterally exited from those rule-bound systems, albeit to their peril.

In closing, one final comment merits attention because it reveals just how confused and confusing the debate about the desirability of a currency boards is. Has the IMF been for or against currency boards? Well, it depends on when you ask. *Ex ante* the IMF has generally been opposed and has employed many of the clichés mentioned. The most notable case was in 1998 when the IMF vehemently opposed the establishment of a currency board in Indonesia (Hanke 2000b; Culp, Hanke, and Miller 1999). This prompted Robert Mundell (cited in IMF 2000b), the 1999 Nobel Laureate in Economics, to chastise the IMF at an IMF economic forum, where he said,

> I have been very disappointed in the way the IMF has treated currency board arrangements, by and large. I think they should have grasped onto it. After all, let's suppose that apart from the fact that the United States dollar would be at the center of this thing, you could imagine a world of currency boards, where all central banks operate like currency boards—not currency boards, but currency board systems. After all, that's what the gold standard was—it was what people nowadays call a currency board system. That's what the adjustment mechanism was. It was automatic until countries decided in the 1930s to go off on independent mone-

tary policies; then they got off on the wrong track.

Ex post the IMF has had nothing but praise for the five currency boards installed in the 1990s, as well as Hong Kong's (IMF 2000a, 2001a, 2001b, 2001c, 2001d, 2001e). According to the IMF, they have strengthened fiscal discipline and the banking systems, have motivated reforms, and have been the linchpins for growth.

ARGENTINA

Even though one might agree that the opponents of currency boards have ignored the evidence and put forward a wide variety of nonsensical arguments, the current travails in Argentina might cause one to pause before embracing the currency board idea. Just how did Argentina become embroiled in yet another financial turmoil? After all, it has a currency board–like system.

Even though Argentina emerged intact from Mexico's tequila crisis of 1995 and its GDP grew by 5.5 percent in 1996 and 8.1 percent in 1997, its economy ran into trouble in 1999, after Brazil's devaluation and before its own presidential elections.

The inauguration of Fernando de la Rua as president in December 1999 engendered some economic optimism, but the de la Rua government was a weak left wing coalition. It quickly proved incapable of reforming the supply side of the economy and bringing order to Argentina's fiscal affairs. A crisis of confidence ensued.

Earlier this year, de la Rua was forced to appoint Domingo Cavallo as his economic czar. Cavallo designed Argentina's unorthodox currency board, which killed the country's hyperinflation. But this time around, Cavallo has made missteps that have worsened Argentina's predicament.

In June, Cavallo introduced a dual-currency regime. Under this setup, all exports (excluding oil) take place with a devalued peso, all imports with a revalued peso. All other transactions take place at a peso-dollar rate of 1:1. Then a law was passed in which the peso's anchor will switch from the dollar to a basket of 50 percent euros and 50 percent dollars once the euro reaches parity with the dollar.

Not surprisingly, these changes were viewed by the markets as moves by Argentina to abandon its currency board. Interest rates shot up in anticipation of a devaluation.

This raises the issue of whether, and how, to drop an exchange rate regime. Countries that exited from pegged regimes and adopted currency boards in the 1990s have all seen dramatic improvements in their macroeconomic indicators. Indeed, a shift from a soft regime to a hard one has always ended currency crises. But not so with shifts from hard regimes to soft. Recall Hong Kong's exit from its currency board in November 1974.

Domingo Cavallo should understand that merely talking about the idea of abandoning a hard regime in the middle of a crisis is playing with dynamite. In July, the dynamite exploded. Military history teaches the same lessons about the dangers of discussing exit strategies. In his new book, *Waging Modern War*, General Wesley Clark showed that every time the U.S. Department of Defense spoke about exit strategies for U.S. troops in Bosnia, the Bosnian Serbs would intensify their efforts, causing no end of problems for the allies (Clark 2001).

THE WAY FORWARD

What is the way forward for currency boards? The analytical poverty of nirvana economics must be eliminated. Hypothetical ideals are operationally irrelevant. Within the feasible subset of real-world options, the relevant test should be whether an alternative can be described that can be implemented with expected gains. It is this remediableness criterion that should be adopted.

When that criterion is applied, currency boards stand head and shoulders above central banks for many developing countries. Just how many pass the test? According to the World Bank, average annual inflation has exceeded 10 percent in sixty-one countries with central banks during the past decade (World Bank 2001). As a rough estimate, then, sixty-one new currency boards could pass the remediableness test. Indeed, for these countries, central banks are an expensive luxury they can ill afford.

References

Bauer, Peter. 1976. *Dissent on development*. Rev. ed. Cambridge, MA: Harvard University Press.

Central Intelligence Agency (CIA). 1999. U.S. Central Intelligence Agency, CIA world factbook. Retrieved from http://www.odci.gov/cia/publications/factbook/index.html.

Clark, Wesley. 2001. *Waging modern war*. New York: PublicAffairs.

Council of Economic Advisers. 1999. *The annual report of the Council of Economic Advisers*. Washington, DC: Government Printing Office.

Culp, Christopher L., Steve H. Hanke, and Merton H. Miller. 1999. The case for an Indonesian currency board. *Journal of Applied Corporate Finance* 11 (4): 57-65.

Dow Jones Newswires. 2001. Argentina's July imports fall 20% on year. 31 August.

Frydl, Edward J. 1999. The length and cost of banking crises. IMF working paper no. WP/99/30. Washington, DC: International Monetary Fund.

Ghosh, Atish, Anne Marie Gulde, and Holger Wolf. 1998. Currency boards: The ultimate fix? IMF working paper no. WP/98/8. Washington, DC: International Monetary Fund.

Gwartney, James, and Robert Lawson. 2001. *Economic freedom of the world: Annual report 2001*. Vancouver, British Columbia, Canada: Fraser Institute.

Hanke, Steve H. 1996/1997. A field report from Sarajevo and Pale. *Central Banking* 12 (3): 36-40.

———. 1999. Some reflections on currency boards. In *Central banking, monetary policies, and the implications for transition economies*, edited by M. Blejer and M. Skreb, 341-66. Boston: Kluwer.

———. 2000a. Indonesia's central bank goes bust. *Asian Wall Street Journal*, 16 February.

———. 2000b. Reforming the IMF: Lessons from Indonesia. *Central Banking* 11 (2): 38-44.

———. 2001. IMF early warning should start on the Web. *Wall Street Journal*, 1 May.

Hanke, Steve H., Lars Jonung, and Kurt Schuler. 1992. *Monetary reform for a free Estonia*. Stockholm: SNS Forlag.

———. 1993. *Russian currency and finance*. London: Routledge.

Hanke, Steve H., and Kurt Schuler. 1991a. *Banco central o caja de conversion?* Buenos Aires, Argentina: Fundacion Republica.

———. 1991b. *Teeth for the Bulgarian lev: A currency board solution*. Washington, DC: International Freedom Foundation.

———. 1994a. *Currency boards for developing countries*. San Francisco: Institute for Contemporary Studies.

———. 1994b. *Valiutu Taryba: Pasiulymai Lietuvai*. Vilnius, Lithuania: Lietuvos Laisvosios Rinkos Institutas.

Hicks, John. 1967. *Critical essays in monetary theory*. London: Oxford University Press.

Horváth, Balazs, and Istvan P. Székely. 2001. The role of medium-term fiscal frameworks for transition countries: The case of Bulgaria. IMF working paper no. WP/01/11. Washington, DC: International Monetary Fund.

International Monetary Fund (IMF). 2000a. IMF concludes article IV consultation with Argentina. Public information notice no. 00/84. 3 October.

———. 2000b. One world, one currency: Destination or delusion? Transcript of economic forum, 8 November. Available from www.imf.org.

———. 2001a. IMF completes final Bosnia and Herzegovina reviews, approves US$18 million credit tranche. News brief no. 01/46. 25 May.

———. 2001b. IMF concludes article IV consultation with Bulgaria. Public information notice no. 01/33. 3 April.

———. 2001c. IMF concludes article IV consultation with Estonia. Public information notice no. 01/62. 9 July.

———. 2001d. IMF concludes article IV consultation with Lithuania. Public information notice no. 01/6. 22 January.

———. 2001e. People's Republic of China—Hong Kong special administrative region: Selected issues and statistical appendix. IMF country report no. 01/146. August.

———. 2001f. *World economic outlook*. Washington, DC: International Monetary Fund.

James, Harold. 2001. *The end of globalization: Lessons from the Great Depression*. Cambridge, MA: Harvard University Press.

Kenen, Peter B. 1978. The role of monetary policy in developing countries. In *The role of monetary policy in developing countries: Theoretical perspective and institutional framework*, edited by Research Department, Central Bank of Gambia, 9-13. Banjul: Central Bank of Gambia.

Klamer, Arjo. 1989. An accountant among economists: Conversations with Sir John Hicks. *Journal of Economic Perspectives* 3 (4): 167-80.

Marsh, David. 1992. *The Bundesbank: The bank that rules Europe*. London: Mandarin.

Organization for Economic Cooperation and Development (OECD). 1999. *OECD economic surveys: Bulgaria*. Paris: Organization for Economic Cooperation and Development.

Polanyi, Michael. 1958. *Personal knowledge*. London: Routledge.

Schuler, Kurt. 1996. *Should developing countries have central banks? Currency quality and monetary systems in 155 countries*. IEA research monograph no. 52. London: Institute of Economic Affairs.

Tignor, Robert L. 1998. *Capitalism and nationalism at the end of empire.*

Princeton, NJ: Princeton University Press.

United Nations Conference on Trade and Development. 2001. *Trade and development report, 2001*. Geneva, Switzerland: United Nations.

Walters, Alan, and Steve H. Hanke. 1992. Currency boards. In *The new Palgrave dictionary of money and finance*, vol. 1, edited by P. Newman, M. Milgate, and J. Eatwell, 558-61. London: Macmillan.

Williamson, John. 1995. *What role for currency boards?* Washington, DC: Institute for International Economics.

Williamson, Oliver E. 1996. *The mechanisms of governance*. New York: Oxford University Press.

World Bank. 2001. *World development report 2000/2001: Attacking poverty*. New York: Oxford University Press.

ANNALS, *AAPSS*, **579**, January 2002

One Region, One Money?

By GEORGE M. VON FURSTENBERG

ABSTRACT: The article explores causes and consequences of the declining usefulness of the separate currency denominations maintained by the large number of small open economies whose currencies play little or no role in international finance. Pressures for currency consolidation arise from several sources related to political liberalization, economic globalization, and the information and communications technology revolution. Freer cross-border provision of financial services and a changed official attitude to foreign establishment and takeovers have encouraged foreign entry. Many regional and global electronic spot markets and electronic trading platforms price in U.S. dollars or, prospectively, in euro. Cross-border e-banking, e-investing, and e-ordering of all kinds may compete not only with domestic financial and business establishments but also with local currencies that provide inferior consumption insurance at currency-crisis cycle frequencies and inadequate intertemporal predictability of purchasing power and other "real" terms of contract at longer frequencies.

George M. von Furstenberg, for many years a titled professor of economics at Indiana University, is the inaugural holder of the Robert Bendheim Chair in Economic and Financial Policy at Fordham University. Work at the International Monetary Fund (division chief, 1978-83) and at USG agencies, such as HUD (1967-68), the President's Council of Economic Advisers (senior economist, 1973-76), and the Department of State (1989-90), alternated with his academic pursuits. In Washington, he also has been a resident fellow, economist, or adviser at both the Brookings Institution and AEI. His interests are consequently policy oriented, broad, and international, with core subjects of macroeconomic theory and international finance. His latest book projects have dealt with Regulation and Supervision of Financial Institutions in the NAFTA Countries *and* Learning from the World's Best Central Bankers, *the latter coauthored with M. K. Ulan. He joined the G8 Research Group in 1999 and in 2000 was president of the North American Economics and Finance Association focusing on integration processes in the Western Hemisphere.*

NOTE: Address correspondence to Professor George M. von Furstenberg, Robert Bendheim Chair in Economic and Financial Policy, Graduate School of Business Administration, Fordham University, 113 W 60 St, New York, NY 10023-7484; e-mail: vonfurstenb@fordham.edu.

THIS article argues, and in small part substantiates, that e-commerce, regional economic integration, and global liberalization have eroded the monopoly of small currencies in their home market. These developments now threaten the continued viability of a number of them over the medium run. If technological and market-driven pressures lead to growing use of the internationally dominant currency denomination of the region in a lengthening list of financial, e-commerce, and other activities in a liberalizing world, the question for government policy becomes how to respond to these pressures. What kinds of institutional arrangements and international architecture for trade in financial services are most suitable for the prospective environment of a greatly reduced multiplicity of currencies? Even partial currency consolidations, such as those afforded by currency boards, are likely to prove unsustainable in the new environment that is leading to regional monetary unions at an increasing pace.

The evolution from the original European Common Market of six countries to European Monetary Union (EMU) took more than forty years. The leisurely pace was due to only gradually growing appreciation of the monetary requirements of deep economic integration as long as the Bretton Woods system provided reasonably fixed exchange rates between the major currencies. Even after the demise of that system in 1973, it still took one or two decades for freedom of capital movement fully to be reestablished in most parts of the world. This made fixed but adjustable exchange rates much more vulnerable to being dislodged until they could not credibly be fixed any more. Maintaining separate currencies, and hence exchange rates, became less desirable when exchange rates, instead of being serviceable shock absorbers, became a growing source of shocks to the economy and its finances. "Really I do believe that you cannot have a common market when you have fluctuating exchange rates in an area," Mundell (2000, 164) said. Abrupt changes in nominal and real exchange rates that reverse themselves only slowly after a currency crisis can drastically change competitive conditions between the members of an economic union and hence of each member with outsiders. Such changes are liable to disturb, rather than to equilibrate, trade relations. The desire to avoid such upsets by using a single money inside economically integrated regions may have contributed to a mutual insurance interest in EMU. Nevertheless, its adoption owed more to the political logic of shared governance and a common anti-inflationary resolve than to overwhelming pressures in financial markets.

Since about the time of the Maastricht Treaty, 1991, the regulatory protections that had allowed many small currencies and fragmented financial markets to continue have been emasculated. Hence, in the future, there will be greater urgency to decide whether to hang on to a financially small and purely domestic currency in which less and less business can be conducted cost-effectively. The alternative is to try merging it into some form of regional monetary union while there still is a choice. Even in the Western Hemisphere, where free trade areas, such as NAFTA, have been formed between countries whose currencies float against each other, the question of monetary unification may not be put aside much longer. Large exchange-rate movements between the partners in an economically integrated region almost inevitably threaten stability. Politically, the resulting changes in trade advantage are liable to be viewed as disruptive and unfair. Monetary union, whether unilateral like dollarization or multilateral like EMU from conception, may be the only reliable way to preclude such disruptions. Indeed, lack of monetary union may detract from economic union because exchange rate movements give a divisive edge to national borders and national trade interests when currency boundaries are maintained.

The medium-term evolution to regional monetary unions that appears to be under way does not denationalize money because the money involved remains a creature of the fiat of a state or group of states. Others already have looked ahead to a more distant future in which privately issued electronic money might no longer need to be convertible into traditional money or supported by legal tender to be widely accepted as a means of settlement and store of value; Cohen (2000) provided an excellent overview. Money would then exist inside global electronic communications and marketing networks. Financial services likewise would be product and by-product of electronic-commerce and communications providers, and dedicated financial intermediaries would be bypassed. As a result, monetary and financial union by government construction could become meaningless. Instead of looking far ahead to new forms of private denationalized moneys, we merely note a historical resurgence of the forces of currency substitution between "official" moneys. These forces are leading to a new wave of currency consolidation across national boundaries.

A GLANCE AT HISTORY AND MEDIUM-TERM PROSPECTS

Briefly looking both back and ahead suggests that, in matters of currency competition, we may be returning to conditions once common in many parts of the world when good moneys knew no boundaries and bad moneys could not yet be forced on people. Gresham's Law could come into operation only when a new form of money was declared legal tender at an overvalued legal exchange rate for money and debt contracts denominated in some older form or substantiation of money.

Over time, many countries sought to strengthen the issuing authority's monopoly power to afford effective protection for the national currency. Such action led away from the production of national money in monopolistic competition with other such moneys to positively reserving the domestic market for its use. To ensure such exclusivity, the domestic currency generally has been required for tax payments and as the denomination for tenders on government projects. It has further been sheltered by capital controls and by banking regulations that strictly limited the booking of foreign-currency assets and liabilities for domestic residents and gave the national denomination exclusive rights in many home-country applications.

These barriers have tended to erode over the past two dozen or more years as worldwide internal and external liberalization have taken hold. As a result, national moneys have been exposed to international competition and had to struggle for survival once again. Doyle (2000), Nuti (2000, 175) and Cohen (2000, 3-4) provided or cited estimates of the extent to which the world's most important currencies, particularly U.S. dollars and DM (henceforth euro) were located outside their country of issue. Barriers to foreign competition have been falling first in developed and then in developing countries as they integrated into the liberal international trade and investment regime and extended national treatment to foreign suppliers with fewer or expiring derogations. Freer cross-border provision of financial services and a changed official attitude to foreign establishment and takeovers have encouraged foreign entry. These developments also have opened the door to more widely denominating and trading domestic claims in international denominations for purchase by both foreign and domestic residents.

Providing such foreign-currency-denominated loan, debt, equity, and reinsurance financing is a business in which foreign providers, domiciled in the country that issues the relevant international currency, tend to have a funding and marketing advantage. Because of this inevitable link to the retention of national ownership and competitive advantage, issues of currency denomination rarely have escaped regulatory and legislative scrutiny, with currency substitution—the domestic use of a foreign money or currency denomination (Cohen 2000, 2)—coming in for particular attention.

Granting market access to both domestic and foreign entrants or potential competitors thus raises the question of whether granting access to foreign-currency denomination of a widening list of financial contracts in the domestic market should follow. Certainly, offering to do business in any international currency, principally U.S. dollar, euro, or yen, that a foreign entrant can call its own may be its best competitive weapon. Simply following the principle of national treatment would outlaw this weapon, thereby crimping effective market access by foreign providers if only local-currency contracts are permitted, as is still frequently the case in insurance. If foreign providers are only allowed to compete in the same (domestic) currency vehicles that their domestic counterparts naturally drive better, giving foreign suppliers national treatment on such a—to them restrictive—standard does not really give them meaningful market access at all. By the same token, imposing a requirement on all insurance providers in the national market to reinsure with a national reinsurance monopoly or to cede to this monopoly part of any non-retention does not violate national treatment on its face. However, effective market access not only to the reinsurance but also the insurance business may be denied to potential foreign competitors if they are subjected to reinsurance requirements of this form.

The prerequisite for liberalized market access, now clearly in view, is that individual and corporate citizens in many small countries will be able to choose to make payments in more than one acceptable currency and freely incur debts and acquire assets denominated in different currencies. Furthermore, using financial derivatives, they will be able to swap, alter, or hedge their currency exposure increasingly at will. However, they can do so only at considerable cost when their own currency is involved: risk premiums that are reflected in interest rates and hence cause the forward exchange rates for small currencies to exceed their expected future spot rates add to the cost of hedging. These risk premiums are almost entirely due to currency risk, in the sense that absent currency risk, very little remains of what was formerly identified as country risk, as southern members of the Euro Area can attest.

It is inconceivable, for instance, that Mexico, if it dollarized completely, would face premiums as high as the 300 to 340 basis points that were observed on its sovereign dollar borrowing in 2000. This is the yield spread over comparable U.S. treasuries that Mexico's central bank (Banco de México 2000, 16) has identified, quite conventionally and yet misleadingly, as pure country risk. Tao and Lau (1998, 22) reported that interest rates even in Panama, a fiscally disorderly and often poorly governed country, "have remained stable at 0-1.3 percent above LIBOR over the past two decades" because it was dollarized. That is much less than what has been charged on sovereign-dollar borrowing by Mexico, even though Mexico of late has been fiscally much more virtuous. Of course, some of the worst governments of small-dollarized countries may not always face lower dollar borrowing costs than some of the best governments of nondollarized countries such as Chile. But that would hardly matter to business because sovereign borrowing risk does not set the lower limit of the risk premiums charged to borrowers in dollarized developing countries. With fiscal and monetary policy risks decoupled and intraregional currency risk eliminated, credit to certain private parties can be less risky than credit to their fiscally unsound governments. Hence, it is no great surprise that Fatás and Rose (2001) found that an international common currency area is not associated with greater fiscal discipline among the lesser members of the area precisely because a lack of fiscal discipline may ruin the credit rating of the government but not of the entire country. When the penalty for any lapse in fiscal discipline becomes less encompassing, it will be less of a deterrent unless mutual supervision and correction, as under European Union's 1997 Stability and Growth Pact, is brought into play. In matters relating to the soundness of the financial and settlement systems, however, any deep monetary and financial union encourages, and is predicated on, the sharing of good regulatory and supervisory practices.

In Mexico as in almost all other countries of the Western Hemisphere farther south, pressures and opportunities for dollarizing more and more of the banking and financial business manifest themselves in several ways. For instance, they are both cause and effect of the widespread takeover of local financial groups by foreign financial conglomerates, particularly those headquartered in the United States. In the end, foreign ownership of banking and finance generally predominates in financially small countries. The insurance subsidiaries in the acquiring U.S. financial groups, like Travelers in Citigroup, will want to offer the same products through the Mexican branches, in this case of what until 2001 used to be Banacci, as they do in the United States. These dollar-denominated products may be far more useful to their Mexican customers than peso-denominated policies not only in pension, life, and annuity applications but also in the insurance of industrial property whose replacement cost is more stable and predictable in U.S. dollars than in local currency.

While "the instability of the insurance sector in emerging market economies can be attributed to a wide range of microeconomic and institutional failings" (International Association of Insurance Supervisors [IAIS] 1997, 5), currency instability surely plays a large role as well. In light of the latest in a number of currency crises, the Turkish lira can be used to visualize the currency substitution dynamics in this regard. If insurance companies licensed to operate in Turkey try to hedge their lira liabilities with lira assets, they will still be subject to exchange risk as asset deflation and currency crisis go hand in hand in emerging markets. Contrary to IAIS (1997, 13) representations, following the principle of currency matching does not ensure protection from exchange-rate risks in such markets because a currency crisis often pulls down the entire economic house. Under these conditions, there is not much insurance value that can reliably be offered by the private sector, particularly if there is double-digit inflation or higher to start with.

It would make more business sense for Turks to buy their insurance in euroland, where many of them work, live, or visit relatives, if they cannot obtain policies settling in euros in Turkey. This in turn puts pressure on Turkish insurance companies, at least after privatization, to offer their own euro-denominated life, pension, and annuity policies. Doing so would create a demand and market for euro-denominated Turkish securities assuming a normal statistical home bias in the allocation of the investment portfolio by Turkish insurance companies. They would favor domestic issues to exploit their information advantage or insider status. Euroization of other balance sheet positions and contracts might well follow, as one decision about currency choice leads to another.

As these circles of currency substitution widen and interlock across ever more markets and services within a country, the question becomes how many currencies will remain in wide use under arrangements in which foreign currencies may effectively compete. Will the local currency be among the survivors? In my view, regionally centralizing tendencies tend to weigh against such a prospect if the country is financially small to start with and if it lacks a very large internal market in which strong network externalities from the use of the domestic money can still be obtained. This naturally leads to the search for a quantitative perspective on what is small and how much countries that lie next to an area with a dominant currency still use their own money.

TO WHAT EXTENT DOES A SMALL OPEN ECONOMY, LIKE MEXICO, USE ITS OWN MONEY?

The Federal Reserve has put forward (Leahy 1998) a new method for estimating summary measures of the foreign exchange value of a currency. The method provides for calculating a set of weights to be applied to a country's most important bilateral exchange rates while also taking account of competition between imports and goods produced and sold in the same country, including the home country. The resulting weights are so comprehensive that they can be used for purposes other than deriving effective exchange rates for which they were originally intended. In particular, the weights sum to unity when including the weight for the 1:1 exchange rate of a country's own currency. The latter weight provides a useful inverse measure of its foreign currency dependence or degree of monetary openness.

Application of the method to Mexico when a total of n countries are considered calls for establishing the following:

- the market shares of Mexican-produced goods in each of their $n - 1$ major foreign markets, $X_{MX,j}$, as well as in Mexico itself, $X_{MX,MX}$;
- the market shares of foreign-produced goods sold in Mexico, $M_{MX,j}$, as well as of Mexican goods sold in Mexico, $M_{MX,MX}$; and
- the market shares of goods imported by each of Mexico's major trading partners in all goods sold in the respective country j, $M_{j,k}$, where $j \neq k$, as well as the share of home-produced goods sold in the respective country, $M_{k,k}$

With these definitions, the weight on the k-currency real exchange rate with the Mexican peso would be the following:

$$W_{MX,k} = \Sigma_{j = 1, \ldots n} X_{MX,j} M_{j,k}. \quad (1)$$

By setting $k = MX$, we can calculate the weight of the Mexican peso in Mexico to gauge how important the domestic currency remains in that country relative to other currencies used in its economic transactions. The United States (US), the Euro Area (E), and Japan (J) are Mexico's major trading partners as they together accounted for 92 percent of its goods exports and 85 percent of its imports in 1999. (These import and export weights are normalized to 100 percent to represent all exports and imports.) With the market-share values for 1999 calculated from data provided by the International Monetary Fund (IMF) (2000a, 2001), application of equation (1) to obtain the weight for the Mexican peso yields the following:

$$\begin{aligned} W_{MX,MX} &= X_{MX,MX}\, M_{MX,MX} \\ &+ X_{MX,US}\, M_{US,MX} \\ &+ X_{MX,E}\, M_{E,MX} \\ &+ X_{MX,J}\, M_{J,MX} \\ &= 0.717\ (0.710) \\ &+ 0.271\ (0.011) \\ &+ 0.010\ (0.001) \\ &+ 0.002\ (0.000) = 0.512. \end{aligned} \tag{2}$$

In the same way, the weight of the U.S. dollar for Mexico is calculated as

$$\begin{aligned} W_{MX,US} &= X_{MX,MX}\, M_{MX,US} \\ &+ X_{MX,US}\, M_{US,US} \\ &+ X_{MX,E}\, M_{E,US} \\ &+ X_{MX,J}\, M_{J,US} \\ &= 0.717\ (0.252) \\ &+ 0.271\ (0.870) \\ &+ 0.010\ (0.022) \\ &+ 0.002\ (0.016) = 0.417. \end{aligned} \tag{3}$$

The conclusion derived from the application of this weighting scheme is that the weight of the U.S. dollar in the Mexican economy has risen to within 10 percentage points of that of its home currency. Furthermore, the Mexican peso's share is barely above 50 percent judged merely by its trade in goods and ignoring services, workers' remittances from the United States, and asset pricing in dollars. The result is conservative also in that it ignores not only U.S. currency circulating in Mexico but also any dollarization that has already occurred inside Mexico's domestic business to insulate some of its cash flow from exchange-rate fluctuations.

This is an important finding that suggests that small open economies in the vicinity of large countries or groups of countries with an international currency already depend importantly on money other than their own. They are much more exposed to currency crises and exchange-rate instability than the share of bilateral trade in relation to GDP ($X_{MX,US}$ = 27.1 percent) or to domestic absorption ($M_{MX,US}$ = 25.2 percent) would suggest.

INTERNATIONAL PORTFOLIO DIVERSIFICATION WORKS BEST IN THE DOMINANT CURRENCY DENOMINATION

Economists have often deduced that, from the point of view of obtaining optimal consumption insurance through portfolio diversification, the investment portfolios of otherwise comparably positioned investors from Canada, France, and Japan should look very much alike. The failure for them to do so, because citizens strongly favor claims on their own country's obligors, has been labeled the home bias puzzle (see Lewis 1999). Hausmann et al. (2000, 142-44) have argued that for emerging-market economies all of which are financially small, there is even a presumption against investing at home from the point of view of consumption insurance. The reason is that in a currency crisis, just when income and output fall and internal and external sources of credit dry up, domestic asset values collapse. Adding a large negative wealth shock to a negative current-income shock would impart a double blow to consumption for investors at home.

Had these investors instead been invested in international foreign-currency claims when the sharp real depreciation of the domestic currency occurred, they would have benefited from the real appreciation of the domestic value of their foreign holdings. This would have reduced, rather than amplified, the blow to consumption from a currency and financial crisis. Hence, to obtain optimal consumption insurance, investors in small emerging-market countries should invest outside their own country and currency to an extent even greater than fitting for the average international investor. When Uruguayans hold 85 percent of their savings in U.S. dollar-denominated accounts in their own country, they are acting to reduce this double exposure to a degree that depends on whether they deposit in domestically owned banks or in local branches of foreign banks.

Even in Uruguay's large neighbor, Argentina, about 50 percent of bank assets are held in foreign-controlled institutions by a variety of measures (IMF, 2000b, 153). Multinational financial institutions are almost always headquartered in the key-currency countries that have long been leading the development of the financial services industry and have determined its international coordination and supervision. They bring their privileged key-currency connection with them wherever they establish around the globe and make that denomination their stock in trade. Cross-border banking via the Internet (see IMF, 2000b, 157) may add to the advantage of the dominant currencies since they yield the widest range of transaction services that are true to the quoted price and match the denomination of the widest range of financial investments and products. Hence, cross-border e-banking may compete not only with local banks but also with local currencies.

Because competitive pressures contribute to their health, large international currencies tend to convey other advantages to foreign users over denominating in small currencies. To protect their international standing, preeminent currencies and their financial infrastructure must be well managed. Lapses in the sound conduct of monetary and financial policy, as in the United States during much of the 1970s and in Japan during and beyond the 1990s, tend to diminish the international role of the respective currency, thereby exerting a powerful disciplining effect. By contrast, emerging-market economies typically have currencies whose purchasing power is unreliable. Even in the absence of persistently high inflation, they commonly experience real exchange rates that are both highly variable and prone to drift up between major corrections, not necessarily around a fixed mean. Hence, denominating annuities and pensions and lump-sum or life insurance settlements of any kind in such currencies would provide far less calculable real-value assurance than denominating in one of the large currencies. The latter are key to international pricing in product and finance markets and reliable stores of value and of future purchasing power over a broad range of goods. The added purchasing-power risk thus detracts from the suitability of small currencies for extended use in intertemporal trades, and this contributes to the case for currency consolidation.

International financial derivatives, such as interest and currency swaps, forwards, futures, and options, received a big boost from the collapse of the Bretton Woods system. As Plender (2001, 12) has pointed out, this occurred because the collapse of that system shifted the task of managing currency volatility from the public to the private sector. Regional currency consolidation will lower currency risk in some respects that are important for production and sales organization and for trade in goods and services in the region. But they will not lower exchange risk between the large currencies, such as dollar, euro, and yen, which have accounted for the bulk of the currencies involved in the construction of international financial derivatives. The U.S. dollar has been most prominent of all on the ground that the underlying debt and equity claims suitable for listing, securitization, and exchange trading in international financial markets are themselves commonly denominated in dollars and, to a lesser extent, in euro and yen. Countries can use only very few other currency denominations for borrowing in international financial markets. Generally, large risk premiums and illiquidity, reflected in wide bid-ask spreads, discourage denominating in peripheral currencies. Since calculability of risk exposure and a high degree of liquidity of positions taken by major participants, including hedge funds, are essential to the functioning of the market in derivatives, standardization on a common currency is convenient in many, although not all, applications.

The dollar may "intrude" even into exchange contracts between other currencies. IMF (1999, 49) explained, for instance, that nondeliverable foreign exchange forwards in emerging markets tend to be settled in U.S. dollars for the difference between the implied exchange rate on the contract and the prevailing spot rate on the maturity date of the contract. The IMF noted further that net settlement in domestic currency existed in many industrial countries in the 1970s and 1980s prior to the removal of exchange controls. The big currencies thus tend to get bigger when capital controls are removed.

COMMON CURRENCY IN E-TRADE AND E-COMMERCE

Many regional and global electronic spot markets and electronic trading platforms price in U.S. dollars or, prospectively, in euro. It may be instructive to consider a simple example. Certain electronic auctions conducted in Canada are bid in U.S. dollars to encourage cross-border participation. One could, of course, reflect on the screen, second by second, what the auction price amounts to in Canadian dollars. However, little would be gained by this instant currency conversion. For instance, if the U.S. dollar price achieved at auction is final and binding, paying with a debit or credit card on a Canadian dollar account could cost an extra 2 percent commission for the exchange conversion. Uncertainty would be added for the Canadian buyer at auction because the exchange rate would be the inter-bank sell rate prevailing when the charge is processed by the bank.

Instead of putting up with this cost and uncertainty, the Canadian could, of course, have a U.S. dollar account with his or her Canadian bank or in the United States. But if the balance in that account must be maintained by drawing on income earned in Canadian dollars, the problem of uncertain settlement costs does not really go away. With digital signatures now having legal effect, validity, and enforceability in the United States (see *Tech Law Journal* 2000) and in a growing list of other countries or country groups, ordering, shopping, and settling in international money anywhere in the region, indeed in the world, have become increasingly attractive. This, however, creates pressures not just to convert to such money but either to be paid in it or to have payments indexed to it.

In business applications, there are even stronger pressures for currency consolidation. Transnational bidding on business that should lead to standing orders is handicapped if persistent exchange-rate movements keep interfering with what subcontractors or component suppliers must ask. To avoid the disruption of continuing relationships by exchange-rate movements whose eventual results for competitiveness cannot be hedged, those who seek to be integrated into the regionwide supply chain try to control their costs, from parts to labor, in the same currency in which they must bid.

SHOULD SMALL COUNTRIES KEEP NOMINAL EXCHANGE-RATE FLEXIBILITY?

Flexible exchange rates are often advertised as a low-cost and fast-acting compensatory mechanism for countries with nominal rigidities that are subject to either real or nominal shocks. The unspoken assumption, frequently falsified (see, for instance, Buiter 1997; Hausmann et al. 2000), is that exchange rates can be counted on to move reliably so as to facilitate efficient adjustment rather than having a disturbing way of their own. Intending more than a facile critique of perfect-foresight models, Buiter (1999) gave a sardonic example of the heroic deeds to be accomplished by monetary policy enabled by flexible rates against a supposedly unitary shock:

> There is assumed to be only one kind of shock, a national aggregate supply shock. The national monetary authority is assumed to observe the national supply shock immediately and perfectly. It then sets national monetary policy instantaneously and optimally to cope with this shock. The national authority knows the true structure of the economy and this structure of the economy makes certainty-equivalent strategies optimal. (P. 50)

Some Canadian (see Laidler 1999) and Mexican (see Schwartz and Torres 2001) economists continue to try to prove that flexible exchange rates work just fine for their countries particularly against well-defined shocks to the relative price of their natural resources. But they have yet to include complete U.S. dollarization or other forms of monetary union among the alternatives seriously considered. In Mexico at least, such a union would preclude the very currency crises from which advocates of flexible rates get their economic "supply shock" observations. As Calvo and Reinhart (2000) explained, in many countries there is deep and cogent doubt that floating exchange rates in fact have tended to move to facilitate adjustment in the goods and factor markets. Small open economies in emerging-market countries rarely find that when things start to go badly—usually first because there is an international-portfolio or private capital-account shock—exchange rate movements quickly reverse the tide and let conditions improve again. Instead, currency crises commonly make things much worse before they start getting better, and, contrary to once popular belief, flexible exchange rates do not preclude such crises.

Even when real exchange rates move in textbook fashion to accommodate the needs of trade balance and production adjustment, some of the other tacit assumptions that make such movement unequivocally beneficial are less and less likely to be satisfied. One of these is that countries are homogeneous internally but heterogeneous internationally in their production structure and shock exposure. Likewise, factor mobility, particularly that of labor, often is assumed to be high internally and low internationally. Mexico's adjustment to the 1999-2000 increase in the price of crude oil shows what can be wrong with these assumptions. The oil price increase and the effect on Mexico's federal budget and current account may have encouraged increased private capital inflows that contributed to an appreciation of the Mexican peso in both nominal and real terms. But only small additional amounts of capital and labor have been attracted to oil and gas exploration and development, while the real appreciation has slowed the development of the non-oil sector in the country at large.

If small countries were indeed internally homogenous and externally heterogeneous so that they had a specialized nationally integrated production structure for final goods, shocks to both domestic supply conditions and to (mostly) foreign demand for the small country's specialized output in theory could be cushioned and adjustment could be speeded by movement in nominal exchange rates. But for many small open economies, this picture of the production structure bears little relation to the reality they confront in a regionalizing, and to a lesser extent globalizing, economic system. Becoming a component part of international, most particularly regional, supply chains means that anything that disrupts this chain anywhere will be felt everywhere else in the region.

By the same token, if many countries in the region share in the production of final goods, such as automobiles or electronic appliances, through the production or assembly of parts, any shock to aggregate demand for the final good will affect all who contribute to its supply as well. Under these conditions, exchange-rate movements among the partners in the region cannot be part of efficient adjustment. Hence, in an economically interlocking world, little remains of the classical case for flexible exchange rates. Once countries are firmly committed to low inflation and do not cherish the freedom to engage in inflationary experiments, they will benefit further by irrevocably relinquishing the option to change their exchange rate with their hard-currency neighbors. Indeed, currency union would enhance the regional integration process by markedly raising trade and GDP within the union (Frankel and Rose 2000).

IS A CURRENCY BOARD ARRANGEMENT (CBA) SUFFICIENT FOR CURRENCY CONSOLIDATION?

A number of business and banking groups seeking some form of monetary union with the United States, for instance in Mexico, recently have come out in favor of a CBA because they view such an arrangement as politically more acceptable than complete dollarization. This section argues quite generally that currency boards may, or may not, advance the objective of monetary union. It all depends on how appropriate the choice of the peg is to their trade and finance and what better alternatives are available in their economic neighborhood.

Currency boards in theory have a fixed reserve ratio against high-powered money and a fixed exchange rate with something "hard" in common with the gold standard. Yet, while there were rules of the classical gold standard that were sufficiently widely observed to make the standard credible and speculation generally stabilizing (Eichengreen 1994, 43), CBAs now make their own rules. For instance, Argentina's and Hong Kong's CBAs have very little in common in the way they operate, in the extent to which they are backed by reserves and constrained by their particular status, and in the fluctuations they have experienced in their credibility. As described in Dodsworth and Mihaljek (1997) for instance, there is little that is classical or ruled out in the operation of Hong Kong's currency board since it was reestablished in 1983. Indeed, some of its defenses against speculative attack, such as using more than 10 percent of its foreign exchange reserves in August 1998 to discourage short selling, by buying shares in the local stock market, have been unprecedented.

Apart from each CBA being increasingly sui generis and thus requiring detailed individual assessment, there is also the question of the choice of currency peg that is appropriate for each. It is not true that any and all of the major hard currencies will do. For instance, Hong Kong, Argentina, and Lithuania, all with a U.S.-dollar-based currency board, are surrounded (or will be surrounded when the renminbi starts to float against the U.S. dollar) by countries whose real exchange rates may develop very differently. Because these countries are unduly exposed to foreign-induced misalignment of their trade-weighted exchange rate, the rationale for sticking with their CBA can become doubtful. When such a misalignment becomes acute, as between Argentina and Brazil in the aftermath of Brazil's currency crisis of January 1999, risk premiums surge. They may feed on themselves by placing the benefits of maintaining the CBA further in doubt.

CBAs that peg unnaturally to a currency from outside their major trading region are prone to stress. Singapore's switch from a sterling-based currency board in 1967 to the U.S. dollar, though precipitated by the desire to disassociate from the pound's devaluation from $2.8 to $2.4, was appropriate to its trade and finance as well. Singapore broadened its exchange-rate reference further a few years later when it made the transition to managed floating. By contrast, Lithuania's perverse insistence on maintaining a dollar-based currency board in what is rapidly becoming a sea of euros has been costly. Real GDP fell more than 4 percent in 1999, and little or no growth has been reported for 2000 as the strength of the dollar against the euro persisted during the year.

Thus, while CBAs incorporate a strong policy commitment to fixed exchange rates that is backed up by a high level of international reserves, this commitment may still not be sustainable politically when it is perceived to be harmful to the economy and to its secure integration in the region. Only currency boards linked to the respective key currency within economically and financially heavily integrated and interdependent regions are likely to provide adequate insurance against disruptive changes in real exchange rates with their main trading partner or partners. U.S.-dollar-based currency board arrangements with Mexico and Central American and Caribbean countries and euro-based CBAs in Eastern European countries thus could qualify as useful precursors to more complete and less reversible forms of currency consolidation. Currency boards established in distant outposts far away from the peg country and its currency area, however, represent false starts from the point of view of currency consolidation: they are likely to lead either to floating or to new forms of monetary union in their region down the road.

Even currency boards with the dominant currency next door may not survive for long when the respective financial systems are placed in direct competition with each other. The strength of trade and finance relations, say of countries in the vicinity of the United States or of euroland, makes the almost complete financial integration and interest rate convergence that is available on formally adopting the U.S. dollar or euro more attractive than staying in the halfway house of a currency board. Hence, if currency consolidation is to be allowed, some form of monetary union is the way to achieve it. Whether that union should take the form of unilateral dollarization or of multilateral and comanaged monetary union as in euroland is another important matter meriting detailed analysis. I have begun to explore some of these alternative ways of achieving currency consolidation elsewhere (von Furstenberg 2000a, 2000b).

CONCLUSIONS

Like centuries ago, small open economies now make much more use of foreign money, especially the dominant currency of their region, than international trade analysis and past measures of effective exchange rates have tended to recognize. The currency denominations of financially small countries, in particular emerging-market countries, are at a distinct disadvantage in both spot transactions in the electronic marketplace and in intertemporal trade and insurance. Even direct consumption insurance counsels residents of emerging-market countries exposed to currency crises to keep away from investing in their own currency at home lest shocks to their income be compounded by shocks to their wealth. Foreign financial institutions from the key-currency countries often bring the financial services that are denominated in those same currencies that the market demands.

Idiosyncratic exchange rate behavior and country risk premiums that are due, in good part, to currency risk are the downside to keeping separate currencies in small countries. Doing so is more likely to discourage and disrupt their membership in international supply chains than to promote adjustment to supply shocks. Even CBAs are unlikely to prove a highly durable substitute for the more complete forms of currency consolidation provided by regional monetary union. However, they may lead the way to such union if they are established with a peg to the currency that is most suitable for intense commercial and financial relations with neighboring countries in the respective region.

As Hoekman and Braga (1997) have pointed out and as devastating currency crises in emerging markets reinforce every few years, foreign exchange transactions and insurance services, together with other services, are an input to the production of most industries and directly and indirectly consumed by households. In addition, an inefficient domestic currency arrangement detracts from the efficiency that can be achieved by other services, such as insurance, in the domestic economy. For these reasons, any failings in the monetary and exchange arrangements to which a country may cling can be very costly to the economy as a whole.

References

Banco de México. 2000. *Inflation report, July-September 2000*. October.

Buiter, W. 1997. The economic case for monetary union in the European Union. *Review of International Economics* 5 (4): 10-35.

———. 1999. Optimal currency areas: Why does the exchange rate regime matter? Sixth Royal Bank of Scotland/Scottish Economic Society annual lecture, Edinburgh, October 26.

Calvo, G. A., and C. M. Reinhart. 2000. Fear of floating. NBER working paper no. 7993, November. Cambridge,

MA: National Bureau of Economic Research.

Cohen, B. J. 2000. *Life at the top: International currencies in the twenty-first century*. Princeton, NJ: Essays in International Finance, No. 221, December.

Dodsworth, J., and D. Mihaljek. 1997. Hong Kong, China: Growth, structural change, and economic stability during the transition. Occasional paper no. 152, August. Washington, DC: International Monetary Fund.

Doyle, B. M. 2000. Here, dollars, dollars . . . —Estimating currency demand and worldwide currency substitution. Board of Governors of the Federal Reserve System discussion paper no. 657, January.

Eichengreen, B. 1994. *International monetary arrangements for the 21st century*. Washington, DC: Brookings Institution.

Fatás, A., and A. K. Rose. 2001. Do monetary handcuffs restrain Leviathan? CEPR discussion paper no. 2692, February.

Frankel, J. A., and A. K. Rose. 2000. Estimating the effect of currency unions on trade and output. NBER working paper no. 7857, August. Cambridge, MA: National Bureau of Economic Research.

Hausmann, R., M. Gavin, C. Pagés-Serra, and E. Stein. 2000. Financial turmoil and the choice of exchange rate regime. In *Wanted: World financial stability*, edited by E. Fernández-Arias and R. Hausmann, 131-164. Washington, DC: Inter-American Development Bank.

Hoekman, B., and C. Primo Braga. 1997. Protection and trade in services: A survey. CEPR discussion paper no. 1705, September.

International Association of Insurance Supervisors. 1997. *Guidance on insurance regulation and supervision for emerging economies*. IAIS—Emerging Market Issues Committee, September.

International Monetary Fund. 1999. *International capital markets: Developments, prospects, and key policy issues*, September. Washington, DC: International Monetary Fund.

———. 2000a. *Direction of trade statistics yearbook 2000*. Washington, DC: International Monetary Fund.

———. 2000b. *International capital markets: Developments, prospects, and key policy issues*, September. Washington, DC: International Monetary Fund.

———. 2001. *International financial statistics*, January. Washington, DC: International Monetary Fund.

Laidler, D. 1999. What do the fixers want to fix? The debate about Canada's exchange rate regime. C. D. Howe Institute commentary, Toronto, December 7.

Leahy, M. P. 1998. New summary measures of the foreign exchange value of the dollar. *Federal Reserve Bulletin* 84 (October): 811-18.

Lewis, K. V. 1999. Trying to explain home bias in equities and consumption. *Journal of Economic Literature* 37 (2): 571-608.

Mundell, R. A. 2000. Exchange rate arrangements in Central and Eastern Europe. In *Eastern enlargement: The sooner, the better?* edited by S. Arndt, H. Handler, and D. Salvatore, 158-65. Vienna: Austrian Ministry for Economic Affairs and Labour.

Nuti, D. M. 2000. The costs and benefits of euro-isolation in Central-Eastern Europe before or instead of EMU membership. In *Eastern enlargement: The sooner, the better?* edited by S. Arndt, H. Handler, and D. Salvatore, 171-94. Vienna: Austrian Ministry for Economic Affairs and Labour.

Plender, J. 2001. The limits of ingenuity. *Financial Times*, May 17, 12.

Tao, D., and J. Lau. 1998. *Dollarisation: An emergency exit for Hong Kong?*

Credit Suisse/First Boston, Code EC0036, August.

Tech Law Journal. 2000. Summary of bills pertaining to electronic signatures and authentication in the 106th Congress. Available from http://techlawjournal.com/cong106/digsig/Default.htm.

von Furstenberg, G. M. 2000a. The case against U.S. dollarization. *Challenge* 43 (4): 108-20.

———. 2000b. US-dollarization in Latin America: A second-best monetary union for overcoming regional currency risk. *Economia, Societá e Istituzioni* 12 (3): 281-317.

ANNALS, *AAPSS*, **579**, January 2002

Monetary Unions and the Problem of Sovereignty

By ROBERT A. MUNDELL

ABSTRACT: Different types of monetary sovereignty are issues in exchange rate agreements monetary unions. Policy sovereignty refers to independence in making exchange rate and monetary policy, legal sovereignty to a country's ability to make its own laws with respect to the unit of contract and medium of exchange. This article traces the history of the concepts and their applications in the history of political philosophy and monetary policies. The first section relates the concepts of legal and policy sovereignty as they emerged in Roman law into the Europe of the Middle Ages and Renaissance. The second part discusses the implication of the sovereignty issue for choice along the road to the European Monetary Union.

Robert Mundell is University Professor of Economics at Columbia University, where he has taught since 1974. He is known as an authority on international exchange rate systems, macroeconomic policies, and supply-side economics. Among his many contributions in books and journals, he is known as the father of the theory of optimum currency areas. He received the Nobel Memorial Prize in Economics in 1999.

NOTE: This article is an abridgement of a paper originally prepared for the International Economic Association Conference in Trento, 4-7 September 1997, forthcoming in the proceedings to be published by Cambridge University Press. The original paper contained a lengthy middle section on the sovereignty issue in the United States.

MONETARY integration involves a consideration of two quite different types or dimensions of sovereignty. One is *policy sovereignty*, and the other is *legal sovereignty*. Policy sovereignty refers to the ability to conduct policy independent of commitments to other countries. Legal sovereignty refers to the ability of a state to make its own laws without limitations imposed by any outside authority. Both concepts need to be considered in plans for monetary unions. What are the implications of a change in legal sovereignty when the national currencies of some of the oldest states in the world abandon national sovereignty, and what will they receive in exchange?

In the middle of the last century, John Stuart Mill ([1848] 1909) recognized but deplored the sentiment that made nations so attached to their own currencies:

> So much of barbarism still remains in the transactions of the most civilized nations, that almost all independent countries choose to assert their nationality by having, to their own inconvenience and that of their neighbours, a peculiar currency of their own. (P. 615)

Has the world—or Europe—changed to such an extent that the national populations are now prepared to scrap those hallmarks of sovereignty that have existed for thousands of years?

What is the nature of the sentiment that makes national currencies so difficult to give up? Some idea of this can be got from British or English history, whose currency goes back at least thirteen centuries. Sir Robert Peel, in 1819, quoted in the House of Commons the evidence of a London accountant given before the Committee on the Resumption of Cash Payments:

> He was required to define what he meant by the pound. His answer was: "I find it difficult to explain it, but every gentleman in England knows it." The Committee repeated the question, and Mr. Smith answered: "It is something that has existed without variation in this country for eight hundred years—three hundred years before the introduction of gold." (Feaveryear 1963, 1)

Peel quoted Smith's opinion only to ridicule it because Peel would become the political champion of those who held the view—with John Locke,[1] Isaac Newton, David Ricardo, John Stuart Mill, and a host of other classical economists—that the "pound sterling could only rightly be defined as a 'definite quantity of gold bullion.' " (Feaveryear 1963, 1). That makes the pound into a commodity rather than a money because the essence of money lies not in the value of the commodity of which it is made but in its overvaluation.

This article will discuss the relation of monetary integration to both types of sovereignty, but its primary emphasis will be on the implications for legal sovereignty of different types of monetary unions. The sections in part 1 will explore the concepts of policy and legal sovereignty and relate these concepts to the history of the monetary sovereignty as it emerged from Roman law into the Europe of the Middle Ages. The sections in part 2 will discuss explicitly some implications of the sovereignty issue for choices made with respect to sovereignty along the road to the European Monetary Union (EMU).

PART 1. TYPES OF SOVEREIGNTY

I shall in this part discuss different types of sovereignty, paying attention to the distinction between legal and policy sovereignty in monetary unions, the concept of monetary sovereignty itself, the early history of monetary sovereignty in the ancient world and the Europe of the Middle Ages, and finally the landmark "Case of the Mixed Moneys," which established a legal precedent on which subsequent legal history has drawn.

Policy sovereignty and legal sovereignty

One step in the spectrum of monetary integration from complete independence with freely flexible exchange rates to complete union with currency unification is a system of fixed exchange rates. When a country opts for fixed exchange rates, it sacrifices monetary policy autonomy in favor of a mechanism of adjustment for correcting the balance of payments. In short, it sacrifices policy sovereignty in the field of money.

Where does the sovereignty go? One possibility is a system in which the sovereignty is transferred to a hegemony. If a small country unilaterally fixes its currency to that of a larger neighbor, it in effect transfers policy sovereignty to that larger neighbor. The fixing country loses sovereignty because it no longer controls its own monetary destiny; the larger country gains sovereignty because it manages a larger currency area and gains more "clout" in the international monetary system.[2] The rate of inflation in the system will be governed by the monetary policy of the hegemony. To a very great extent, this was the type of system practiced within the great empires of the major powers leading up to World War I.

If, on the other hand, several countries agree to cooperate in forming a currency area, the "$n - 1$" or "redundancy problem" leaves open for policy the rate of monetary expansion of the area as a whole and therefore its rate of inflation. Some kind of monetary authority would determine the monetary policy for the area as a whole, and each country would share in the area's sovereignty according to the political terms of the monetary agreement. Each country sacrifices its complete sovereignty over its own monetary policy in exchange for its share—however allocated—in the more powerful sovereignty exercised by the joint monetary authority.

A system of fixed exchange rates with a central control over the currency area's monetary policy is by no means a complete monetary union. A further step along the road to monetary integration is the creation of a joint currency. Whether the creation of a joint currency represents an important or an unimportant change in sovereignty depends on its legal attributes. In the events leading up to the Bretton Woods meeting, both the White and Keynes plans had made provisions for a world currency that would have had a kind of legal tender power—bancor in the Keynes plan, unitas in the White plan. Both these proposals were rejected by the United States, undoubtedly because it would have involved a loss of monetary sovereignty to the largest power.

The creation of the SDR, however, was acceptable because it was not explicitly a reserve asset, and a country's liability was limited. Initially, when established in 1968, the SDR had a gold weight guarantee. As soon as the price of gold soared, however, the gold guarantee was stripped away from it, and further allocations were too small to have an important impact on the international monetary system. Countries—and this meant especially the largest countries—were not willing to confer either policy sovereignty or legal sovereignty in the field of money to a supranational institution. The important decisions in the field of international economic policy have been made by the large powers unilaterally or in groups like the G5 or G7.

A more interesting case, perhaps, has been the creation of the ECU, which is scheduled to be the unit from which the euro evolved in 1999. The European Monetary System, established in 1978, was a loose system in some respects patterned after the arrangements set up at Bretton Woods but with the addition of the ECU as the unit of account for the system. The setting up of the ECU did not itself involve much transfer of policy sovereignty and almost no transfer of legal sovereignty. The national currencies were still sole legal tender in their respective authorities and—except for the transactions of the European Commission (which, admittedly, have become increasingly important)—the use of the ECU was purely voluntary.

The Exchange Rate Mechanism (ERM), however, did involve a transfer of policy sovereignty. Although the pegging arrangement was intended to be multinational, forces in the exchange market took over, and it soon gravitated to a DM zone, with monetary policy determined by the Bundesbank. Policy sovereignty was therefore shifted from the other nation-states in the ERM to Germany. The aftermath of German spending after the unification shock in 1990, however, brought about a conflict between stability in the German economy and its neighbors, and the system had to be modified.

When EMU came into being, important changes ensued for policy sovereignty. The exchange rates of members were irrevocably fixed, and the monetary policy of the area as a whole was under the control of the European Central Bank (ECB). Thus, each country sacrificed its policy sovereignty in the field of its own money in exchange for its share of policy sovereignty in the direction of the ECB. The governors of the national central banks are members of the Governing Council of the European System of Central Banks, and as many as six of the countries are on its six-member Executive Board, each of whom also has a vote on the Governing Council. Even though the principle is one country, one vote (probably a mistake), in practice the large countries will have a greater voice in dominating the ECB and staffing its top officers.[3] From the standpoint of policy sovereignty, EMU will be different from the ERM in that it will be irrevocable and the supranational policy sovereignty will be shared.

The EMU plan, however, goes far beyond policy sovereignty and the creation of a new currency. It involves also the *replacement* of national currencies by the euro, which will take place for the first entrants starting on 1 January 2002 and extending no later than 30 June of the same year. The implications of this change for legal sovereignty are extremely important for the countries involved. The right to produce a national currency has for centuries—even millennia—been looked on as a principal dimension of political independence and a badge of legal sovereignty. Yet, the decision to opt for a monetary union that replaces national currencies with a single currency seems to have been taken up and accepted with little discussion.

The Maastricht plan for a single currency to replace the national currencies was a key feature of the Delors Report, which stated the following:

> The adoption of a *single currency*, while not strictly necessary for the creation of a monetary union, might be seen—for economic as well as psychological and political reasons—as a natural and desirable further development of the monetary union. A single currency would clearly demonstrate the irreversibility of the . . . union, considerably facilitate the monetary management of the Community and avoid the transactions costs of converting currencies. . . . The replacement of national currencies by a single currency should therefore take place as soon as possible after the locking of parities. (Quoted in Kenen 1995, 14)

The Delors Committee was not assigned to make a case for EMU but rather to make recommendations as to how it should be brought about. The committee's report found its way into the Maastricht Treaty, but it did not explicitly outline the implications of scrapping national currencies. If countries give up their legal national sovereignty, what will be the nature of the share in sovereignty they get in exchange? What are the psychological effects of abandoning the heritage? Can monetary sovereignty be sacrificed without political sovereignty? Where will the sovereignty go? What will citizens get in exchange? What are the "psychological and political reasons" mentioned in the Delors Report?

Every member of the International Monetary Fund (IMF) has an independent currency, which it currently regards as a mark of its political independence and national sovereignty[4] as well as a part of its national heritage and patrimony. This is despite the fact that twentieth-century governments without exception abused that sovereignty by resorting to inflationary policies. Will European Union (EU) members of the Executive Board of the IMF be content to be represented by a single monetary authority, or will they want to maintain their national representations? What are the implications for the "law of payment," that rule known in law since antiquity that specifies that an independent country has the right to determine that which is acceptable as legal tender in payment of debt? Other issues concern the potentially inflationary impact of replacing several national currencies by a single "more liquid" currency, the sacrifice and redistribution of seigniorage in the union, and the mental and psychological transactions costs and even trauma of changing units of account.

Much attention in the literature has been given to the difference between monetary systems based on fixed and flexible exchange rates. Strictly speaking, this is a false issue since the two are incomparable. A fixed exchange rate is a monetary rule, and such a system should be contrasted with other monetary rules, not the absence of a monetary rule. Within the category of fixed exchange rates, however, there are several options depending on such factors as the irrevocability of the commitment to the parity, the width (if any) of the exchange rate margins, the asymmetry of the intervention responsibilities, and the degree of unification of the units of account. We shall have to touch here on the difference, relevant to the sovereignty issue, between a system of rigidly fixed parities and a single currency.

The sovereignty issue

We now need to turn to the issue of monetary sovereignty itself. What is it? Where is it located? When did it come into being? What are the implications of giving it up or sharing it? By what legal process is it transferred? Who has the right to transfer it? Is transfer irrevocable? Does the state exist without it? Where does sovereignty lie in a monetary union of independent states? These are some of the questions that could be asked about monetary sovereignty in a future monetary union.

Monetary sovereignty might be thought of as one of the dimensions of political sovereignty. But therein lies a problem. According to political scientists, the concept of political sovereignty was developed in Renaissance times, starting importantly with Jean Bodin in 1576. But the concept of monetary sovereignty is far older. It goes back to the Romans and before; quite probably it goes back to the ancient empires of Sumer, India, Babylon, and Egypt. The literature in the ancient world is explicit and substantial.

First, however, let us see what sovereignty means in political science. According to one view, the concept of sovereignty "implies a theory of politics which claims that in every system of government there must be some absolute power of final decision exercised by some person or body recognized as competent to decide and able to enforce the decision" (Crick 1968). The simplest form of the theory is the common assertion that "the state is sovereign," which is usually a tautology, just as the expression "sovereign state" can be a pleonasm (Crick 1968). The concept of the state came into being about the same time as the concept of sovereignty, and it served the same purpose and had the same meaning (Crick 1968).

Not surprisingly, the concept of political sovereignty came into being at a time when it became a necessity. The concept received extensive treatment in the hands of Jean Bodin writing soon after the Massacre of the Huguenots on St. Bartholomew's Day in 1572. Bodin was a kind of polyhistor—an economist as well as a jurist. He was the originator of the partly correct quantity-of-metal theory of the value of money and held and tested the proposition that the great increase in prices in the sixteenth century was due to the influx of metals (Bodin [1568] 1946) from America, a theory Earl Hamilton would test but only partially validated four centuries later.[5] Bodin was writing in the midst of the great religious wars associated with the counterreformation. He saw civil war as the worst of all evils, held that the state was primarily concerned with the maintenance of order and not the establishment of true religion, and introduced his concept of sovereignty to bolster the power of the French king over the rebellious feudal lords and the church: "It is clear that the principal mark of sovereign majesty . . . is the right to impose laws generally on all subjects regardless of their consent. . . . If he is to govern the state well, a sovereign prince must be above the law." Bodin thought he had found in this principle a universal recipe for political stability (Crick 1968, 79). Bodin's views were taken up by Hobbes (1651) who also was preoccupied with the problem of civil war. In their theories, sovereignty was more or less absolute except insofar as they conflicted with divine right (Bodin) or the laws of nature (Hobbes).

Earlier, Machiavelli, in *The Prince*, did not develop the concept of sovereignty, but he did recognize the distinctions in power necessary for two quite different situations—peace where republicanism can rule and war where dictatorship is, if not inevitable, more likely. This distinction can be seen in the doctrine of constitutional dictatorship in the Greek states and in the Roman Republic, as also in the assumption of emergency powers by Lincoln during the Civil War and by Churchill in World War II. "Is there, in all republics," asked Lincoln in 1861, "this necessary and fatal weakness? Must a government, of necessity, be too strong for the liberties of its people, or too weak to maintain its own existence?" (Crick 1968, 80).

Later developments of the concept tried to reconcile the theory of sovereignty with that of consent, with not much success. During the French Revolution, it was asserted that "Sovereignty is one, indivisible, unalienable and imprescriptible; it belongs to the Nation; no group can attribute sovereignty to itself nor can an individual arrogate it to himself." The idea of popular sovereignty became identified with the slogan "sovereignty of the people," which Alexis de Tocqueville and John Stuart Mill both identified with the "tyranny of public opinion" (Crick 1968, 80).

Recent monetary literature has not paid much attention to sovereignty. Fred Hirsch (1969), however, recognized the intimate connection between sovereignty and the right to issue money:

> One of the hallmarks of national sovereignty throughout the ages has been the right to "create money"—that is for the sovereign to lay down what is or is not legal tender, to require that it shall be accepted in settlement of debt within the country's borders, and to maintain the sole right of issuing this national money.

None of these sovereign powers will itself control the way in which individuals choose to use this money—that will depend on the "quality" of the money itself, on its real worth in relation to the goods it buys or to other forms of money that individuals can get hold of or spontaneously create. But the ability to create its own domestic money is the key financial distinction of a sovereign state. (P. 22)[6]

Early concepts of monetary sovereignty

As already noted, the concept or doctrine of political sovereignty entered the literature of political science in the sixteenth century, thousands of years after the concept of monetary sovereignty had been proclaimed by the rulers or priesthood of the ancient theocracies. Different metals received different treatment. In early times, gold was a sacred metal, under the control of the top prelate, a position often combined with the top ruler. The earliest mints were temples; indeed, our word for money derives from the surname of Juno: the earliest Roman money was coined in the temple of Juno Moneta, from the Latin word *monere*, meaning "to warn": Juno "the Warner" was said to have promised that if the Romans fought only "just" wars they would never be short of money.[7]

The authority to create money was a prerogative of the sovereign or the priesthood from very early times. Coins were a fiscal resource to the extent that they were overvalued. Overvaluation requires a monopoly, which must be enforced by control over the supplies of the precious metals, laws against counterfeiting, and the law of payment that make money legal tender. In ancient India, laws regarding the use of the precious metals (including copper) were precise: the Code of Manou classifies robbery of sacred gold or the gold of a priest with the highest crimes, debasers of metals are classed with rogues, and a goldsmith who commits fraud "shall be cut piecemeal with razors." (Del Mar 1885, 62).

From the very beginnings of coinage in ancient Lydia (or some as yet undiscovered place), coinage was overvalued. The Lydian kings, perhaps starting with the usurper Gyges, maintained the overvalued one-third stater electrum coins that were the staple of the Mermnadae dynasty that ended with the self-immolation of Croesus in 546 B.C. The Persian conquerors of Lydia maintained an overvalued gold coinage, with an artificial bimetallic ratio of 13:1 at a time when the silver price of gold outside the empire was half that. The coinage prerogative was rigorously asserted by the Persian state. Herodotus tells us that Darius, having coined gold money that was stamped with his own image, accused and condemned to death Ariander, his viceroy in Egypt, for having coined similar pieces in silver. (Grimaudet [1579] 1900, 12).

A similar system was adopted by the Romans after 46 B.C. but at a ratio of 12:1, which was maintained, through Rome's successor in Constantinople, until the sacking of that great city by the Crusaders in 1204. Protection of the monetary prerogative required draconian laws against and gruesome tortures for infringements on it. The Christian states of Western Europe acknowledged the de jure sovereignty in matters of gold coinage of the god-emperor at Constantinople and abstained from it as long as that authority lasted.

The formation of the Holy Roman Empire with the crowning of Charlemagne in 800 set in motion the running battle between church and state in the West and between the Western papacy and the Eastern church. The second battle ended in 1204, but the struggle between the empire and the Western papacy would last through the Middle Ages. Within its own geographical domain, the Holy Roman Empire was sovereign, and the communes of the Empire were on occasion granted charters to coin money. In the case of Siena, this was granted by Henry VI, king of the Romans (eldest son of the Emperor):

> In the name of the Holy and Indivisible Trinity, We, Henry VI, by divine favor, King of the Romans . . . make known to all the faithful of the empire, present as well as future, that in view of the merits of our trusty subjects, the citizens of Siena, we grant them . . . the privilege of coining money in the city of Siena. (Schevill 1909, 57)

Early money for these satellite states was coined "by the grace of Caesar."

The Western emperors had local power, but their sovereignty was qualified. The right to coin gold had been from early history the mark of complete sovereignty. Neither Charlemagne nor any of his successors—until Frederick II—coined gold. The gold coinage of Europe was the bezant, which was produced in Constantinople by the lawful descendants of Constantine. The circulation of gold bezants and its fractions served throughout Europe not only as a standard for weights and measures but also as a check on debasement and devaluation. The one-quarter bezant piece had exactly the same weight as an English (silver) penny. The pretensions of Charlemagne were immense, but they did not challenge the monopoly of gold that had been jealously guarded in Rome or Constantinople since the time of Julius Caesar.

The Holy Roman Empire was, it has been said, a fiction: neither holy, Roman, nor an empire. The German emperors had nominal authority over the smaller communes and could grant charters and licenses, but the Basileus at Constantinople had legal sovereignty.

With the sack of Constantinople in 1204, however, that empire collapsed. It was not at first clear where the coinage prerogative would go. But in 1225, Frederick II leaped into the breach with his magnificent augustal coins. With Frederick's death in 1250, the empire fell (temporarily). The gold prerogative was now up for grabs. Who would fill the gap? Gold coinage suddenly flourished in France, Florence, Genoa, and even England[8] in the interregnum, while other countries followed later. But the gold currencies that became the "dollars of the Middle Ages" were the ducats, sequins, and florins—virtually interchangeable coins—produced by the Italian city states.

In one sense, these coins were not yet legal. The empire had lost the mantle of sovereignty, and a few states had produced gold coins, but there was no formal transfer of sovereignty. Edward III had issued his gold nobles in his capacity as vicar-general of the Holy Roman Empire. It was not until the year 1356 that the empire (which had been reformed) issued its "golden bull," formally ceding the gold prerogative to the kings of Europe.[9]

Before this final event, the nations of Europe had been gradually building up their independence from the emperor and the pope in a series of steps that gave their kings complete control over the precious metals. There were various steps in this process: the assertion of mines royal, treasure trove, coinage of gold, demonetization of the Imperial bezant and other coins, control over the movement of the precious metals, the suppression of episcopal and baronial mints, the trial of the pix, the regulation of the standard, and the doctrine of national money. In England, these were accomplished by the monarch in the thirteenth and fourteenth centuries (Del Mar [1895] 1968, 277).

An early treatise on English law, ascribed to Ranulf de Glanvill (1187-89), starts off in the tone of Justinian's *Pandects* asserting the famous maxim of absolutism: "The will of the prince has the force of law," with no mention of consent of the governed; he does, however, attempt to justify the laws of England against the charge that they have not been written down. The main body of the work begins with a specification of crimes and jurisdictions, in the course of which he outlines the dimensions of *crimen laesae maiestatis*:

> Of please some are civil, some are criminal. Again, of criminal pleas some pertain to the crown of our lord the king, others to the sheriffs of the counties. To the king's crown belong these: the crime which in the *leges* [i.e., the Roman laws] is called *crimen laesae maiestatis*,—as by slaying the king or by a betrayal of his person or realm or army,—the concealment of treasure trove, breach of his peace, homicide, arson, robbery, rape, forgery, and the like. (Haskins [1927] 1957, 219)

The doctrine of mines royal holds that all mines producing one or both of the precious metals belongs to the crown. Louis IX of France was the first Christian king to assert it, and he was followed by Henry III in 1262. Henry, however, was bullied out of this right by the pope, and it never came into force again until the reign of Edward III. With respect to the doctrine of treasure trove—a modern version is "finder's keepers"—Edward the Confessor had declared that all the gold and one-half of the silver belonged of right to the king; a later version of it in France and also England was that all the gold belonged to the king, while all the silver was relinquished to the nobles. By the time of Edward III, however, the crown claimed all the gold and all the silver.

Gold coinage, as we have seen, was first asserted—timidly—by Henry III but boldly by Edward III in the next century. Before that time, until 1204, it was conceded universally to have been the lawful successor of Constantine and therefore the lawful suzerain of the empire to which in certain respects kings owed fealty (Del Mar [1895] 1968, 279). In an important sense, England achieved her complete independence only in 1356 or perhaps 1366 or even later.[10]

It was around the year 1291 that Edward I ordered that no foreign coins should be admitted into the kingdom except such as might be in use by travelers and others for casual expenses; and to these, he provided public offices where they might be exchanged. This law was probably aimed at the bezant, the most important foreign coin in circulation; other coins continued to circulate as before (Del Mar [1895] 1968, 279).

The power to regulate gold and silver movements had not been asserted before the thirteenth century, and the assumption of this regalian right, along with the purging of baronial and episcopal mints, was an important part of the process of centralizing the money power in the hands of the sovereign. A related development was the appointment of the Monetary Commission of 1293, in the twenty-second year of the reign of Edward I, with the mandate to examine the coins employed in the kingdoms and report on them to the king.

The "trial of the pix" is a test for the standard of the coinage.[11] Of Roman origin,[12] it was introduced in the reign of Henry I and became widespread two centuries later in the reign of Edward I. Its widespread use was a telltale indication that the coinage had deteriorated. So long as the sacred empire remained, the coinage prerogative of the Basileus acted as a continual check on any tendency to adulterate the coinage. Yet, once this yoke was thrown off, adulteration became prevalent in all parts of Europe.[13]

The right to produce and control money is a clear-cut test of a country's independence and sovereignty. The most important dimension of this monetary sovereignty, however, is the right of a state to declare that which counts as legal tender. This principle, called the law of payment, goes back to ancient times, to Paulus and the Pandects of Justinian. But nothing is heard of it before the downfall of the sacred Empire, and it is first noted in England in the reign of Edward III.

The countries of Europe not only had to deal with the residual powers of the Empire but also with the Church, which at all times in the Middle Ages was a multinational power seeking to impose its authority over the nations of Europe. But the larger nations did not always comply. When Pope Boniface VIII wrote to Philip le Bel, claiming him as "a subject both in spirituals and temporals," Philip replied, "We give your Foolship to know that in temporals we are subject to no person" (quoted in Del Mar [1895] 1968, 279). This made clear France's independence of both the empire and the papacy—in this reign at least. In England, however, the test came somewhat later. It was not until 1366, in the fortieth year of the reign of Edward III, that England broke free of Rome. In that year, it was ordered that Peter's-pence should no more be gathered in England or paid to Rome (Del Mar [1895] 1968, 283). Finally, in that year, England could be considered an independent, if not completely sovereign state, free at last from the ghost of Roman authority and monetary tribute to—if not spiritual authority from—Rome.

The concept of political sovereignty was borne out of need: civil war created the need for authority and the power of the church created the need for an independent temporal power. England broke free of the Church and established her spiritual sovereignty early in the sixteenth century, but France was still Catholic, and the counterreformation was in full swing on the frightful day of St. Bartholomew in 1572. Bodin's doctrine of sovereignty filled the need of the nationalist party (led by Bodin's patron, the king's brother),[14] which, while still Catholic, wanted to end the persecution of the Huguenots and reestablish civil order. Bodin's concept of sovereignty explicitly incorporated the money prerogative (Bodin 1576 I, chap. 11, 213; quoted in Nussbaum 1950, 34).

Bodin's conception of sovereignty was not original with him. A contemporary, François Grimaudet (1520-80), born ten years earlier than Bodin, had already printed a book in 1560 that explicitly proclaimed the doctrine "That the welfare of the State demanded the subjection of the ecclesiastical to the civil power, in whose hands all the functions of society were legally invested." It would be surprising if Bodin had not seen this work. Grimaudet also wrote several books on money and the law, including a major treatise on the law of payment. At one point, he insisted the following:

> The value of money depends on the State; that is to say, in a monarchy, upon the prince, and in an oligarchy, upon the State, which alone has the right to coin money, or to have it coined and to stamp a valuation upon it. (Grimaudet [1579] 1900, 11)

The case of the mixed moneys

Monetary sovereignty can be broken into three parts: (1) the right to determine what constitutes the unit of account—the commodity or token in which price lists are specified; (2) the right to determine the means of payment—legal tender for purposes of the discharge of debt; and (3) the right to produce money—or else determine the conditions under which it is to be produced by others.

Under a pure commodity money system, the relevance of monetary sovereignty was restricted to debtor-creditor problems of intertemporal exchange arising from changes in relative prices. In the ancient empires, this right was manifested in debt-reduction-cancellation decrees, which were not uncommon among the early empires.[15]

Monetary sovereignty took on its great importance in the age of overvalued money.[16] Whether the overvalued money arose as a result of coinage, paper money, or bank money, the question of profit or seigniorage arose. In the transition from commodity money to overvalued money, the government had access to a great fiscal resource that it could either exercise itself or sell (e.g., in the issue of charters to banks) to the private sector. To overvalue a money, the state had to keep its supply restricted, by means of a monopoly, and thus arose the draconian penalties[17] that became associated with the infringement of monetary laws. Infringement of monetary sovereignty was invariably classified with crimes of high treason.

The right of the sovereign to determine what constitutes legal tender was unquestioned in Roman times and reaffirmed in the modern age. A landmark case in England arose in the wake of the Irish rebellion of 1598. To stretch the royal budget, Queen Elizabeth I issued a special "mixed" money that was forbidden in England—in short, occupation script:

> Sometime before this proclamation, an Irish merchant had bought some goods for which he specifically promised to pay one hundred pounds in English sterling. He appeared in Dublin on the day fixed for payment and tendered one hundred pounds—in occupation coinage—in settlement of the debt. The creditor refused to take the debased money and sued for payment in sterling. However, in 1604, the court held for the debtor. (Dunne 1960, 3)

This landmark decision, referred to as the Case of the Mixed Moneys, became the law of the land.[18] The importance of the decision is not so much in the great injustice associated with changing monetary rules ex post facto but rather the great importance of the institution of legal tender[19] and the authority of the sovereign to determine what that legal tender is.

PART 2: SOVEREIGNTY AND MONETARY UNIONS

Part 2 will discuss explicitly monetary unions as they relate to the sovereignty issue. The first section will discuss different types of currency areas, reviewing the distinction between "true" and "pseudo" currency areas. The second section will identify key differences in policy and legal sovereignty in three different types of monetary unions. The third section will discuss the choices made for EMU and its alternative that involve different commitments of sovereignty.

Types of currency areas

I have elsewhere defined a currency area (Mundell 1961) as a zone of fixed exchange rates and made a distinction between true and pseudo currency areas (Mundell 1997a, 1997b). A true currency area is a zone of fixed exchange rates in which the adjustment mechanism works because the balance of payments determines (or at least dominates) monetary policy. By contrast, in a pseudo currency area, monetary policy may be allocated to domestic objectives.

The anchored dollar system (often called the Bretton Woods arrangements because they were endorsed by the major countries at the Bretton Woods Conference in 1944) that extended from 1936, the date of the Tripartite Agreement, until 1971 was a pseudo currency area because reserve currency countries like the United States and Britain automatically sterilized the monetary impact of gold flows. Such sterilization was the exception rather than the rule under the international gold standard that existed between 1873 and 1914 and under the bimetallic system that characterized the international monetary system between 1815 and 1873.

The bimetallic system covering most of the world from 1815 to 1873, and also the gold bloc from 1874 to 1914, could be characterized as true currency areas; there was both a commitment to parity and at least a semiautomatic system of adjustment: sterilization of the monetary impact of gold flows was the exception rather than the rule. Any departure from parity arising from an emergency would be corrected after the emergency passed, with the result that interest costs were kept down and speculation tended to be stabilizing.

The international gold standard that was restored between 1924 and 1933 was intended to be a true currency area, but its reconstruction was based on a fatal defect, and it had overtones of a pseudo currency area. The dollar had become the dominant currency in the system, and dollar prices ruled the roost. Unfortunately, because of wartime price increases that were not completely reversed in the 1921 deflation, the U.S. price level was still 40 percent higher than the prewar price level, shrinking drastically the gold base of the new system. This meant that gold was undervalued by 40 percent. When in the middle of the decade other countries restored their currencies at new exchange rates, they related them to dollar prices generalizing the undervaluation of gold and creating potential deflationary pressure. The United States, now the dominant financial power, had adopted a new policy of stabilizing the domestic price level in the 1920s. However, in the early 1930s, with deflation and the onset of the depression, followed by the depreciation of the pound sterling in 1931, the Federal Reserve shifted to tight money policies and doomed the world economy to depression.

The anchored dollar standard that characterized the system from 1936 until 1971 was also a pseudo currency area. The responsibility for fixing the price of gold was left to the United States, and the responsibility for fixing exchange rate parities was left to the other countries. There was a commitment to parities, but it was by no means absolute: James Meade dubbed the arrangements an "adjustable peg system." Countries made an effort to maintain the parities, but they did not allow the self-adjusting monetary mechanism to operate as a matter of course. This period was characterized by a deterioration of the understanding of how a fixed exchange rate system was supposed to operate and it was not generally realized that the new arrangements constituted a "disequilibrium system."[20] Most important, the key-currency country and major reserve center, the United States, automatically sterilized the impact of gold flows on bank reserves and the money supply, undermining the global adjustment mechanism and shifting its burden to the rest of the world.[21]

The reformed fixed exchange rate system established at the Smithsonian Institution in December 1971 was similarly a pseudo currency area. It was a pure dollar standard in which the rate of inflation was determined by the Federal Reserve System acting to implement national rather than international interests. It broke down because U.S. monetary policies were too inflationary for the European countries.

Parts of the ERM of the European Monetary System were likewise a pseudo currency area. Exchange rates were fixed, but the balance of payments did not automatically determine monetary policies in every country; as a result, there were frequent exchange rate changes, and speculators won in every battle with the authorities. Exceptions were the "inner DM area" that included Austria and the Benelux countries.

The ERM system was defective also for the same reason that the Smithsonian system broke down: the policies of the center country collided with the interests of the other participants. The ERM became a DM area with monetary policy in the ERM zone determined by the Bundesbank, which had a legal mandate to pursue policies appropriate for Germany alone. When the unification shock created a major conflict between the interests of Germany and the other members of the ERM, the Bundesbank followed its legal mandate to protect internal balance in Germany, leaving other countries the option of staying with the mark and appreciating against the dollar and other third currencies or leaving the system. Italy and Britain left the system, Spain devalued within it, and France sought and obtained a transmogrification of the system in the form of drastically widened exchange rate margins.

There were two important differences between the breakup of the Smithsonian system in 1973 and the ERM system in 1992: One was that, *from the standpoint of its partners*, U.S. monetary policy in 1973 was excessively expansionary, whereas Germany's in 1992 was excessively contractive. The other major difference was that, unlike the situation in 1973, when the international monetary system was falling apart amidst the atrophy of U.S. leadership, the ERM countries had signed an agreement to pursue monetary union by 1999, and Germany, in partnership with France, was still willing to lead. The flaw in the ERM arrangements was the absence of an agreed procedure for determining the common rate of inflation in the early stages of the integration process.

Under a true currency area, interest rates converge and speculation is stabilizing; adjustment takes place between countries just as it does between regions sharing a common currency. Under a pseudo currency area, on the other hand, interest rates diverge by an extent determined by expected exchange rate changes; speculation, based typically on a one-way option, is destabilizing. A pseudo currency area falls uncomfortably between two stools and has little to recommend it as an alternative to more fixed or more flexible systems.

Recent history is replete with stabilization programs using pegged exchange rates to break inflation but with little recognition that the stabilization policy will fail unless central bank credit is curbed. As a result of the failure of pseudo-stabilization policies in such countries as Argentina and Brazil in the 1980s and Mexico in the 1990s, many policy makers, not understanding the subtle distinction between pegged or pseudo-fixed and fixed exchange rates, have rejected entirely the idea of fixed exchange rates.

Failure to make the necessary distinction between true and pseudo currency areas has frequently led policy makers to lump both types together under the umbrella of "fixed exchange rates." Even today, there is a surprisingly influential view that holds that, under fixed exchange rates, there is no mechanism for adjusting the balance of payments. Yet, these attacks on fixed exchange rates are only valid for the pseudo-fixed exchange rates of pseudo currency areas. They do not apply to true currency areas. A hard fixed exchange rate system does not break down because it contains within it a mechanism that automatically enforces adjustment.

If there were no mechanism for adjusting the balance of payments under fixed exchange rates—as it is often claimed by advocates of flexible rates—how does adjustment take place between regions sharing a single currency? This is a problem for those who reject fixed exchange rates between countries yet would abhor the thought of breaking up a common currency area like the United States. For a time, some economists argued that fixed exchange rates were workable between different regions of large countries like the United States only because of fiscal stabilizers, intergovernment transfers, and big government. One heard this even a few years ago from economists who argued that monetary union in Europe would lead to civil war! Yet, this neglects the fact that the United States has had a common currency since 1792 (leaving aside the four years of the Civil War), long before the movement to big government that came in the wake of the two world wars. It also ignores the evidence of national and imperial monetary systems since coinage was invented. It also neglects the fact that the bimetallic and gold standard systems worked perfectly well, from the standpoint of international adjustment, at a time when there was a complete absence of international transfers or fiscal "stabilizers." The idea that balance of payments adjustment requires fiscal stabilizers or big government is the opposite of the truth.[22]

In view of the skepticism that greets stabilization efforts, some countries have resorted to partial or complete currency board systems. Currency board systems fall into the category of true fixed exchange rate systems because they prohibit, or drastically curtail, purchases of domestic assets; the money supply therefore rises and falls with purchases and sales of foreign exchange reserves imposing the self-equilibrating adjustment of the balance of payments. A currency board system, like any truly fixed exchange rate system, is not subject to destabilizing speculation[23] and leads eventually to the same rate of inflation as that country whose currency is the partner in the fix.[24]

A currency board system represents an ideal monetary arrangement for a small country economically close to a large one with a stable inflation rate if the country is willing and able to achieve the monetary and fiscal discipline without which any fixed exchange rate system would founder. A successful currency board system closes the exchange rate margins, equates domestic reserve creation with changes in foreign exchange reserves, and rules out exchange rate changes. Spot and forward exchange rates against the partner currency are fixed and equal, and interest rates converge to those in the partner country.

In a pure currency board arrangement, central bank money is completely backed by foreign exchange reserves. Some of the seigniorage lost by this arrangement can be made up by investing the foreign exchange in interest-bearing liquid assets, such as U.S. Treasury Bills. But larger countries that lack full cover for central bank money may choose a currency-board arrangement that involves less than 100 percent cover.[25] A currency board that operated initially with 50 percent foreign exchange cover could still maintain 100 percent cover for *increments* in reserve money.

Countries with exchange rate arrangements as diverse as Hong Kong, Panama, Estonia, Luxembourg, Argentina, Bulgaria, Bosnia, and members of the euro zone have diverse fixed exchange rate arrangements that have in common a strong commitment to parity combined with a monetary policy that is committed to equilibrium in the balance of payments. However, the experiences of countries like Austria and the Netherlands, which have had fixed parities with the mark in conjunction with a commitment to systematic adjustment of monetary market conditions to preserve equilibrium in the balance of payments, have shown that fixed exchange rate arrangements short of currency boards can also be credible. The essential distinction is not so much whether a country has a currency board system, whether its exchange margins are one-half of a percent or 2 percent, or whether its international reserves backing domestic notes are 50 percent or 100 percent. It is rather whether a country has committed itself to the parity and to an adjustment mechanism that ensures that economic conditions are maintained consistent with that parity.

Three approaches to Monetary Union

Let us suppose that two countries are considering different forms of monetary integration. There are three possibilities to consider:

1. fixed exchange rate systems in which two or more currencies are locked irrevocably together, and monetary policy is determined by the balance of payments;
2. a currency board regime combined with the creation of a parallel currency and a supranational central bank in which
   - the parallel currency is *not* legal tender,
   - the parallel currency *is* legal tender along with the national currencies, and
   - the parallel currency is the *sole* legal tender; and
3. a supranational central bank and a legal tender common currency that completely replaces national currencies.

I shall discuss each of these in turn. (1) Fixed exchange rate systems (including currency board systems) often result from asymmetrical sizes of the countries. One country is large and, with a stable and low inflation rate, is looked on as a good monetary leader. In this case, a natural assignment of instruments to targets results: the large country determines the inflation rate of the area, and the small country or countries fix the exchange rate (with or without the cooperation of the large country).

If the two countries are of roughly equal size, a hegemonic relationship is unlikely. Both parties would contribute to the fixing. One possibility is for each country to defend its own currency when it is weak; this is a potentially deflationary solution because intervention reduces aggregate reserves. Alternatively, each country could defend the partner's currency when it is weak—a potentially inflationary solution because intervention adds to reserves. Whichever method of fixing is adopted, joint decision making will be required to determine the common monetary policy and the rate of inflation of the area as a whole. Although this policy could be determined by fixed rules regarding annual increments of domestic assets, it would more probably be facilitated by a formal institution designated as the monetary authority. For small countries forming a monetary union, a good solution to the "*n*th" or "redundancy" problem would be to fix the joint currency to a stable external currency bloc.

(2). Consider next the case of a currency board combined with a parallel currency (G-currency) and a group central bank (GCB). Suppose that the currency is (like the ECU) a weighted average of the national currencies and that it is to be used as the focus of intervention. National central banks cease their purchases of domestic assets and lock exchange rates with each other by fixing the national currency to the central currency. Monetary expansion in the group is determined by asset expansion of the GCB over and above any purchases of the national currencies.

In this setup, the central currency and the national currencies are, except for calculation purposes, close substitutes. The degree to which they are substitutes, however, depends on their legal tender status. There are three approaches to consider in ascending order of proximity to true monetary union:

1. The G-currency is not legal tender. In this case, the demand for G-currency would depend on its convertibility into the other currencies; it is unlikely that the G-currency would become an important unit of account, and it is difficult to see how this approach would provide the momentum needed for a unified currency system.
2. The G-currency is made legal tender along with the other national currencies. In this case, the demand for the G-currency would grow over time as the countries become familiarized with it, and, if it is also used as an invoice currency, it could in the long run become an important share

in the total legal-tender money supply.

3. The G-currency enters as legal tender, while the national currencies are scheduled to be phased out as legal tender. The national central banks cease their purchases of domestic assets and lock exchange rates with each other by fixing the national currency to the central currency. The GCB opens a window at which it stands willing to buy (from commercial banks) national currencies in exchange for the G-currency. Monetary expansion in the group is determined by asset expansion of the GCB over and above any purchases of the national currencies.

After a certain period of time—three years in the case of the EMU—the national currencies will cease to be complete legal tender. Because this represents a conspicuous shift of sovereignty, the process may have to be accomplished by stages.[26] But whatever the progression, the recognition that national currencies will cease to be complete legal tender after a date will greatly strengthen the use of the G-currency as unit of quotation and contract for deferred payments. Of the three approaches thus far considered, this is the route to monetary union, but it is also flexible as to the timing for national currencies to be phased out.

(3). Consider now the case where national currencies are scrapped in exchange for the G-currency and the ECB becomes a full-fledged independent monetary authority. Exchange rates are locked, national central banks cease purchases of domestic assets, and the ECB stands willing to exchange all national currencies for G-currency in addition to carrying out the monetary policy of the group with open market operations in community assets or foreign exchange.

This sudden-death approach—adopted by the EU—is the most direct approach to monetary union. All of a sudden, national currencies are demonetized, and a supranational authority conducts monetary policy in what appears to be an irrevocable monetary union. Through this approach, a country relinquishes national sovereignty over money in return for a share in the supranational sovereignty. This approach has the merit that the location of the sovereignty is unambiguous, and it creates the impression—whether justified or not—that the transformation is irrevocable. Its disadvantage is that the sacrifice of the national currency may dissuade countries to take the final step. The Delors Report approach, enshrined in the Maastricht Treaty, was a colossal gamble that might not have worked out had it not been for the political pressures imposed by the felt need to lock a united Germany into a European framework. Even so, because EMU came close to not working, it is not necessarily the right model for other monetary unions.

An alternative approach to monetary union

Abolition of national currencies is not a prerequisite for a common monetary policy. This was recognized in both the Werner Report of the early 1970s and the Delors Report of the late 1980s, which proposed three necessary conditions: (1) the total convertibility of currencies, (2) the complete liberalization of capital flows and full integration of financial markets, and (3) an irrevocable locking of exchange rates. If these three conditions were achieved, the European Community or Union would function as if it were a single monetary area (see Kenen 1995, 14), except, of course, for the information economies of a single unit of account. Although the Delors Report recommended a single currency, it was recognized as the preferred course, not a prerequisite.

To be sure, these three conditions leave unclear the nature of the mechanism for controlling the monetary policy of the monetary area. Suppose all national currencies are fixed to one another with no margins. If the fix is irrevocable, speculation would make all forward rates equal to spot rates, and interest rates on credit instruments with the same noncurrency risk would converge despite being denominated in different currencies.

Nevertheless, this arrangement leaves open-ended both the nature of the mechanism for fixing exchange rates and the mechanism for ensuring appropriate monetary growth in the area as a whole. A requirement that each country buy and sell its partners' currencies at fixed prices forever would be sufficient to keep spot and forward exchange rates fixed, but it would not guarantee either adequate monetary growth or price stability. If national central banks had no restrictions on the purchase of domestic assets, competition for seigniorage could lead to hyperinflation. A monetary union without a centralization of decision making with respect to monetary policy would quickly fail. To these three provisions must therefore be added a fourth: the centralization of monetary policy in an institution for determining the monetary policy of the area as a whole.

Collective management of monetary policy in a framework of, say, *n* currencies is by no means simple or automatic. It is a great help initially to have a dominant currency that becomes the unit of account of the union and the focus for monetary discipline of the others. Suppose then that one existing currency is designated as the "pivot"[27] and that all other central banks fix exchange rates to that pivot currency, at the same time eschewing any further purchases of domestic assets. Exchange rates would then be fixed, and monetary growth would depend entirely on the purchase of assets by the designated pivot central bank, which would now have complete control over monetary policy.

This approach to monetary union is less draconian than the sudden-death approach recommended in the Delors Report and adopted by the EMU. Legal sovereignty would be retained even while policy sovereignty is given up. In return, the other countries would get automaticity of monetary policy and the inflation rate and interest rate of the dollar area. There would be no coercive phasing out of cherished national currencies except insofar as countries decided to take that more irrevocable step.

The transactions and leadership costs in forming monetary unions are greatly reduced by the use of a "living" currency as a safeguard against mistakes made by inexpert monetary doctors. This was the mechanism I suggested in my plan for a European currency presented for the first time in December 1969.[28] It is more flexible than the Maastricht approach because it does not involve the same commitment of legal sovereignty. National currencies, far from being suddenly scrapped, would continue in existence while habit and efficiency are allowing the euro to take over.

The approach to monetary union through the use of a national currency did not work in Europe, however, because of several relevant objections: First, such a solution would have involved, at least initially, German rather than European control of monetary policy, with German rather than European inflation preferences. This was indeed the problem with the exchange rate mechanism of the European Monetary System, which, in the 1980s, gravitated to a DM area. It could have been mitigated by the introduction of non-German directors in the Bundesbank, but the political transactions costs would have defied solution.

Second, the mark was a national symbol peculiar to Germany.[29] Non-Germans would have to change their currency, while Germans would have the benefit of continuing to use their own currency. Of course, the extra benefit to Germany would be restricted to the transition period. The problem in the transition period could be mitigated by putting an overstamp on marks, designating them as Europeanized marks. After the transition, all member countries would use the new currency, the euro, with European symbols, so the end result would be the same. Nevertheless, it must be admitted that the asymmetric prestige element involved in the transition would have been hard to swallow in France.

It should be recognized, however, that the European use of the mark could have been looked on as a sacrifice for Germany too. Whereas the other countries lose policy sovereignty, Germany, while retaining a high measure of policy sovereignty, would, in effect, lose legal sovereignty as the mark-euro became the currency of the EU rather than the nation-state of Germany.

Third, the use of the mark would confer on Germans the great benefit of not having to change their unit of account and learn a new system of reckoning. In every other country, citizens would have to go through the agonizing, if once and for all, mental process of recalculating prices. Germany would be specially favored by the continued use of its national unit of account as the euro.

Against these costs, however, there are other considerations. First, the cost to the other countries of changing units of account would not be harder in using the mark-euro than it would be in using the ECU-euro; use of the mark is a benefit to Germany, not a cost to the others. Because the mark is the most important European currency in most EU members' exchange markets, exchange rates on the mark are more familiar than any other exchange rate (except the dollar). By contrast, the ECU exchange rate was not well known at all to the general public. Second, the fact that German citizens will not have to change their unit of account can be looked on as a benefit not a cost because it would give Germans some compensation for their sacrifice of the most important currency in Europe and the currency that, since 1948, has had one of the best inflation records in the world. From a narrow economic perspective, at least, Germany had the most to risk and the least to gain by scrapping the mark for the euro.[30] Third, the identification of the euro with the mark would fit in more conveniently with the rest of the international monetary system, where the three most important currencies quoted are the dollar, the mark, and the yen. The euro-mark, being a known commodity externally, would allow the euro to fit into the international monetary system with the least disruption.

These factors might have lent support to the use of the mark as the foundation for the euro. The successful launching of the euro in January 1999 makes some of the concerns raised above irrelevant. It now appears that the birthing difficulties faced by the launching of a new currency will be overcome and that EMU will be a permanent feature of the international monetary landscape in this century. Nevertheless, it might be a mistake to believe that the success of the euro would carry over to other monetary unions. It is worth therefore keeping the approach that seemed appropriate to me three decades ago alive as an option in other cases in which political integration is not on the agenda.

Application to other currency areas

What has worked for Europe is not necessarily the best model for other areas considering closer monetary integration or even monetary union. It generally can be assumed that the creation of the euro will create a huge monetary area in Europe that will be on the same scale of importance as the dollar and the yen and, moreover, that it is likely to be an expanding monetary area increasing in importance over time. The creation of the euro cannot fail to have a "demonstration effect" leading to the formation of currency areas elsewhere. There are at least two reasons for this. One is the effect on economic ideas. Prior to 1971, the dominant international paradigm was an international monetary system based on fixed exchange rates anchored, by at least one country, to one or both of the precious metals. After this system broke down in August 1971, flexible exchange rates became the fashion, and any attempt to fix exchange rates in currency areas or by currency boards was looked on in horror by the international monetary authorities, partly on the spurious grounds that a system of fixed exchange rates lacks a feasible mechanism of adjustment. But when eleven (now twelve) countries in Europe decide to not only have absolutely fixed exchange rates but also scrap their currencies to boot, it requires a reappraisal of theories and policies.

The other reason is that the creation of a huge and expanding monetary bloc in Europe will lead competing areas to reconsider their international currency arrangements. As the European monetary area expands into Central and Eastern Europe, the coastal states of the Mediterranean, and Africa, it seems likely that there will be renewed interest in the idea of monetary integration in the Western Hemisphere and the Pacific Area. Bigness begets bigness.

Our interest here is not in precise proposals but in the lessons of monetary integration from our study of sovereignty and the example set by Europe. Most other large areas lack the political and economic prerequisites for a single-currency area but would nevertheless benefit from the economic benefits of large and stable currency areas. Let us therefore consider the possibility of the creation of an international dollar area to include countries outside the United States.

Suppose, for example, a group of countries associated with the United States—in the Western Hemisphere or elsewhere—decide to integrate their monetary policies with that of the United States but without, at least initially, abolishing their national currencies.[31] Let us assume that the dollar is chosen as the lead currency and that the U.S. Federal Reserve[32] is designated as the monetary leader. All other countries would fix their currencies to the dollar at specified parities and the other national central banks cease all purchases of domestic assets.[33] Monetary growth in the currency area as a whole would then depend only on the balance sheet of the Federal Reserve System. Money supplies in the other countries would increase through surpluses in their balances of payments. With absolutely fixed exchange rates (possibly guaranteed by the U.S. Treasury) interest rates in the entire area, apart from any default risk or differential tax rates, would converge. The other countries would get more or less the same rate of inflation as the United States.

Thus far, such an arrangement would be asymmetric with policy (but not legal) sovereignty in the United States. At the same time, the United States would capture the seigniorage from monetary growth. If such an integrated monetary arrangement came into being, it would be useful to establish a monetary institution for the area as a whole that would have an input into the policy decisions regarding the inflation (or exchange rate) target for the area as a whole and to make provisions for a fairer distribution of seigniorage. Within such a framework, it would be possible to make decisions, if applicable, as to whether the dominant currency should be overstamped or redesigned, whether it would be desirable to phase out some or all of the other currencies, and whether it would be desirable to engage in operations in the external exchange markets to mitigate volatility of the dollar against other major currencies.

A concluding comment

Members of the European Community signed the Treaty of Maastricht that formed the EU and developed a plan for the EMU to begin in 1999. This plan involved the sudden sacrifice of policy and legal sovereignty to the central government in which, of course, each member shares control. It remains to be seen, however, whether, in the final analysis, many countries in different situations would be willing to completely scrap their legal sovereignty in the way prescribed.

The choice made at the time of Maastricht will remain one of the most intriguing questions for historians. That the Maastricht Plan followed the Delors Report is well known. But the Delors Report said (to repeat), "The adoption of a *single currency*, **while not strictly necessary for the creation of a monetary union . . . would clearly demonstrate the irreversibility of the . . . union**" The replacement of national currencies by a single currency should therefore take place as soon as possible after the locking of currencies" (my emphasis). The national currencies are scheduled to disappear by the year 2002, three years after locking currencies.

There is no doubt that a single-currency monetary area offers important advantages over a monetary area in which multiple currencies remain. The single currency imposes quick adjustment day in and day out and does not leave time for large imbalances to build up. It rules out speculation about intraunion exchange rate changes. It is also true that the single-currency approach is more difficult to reverse. Moreover, transactions costs and information costs of trade in a single-currency area are much less than in a multicurrency union. These great advantages of the Delors-Maastricht approach must be acknowledged.

As it is turning out, the approach adopted seems to have had unparalleled success. It has shown that some of the leading countries of Europe will have lost the "barbarism" noted by John Stuart Mill ([1848] 1909), "that almost all independent countries choose to assert their nationality by having, to their own inconvenience and that of their neighbours, a peculiar currency of their own." It is quite another question, however, whether the European model will travel well. Without a complementary development of deeper political integration, other emerging currency areas would be better advised to exploit the advantages of credible currency-board-like arrangements centered around a hegemonic leader or else a parallel-currency arrangement linked firmly to one or more of the largest currency area.

Notes

1. Locke, however, would have insisted that money is a quantity of silver.

2. That a country's "power" or "clout" in the international system is increased by the use of its currency, as a key currency can be readily illustrated by the weights of the three largest countries in making up the International Monetary Fund (IMF) unit of account, the SDR. The United States with a GDP of 24 percent of the world economy has a weight of 40 percent; Germany, with a GDP of less than 8 percent of the world economy, has a weight of 21 percent; and Japan, with a GDP of 14 percent of the world economy, has a weight of 17 percent. The ratio of SDR weight to GDP share in the world economy is 2.6 for Germany, 1.6 for the United States, and 1.2 for Japan. These weights were determined before 1 January 1991, when several large countries, including France, the United Kingdom, and Italy, were tied in effect, through the Exchange Rate

Mechanism (ERM), to the DM; the IMF would probably justify Germany's excessive weight in the SDR on the grounds that the clout of the mark was much greater before the partial breakup of the system in the crisis of September 1992. The SDR was modified to allow for the euro beginning on 1 January 1999, when the new weights were 39 percent for the U.S. dollar, 32 percent for the euro (replacing 21 percent for the DM and 11 percent for the French franc), 18 percent for the Japanese yen, and 11 percent for the pound sterling. Two years later, on 1 January 2001, new weights were established in the following amounts: 45 percent for the U.S. dollar, 29 percent for the euro, 15 percent for the Japanese yen, and 11 percent for the pound sterling.

3. This is as it should be because large countries have more to lose and less to gain by monetary union.

4. A few of the tiny countries may be exceptions. Panama and Liberia have national coinages but use the U.S. paper dollar for the bulk of their transactions. Luxembourg has been a passive member of a monetary union with Belgium since 1924 and thus has transferred policy sovereignty while retaining legal sovereignty.

5. Like all "valid" theories, Bodin's was only partly correct. At the time Bodin was writing (middle of the 1560s), prices measured in metallic units had hardly changed at all; Jehan Cherruyt de Malestroict was correct in attributing the rise in French prices to the debasement of the unit of account. Gold and silver prices did rise substantially, however, between 1565 and 1594; using English prices (where Elizabeth I's unit of account remained constant) as a measure, prices rose 50 percent between 1565 and 1593. Bodin's theory that the price increases were due to the influx of silver from Spanish America was not correct at the time he wrote, but it was correct for future price increases. His argument was timelier when he repeated it in 1576 in his major work, *The Six Books of the Republic.*

6. Charles Goodhart goes even further in emphasizing the implications of a single currency for the need for a strong centralized fiscal authority:

> It is, however, unrealistic to discuss "optimal" currency areas without giving explicit consideration to the close links between control of the currency and national sovereignty . . . the right to issue legal-tender currency is one of the most important, and prized, aspects of independent, sovereign power. Monetary independence entails the power also to change the exchange rate of the country vis-à-vis the currencies of other areas. If, say, British Columbia, or Florida, or Scotland, were given a separate Central Bank, a separate currency and the power to vary its exchange rate vis-à-vis the Canadian dollar, or US dollar or English pound, how much would be, or could be, left of national union between the two areas? Not only monetary policy, common currencies and integrated markets would have gone, but it is also extremely difficult to see how it would be possible to maintain any coherent common fiscal policy between the two areas. . . .
>
> I have argued both that a single-currency area requires a strong, centralized fiscal authority, ready and able to ease regional adjustment problems, and also that it will be difficult to establish any effective centralized fiscal authority covering areas with independent, separate currencies (i.e., both that a single-currency area cannot cover several, independent, uncoordinated fiscal areas, and the converse that an integrated fiscal area cannot extend over several independent currency areas).

Goodhart goes on to note, however, that the 1880-1914 gold standard constitutes an exception to the rule.

7. Cicero, however, in his *Treatise on Divination*, says it was due to a warning voice that issued from the enclosure when Rome was besieged by Gallic Senones. See Grimaudet ([1579] 1900, 14).

8. The gold coin issued in 1257 by Henry III was an imitation of an Arab maravedi and was almost immediately withdrawn.

9. More than a decade before the bull was issued, Edward III of England had already issued his gold nobles, under the authority of his position as vicar-general of the Holy Roman Empire.

10. England would not finally achieve spiritual sovereignty until 1532, when the final breach with Rome over the annulment of Henry VIII's marriage with Catherine of

Aragon was decided in an English court; thereafter, the Catholic Church in England was a national institution.

11. What came to be called the "trial of the pix" was instituted as a test of the fineness of coins submitted to the Exchequer for payments of taxes or debt. The Exchequer's problem was to test the adequacy of the coins received. To allow payments by tale would invite bad coins, while to test every coin was clearly impossible. The first precaution taken was to exact from the debtors an extra sixpence with each pound to make up a presumed shortness of weight; this was payment *ad scalum*. This was found not to be enough, so each counted pound was weighed, and the debtor could either make up the difference or pay an additional shilling for any shortfall; this was payment *ad pensum*. These precautions protected against the lightness of the coinage, but they were of course no protection against debased money. In Henry I's reign, Roger of Salisbury introduced a new plan of "blanching" money, that is, testing the fineness (or whiteness) of it. When any payment was made, forty-four shillings' worth of coin was selected at random out of the heap, weighed, and handed to the Master of the Assays, who carried off a pound's weight of it and, accompanied by the sheriff and his own subordinates, proceeded to the furnace to make the assay. The coins were melted and the dross skimmed off until pure silver alone remained. So long as the surface of the melted mass was clouded, there was still dross to be removed, but when the surface was bright and mirror-like, the impurity was gone, and nothing but silver remained. Both sides watched the operation, the sheriff anxious to prevent any waste of silver, the Exchequer officials careful to see that all dross was removed. The assayer had an interest in being accurate, for if either side challenged the assay, he had to make a second, for which he received no fee. When the operation was complete the mass was weighed and if it was short of its proper weight, the sheriff had to cast in enough pence to turn the scale. These pence were counted, and the sheriff had to pay that number on each pound of his total "form" as a quittance. See Warner (1907, 72-73).

12. During the Roman social wars, around 91 B.C., Livius Drusus, a tribune of the people, authorized the coinage of silver denarii, alloyed with one-eighth part copper, lowering the established standard. Later, copper pieces were plated to resemble silver. The discontent produced by this law induced the College of Praetors (84 B.C.) to restore the silver money to the ancient standard by instituting what would later be called the "trial of the pyx." Sylla was so enraged by this interference with the coinage that he annulled the decree of the praetors; proscribed their leader, Marius Graditidianus, as a traitor; and handed him over to the ferocious Cataline, who "slew him barbarously" (Del Mar, 123).

13. Dante produced a colorful account of the passions aroused by monetary crimes in the Middle Ages in the case of Master Adam, who adulterated the florin:

And there I saw another husk of sin,
who, had his legs been trimmed away at the groin,
would have looked for all the world like a mandolin . . .
He strained his lips apart and thrust them forward
the way a sick man, feverish with thirst,
curls one lip toward the china and the other upward.
"O you exempt from every punishment
of this grim world (I know not why)," he cried,
"look well upon the misery and debasement
of him who was Master Adam . . .
Inflexible Justice that has forked and spread
my soul like hay, to search it the more closely,
finds in the country where my guilt was bred
this increase of my grief; for there I learned,
there in Romena, to stamp the Baptist's imagine
our alloyed gold—till I was bound and burned . . .
Because of them I lie here in this pigpen;
it was they persuaded me to stamp the florins
with three carats of alloy.

14. Duc d'Alençon.

15. Saggs (1955) wrote the following:

> One facet of this [the king Lipit-Ishtar's sense of social justice] was his claim that he had "made justice." This claim, not unusual among old Babylonian rul-

> ers, referred to the cancellation by royal decree of certain debts, such as any which had forced free people to sell themselves or their families into slavery. (P. 97)

Debt cancellations occurred from time to time in all the ancient empires, including the Roman; Julius Caesar, as consul in 48 B.C., eliminated interest already paid on debts prosecuted in magistrate's court, in effect making the loan interest free.

16. In his *Treatise*, Keynes (1930, chap. 1) used the term *representative money* to mean what I mean by overvalued money.

17. The following account related by Nussbaum (1950) illustrated the situation in France in the fifteenth century:

> Among the numerous trials of counterfeiters in the Middle Ages, records of which have been preserved for us in the public archives, certainly one of the most moving is that of the goldsmith Louis Secretain, condemned at Tours, 1486, to be boiled and hanged after having been convicted of the crime of counterfeiting. On the day of the punishment, Secretain was led from the prison to Foire-le-Roi Square, in Tours, where a huge caldron filled with water had been set upon a blazing fire. The unfortunate one was bound by the executioner and thrown into the caldron; but the water had not yet reached the boiling point and in his struggles the victim disengaged himself from his fetters. He reappeared on the surface of the water holding out to the crowd, which was speechless with pity, his suppliant arms and crying out "Jesus! Mercy!" The executioner, armed with an iron fork, smote him on the head several times to make him sink again to the bottom of the vat. The crowd and the judges, themselves exasperated, cried at last: "Death to the executioner!" An affray ensured in which the executioner was killed and Secretain rescued. The half-cooked unfortunate one was carried into a neighboring church where he found refuge until the king's pardon was brought at last, returning him his freedom.

18. Dunne (1960, 3). The landmark decision read as follows:

> as the king by his prerogative may make money of what matter and form he pleases and establish the standard of it, so he may change his money in substance and impression, and enhance or debase the value of it or entirely decry or annul it.

Moreover, "although . . . at the time of contract . . . pure money was current in the kingdom . . . yet mixed money being established . . . before the day of payment . . . may be tendered . . . and the obligee is bound to accept it."

19. "Legal tender" is a term of the courtroom; a plea of legal tender is what lawyers call a "plea of avoidance," an admission whose damaging effect is immediately nullified by bringing in some addition factors. Thus, a defendant charged with debt might admit the borrowing and plead "legal tender"—namely, that at some previous time he physically had offered his creditor money that the law deemed acceptable for debt payments and had been refused. Such a suit, if proved in an early English tribunal, ended the creditor's suit then and there. The creditor's total loss was "accounted his own folly that he had refused the money when a lawful tender of it was made him." See Dunne (1960, 4).

20. See Mundell (1961) for an analysis of the disequilibrium system.

21. This is not to say that the alternative policy of allowing U.S. gold losses in the 1950s and 1960s to contract the U.S. monetary policy would have been desirable. Because of wartime and postwar inflation, gold in the 1950s again had become undervalued, and strict adherence to the "discipline" would have brought on another deflation and depression.

22. The theory that international adjustment is made easier by such "built-in-stabilizers" as high marginal tax rates is a colossal fallacy. On the contrary, the phenomenal increases both in marginal tax rates and in the ratios of government expenditure to GDP in all the European countries has clogged the arteries of commerce, raised unemployment, and reduced mobility, making international adjustment more rather than less difficult.

23. There are, of course, many different types of currency boards, differences based primarily on the size of exchange rate margins, the reserve ratio (which may be less or greater than 100 percent), and the legislative procedure for changing either the exchange rate or

the target currency. See Hanke and Schuler (1994) for a good recent discussion of currency boards.

24. It should be understood that when one country fixes its currency to another as in a currency board regime, the two members of the currency area will enjoy the same rate of inflation, provided the index of inflation is the same in both countries. It does not mean, however, that national price indexes will record the same rate of increase inasmuch as these have different weights. Since 1983, for example, when Hong Kong inaugurated its currency board with the U.S. dollar, the index of inflation has consistently been higher than that in the United States to the extent that the "real exchange rate" of the Hong Kong dollar has appreciated substantially against the U.S. dollar. This appreciation can be explained partly by an initial undervaluation of the Hong Kong dollar, requiring a correction, and partly by rapid productivity growth in the traded-goods industry.

25. Some small countries find it advisable to maintain more than 100 percent reserves so that the excess can be used as cover for the central bank's role (if it is maintained) as lender of last resort to the commercial banking sector. Several writers have made the mistake of asserting that currency board systems are flawed because of the risks to the commercial banking sector. However, it is not a currency board system as such that presents the danger to the commercial banks as much as the impact of stabilization policies of any kind, as real interest rates rise and the quality of commercial bank assets fall.

26. Phasing out the national currencies as legal tender could be done in stages, making it legal tender for small but not large transactions.

27. *Pivot currency* is one of the useful terms first used by Susan Strange in the 1960s.

28. "A Case for a European Currency" (Mundell 1969) was first presented at an American Management Association Conference in New York in December 1969; a revised version of this paper with the title "A Plan for a European Currency" was presented at the Optimum Currency Areas Conference in Madrid in March 1970 and published in Mundell (1973). In 1969 and 1970, I suggested the use during the transition period of the pound as the pivot, with its key position in the London foreign exchange market. It was soon apparent, however, that the mark had superseded the pound as the second most important currency in the world, and indeed the mark did later become the pivot in the exchange rate mechanism of the European Monetary System.

29. The mark did not originate, however, as a German currency. It was an ancient Norse unit of money and weight that came to be widely used all over western and especially northern Europe. The Norse coinage system consisted of stycas, scats, and oras, such that 8 stycas = 1 scat and 8 scats = 1 ora. Scats and oras had the same weight, so it appeared that the bimetallic ratio was intended to be 8:1. According to one plausible theory, the mark came to be the name for the amount of silver that exchanged for a Roman libra composed of five Roman gold pieces, that is, aurei and later bezants. The British pound of 240 silver pieces called pence was likewise the amount of gold that exchanged for one pound of 240 silver pence was likewise the amount of silver that exchanged for one Roman pound (pondus or libra) of five aurei. But when the British bimetallic ratio was brought into harmony with the Roman ratio of 12:1, for the first time in the third coinage reform of Alfred the Great (between AD 878 and 899), the pound meant 12 ounces, whereas the mark meant 8 ounces. When bimetallic ratios became unified the mark came to mean 160 pennies or 14 2/3 shillings.

30. I have elsewhere argued (e.g., Mundell 1994) that dominant countries have the least to gain and the most to lose by giving up monetary sovereignty to a supranational institution, and that is the reason why, historically, the dominant powers have always resisted international monetary reform. This was true of Britain in the nineteenth century, of the United States at Paris in 1933, and at Bretton Woods in 1944, and it has underlay the German insistence on convergence before locking exchange rates, instead of locking exchange rates as a route to convergence. If Chancellor Kohl's enthusiasm for monetary and even political union is seen as an exception to this theory, it could be pointed out that Kohl's position can be explained completely by his commitment to Europe on the eve of German monetary unification.

31. For a proposal for a North American Monetary Union based on a single currency, the "Amero," see Grubel (1999).

32. The Treasury is the senior monetary institution in control of exchange rates in the United States (e.g., the Secretary of the Treasury is the "governor" of the IMF for the United States, and the Chairman of the Federal Reserve System is its alternate governor), and the role of the Central Bank as the institution representing the United States in an international monetary integration framework would have to be, at least partly, as a designee of the Treasury.

33. An alternative arrangement would allow for a specified increase in domestic assets with the rate of growth or the purchase periodically of "fiduciary assets" to reduce the proportion of foreign assets in the central bank's balance sheet.

References

Bodin, Jean. [1568] 1946. *The response of Jean Bodin to the paradoxes of Malestroit*. Chevy Chase, MD: Century Dollar.

———. 1576. *Six Livres de la République*.

Crick, Bernard. 1968. Sovereignty. In *Encyclopedia for the social sciences* Vol. 15, 77-81. Chicago: Macmillan and Free Press.

Del Mar, Alexander. 1885. *A history of money in ancient countries*. New York: Burt Franklin.

———. [1895] 1968. *History of monetary systems*. London: Effingham Wilson, *Royal Exchange*.

Dunne, Gerald T. 1960. *Monetary decisions of the Supreme Court*. New Brunswick, NJ: Rutgers University Press.

Feaveryear, Sir Albert. 1963. *The pound sterling: A history of English money*. Oxford: Clarendon.

Grimaudet, Francois. [1579] 1900. *The law of payment*. New York: Cambridge Encyclopedia Britannica.

Grubel, Herbert G. 1999. The case for the Amero: The economics and politics of a North American monetary union. In *Critical issues bulletin*. Vancouver, Canada: Fraser Institute.

Hanke, Steve H., and Kurt Schuker. 1994. *Currency boards for developing countries*. San Francisco: International Center for Economic Growth.

Haskins, Charles Homer. [1927] 1955. *The twelfth century Renaissance*. New York: Meridian, World.

Hirsch, Fred. 1969. *Money international*. New York: Doubleday.

Kenen, Peter. 1995. *Economic and monetary union in Europe: Moving beyond Maastricht*. Cambridge: Cambridge University Press.

Keynes, John Maynard. 1930. *A treatise on money*. London: Macmillan.

Mill, John Stuart. [1848] 1909 (Ashley ed.). *Principles of political economy*. London: Longmans, Green.

Mundell, Robert A. 1961a. The disequilibrium system. *Kyklos* 2, reprinted in Mundell (1968).

———. 1961b. *A theory of optimum currency areas*.

———. 1969. A case for a European currency. Paper presented at the American Management Association Conference, December.

———. 1973. A plan for a European currency. In *The economics of common currencies*, edited by H. G. Johnson and A. K. Swoboda. London: Allen & Unwin.

———. 1995. The International Monetary System: The missing factor. *Journal of Policy Modeling* 17 (5): 479-492.

———. 1997a. Currency areas, common currencies, and EMU. *American Economic Review* 87 (2): 214-16.

———. 1997b. Updating the agenda for monetary union. In *Optimum currency areas*, edited by Mario I. Blejer, Jacob A. Frenkel, Leonardo Leiderman, and Assaf Razin, in cooperation with David M. Cheney. Washington, DC: International Monetary Fund.

———. 2000. Money and the sovereignty of the state. *Zagreb Journal of Economics* 4 (5): 3-54.

Nussbaum, A. 1950. *Money in the law.* 2d ed. Brooklyn, NY: Foundation.

Saggs, H.W.F. 1995. *Babylonians.* Norman: University of Oklahoma Press.

Schevill, Ferdinand. 1909. *Siena: The history of a medieval commune.* New York: Harper & Row.

ANNALS, *AAPSS*, **579**, January 2002

The Euro, the European Central Bank, and the International Monetary System

By DOMINICK SALVATORE

ABSTRACT: The creation of the euro at the beginning of 1999 represents one of the most significant events in international finance since the end of World War II. Never in the past had a group of sovereign nations voluntarily given up their national currency for a common currency. The article begins by reviewing the benefits and costs of the euro on the participating countries; it then examines the role of the European Central Bank (ECB) in the conduct of monetary policy in the European Monetary Union, as well as its effect on the euro/dollar and euro/yen exchange rates; finally, the article analyzes the effect that the ECB has and is likely to have on the functioning of the international monetary system.

Dominick Salvatore is Distinguished Professor of Economics at Fordham University in New York. He is chairperson of the Economics Section of the New York Academy of Sciences and was president of the International Trade and Finance Association in 1994-95. He has taught at the Universities of Vienna, Rome, Triest, and Krems. He published extensively in the field of international trade and finance and is editor of the Economics Handbook Series for the Greenwood Press.

THE creation of the euro at the beginning of 1999 represents one of the most significant events in international finance since the end of World War II—second in importance only to the formation of the Bretton Woods System in 1947 and its collapse in 1973. Never in the past had a group of sovereign nations voluntarily given up their national currency for a common currency. Eleven of the fifteen members of the European Union (EU) adopted the new currency at its inception, and Greece joined them in January 2001. Only the United Kingdom, Sweden, and Denmark have thus far refused to participate, but they reserved the right to join later.

The euro will begin to circulate as the currency of the European Monetary Union (EMU) in January 2001, and the national currencies of the participating countries will be completely withdrawn from circulation by February 2002, when the euro will become the sole currency of the EMU.

This article begins by reviewing the benefits and costs of the euro for the participating countries; it will then examine the role of the European Central Bank (ECB) in the conduct of monetary policy in the EMU, as well as its effect on the euro/dollar and euro/yen exchange rates; finally, the article will analyze the effect that the ECB has and is likely to have on the functioning of the international monetary system.

THE BENEFITS OF THE EURO

The effects of the introduction of the euro have been amply examined in both Europe and in the United States, and most economists on both sides of the Atlantic generally agree with the analysis and with the benefits and costs that are likely to result from its introduction. The benefits are the following: (1) the elimination of the need to exchange currencies among EU members (this has been estimated to save as much as $30 billion per year), (2) the elimination of excessive volatility among EMU currencies (fluctuations will occur only between the euro and the dollar, the yen, and the currencies of other non-EMU nations), (3) more rapid economic and financial integration among EU members, (4) the ability of the ECB to conduct a more expansionary monetary policy than that practically imposed in the past by the Bundesbank on the EU countries, and (5) greater economic discipline for countries, such as Italy, Belgium, and Greece, that seemed unwilling or unable to bring their fiscal house in order without externally imposed conditions.

Other benefits of the euro for EMU members are (6) seignorage from the use of the euro as an international currency (the use of the dollar as an international currency confers about 10 to 15 billion dollars in benefits to the United States, and the expectation is that the euro could provide as much seignorage to the EMU), (7) reduction in the cost of borrowing in international financial markets (it has been estimated that the U.S. cost of borrowing on international financial markets is about 0.25 to 0.50 percentage points lower than it would have been the case if the dollar were not used as an international currency, for a total savings of about 10 to 15 billion dollars, and the expectation is that the EMU could gain as much from the use of the euro as an international currency), and last but not least, (8) the greater economic and political importance that the EU will acquire in international affairs.

There is, however, a concern in the United States that the EU might use this increased power to become more confrontational in transatlantic relations (see Feldstein 2000). To be sure, when there are real and important disagreements, it is only proper and fair for the EU to use its newly acquired clout to protect and foster its economic and political interests. The hope, however, is that it will not pursue anti-American policies to provide the glue that unites and keeps the union together, or for its own sake simply to assert its power. Similarly, the increased economic and political importance of the EU in international affairs will check American power now that the fear of communism has vanished and the Soviet Union has collapsed as a military superpower. While some Americans may fear the competition that the euro will provide for the U.S. dollar as an international or vehicle currency, this competition will be beneficial, not harmful, to the United States in the long run because it will impose more discipline in the conduct of its economic policies than has been the case in previous decades.

THE MAJOR PROBLEM WITH THE EURO

The most serious (and yet untested) problem that the establishment of an ECB and the euro may create for the EMU is a member nation's response to an asymmetric demand or supply shock. It is practically inevitable that a large and diverse single-currency area as the EMU will face periodic asymmetric shocks that will affect various member nations differently and drive their economies out of alignment. In such a case, there is little that a nation adversely affected can do. It is clear that the nation cannot use expansionary monetary policy or devalue (or allow its currency to depreciate) to overcome a recession or an excessive slowdown in growth because of the existence of the single currency. Fiscal discipline also prevents the nation from adopting an expansionary fiscal policy (see Salvatore 1996, 1997, 1998b). The only possibility is downward wage adjustment. Since wages are rigid downward, however, this instrument has never been used, and it is very likely that labor would not allow it to be used (see Salvatore 1998b).

A single currency works well in the United States because if one of its regions suffered from an asymmetric shock, workers would move quickly and in great numbers out of the region adversely affected by the shock and toward areas of the nation with greater employment opportunities. This escape hatch is not generally available to Europe to the same extent as in the United States because of much lower labor mobility. The Organization for Economic Cooperation and Development (OECD) (1986), the European Commission (1990), and the International Monetary Fund (IMF) (2000b, chap. 6) found that labor mobility among EU members is one-third to one-half that among U.S. regions. The main reasons for lower labor mobility among EU members are language barriers, inflexible housing markets, and the short period since free labor movement has been possible (the single market was established only in 1992). Otherwise, how could we account for the persistence of a rate of unemployment of 9 percent in Germany and 5 percent in nearby Netherlands? This difference in unemployment rates among EU member nations is much higher than among U.S. regions.

It is true that Bini-Smaghi and Vori (1993) showed that the present twelve member states of the EMU are more alike than the fifty states of the United States. But this comparison does not make much sense. First of all, we simply cannot compare twelve countries of the EMU with the fifty states of the United States. If we used for the comparison the different regions of the EMU (i.e., looked at the German *lander* and the Italian *regioni*, as we should) we would very likely find that this larger group of EMU regions is more different than the fifty states of the United States. But even this completely misses the point. What is important is not how different the regions of the United States are as compared to the EMU regions but rather how much economic flexibility and labor mobility there is in the United States as compared to in the EMU—and these, as we have seen, are much lower in the EMU than in the United States. In addition, in the United States there is a great deal of federal fiscal redistribution in favor of an adversely affected region (see Bayoumi and Masson 1994). In the EU, on the other hand, fiscal redistribution cannot be of much help because the EU budget is less than 1.5 percent of the EU's GDP, and almost half of it is devoted to its Common Agricultural Policy. Furthermore, real wages are more downwardly flexible in the United States than in the EU.

Facing an asymmetric shock, the United Kingdom and Italy opted to leave the Exchange Rate Mechanism (ERM) of the European Monetary System (EMS) in September 1992 and, by allowing their currencies to depreciate and by lowering their interest rates, were able to move out of the deep recession in which they found themselves. With a single currency, this policy move would have been impossible. Remaining in the ERM in September 1992 would have meant Britain and Italy standing idly by and watching their unemployment rates increase from already very high levels until the recession came to an end by itself, gradually, over time. No government can afford to stand idly by and remain inert in such a situation. In any event, massive speculation against the pound and the lira forced a depreciation of those currencies in September 1992, an event that helped them overcome the recession. It is true that the establishment of a single currency will prevent such speculative attacks, but that also means that with a single currency, the nation will have almost no policy choice available to overcome a negative asymmetric shock. It will simply have to wait for the recession to be cured by itself.

Supporters of the single currency reply that the requirements for the establishment of single currency will necessarily increase labor market flexibility, and by promoting greater intra-EU trade, a single currency will also dampen nationally differentiated business cycles. Furthermore, it is pointed out that highly integrated EU capital markets can make up for low labor market flexibility and provide an adequate automatic response to asymmetric shocks. These automatic responses may not be sufficient, however. It is also true that meeting the Maastricht criteria will increase labor market flexibility, but this is at best a slow process, and it may not be allowed to take place to a sufficient degree if EU labor insists on retaining many of its present benefits (such as strong job security and high unemployment pay). Furthermore, "excessive" capital flows may work perversely by reducing the incentive for the introduction of fundamental labor-market-liberalizing measures, and by pushing up the euro exchange rate, they may even produce supply shocks of their own in the EMU member.

In the final analysis, a major asymmetric shock may result in unbearable pressure within the EU because of limited labor mobility, grossly inadequate fiscal redistribution, and a ECB that will probably want to keep monetary conditions tight to hold inflation at bay and to make the euro as strong as the dollar. Some indication of the type of problem that the EU may be facing is given by the fact that during the past two years, Ireland has faced very high growth and inflation rates while

TABLE 1

PROBABILITY OF ASYMMETRIC SHOCKS AND LABOR MARKET INFLEXIBILITY

Probability of Asymmetric Shocks	Labor Market Inflexibility	
	Low	High
Low	Austria Netherlands	Belgium France Germany Denmark[a]
High	Ireland Portugal United Kingdom[a]	Finland Greece Italy Spain Sweden[a]

SOURCE: International Monetary Fund (2000a, 194),

a. European Union but a non–European Monetary Union member.

Germany and Italy were growing sluggishly. This meant that the ECB should have tightened monetary policy to cool Ireland off and adopted an expansionary monetary policy to stimulate growth in Germany and Italy. A much larger asymmetric shock could create a much greater problem in the EMU, and it is impossible to anticipate a key EMU member's reaction to it. It is true that in an international financial system ever more integrated, the ability of a nation to conduct even a semi-autonomous monetary and exchange rate policy is very limited, but with a single currency, a nation will not be able to conduct any monetary or exchange rate policy.

Table 1 identifies the EMU and the EU members with a lower and a higher-than-average probability of facing an asymmetric shock and with a lower and a higher-than-average labor-market inflexibility. The table shows that Finland, Greece, Italy, and Spain among EMU members (as well as Sweden, an EU but a non-EMU member) have a high probability of facing an asymmetric shock (in relations to the EMU average) and have the most inflexible labor markets. These are the countries that are likely to face the greatest problems and costs from belonging to the EMU in the future.

As to whether economic integration within the EMU reduces or increases the frequency and magnitude of asymmetric shocks, there is a great deal of disagreement. Bayoumi and Eichengreen (1993, 1996) provided econometric evidence that asymmetric shocks among EMU countries are more frequent and of greater magnitude than among U.S. states. This conclusion is shared by Krugman (1993), who pointed out that the adoption of a single currency was likely to lead to greater regional specialization and, therefore, to a greater likelihood of asymmetric shocks over time. Frankel and Rose (1998), on the other hand, argued that greater economic integration (through trade and capital flows) was likely to result in more highly correlated cyclical conditions as the economic structure of EMU members adapts to the currency union. Although the available data to date are insufficient to resolve this disagreement, most economists do believe that greater economic and financial integration does enhance the effectiveness of the common monetary policy in member nations (see Fratianni, Salvatore, and von Hagen 1997; OECD 1999, 2000a; Angeloni and Mojon 2000).

THE EUROPEAN CENTRAL BANK AND THE COMMON MONETARY POLICY

On 30 June 1998, the ECB was inaugurated in Frankfurt with Wim Duisenberg, the former head of the Dutch Central Bank, as its first governor. The ECB was established as the operating arm of the European System of Central Banks or Eurosystem, a federal structure of the national central banks (NCBs) of the euro area. The ECB assumed responsibility for unionwide monetary policy for the eleven countries of the euro zone forming the EMU, as scheduled, on 1 January 1999. ECB's monetary decisions are made by a majority vote of the Governing Council, composed of a six-member executive board (which includes the ECB president, Wim Duisenberg, and its chief economist and former chief economist of the Bundesbank, Otmar Issing) serving a single, nonrenewable eight-year term and the heads of the eleven NCBs (twelve since January 2001 when Greece was admitted).

The Maastricht Treaty entrusted the ECB with the sole mandate of pursuing price stability, defined as an annual inflation rate of less than 2 percent in the medium term for the euro area as a whole (Duisenberg 1999; Issing 2000a). Specifically, the Governing Council adopted the following definition of price stability: "Price stability shall be defined as a year-on-year increase in the Harmonized Index of Consumer Prices (HICP) for the euro area as a whole of less than 2% to be maintained over the medium term" (ECB 1999, 40). This fact makes the ECB the world's most independent central bank. The ECB is only required to brief regularly the European parliament on its activities, but the European parliament has no power to influence ECB's decisions.

This situation contrasts sharply to that under which the U.S. Fed, which is constitutionally required to pursue both price stability (by the Federal Reserve Act of 1913) and full employment (by the Employment Act of 1946 and the Employment and Balanced Growth Act of 1978), operates, a circumstance that limits somewhat its effectiveness as an inflation fighter when a conflict arises between its two goals. Furthermore, while the U.S. Congress could pass laws reducing the independence of the Federal Reserve Board, the Maastricht Treaty itself would have to be amended by the legislatures or voters in every member country for the ECB's statute to be changed. The almost total independence of the ECB from political influences was deliberate so as to shield the ECB from political influences that might force it to provide excessive monetary stimulus and thus lead to inflation. But this also led to the criticism that the ECB is distant and undemocratic and not responsive to the economic needs of EMU citizens.

The conduct of monetary policy (i.e., the setting of interest rates) is based on the analysis of the so-called two pillars. The first pillar of the Eurosystem's monetary policy strategy is the announced money-supply target or, more precisely, the quantitative reference value for monetary growth by the Governing Council. This is a growth of the broad money aggregate M3 of 4.5 percent, which is believed to be compatible with price stability. However, since it may be difficult to define and interpret measures of the eurowide money supply and guarantee that a stable relationship exists between the money supply and inflation, the Governing Council decided to supplement its announced quantitative reference value for monetary growth with a second pillar in the form of a broadly based assessment of the outlook of price developments and risks to price stability to monitor performance against its inflation target better. This assessment of the outlook for prices or second pillar is made by using a wide range of financial and other economic indicators that include wages and unit labor costs, fiscal policy indicators, financial market indicators (such as asset prices), and the exchange rate of the euro (Ising 2000b).

The Eurosystem adopts a neutral stance about the international role of the euro. That is, its stated aim is neither to hinder nor to promote its international role (say, as a challenger to the U.S. dollar) but to leave its value entirely to market forces. The belief is that doing otherwise would compromise the achievement of its main goal of price stability. Of course, to the extent that the Eurosystem succeeds in maintaining price stability, it will also inevitably increase the international role of the euro. The Eurosystem's choice not to use exchange rate targets for the euro is based on the correct conviction that the exchange rate of the euro is the outcome of monetary and fiscal policies, as well as of cyclical and structural forces, in the euro area and abroad, and should not itself be an objective or aim of the Eurosystem. Only if the euro were to become grossly misaligned would the EMU Ministers of Finance (who are ultimately responsible for the exchange rare of the euro) issue general orientation statements on what it considers an appropriate range for the international value of the euro.

Although the Eurosystem has neither an explicit nor an implicit exchange rate target or range for the euro, the exchange rate of the euro has important implications for prices in the euro area because it directly affects import prices and indirectly determines the international competitiveness of the euro area. Those implications are the reason that the Eurosystem included the exchange rate of the euro among the second-pillar indicators. In general, then, the exchange rate policy of the euro is ultimately in the hands of politicians rather than of the ECB. This situation is somewhat puzzling because monetary and exchange rate policies are closely related, and it is impossible to conduct a truly independent policy in one without the other in a world of mostly unrestricted international capital flows.

Be that as it may, the first two and a half years of operation of the EMU (i.e., until the middle of 2001) were somewhat turbulent, with politicians almost continuously demanding lower interest rates to stimulate growth and the ECB increasing them for fear of resurgent inflation in the euro area (only in May 2001 did the ECB reduced the interest rate by a token 0.25 percentage point from 4.75 percent to 4.50 percent)—probably to placate its critics. The conflict in the conduct of a unionwide monetary policy was also evidenced during this period by the fact that nations such as Ireland and Spain faced excessive growth and inflationary pressures, requiring a more restrictive monetary policy, while other nations (such as Germany and Italy) faced anemic growth, requiring lower interest rates. As it was, the ECB adopted an intermediate monetary policy, with interest rates possibly being too low for Ireland and Spain and too high for Germany and Italy (OECD 2000b).

There is also the question of the effectiveness of a eurowide monetary policy on the various EMU members. Previous research by the IMF (1998) indicated that a rise in interest rates took twice as long to have a significant effect in Austria, Belgium, Finland, Germany, and the Netherlands than in France, Italy, Portugal, and Spain but that the final impact was almost twice as large, on average, in the first group of countries than in the second because of their different financial structure. For example, the IMF found that Spanish banks passed an interest rate increase on to customers within three months, while German banks took one year or more because of their closer relationship with customers. Similarly, a country such as Italy, where adjustable-rate debt is common, responds faster to interest-rate changes than countries such as Germany, where fixed-rate debt is more common. Although the euro will very likely lead to the narrowing of these country differences over time, they are likely to persist at least for several years to come.

A related problem that the EU is likely to face in the conduct of its monetary policy is that various nations are likely to experience very different growth rates (from the estimated trend of real EMU's GDP growth of between 2.0 percent and 2.5 percent per year). Would Germany accept a growth rate much lower than France's, year in and year out, if that is what would result from a common monetary policy without Germany's being able to provide much fiscal stimulus (because of budget restrictions imposed by the Maastricht Treaty) or other strategic help to some industries deemed important for growth? It is true that long-run growth depends primarily on structural conditions and market liberalization and deregulation, but the demand for monetary policy to do its part may be irresistible in a large country facing a constantly lower growth rate than the other EMU member countries and may result in great political conflicts within the EMU? This proposition is especially true in the current situation in which most EMU countries face strong opposition from organized labor to the reduction in social benefits, the increase in the pensionable age, and the ability of firms to fire workers when justified by economic conditions.

It is true that many of these changes would have to be made anyway in the long run, but the euro is creating more pressure to accelerate the time framework for restructuring the economy, and this fact is likely to impose more pressure on the ECB to conduct a monetary policy more accommodating to long-run growth. The ECB and politicians will certainly blame market forces when introducing these changes, but they will have to answer to an electorate that does not necessarily accept the American model of capitalism and that many European politicians themselves have in the past attacked severely to justify the much higher unemployment rate and lower growth rate in Europe than in the United States.

In addition, fiscal policy (which remains a national prerogative) cannot be of much help in overcoming differences in cyclical or growth conditions among EMU members because the Stability and Growth Pact mandates that member countries keep budget deficits below 3 percent of GDP and the debt at less than 60 percent of GDP. With most countries either at or above the permitted limits, fiscal policy cannot be of much use to overcome differences in growth rates among EMU members. In the case of Italy, fiscal policy will have to be restrictive to lower government debt to the allowed limit precisely at the time when its growth is slowest among EMU members.

THE ECB AND THE INTERNATIONAL VALUE OF THE EURO

The euro was introduced on 1 January 1999 at the value of $1.17; it rose to $1.18 on 4 January (the first business day of the new year), but defying almost all predictions, it declined almost continuously, reaching near parity to the dollar at the

FIGURE 1
DAILY EXCHANGE RATE: U.S. DOLLAR AND THE EURO

SOURCE: Federal Reserve statistical release—foreign exchange rates historical data.

FIGURE 2
DAILY EXCHANGE RATE: JAPANESE YEN AND THE EURO

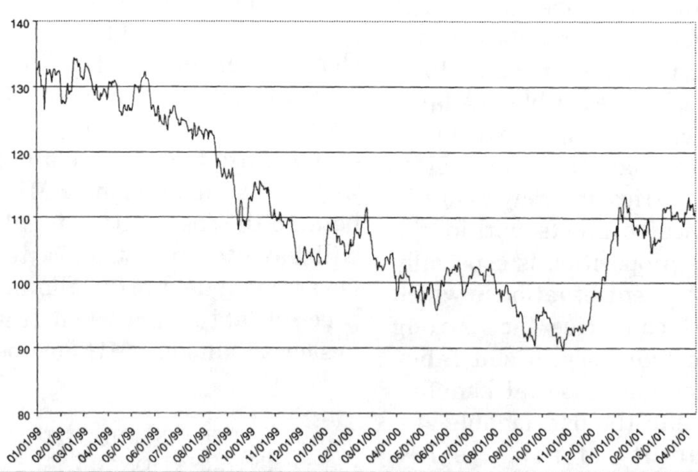

SOURCE: Historical currency exchange rate; see www.oanda.com.

end of 1999 then falling to a low of $0.82 on 26 October 2000 (see Figures 1 and 2).

Much has been written on the reasons for the continued depreciation and weakness of the euro with respect to the U.S. dollar and the Japanese yen (see Salvatore 2002a). The fact remains that, defying almost all explanations, the euro has weakened and remained relatively weak since its introduction two and a half years ago. One proposal advanced for strengthening it was the adoption of a target zone for the euro-dollar and euro-yen exchange rates. These were forcefully advanced during mid-1999 by the finance ministers of France (Dominique Stauss-Khan) and Germany (Oscar Lafontaine). But then, the discussion of target zones subsided. Historically, target zones have never really worked. For example, the implicit target zones established by the 1987 Louvre Accord soon collapsed. Even when intervention in foreign exchange markets seems to work (as in the case of the 1985 Plaza Agreement), that intervention was moving in the direction of markets. When counter to markets trends, foreign exchange interventions almost never work.

Nevertheless, the ECB in concert with the New York Fed (which operates as the U.S. central bank for international operations) and the central banks of Japan, France, the United Kingdom, and Canada, in a move that caught the markets by surprise, intervened in foreign exchange markets for the first time on Friday, 22 September 2000, in support of the euro, which had fallen in previous days to its all-time low of $0.82. By the end of the day, the euro had risen to $0.88, but in the following days, the euro fell back to its preintervention level. At the beginning of November 2000, the ECB intervened again several times (but alone) in foreign exchange markets in support of the euro but to no avail. Not even the uncertainty surrounding the election of the president of the United States was sufficient to lift the value of the euro. Only when it became evident, toward the end of November 2000, that the growth rate of the United States had declined sharply and that, as a result, the EU was expected to grow more rapidly than the United States in 2001 did the net capital outflow from Europe to the United States dry up and the euro started to appreciate significantly against the dollar (it reached the value of $0.96 on Friday, 5 January 2001). At the time, this trend was expected to continue with the euro reaching parity with the U.S. by mid-2001.

By the end of May 2001, however, the euro had fallen back to below $0.90 (it was $0.86 on 23 May 2001) as markets anticipated that growth and profitability in the United States would resume in the second half of 2001. Another possible explanation for the strength of the dollar relative to the euro was the continued higher growth of labor productivity in the United States than in the EU. Only if the current U.S. slowdown kills the growth of its labor productivity—so the argument goes—will the euro probably appreciate significantly with respect to the dollar. Still another possible reason for the continued strength of the dollar (and weakness of the euro) is that perhaps investors still see the United States as a safe haven in times (such as the present one) of economic turmoil (due to the financial crisis in Turkey and Argentina, the continued economic crisis in Japan, and danger of renewed financial instability in Brazil and Russia).

As is clear from the above, there is no shortage of explanations for the current strength of the dollar and weakness of the euro, and, as some older explanations are contradicted by emerging facts and evidence, new ones are confidently introduced. Of course, should the dollar begin to depreciate heavily with respect to the euro in the future, all sorts of reasons will be advanced to explain it. In short, there is no economic model or theory that can consistently and accurately predict exchange rate movements in the short run because fundamental forces at work are easily and frequently overwhelmed by transitory ones and "news." One cannot forget the glaring forecasting mistake made by Richard Portes and Helen Rey (1998) at the time the euro/dollar exchange rate was set in the fall of 1998 that that the euro would soon become very strong (i.e., appreciate heavily against the dollar) and could even replace the dollar as the leading international currency within a year of its introduction.

Also important is the relationship between the euro and the currencies of the EU countries that have so far refused to join the euro (the British pound, the Swedish krona, and the Danish krone). The exchange rate between the euro and these other currencies is also likely to be subject to high volatility and misalignments without the establishment of an exchange rate mechanism similar to the ERM. But, as the experience with the 1992-93 ERM crisis showed, such a system is unstable and crisis prone (Salvatore 1996). It is, however, in the interest of Britain, Sweden, and Denmark to enforce strong limits on the fluctuation of their currencies with respect to the euro in anticipation of their possible joining it in the future and to avoid importing financial instability in the meantime.

THE ECB, THE EURO, AND THE FUNCTIONING OF THE INTERNATIONAL MONETARY SYSTEM

The introduction of the euro on 1 January 1999 proceeded smoothly and did not create problems for the working of the international monetary system (Salvatore 2002b). What may create problems is the fact that with most trade and financial relations conducted within, rather than among, the three major trading blocks (the EU, NAFTA, and Asia centered on Japan), there will normally be less concern about the euro/dollar and euro/yen exchange rate than intrablock rates and less interest in intervening in foreign exchange markets to stabilize exchange rates (only with the deepening depreciation and undervaluation of the euro in 2000 did interest in the euro exchange rate came to the forefront). With less interest and less intervention, it is likely that the euro/dollar and euro/yen exchange rate will continue to be volatile in the future. This tendency arises also because the exchange rate is one of only a few market-equilibrating mechanisms operating among the three major trading blocks. Exchange rates among the three leading currencies are likely to be especially volatile when the three blocks face different cyclical conditions and shifting market perceptions about economic and financial prospects (Buiter 2000).

By adding to transaction costs, large exchange rate volatility will affect the volume and pattern of international trade. These costs, however, are not very large, and firms engaged in international trade and finance can easily and cheaply cover their foreign exchange risk. Potentially more damaging to the flow of international trade and investments than excessive exchange rate volatility are the wide and persistent exchange rate misalignments (as they seem to have developed in 2000 and 2001 between the euro, on one hand, and the dollar and the yen, on the other). An overvalued currency has the effect of an export tax and an import subsidy for the nation, and as such, it reduces the international competitiveness of the nation or trading block and distorts the pattern of specialization, trade, and payments. A significant exchange rate misalignment that persists for years cannot possibly be hedged away and can impose significant real costs on the economy in the form of unemployment, idle capacity, and bankruptcy, and these may lead to serious protection and trade disputes. This is exactly what happened when the U.S. dollar became grossly overvalued in the mid-1980s.

The only way to limit excessive exchange rate misalignment among the euro, the dollar, and the yen is by greater macroeconomic policy coordination among the three major trading blocks than has hereto been practiced. Successful international policy coordination did prevent the financial crises in emerging markets (Mexico in 1994-95, East Asia in 1997-99, Russia in summer 1998, Brazil in early 1999, and Argentina and Turkey in 2000-01) from spreading or having a lasting damaging effect on other emerging markets and on advanced market economies. But policy coordination among the Untied States, the euro area, and Japan has been only limited and sporadic rather than extensive and continuous effect in the past, and it is difficult to expect that it will be much higher in the near future. Yet, more policy coordination is exactly what seems to be required to prevent the further development and crystallization of the tripolar (New York, London-Frankfurt, and Tokyo) world financial system, characterized, as it is, by the huge and rapid international capital flows among them, from leading to large exchange rate misalignments and financial instability in the future (IMF 2000a, chap. 4).

To be sure, by reducing the number of key currencies, the euro simplifies international cooperation among the major economic areas and makes exchanging information and views more efficient. This simplification will be even greater if and when the United Kingdom adopts the euro. At the same time, a trade or exchange rate dispute that before the creation of the euro could have been between the United States and, say, France now becomes a dispute between the United States and the entire euro area. In short, simplification, by having to deal with far fewer major currencies with the euro than without it, also brings the danger that future disputes will be disputes among titans and that trade and exchange rate relations among the major three currency blocks will be governed by strategic behavior and policies—with all of their inherent uncertainties and dangers. The world was certainly simpler (although not necessarily fairer) when there was one hegemonic power (the United States) and only one dominant international or vehicle currency (the dollar) (Tavlas 1997).

Finally, there is the challenge of the representation of the ECB on international bodies such as the IMF, OECD, and Bank for International Settlements (BIS). As it is, the ECB participates in many international meetings and fora, such as those held by the IMF, OECD, BIS, G7, G20, and so forth, but as an observer rather than a full voting member because most of these institutions and forums restrict membership to individual nations rather than to currency areas. Nevertheless, the ECB's observer status allows it to make its views known. Of course, this situation could change in the future, and the ECB might come increasingly to represent the entire euro area in international bodies and deliberations.

References

Angeloni, I., and B. Mojon. 2000. After the changeover: Three conditions for a successful single monetary policy. *Euro* 50:19-28.

Bayoumi, T., and B. Eichengreen. 1993. Shocking aspects of European monetary unification. In *Adjustment and growth in the European monetary union*, edited by F. Torres and F. Giavazzi, 241-60. Cambridge: Cambridge University Press.

———. 1996. Operationalizing the theory of optimum currency areas. CEPR discussion paper no. 1484. London: Center for Economic Policy Research.

Bayoumi, T., and P. Masson. 1994. Fiscal flows in the United States and Canada: Lessons for monetary union in Europe. CEPR Discussion paper no. 1057. London: Center for Economic Policy Research.

Bini-Smaghi, L., and S. Vori. 1993. *Rating the EC as an optimal currency area*. Rome: Bank of Italy.

Buiter, W. H. 2000. Optimal currency areas: Why does the exchange rate regime matter? CEPR discussion paper no. 2366, January. London: Center for Economic Policy Research.

Duisenberg, W. F. 1999. Economic and monetary union in Europe—The challenges ahead. In New Challenges for Monetary Policy, symposium sponsored by the Federal Reserve Bank of Kansas City.

European Central Bank (ECB). 1999. The stability-oriented policies monetary policy strategy of the Eurosystem. *ECB Monthly Bulletin*, January, 39-50.

European Commission. 1990. One market, one money. *European Economy* 44:29-34.

Feldstein, M. 2000. The European Central Bank and the euro: The first year. *Journal of Policy Modeling*, May: 345-54.

Frankel, J., and A. Rose. 1998. The endogeneity of optimum currency criteria. *Economic Journal* 108:1009-25.

Fratianni, M., D. Salvatore, and J. von Hagen, eds. 1997. *Handbook of macroeconomic policies in open economies.* Westport CT: Greenwood.

International Monetary Fund. 1998. The real effects of monetary policy in the European Union. Working paper no. 160. Washington, DC: International Monetary Fund.

———. 2000a. Exchange rate regimes in an increasingly integrated world economy. Occasional paper no. 195. Washington, DC: International Monetary Fund.

———. 2000b. World economic outlook supporting studies. Washington, DC: International Monetary Fund.

Issing, O. 2000a. The ECB's monetary policy: Experience after the first year. *Journal of Policy Modeling* May:325-43.

———. 2000b. The monetary policy of the ECB in a world of uncertainty. In *Monetary policy-making under uncertainty* ECB and Center for Financial Studies, 3-9. University of Frankfurt.

Krugman, P. 1994. Lessons of Massachusetts for EMU. In *Adjustment and growth in the European Monetary Union*, edited by F. Torres and F. Giavazzi, 241-60. Cambridge: Cambridge University Press.

Organization for Economic Cooperation and Development. 1986. *Flexibility in the labor market*. Paris: OECD.

———. 1999. *EMU: Facts, challenges and policies*. Paris: OECD.

———. 2000a. *EMU: One year on*. Paris: OECD.

———. 2000b. *Financial market trends*. Paris: OECD.

Portes, R., and H. Rey. 1998. The emergence of the euro as an international currency. In *Prospects and challenges for the euro*, edited by D. Begg, J. von Hagen, C. Wyplosz, and K. Zimmermann, 305-43. Oxford: Blackwell.

Salvatore, D. 1996. The European Monetary System: Crisis and future. *Open Economies Review*, December:593-615.

———. 1997. The unresolved problem with the EMS and EMU. *American Economic Review* May:224-26.

———. 1998a. Europe's structural and competitiveness problems. *World Economy*, March:189-205.

———. 1998b. The operation and future of the International Monetary System. In *Ideas for the future of the International Monetary System*, edited by M. Fratianni, D. Salvatore, and P. Savona, 5-45. Hingham, MA: Kluwer.

———. 2002a. The euro: Expectations and performance. *Eastern Economic Journal*, January.

———. 2002b. The architecture and future of the international monetary sytem. In *The open economy macromodel: past, present and future*, edited by W. Young. Hingham, MA: Kluwer.

Tavlas, G. S. 1997. The international use of the U.S. dollar: An optimum currency area perspective. *World Economy*, 709-47.

ANNALS, *AAPSS*, **579**, January 2002

The Road to the Euro: Exchange Rate Arrangements in European Transition Economies

By EDUARD HOCHREITER and HELMUT WAGNER

ABSTRACT: This article examines the monetary policy road of the ten candidate countries from central and eastern Europe (CEE-10) on their way to EU accession and ultimately to adoption of the euro. The authors proceed in three steps. First, they describe the evolution of the monetary regime of the CEE-10 since the demise of the centrally planned economic system. Second, they deal with the currency crises of emerging market economies in the 1990s and develop potential lessons for the CEE-10. Third, they delineate the road map for the candidate countries by looking at both formal requirements and economic challenges that these countries have to meet before they can adopt the euro.

Eduard Hochreiter serves as senior adviser and head of economic studies of the Oesterreichische Nationalbank. He teaches at the University of Economics and Business Administration, Vienna, and at the University of Vienna. He also serves at the Council of Management of SUERF and since 2000 as its secretary general. In addition, he is an alternate member of the Economic and Finance Committee of the EU, a member of the Board of the Konstanz Seminar on Monetary Theory and Policy, of the Research Advisory Board of the Czech National Bank, of the Board of the Friends of the Summer School of the University of Vienna, and of the Editorial Board of Perspectiven der Wirtschaftspolitik.

Helmut Wagner is a professor in economics and chairholder in macroeconomics at University of Hagen. He has been a visiting professor at the University of California (1982-83), MIT (1987), the Bank of Japan's Institute for Monetary and Economic Studies (1988), Princeton University (1991-92), AICGS / The Johns Hopkins University (1997), and Harvard University (2000) and has served as a consultant to the International Monetary Fund. He has published numerous books and articles in refereed journals on macroeconomics and monetary economics, international economics, and development economics.

TEN countries in central and eastern Europe (CEE-10) as well as Cyprus and Malta ("the candidate countries") are presently negotiating their entry into the European Union (EU).[1] A precondition for EU accession is the fulfillment of the so-called Copenhagen criteria, which were decided on at the European Council at the level of heads of states or government in Copenhagen in June 1993. The Copenhagen summit defined the following criteria for EU membership for the candidate countries: (1) the stability of institutions guaranteeing democracy, the rule of law, human rights, and respect for the protection of minorities; (2) the existence of a functioning market economy and market forces within the union; and (3) the ability to take on the obligations of membership, including adherence to the aims of political, economic, and monetary union. This article will deal with issues relevant for monetary policy only.

According to the current schedule, a first wave of candidate countries can be expected to enter the EU around 2005. However, it is often forgotten that the new entrants will, at the time of EU entry, also become members of Economic and Monetary Union (EMU) as phase 3 of EMU commenced on 1 January 1999, and an opt-out clause like the one granted to the United Kingdom and Denmark will not be available to them. Yet, as they will not be able to adopt the euro at that time, they will become EMU members with a derogation until they fulfill the Maastricht convergence criteria. These criteria are contained in article 109j of the treaty establishing the European Community and defined in protocol 6 of that treaty (the Maastricht Treaty), and they comprise the

1. inflation criterion (an inflation rate not more than 1.5 percent higher than those of the three best performing EU countries over the latest twelve months);
2. fiscal convergence criteria: these criteria restrict the government budget deficit and the government debt to certain (politically accepted) levels. A country that wants to participate in the EMU may not have

   - a government budget deficit higher than 3 percent of GDP or
   - a government debt ratio of more than 60 percent of GDP or sufficiently fast approaching that level;

3. interest rate criterion (an average nominal long-term interest rate that does not exceed by more than two percentage points that of the three best performing member states in terms of price stability);
4. exchange rate criterion (participation in the Exchange Rate Mechanism (ERM) of the European Monetary System within the normal fluctuation margin without severe tensions for at least two years).

On fulfillment of these criteria, they can adopt the euro and thereby relinquish their own currencies. The shortest possible period from EU membership to the adoption of the euro is two years. Consequently, counted from today (2001), the new member states could adopt the euro in some six years from now, that is, around 2007-08 at the earliest. Six years seems to be quite a short period of time in view of the real economic adjustments that are still necessary. Yet, from the perspective of financial markets, six years is a very long time that can be beset with vulnerabilities and risks.

In this article, we travel the (monetary policy) road of the CEE-10 on their way to accede to the EU and ultimately to adopt the euro. In doing so, we also point to any lessons that might be drawn from the monetary policy experience of emerging market economies in Asia and the Western Hemisphere during the past decade.[2] Considering the very specific economic and political circumstances in which the CEE-10 have found themselves since the demise of the centrally planned economic system, a number of distinct and unique features relative to other emerging market economies in the Western hemisphere and in Asia have to be borne in mind. First and foremost, the CEE-10 (and the other transition economies) need to construct their economic and political system from scratch. Second, they desire to accede to the EU as soon as possible. Third, their trade with the EU accounts for more than 60 percent of their total foreign trade. Fourth, they need to complete capital account liberalization before EU entry, that is, within three to four years.

The article proceeds as follows: section 2 sketches the evolution of the monetary regime of the CEE-10 since the demise of the centrally planned economic system. Section 3 deals with the currency crises in the 1990s and develops potential lessons for the candidate countries. Section 4 contains a road map to the adoption of the euro for the CEE-10. Section 5 concludes.

THE EVOLUTION OF EXCHANGE RATE ARRANGEMENTS IN THE CEE-10 IN THE 1990s

The design of the monetary framework and the decision on the exchange rate regime form an integral part of any macroeconomic policy set. The choice will, inter alia, be influenced by the country's size, the rate of inflation, the degree of capital account liberalization, and the state of development of the financial sector, the level of foreign exchange reserves, and the country's institutional structure. For the candidate countries under review, the task has been especially daunting as each of them needed to build democratic and market-oriented structures while implementing stability-oriented macroeconomic policies in a way that included the earning of monetary policy credibility quickly without increasing the real cost of stabilization.

Thus, given the high but greatly varying levels of inflation prevalent in all countries, their need to integrate quickly into the world economy (while rectifying their relative prices), and to earn credibility quickly, most of the CEE-10 initially opted for one form of a peg or another (see Table 1).

TABLE 1

EXCHANGE RATE ARRANGEMENTS IN CENTRAL AND EASTERN EUROPEAN COUNTRIES

	Exchange Rate Arrangements					
	Fixed		Limited Flexibility		More Flexibility	
Country	Currency Board Arrangement	Conventional Peg	Explicit Narrow Band	Implicit Target	Broad Band	Relatively Free Float
Czech Republic		• ———	———	• ———→	X	
Estonia	X					
Hungary		• ———	• ———→	X		
Poland		• ———	• ———→	• ———→	X	
Slovenia			X			
Bulgaria	X←———	———	———	———	•	
Latvia		X———	———	———	•	
Lithuania	X←———	———	———	———	•	
Romania			• ———	———	→X	
Slovakia		• ———	• ———	———	X	

SOURCE: Adapted from Keller (2000), Figure 7; national sources.

NOTE: An "X" indicates the current exchange rate regime, a • denotes a previous regime, and a → indicates a regime change; cutoff date: 10 May 2001.

A wide range of exchange rate regimes has been used in the ten countries under consideration. Moreover, regimes have been changed, in some cases several times, in all countries except Estonia (currency board since 1992) and Slovenia (managed float also since 1992).[3]

A clear trend toward the corners of fixed and flexible options has occurred in the evolution of exchange rate arrangements among the CEE-10. At the same time, as is shown in Table 2, this movement has been asymmetric. More flexible arrangements have become—relatively speaking—more popular than fixed hard pegs. Fischer (2001) and Buiter and Grafe (2001) arrived at the same conclusion for the emerging market economies as a whole. Yet, a high degree of flexibility might be quite elusive as transition countries and emerging market economies alike, especially the smaller ones, typically show "fear of floating" (Calvo and Reinhart 2000; Bailliu, Lafrance, and Perrault 2000).[4] Most of these countries manage the exchange rate quite heavily, as in the case in Slovenia. Moreover, for the CEE-10, the euro constitutes—except for Lithuania, which, at the time of writing, continues to tie its currency to the U.S. dollar but plans to switch its peg to the euro by 2002, and Latvia, which still pegs to the SDR—at least an indirect anchor. This situation is not surprising given the close trade relationships with the euro zone and their political aspirations.

Even so, the range of exchange rate regimes currently followed still covers the whole spectrum of possibilities from free floating to currency board hard pegs (cf. Table 2).[5] In contrast to the widely differing exchange rate arrangements, the CEE-10 have moved swiftly and quite uniformly (albeit with some remaining differences) to liberalize capital account transactions. This policy of liberalization stands in sharp contrast to the policies followed in western European countries after World War II, where capital account liberalization was not completed until 1991![6]

Regardless of the present exchange rate arrangement, the CEE-10 have already decided that they want to replace their own currencies with the euro. Countries that currently implement free-floating regimes, crawling pegs, and conventional pegs against currencies other than the euro will, at some point before its adoption, have to change their current arrangements. The questions therefore are the following: which way to go, where are the risks, and is there anything to be learned from the experience of emerging market economies in the 1990s?

TABLE 2

EXCHANGE RATE ARRANGEMENTS IN THE CANDIDATE COUNTRIES AS OF MAY 2001

Country	Exchange Rate Arrangement
Bulgaria	Currency board
Czech Republic	Managed floating
Estonia	Currency board
Hungary	Crawling peg
Latvia	Fixed peg
Lithuania	Currency board
Poland	Floating
Romania	Managed floating
Slovak Republic	Managed floating
Slovenia	Managed floating

SOURCE: International Financial Statistics, March 2001, national sources.

SOME LESSONS FROM THE CURRENCY CRISES OF THE 1990s

In the previous section, we looked at the monetary regimes that the CEE-10 implemented and sketched their evolution. Recall that while most of them started out with some form of a peg, some of them have moved away from this type of arrangement.[7] This latter tendency has been a general trend in the 1990s. While in 1991, 78 percent of all International Monetary Fund (IMF) members in some way followed a fixed or pegged exchange rate regime (hard or soft peg), this number dropped to 58 percent in 1998 (Fischer 2001). Hence, countries appear to have moved away from the middle ground of pegged but adjustable fixed exchange rates (soft pegs) toward the two corner regimes of either flexible exchange rates or hard pegs.

The lesson of the 1990s seems to indicate that adhering to a pegged exchange rate regime can be a useful strategy for controlling inflation. Yet, it may, at some point, contribute to financial instability (cf. Mishkin 2001). Indeed, emerging market economies that were loaded with foreign-denominated debt experienced serious financial and currency crises.[8]

It appears that increased financial market integration has led the majority of emerging market economies to view more flexible exchange rate arrangements as more attractive.[9] At the same time, the policy requirements for maintaining a pegged exchange rate have become more demanding (Mussa et al. 2000).

Beyond the relatively few "emerging markets,"[10] however, there are some 130 developing and transition economies. These economies—in particular, the transition economies that arose from the former Soviet Union, with exception of the Baltics, and those that emerged from Yugoslavia, except Slovenia[11]—still have only embryonic domestic financial systems. In addition, they often resort to quite extensive controls on capital account transactions.[12]

For such economies, pegged exchange rate regimes (in whatever form) can be viable for extended periods, provided monetary and fiscal policy can maintain reasonable discipline. Nonetheless, when these economies become more developed and financially more sophisticated and when they are more integrated into global financial markets, they may consider arrangements that offer greater exchange rate flexibility.[13] Alternatively, they may adopt very hard pegs (euroization/dollarization and monetary union).[14]

Moreover, the Asian crisis also taught us that good economic fundamentals alone are not enough to prevent contagion and currency crises (cf. Baig and Goldfajn 1999; Yeyati and Ubide 2000). A speculative attack may occur even if the fundamentals are consistent with the fixed parity, and speculation against a currency may be self-fulfilling (cf. Obstfeld 1996; Jeanne 1997; with regard to the Asian crisis, see Chang and Velasco forthcoming).

While the bipolar view drew widespread academic support in the aftermath of the Asian crisis and appeared to become a new consensus, it has lost attraction more recently.

On one hand, several authors asserted that often intermediate solutions might be more appropriate than corner solutions. In this context, Frankel (1999, 30) argued that "intermediate solutions are more likely to be appropriate for many countries than are corner solutions. This is true, for example, for some developing countries for which large-scale capital flows are not an issue." Similar arguments were advanced by Williamson (2000).

On the other hand, the fear of floating school questions the feasibility of free-floating arguing that, because of credibility problems, central banks do heavily sterilize to reduce movements in the exchange rate even though they are officially floating.

Yet, the argument that the pure floating corner solution is no real alternative since in practice there is always "dirty floating" (Calvo and Reinhart 2000) can also be turned around and into an argument in favor of a hard peg corner solution such as dollarization or euroization (see Reinhart 2000). If countries are not willing to adopt a freely floating exchange rate, and if, as we have argued, a soft peg or managed floating might be a serious danger for the economic and financial stability because of a lack of credibility, the other corner solution (dollarization/euroization) may seem to be the best alternative.

However, to make such a corner solution successful or appropriate, it needs to be supplemented by further institutional measures or innovations to minimize risks of future currency and financial market crises. These include proper macropolitical behavior (financial soundness, in particular) and the implementation of a sound banking system, sound accounting practices, and appropriate standards of disclosure and the adoption of appropriate auditing and accounting standards, principles of good corporate governance, and efficient bankruptcy procedures (Fischer 1999).

As noted above, a pegged exchange rate regime, while being a successful strategy for controlling inflation, may also increase financial instability. Such a risk remains significant for the most advanced of the CEE-10.[15] To minimize this danger, in particular a healthy banking system and tighter financial supervision have to be effected. These steps, together with a decrease in short-term debt denominated in foreign currencies and an increase in holdings of international reserves, may insulate countries from financial crises.

THE ROAD MAP TO THE EURO FOR THE CEE-10

In this section, we plot the road map to the euro for the candidate countries by looking at both formal requirements and economic challenges that lie ahead before these countries irrevocably fix their exchange rate and abolish their national currencies. We will also touch on the thorny issue of which kind of exchange rate regime might contribute most to a smooth phasing out of the national currency.

Formally, there are three stops ahead to the introduction of the euro.[16]

1. Until EU entry, the exchange rate policy of the candidate country remains its own concern, implying freedom of choice of the monetary framework/exchange rate regime.
2. On EU entry, the exchange rate policy becomes a common concern of the EU. New entrants are expected to enter at some stage but not necessarily at EU entry, the Exchange Rate Mechanism (ERM2), for at least two years.
3. Finally, after fulfillment of the Maastricht criteria, these countries will have to adopt the euro.[17] This step requires a unanimous decision by the European Council at the level of heads of states or government.[18] Recall that the fulfillment of the Maastricht convergence criteria is not required for EU entry but only for the adoption of the euro.

Given these formal requirements, is there a need to change exchange-rate regimes between today (2001) and the adoption of the euro? The interest in this issue arises from not only possible lessons that emanate from the experience of emerging market economies with various exchange rate regimes during the past decade but also—and directly relevant to policy makers in the CEE-10—whether the inevitable risks of a temporary regime shift in terms of loss of policy credibility and increased market uncertainty can be avoided.

The argument has two components, a formal and an economic one. We will deal with them in turn. Formally, the ECOFIN[19] Council (European Commission 2000) already voiced its opinion that all exchange rate regimes except a free float, a crawling peg, and a peg to a currency other than the euro are, in principle, compatible with the ERM2. Therefore, no intermediate regime switch is required for countries following other exchange rate practices at the present time. Depending on the exact interpretation of what constitutes a managed float (which is deemed to be compatible with the ERM2—yet the ECOFIN has not yet specified what constitutes a managed float) and considering that the compatibility of currency board arrangements will be considered on a case-by-case basis, it is clear at present only that Latvia (SDR peg), Lithuania (hard peg against the U.S. dollar), and Hungary (crawling peg as of May 2001 with a broad fluctuation band) will have to have an intermediate switch.

As the CEE-10 continue to adjust to free markets, it is to be expected that there will be related idiosyncratic real and nominal shocks. The policy response to such shocks and, possibly, also the choice of the exchange rate arrangements during the transition to the euro will depend on the effectiveness of the available instruments. That is to say, countries that already have working market structures, flexible prices, and wages (downward as well as upward) will much more easily be able to forgo the exchange rate instrument during this period than others that do not. Thus, countries that suffer substantial price and wage inflexibility and, simultaneously, immobility of labor will likely to be hit by an increase in unemployment if adverse country-specific real shocks arise and they have fixed exchange rates. Therefore, it might be rather costly for the latter group of countries to forgo the exchange rate as an adjustment instrument. If they did so, the loss in economic growth would slow down real convergence, which, by itself, is a goal of European integration.[20]

The prime economic rationale for the CEE-10 (and other developing countries) to join the EU is the hope of approaching the material standard of living of the member states more quickly than they could if they remain outside the EU. For real convergence to happen, faster overall productivity growth than in the current EU is required. Since productivity advances are higher in the tradable sector of the economy that is exposed to international competition than in the domestic sector, under conventional assumptions, the "catching up countries" will experience a higher inflation rate than countries with lower real growth rates (the "Balassa-Samuelson effect" [BS]). Therefore, the (equilibrium) real exchange rate has to appreciate. A real appreciation can also be brought about if the exchange rate appreciates or if there are explicit revaluations. The choice of route to a higher real exchange rate will be influenced not only by formal criteria (see above) but also by institutional conditions in the country concerned. The choice of exchange rate at which the country should enter the ERM2 is a separate issue.

It is in the interest of all parties concerned that the candidate countries enter EMU with an appropriate real exchange rate to avoid economic costs. By "appropriate," we understand a rate that is near to its (unknown) equilibrium level at the time. In this context, the arguments brought forward by Poland to explain its switch to a flexible exchange rate and inflation targeting are of interest. The National Bank of Poland (NBP) (1998) explicitly argued that "The entry to the ERM2 should take place at the equilibrium rate, difficult to determine without resorting to market forces. *A fixed rate would offer little guarantee of attaining this goal*" (p. 9, emphasis added). Thus, in the view of the NBP, participation in the ERM2 requires an intermediate regime shift to prevent an exchange rate misalignment. The NBP's position testifies to great (perhaps too great) faith in market forces to produce the equilibrium exchange rate at the right moment. Experience with floating exchange rates up to now does point to long lasting misalignments and inherent high short-term volatility. Therefore, it would be a stroke of luck if the market rate, say on 1 January 2006, coincides with the equilibrium rate.

In any event, the NBP argument is an argument against a too-early fixing of the exchange rates of candidate countries. On the other end of the spectrum are the hard peggers like Estonia, which want to stick to the current exchange rate (8 kroon for 1 DM) and let the price level adjust to give the appropriate real exchange rate at the time of ERM2 entry. In this context, the statement contained in the letter of intent of February 2000 is relevant and should be read together with the statement of the NBP above:

> Our economic objectives will be pursued in the context of our long-standing currency board arrangement, which continues to provide a stable, transparent, and consistent policy framework. As demonstrated by the sharp improvement in our current account position and solid export growth to western markets, the current exchange rate peg remains appropriate. We intend to maintain the current fixed relationship between the kroon and the DM and euro until Estonia becomes a full participant in the EMU, at which point the euro will become Estonia's currency. (Eesti 2000, para. 12, p. 4, emphasis added)

In this section, we will focus on the challenges posed by the requirement to fulfill the Maastricht convergence criteria. When the Maastricht criteria were agreed, their levels were set with only the then-participating EU members in mind. Possible eastern enlargement played no role. The inflation criterion was determined in a way that should ensure convergence at the level of the three most stable countries, politically to alleviate inflation fears mostly in Germany and economically to bring about a high degree of price stability to foster economic growth. The ECB Council in 1998 quantified price stability for the euro zone as an increase of the harmonized consumer price index below 2 percent over the medium term. The fiscal criteria (and subsequently the Stability and Growth Pact) were deemed necessary to prevent potential free riding of formerly fiscally prodigal states.

There is political agreement that there will be no additional convergence criteria for the current candidates to adopt the euro. In this context, a number of difficult challenges arise for the candidate countries.

First, we above addressed the BS effect, which explains the higher inflation rate prevalent in catching-up countries that experience higher productivity and real growth rates than the core. The need to satisfy the inflation criterion could require the candidate countries to dampen demand to reduce inflation to the required level. Yet, the existence of the BS effect hinges on the assumption that there are nominal wage and price rigidities. If prices were fully flexible (in both directions) in the candidate countries, the problem would disappear; however, prices and wages are quite sticky in these countries.

In addition, once these countries have joined and the catching up continues, some observers fear that a problem might arise for the core countries. As the ECB sets the inflation rate in the euro area as a whole, monetary policy tends to have more restrictive effects in the core countries than in the accession countries. Hence, the economic growth in the core countries will likely to be dampened. The faster the economies of the new members converge with those of the existing EU states, the higher will be the real growth loss in the core countries—unless prices and wages are flexible in both directions in the new EU members.

Such arguments help to understand the fears voiced in some quarters regarding quick adoption of the euro. In our reading, such fears tend to overstate the issue. First, EU entry requires the candidates to show that their economies can withstand the competitive pressures of the single market. Second, at present, price and wage flexibility tends to be greater in the candidate countries than in the current member states. Third, the economic impact in the acceding states is so small that the effect on the EU inflation rate is no more than 0.2 to 0.3 percent (Sinn and Reutter 2001).

Second, we addressed adjustment to asymmetric shocks above. As long as there are no constitutional provisions with respect to regional redistribution such as the German system of Finanzausgleich (according to the Maastricht Treaty, such a centralization of the budgetary process is not planned in EMU), political conflicts may arise. These will pertain to the discretionary redistribution associated with financial transfers that are necessary if countries forgo the exchange rate instrument and prices and wages are inflexible and labor immobile, but an EMU that tends to produce political conflicts about permanent discretionary redistribution will destabilize itself.

This scare scenario, however, overlooks the fact that the introduction of EMU may create greater price flexibility and labor mobility, possibly offsetting the abolition of the exchange rate as an absorption mechanism of country-specific shocks: under the EMU, there will be only one currency; hence, there will be more price transparency. This greater price transparency will lead to more intense competition within the EMU and yield not only lower product prices but also higher price flexibility (see Wagner 1998, 8-9).

Third, we argued above that a pegged exchange rate regime, although it may be a successful strategy for controlling inflation, might increase financial instability. This danger arises in particular in emerging markets with a weak banking and financial system. An exchange rate peg that has been stable for a rather long period of time might lead market participants to underestimate—or even totally neglect—the exchange rate risk, inducing excessive capital inflows. The danger is heightened if countries sterilize the capital inflows, thereby raising domestic interest rates far above the international rates. Thus, a large amount of foreign-denominated debt that makes a country vulnerable to sudden shifts in market sentiment is accumulated. (A common feature of the recent emerging market crises was that the stock of foreign exchange reserves available in the short run typically was far lower than the volume of foreign debt.)

Furthermore, if bank supervision does not meet international standards, as is often the case in emerging markets, the likelihood of a financial crisis rises significantly (cf. Mishkin 2001). The capital inflows typically lead to a lending boom and a financial or real estate bubble. If these bubbles burst, banks are left with a huge amount of bad loans and exploding foreign debt if the financial crisis is accompanied by a successful speculative attack. The severe deterioration of banks' and domestic firms' balance sheets not only jeopardizes financial stability but also hampers economic growth.

This recurrent pattern of emerging market crises led the IMF and most observers to advise countries to take care of a sound and stable financial system before fully opening the capital account.

SUMMARY

This article examined the monetary policy path of CEE-10 on their way to EU accession and, ultimately, adoption of the euro. It proceeded in three steps. First, it described the evolution of the monetary regime of the CEE-10 since the demise of the centrally planned economic system. Second, it dealt with the currency crises of emerging market economies in the 1990s and developed potential lessons for the CEE-10. Third, it delineated the road map for the candidate countries by looking at both formal requirements and economic challenges that these countries have to meet before they can adopt the euro.

The article showed that the range of exchange rate regimes followed by the candidate countries has covered the whole spectrum of possibilities from free floating to currency board hard peg; however, some candidate countries appear to have moved away from the middle ground of pegged but adjustable fixed exchange rates (soft pegs) toward the two corner regimes of either flexible exchange rates or hard pegs. The latter tendency has been a general trend in the 1990s that resulted from the disappointing experiences of emerging market economies with soft pegging during the decade.

When analyzing the formal requirements and economic challenges for the adoption of the euro, the article focused on the challenges for the candidate countries of adjusting to asymmetric shocks, appreciating the real exchange rate at least cost, and selecting the "correct" real exchange rate before adopting the euro. Potential problem areas that may arise on the road to an enlarged euro zone and may delay the process were highlighted in the last section of the article: a real growth loss in the core countries (because of the BS effect); discretionary redistribution associated with financial transfers, which are necessary if countries forgo the exchange rate instrument and prices and wages are inflexible and capital immobile; and financial instability, which may arise if the exchange rate is pegged in candidate countries with a weak banking and financial system and which is not supported by consistent, stability-oriented macro policies.

Notes

1. The process of enlargement of the European Union (EU) was launched on 30 March 1998. Negotiations are currently being held with the following twelve applicants: Bulgaria, the Czech Republic, Estonia, Hungary, Latvia, Lithuania, Poland, Romania, Slovakia, and Slovenia, as well as Cyprus and Malta. See also Oesterreichische Nationalbank (1999, 11 ff). Since the meeting of the European Council at the level of heads of states or government in December 1999, Turkey has also been a candidate for EU accession. Negotiations have not yet started because the conditions for their commencement are not yet met.

2. For a discussion of potential lessons to be drawn from the Austrian exchange rate experience for the CEE-10, compare Glück and Hochreiter (2001).

3. For a more detailed description of the evolution of exchange rate regimes in the early years of transition, see Hochreiter (1995), and for the 1990s as a whole, see Tullio (1999).

4. Calvo and Reinhart "find that countries that say they allow their exchange rate to float mostly do not—there seems to be an epidemic case of 'fear of floating'" (p. 4). Bailliu et al. found that "measurement error in the classification of exchange rate arrangements is an important issue" (p. 25).

5. See also Buiter and Grafe (2001).

6. For a comparative overview of capital account sequencing in Austria and Finland, see Hochreiter (2000).

7. This occurred most recently in May 2001, when Hungary—as a first step to discontinue the crawling peg altogether—widened the fluctuation band from ± 2¼ percent to ± 15 percent.

8. A main element of these crises was the weakness of the bank supervisory process, which often is prevalent in emerging market and transition countries. Compare Berg (1999); Alba, Bhattacharya, and Classens (1998); and Furman and Stiglitz (1998).

9. Compare Eichengreen et al. (1999).

10. Fischer (2001) listed thirty-three emerging market economies out of 182 Inter-

national Monetary Fund members at the end of 1999.

11. We shall not deal with these countries here in this article as our focus is the CEE-10.

12. Compare European Bank for Reconstruction and Development (2000).

13. Compare Wagner (2000a, 2000b) and Mussa et al. (2000).

14. Fischer (2001) stated, "It is reasonable to believe, as EMU expands, and as other economies reconsider the costs and benefits of maintaining a national currency . . . that more countries will adopt very hard pegs, and that there will in the future be fewer national currencies" (p. 10).

15. The informal Malmö ECOFIN in April 2001 specifically pointed to the economic vulnerabilities the candidate countries are exposed to due to their weak financial systems.

16. Compare European Commission (2000).

17. Recall that the candidate countries have no right to opt out.

18. The European Council brings together the heads of state or government of the fifteen member states of the EU and the president of the European Commission. It should not be confused with the Council of Europe (which is an international organization) or with the Council of the EU (which consists of ministers of the fifteen member states).

19. ECOFIN is the European Council at the level of ministers of economics and finance of the fifteen member states. The council is the EU's legislative body. The work of the council is led by the member state holding the presidency. The council is situated in Brussels, but a number of council meetings take place in Luxembourg.

20. Note that the preamble of the European Community Treaty emphasizes real convergence as a central goal of European integration.

References

Alba, P. A., S. Bhattacharya, and S. Ghosh Classens. 1998. Volatility and contagion in a financially-integrated world: Lessons from East Asia's recent experience. Mimeo.

Baig, Tamur, and Ilan Goldfajn. 1999. Financial market contagion in the Asian crisis. *IMF Staff Papers* 46:167-95.

Bailliu, Jeannine, Robert Lafrance, and Jean-Francois Perrault. 2000. Exchange rate regimes and economic growth in emerging markets. Mimeo, Bank of Canada.

Berg, Andy. 1999. The Asia crisis: Causes, policy responses, and outcomes. IMF working paper no. 99/138. Washington, DC: International Monetary Fund.

Buiter, Willem H., and Clemens Grafe. 2001. Central banking and the choice of currency regime in accession countries. SUERF study no. 11, Vienna.

Calvo, Guillermo A., and Carmen M. Reinhart. 2000. Fear of floating. NBER working paper no. 7993, November.

Chang, Roberto, and Andres Velasco. Forthcoming. Financial fragility and the exchange rate regime. *Journal of Economic Theory*.

ECOFIN. 2000. Questions relating to the applicant countries' economic stability and exchange rate strategy—Conclusions. 2283rd council meeting, Brussels, 17 July.

Eesti, Pank. 2000. Memorandum of economic policies 2000-2001. Bank of Estonia, Tallinn.

Eichengreen, Barry, Paul Masson, Miguel Savastano, and Sunil Sharma. 1999. Transition strategies and nominal anchors on the road to greater exchange rate flexibility. In *Essays in international finance*. Vol. 213. Princeton, NJ: Princeton University Press.

European Bank for Reconstruction and Development. 2000. *Transition report*. London: EBRD.

European Commission. 2000. Exchange rate strategies for EU candidate countries. European Commission ECOFIN (521/2000-EN), August. Brussels: European Commission.

Fischer, Stanley. 1999. Reforming the international financial system. *Economic Journal* 109:557-76.

———. 2001. Exchange rate regimes: Is the bipolar view correct? *Papers and Proceedings of the AEA*, May.

Frankel, Jeffrey A. 1999. No single currency regime is right for all countries or at all times. In *Essays in international finance*. Vol. 215. Princeton, NJ: Princeton University International Finance Section.

Furman, Jason, and Joseph E. Stiglitz. 1998. Economic crises: Evidence and insights from East Asia. *Brookings Papers on Economic Activity* 2:1-133.

Glück, Heinz, and Eduard Hochreiter. 2001. Exchange rate policy in the transition to acccession: Any lessons from the Austrian experience? Paper presented at the conference, When Is a National Currency a Luxury? London Business School, March.

Hochreiter, Eduard. 1995. Central banking in transition. In *Establishing monetary stability in emerging market economies*, edited by Thomas D. Willett, Richard C. K. Burdekin, Richard J. Sweeney, and Claas Wihlborg, 127-44. Westport, CT: Westview.

———. 2000. Exchange rate regimes and capital mobility: Issues and some lessons from central and eastern European applicant countries. *North American Journal of Economics and Finance* 11:155-71.

Jeanne, Olivier. 1997. Are currency crises self-fulfilling? A test. *Journal of International Economics* 43:263-86.

Keller, Peter M. 2000. Recent experience with currency boards and fixed exchange rates in the Baltic countries and Bulgaria and some lessons for the future. Seminar on Currency Boards, Experience and Prospects, organized by the Bank of Estonia, May.

Mishkin, Frederic S. 2001. Financial policies and the prevention of financial crises in emerging market countries. NBER working paper no. 8087.

Mussa, Michael, Paul Masson, Alexander Swoboda, Paolo Mauro, and Andy Berg. 2000. Exchange rate regimes in an increasingly integrated world economy. IMF occasional paper no. 193. Washington, DC: International Monetary Fund.

National Bank of Poland. 1998. *Medium-term strategy of monetary policy (1999-2003)*. Warsaw, Poland, September.

Obstfeld, Maruice. 1996. Models of currency crises with self-fulfilling features. *European Economic Review* 40:1037-47.

Oesterreichische Nationalbank. 1999. Focus on Transition 2/1999. Wien.

Reinhart, Carmen M. 2000. The mirage of floating exchange rates. *American Economic Review, Papers and Proceedings* 90 (2): 65-70.

Sinn, Hans-Werner, and Michael Reutter. 2001. The minimum inflation rate for euroland. NBER working paper no. 8085, January.

Tullio, Guiseppe. 1999. Exchange rate policy of central European countries in the transition to European monetary union. In *Inclusion of Central European countries in the European Monetary Union*, edited by Paul De Grauwe and Vladimir Lavrac, 63-104. Dordrecht, the Netherlands: Kluwer.

Wagner, Helmut. 1998. Perspectives on European monetary union. American Institute for Contemporary German Studies (AICGS) research report no. 7. Washington, DC: Johns Hopkins University Press.

———. 2000a. Central banking in transition countries. *Eastern European Economics* 38 (4): 6-53. [See also IMF working paper no. 98/126.]

———. 2000b. Which exchange rate regimes in an era of high capital mobility. *North American Journal of Economics and Finance* 11:191-203.

Williamson, John. 2000. *Exchange rate regimes for emerging markets: Reviving the intermediate option*. Washington, DC: Institute for International Economics.

Yeyati, Eduardo Levy, and Angel Ubide. 2000. Crises, contagion, and the closed-end country fund puzzle. *IMF Staff Papers* 47:54-89.

ANNALS, *AAPSS*, **579**, January 2002

International Financial Architecture and International Financial Standards

By MICHELE FRATIANNI and JOHN PATTISON

ABSTRACT: The international financial architecture literature is concerned with a set of best principles and practices that may lower the risk of financial crises and spillover effects. The financial world has grown enormously more complicated since the end of Bretton Woods. The valuable work of several standard-setting institutions must be judged as minimum requirements for good practice, which are below the perceived needs of the leading financial centers. The paper proposes a "portal" solution, in which the two most important financial centers, the United States and the United Kingdom, set best practices on international financial standards. Since these two centers control access to international markets, and thus, are the conduit of systemic risk, they can establish both the rules for market access and the core regulatory and supervisory framework to deal with international systemic issues. The regulators of the two portals therefore play the fundamental international regulatory role.

Michele Fratianni is the W. George Pinnell Professor of Business Economics and Public Policy at Indiana University. He has held academic positions in Belgium, Germany, and Italy. He has been the economic adviser with the European Commission and senior staff economist with the President's Council of Economic Advisers. He is the founder and managing editor of Open Economies Review *and writes on monetary economics, international finance, and economic history.*

John Pattison is a senior vice president with the Canadian Imperial Bank of Commerce. He has had academic positions at the University of Western Ontario and has been an economist for various governmental and international organizations. He writes on the subjects of international economics, international organizations, and financial regulation.

DEFINING THE ISSUES

The literature on international financial architecture, with its focus on micro and institutional questions, is searching for a set of best principles and practices that may influence the behavior of both private and official agents operating in the international financial community. A key challenge in this area is the regulatory framework for safeguarding integrated national financial systems from systemic risk.

Regulation and prudential supervision of banks and financial intermediaries is, to a large extent, a post–Bretton Woods phenomenon. Before, the regulatory framework was structured primarily around the incorporation of banks, note issuance, and legislation dealing with frauds. Financial regulation is a response to financial liberalization, which followed the demise of Bretton Woods and the end of restrictions on domestic and international transactions. Not surprisingly, the first significant bank failure, Bankaus Herstatt, occurred in 1974, a year after the end of Bretton Woods. The Bundesaufsichtsamt fur das Kreditwesen closed Herstatt, after counterparties in foreign exchange transactions had paid claims by Herstatt in deutsche marks but before Herstatt had paid due amounts in U.S. dollars. This episode marked the beginning of the work of the G10 central banks and the Basel Committee on Banking Supervision in creating international financial standards, both for financial institutions and their regulators.[1] It also created the rationale for the original BIS "Concordat" concerning the supervision of foreign banking establishments by home and host authorities.

Additional challenges ensued. The first was the failure of important financial institutions—such as Drexel Burnham Lambert in 1990, BCCI in 1991, and Barings in 1995—and the rising frequency of banking crises. In the period 1980 to 1995, banking crises occurred at an average rate of 1.44 a year, in contrast to an average rate of 0.30 a year in the period 1970 to 1979 (Kaminsky and Reinhart 1999, Table 1). The second rose from the globalization of financial markets. The vast majority of new entrants in the global marketplace had undeveloped financial structures; poor legal, accounting, and regulatory frameworks; inadequate supervisory methods and staffing; and a history of political interference, favoritism, and cronyism. This raised the prospect of the transmission of more frequent local failures to the international financial system. Claims of financial contagion were made in connection with the Mexican crisis of 1994-95, the Asian crisis of 1997, and the Russian crisis of 1998. The final challenge, related to the second, stemmed from inappropriate national economic policies—especially concerning the exchange rate regime—that led to financial failures and international spillovers.

There is no single international agency with oversight, monitoring authority, or jurisdictional authority over international financial safety and soundness. Equally, there is no combination of international financial institutions with a comprehensive, logically integrated mandate of managing financial safety and soundness. As Kane (2000) put it, "global regulatory redesign is too complex a problem for diverse national regulators to expect to solve by negotiation" (p. 2). Nonetheless, the current architecture is converging to a set of minimum financial standards covering consolidated supervision, capital adequacy, supervision of cross-border banking, securities markets, insurance, accounting standards, auditing standards, standards for specific risks, money laundering requirements, and so on.

The focus of our article is on international financial standards and their role in promoting "good" practices and as a precondition for acceding to the international lender of last resort (ILOL) facilities (Meltzer Commission 2000). Our main contention is that the promulgation of an international financial standard is only the first step in reducing financial risk worldwide. The critical parts of the approach lie in what follows, namely, verification and implementation. Standard verification and implementation, especially in countries outside the G10 group, has been overlooked in the literature. We stress this aspect and propose a market-friendly solution, based on the incentive and leadership of a few financial centers and the incentives of other countries to adhere to the standards set by the leaders.

WHY REGULATION AND SUPERVISION

There are three basic reasons for regulating banks. The first is to prevent the failure of a bank spreading to healthy institutions. Bank depositors tend to panic because they have incomplete information on the quality of a bank's assets. Prudential rules are designed to constrain the risk exposure of banks and, consequently, to reassure depositors that the system is sound. The second is to protect small savers who have relatively low information endowments, inadequate incentives to acquire new information, and a strong preference for holding liabilities of financial institutions that do not carry default, monitoring requirements, and interest-rate risk. The safety of bank deposits is guaranteed either by deposit insurance schemes or by central banks extending the protection of the lender-of-last-resort function. The final reason is to protect producers from the effects of competition and thereby lower the demands of financial institutions on the safety net. Typically, governments provide the regulatory structure and the safety net to financial institutions. These two aspects are intertwined. Since taxpayers bear the cost of financial crises, governments, acting on behalf of taxpayers, limit and constrain the risk that financial intermediaries can take to minimize the burden on taxpayers.

Before the Great Depression, the burden of financial crises fell directly on the affected parties; the taxpayer's deep pockets were seldom called on. The experience of the Great Depression altered fundamentally the rules of the game. To avoid the large consequences on output and unemployment from financial crises, governments erected safety nets. But those safety nets altered the propensity of financial institutions to take risk with the expectations that prospective losses would be collectivized. Safety net and moral hazard are the horns of the dilemma for public policy (International Monetary Fund [IMF] 1999, 74). One cannot exist without the other. There is a general consensus today that risk taking has increased (IMF 1998, 95-96 and 103). For some authors, this higher risk is largely attributable to moral hazard behavior (Calomiris 1998; Schwartz 1998; Meltzer 1999; Calomiris and Meltzer 1999).

Deregulation and liberalization have contributed to a riskier environment. There is some evidence that countries caught in a financial crisis had previously deregulated their financial system (Williamson and Mahar 1998; Kaminsky and Reinhart 1999; Goldstein and Folkerts-Landau 1993). These findings are consistent with the hypothesis that banks seek more profit opportunities as economic rents are eroded by the liberalization program. Unfamiliar with the unregulated environment, banks take excessive risk before finally learning the new risk management techniques and settling into a new steady-state equilibrium (Llewellyn 2000). Equally, regulators and supervisors tend to underestimate the consequences of deregulation on risk taking.

In sum, the case for regulation and supervision stems from the safety net governments provide to the financial system. Governments can react to increased risk taking either by making the safety net less predictable or by tightening the regulatory regime or by a combination of both.

REGULATION AND SUPERVISION IN AN INTERNATIONAL CONTEXT

There are three possible approaches to financial regulation and supervision in a world of integrated financial markets: national regulatory competition, one world financial authority, and a coordinated approach with national enforcement.

National regulatory competition

National regulatory competition is the principle adopted by the European Union (EU) in the sense that the authorities of the home country have the right and obligations of regulating banks they have licensed regardless of where they operate in the defined area of integration. Since each member state accepts this principle, national regulatory standards are mutually recognized. The advantage of this principle is twofold. "Excessive" or "lax" regulation faces competition. Regulated firms can engage in regulatory arbitrage by changing location and regulator. This arbitrage, however, is subject to the policing of the market; for example, risk-averse depositors may prefer a more regulated to a less regulated environment. Furthermore, regulatory competition is an efficient institution to achieve a market-determined convergence of regulatory standards among countries that trust each other's regulation.

Regulatory competition has two disadvantages. The first, as Kane (2000) noted, is that "information asymmetries and entry and exit costs limit opportunities for efficient regulators to discipline inefficient regulators by hit-and-run entry" (p. 21). This applies more to countries with sharply different preferences than to the EU. The second is that the equilibrium solution may entail chasing the lowest common denominator, that is, a standard so low as to make the financial system excessively prone to crises and taxpayer's bailouts. To avoid the chase to the lowest common denominator, the EU has set a minimum floor through a large number of directives affecting the financial system (Fratianni 1995, 162). But the larger the number of countries involved—and hence the more heterogeneous—the more difficult it is for member countries to accept the principle of mutual recognition. This is quite natural because mutual recognition is based on trust: members share a similar approach to risk and regulation, understand the rules, and communicate with one another to make the system work.

A world financial authority

The polar case of national regulatory competition is a World Financial Authority, as Eatwell and Taylor (2000) called it. The argument for creating a single world regulatory authority is that it would eliminate the wasteful activity connected with regulatory arbitrage and would achieve the efficiency and the externalities of a regulator whose reach coincides with the market reach of internationally active banks. How can regulation remain national if markets are internationally integrated? A single world regulator would not suffer from the inconsistencies of numerous national regulators. A world regulator would not face the coordination costs of getting national regulators to agree on a standard. A world regulator would not have the incentive to deviate from the coordination strategy, as is likely in a regulatory cartel.

The affection for a world financial authority is reminiscent of the utopian solution of a world government to solve violent conflicts among nation states. A single, benevolent supranational regulator—it is claimed—would not deviate from the "best" solution, whereas a national regulator in a regulatory cartel would be tempted to "cheat" or deviate from the cooperative equilibrium.

But is it not far fetched to think that an all-powerful world regulator would be benevolent? Without accountability, there is the danger that a single authority would be so singly focused to prevent a financial crisis that it would set an excessive regulatory burden, with the consequence that the world community would pay the cost of stymied competition, innovation, and product differentiation. Competition is just as much of an engine of discovery in regulation as it is in markets. How could one stop a single authority from becoming bureaucratic, narrow, and inflexible? As the power of the single authority rises, so would the rewards for pursuing a strictly regulatory approach over the alternative of market friendly regulation. In the absence of competition, the only route for forcing change would be to amend the international agreement that created the single authority. The exit cost to a single country would be very high. This, in turn, would keep the system stable but would also encourage the single authority to be unresponsive to the wishes of the constituencies. Furthermore, would a single authority be able to assess risk in every corner of the world better than the local regulatory authority? What would be the legitimacy of such an institution relative to national regulatory bodies that respond directly to national parliaments and ultimately to voters? Would it not be unmanageable to administer regulation and supervision to the global financial system? Finally, a world financial authority would not be politically acceptable. Even within the confines of a homogeneous group like the EU, financial regulation and supervision remain at the national level. As White (1999) put it, "oversight and supervision must be a very hands-on affair. This was one of the arguments used in Europe when it was decided that banking supervision would stay at the national level rather than migrating to the European Central Bank" (p. 13).

International standards and the coordinated strategy

The third and most promising approach to international regulation and supervision is to set international standards and let national bodies implement regulation and supervision. Goldstein (1997) has forcefully argued the case for standards of best practices—or what he calls an international banking standard—not imposed from above but accepted voluntarily by countries with the stated purpose of increasing "the scope and pace of banking reform in both developing and industrial countries" (p. 61). Eichengreen (1999b) has adopted Goldstein's international banking standard for his proposal to reengineer the international financial architecture. The establishment of international standards is an exercise in coordination, necessitated by the erosion of national borders in matters of banking and finance. This erosion, in turn, reduces the power of regulators to contain systemic risks and protect consumers within their jurisdictions.

The 1997 currency turmoil in East Asia heightened the sense of urgency in reducing systemic risk. For our purposes, it is useful to distinguish between "normal" or fundamentals-driven interdependence and exceptional, but temporary, interdependence caused by a shock to an individual country or set of countries (Dornbusch, Park, and Claessens 2000). Normal interdependence, as we have noted, has been rising since capital liberalization of the 1980s and 1990s. Controls on capital movements and foreign exchange markets were responsible for large deviations from covered interest rate parity and for large differences between offshore and onshore interest rates (Frankel and MacArthur 1988, Table 3). After France and Italy eliminated those controls in the late 1980s, onshore interest rates quickly converged to the level of their offshore counterparts (Obstfeld 1995, 209-10). In his study on financial integration for the G5 countries, Marston (1995) pointed out that "by the early 1990s . . . the distinction between national and international money markets, at least at the wholesale level end, ceased to be important" (p. 69).

The extent of financial integration can also be gleaned from the size of private capital flows. At the end of the 1980s, capital flows to the developing countries surged. The trend continued through the 1990s, with the exception of bank loans. Emerging market economies were steady recipients of foreign direct investment and portfolio investment in the period 1990 to 1998 (IMF 1999, 53). Bank loans, instead, fluctuated. Large reversals of bank loans took place in 1995, following the Mexican currency crisis, and in 1997-98, following the East Asian and Russian crises. Even more impressive is the extent of cross-border transactions in bonds and equities for the major industrialized countries. As an example, cross-border transactions for Italy literally took off at the end of the 1980s, when controls on capital flows and foreign exchange transactions were abolished.

Financial contagion refers to an exceptional degree of interdependence that cannot be explained by fundamentals. Financial contagion puts at risk countries with acceptable fundamentals and raises the question of what type of assistance the international community needs to provide to those countries that find themselves in financial turmoil through no fault of their own. This is comparable to a situation in which the failure of one bank, because of limited information, spreads to others.

The existence of a significant degree of normal interdependence justifies the establishment of minimal levels of international regulation and international standards; the existence of contagion, instead, may justify the intervention of an international agency acting as a disciplined ILOL. Normal interdependence means that what happens to one country spills over to other countries, through trade and capital account links. The geographical scope of regulation and standards must expand beyond national boundaries if financial institutions based in one country are to be acceptable counterparties to transactions with financial institutions in other countries. If the scope of regulation were to remain national, financial institutions would spend valuable resources in arbitraging regulatory differences.

Contagion places at risk well-behaved countries, that is, countries that adhere to good macroeconomic policies and financial standards. These countries may require access to liquidity to deflect the consequences of contagion. The Meltzer Commission (2000) recommended that the IMF be the ILOL institution. In the commission's recommendation, IMF lending would be short term, at penalty rates, and conditional on ex-ante standards of financial soundness. However, the implementation of standards must be observed and concretely verified rather than merely monitored by the ILOL agency (Fratianni and Pattison 2001b).

One may argue that the important distinction between fundamentals-driven interdependence and exceptional interdependence is not yet fully operational as a practical guide to policy. In fact, the literature has had some difficulty in differentiating, theoretically and empirically, normal interdependence from contagion. On one hand, Schwartz (1998) spoke of the myth of contagion, and Bordo (1999) stated unequivocally that "[he] know[s] of no evidence of pure contagion" (p. 372). On the other hand, Calvo and Reinhart (1996) presented evidence that more than fundamentals were involved in the spillovers following the Mexican crisis; the same qualitative conclusion was reached by Baig and Golfajn (1998) for the 1997 East Asian currency crisis.

The balance of the evidence to date is that contagion is difficult to measure separately from fundamentals-driven spillovers (Dornbusch, Park, and Claessens 2000). Yet, the inability to distinguish between the two is not a justification for inaction. The implementation of international norms for regulation, including rules for competition, and best financial practices can reduce the risk of financial contagion by inducing countries to adopt better fundamentals. By improving its fundamentals, a country has a better chance of reducing contagion. The distinction between fundamentals-driven interdependence and pure contagion is critical, instead, for the administration of ILOL. While drawing that distinction is hard, it is no more difficult than sorting out Walter Bagehot's distinction between illiquidity and insolvency, which is at the heart of the administration of the lender-of-last-resort function.

In sum, international coordination of minimum national regulation and financial standards promises to yield better results than either national regulatory competition or a single supranational regulatory agency. Also, this solution is consistent with the political realities that would make it impossible to delegate regulation to a nonaccountable and unresponsive World Financial Authority. The international coordination approach is neither easy nor fast. By the sheer number, size, complexity, and financial importance of the players involved, progress will not be linear: crises will accelerate coordination, and financial calms will slow it down.

THE IMPLEMENTATION OF STANDARDS

We have argued that international coordination of national regulation and financial standards is a superior strategy to either national regulatory competition or a single supranational regulatory agency. The political advantage of the coordinated solution is that it is consistent with the aspirations of many countries not to relinquish complete control of financial regulation to a nonaccountable and unresponsive World Financial Authority.

Space does not permit a review of international standards; for that, the interested reader may want to consult Goldstein (1997), Eichengreen (1999b), Fratianni and Pattison (2001a), and the Web site of the Financial Stability Forum (FSF).[2] At the time of writing, standard-setting bodies have formulated and proposed sixty-four standards dealing with a broad set of issues: economic, financial, accounting and auditing, financial conglomerate supervision, market integrity, and market functioning (FSF 2000a, 20-21). Some of the standards pertain directly to banks and other financial intermediaries, others to national regulators and supervisors. These standards are often expressed in rather general language, which is open to different meanings by different people living in different cultures. To reduce or eliminate ambiguities, each standard is accompanied by a set of clarifying statements and operating procedures, called methodologies (FSF 2000a, 24). The entire exercise is complex and in rapid evolution. To simplify matters, the FSF (2001) has identified twelve standards (see Table 1) "as key for sound financial systems and deserving of priority implementation, depending on country circumstances. The key standards are broadly accepted as representing *minimum requirements* for good practice" (p. 3, our emphasis).

International standards are referred to alternatively as codes, principles, good regulatory practice, and recommendations. Regardless of their name, the important point to remember is that these standards do not portray best practices but rather minimum accepted levels. On this point, the Basel Committee on Banking Supervision (1997) was clear: "The Principles are minimum requirements and in many cases may well need to be supplemented by other measures" (p. 16). The above citation from the FSF reinforces this assessment.

International standards have no independent legal standing. As Giovanoli (2000) stated, "the standards . . . are simply recommendations, which are neither legally binding at the international level nor self-executing in any country" (p. 45). The FSF was quick to recognize this aspect and set up an appropriate task force (FSF 2000a, 2000b). The task force openly acknowledged the difficulty of implementing and monitoring standards and the incentives of many countries not to make monitoring reports public. The task force believed, however, that standard adoption and implementation could be fostered through "country ownership," market and official incentives, and tighter partnerships. For example, the IMF and the World Bank are international organizations with a high degree of legitimacy because of their universal membership. In addition to legitimacy, these two institutions have the ability to structure incentives and are uniquely placed to monitor adherence to standards through their joint Financial Sector Assessment program and Reports on Observance of Standards and Codes.[3] Notwithstanding the endorsement of the FSF, significant concerns remain about the ability of the IMF to monitor standards given the conflicts of interest inherent in its many roles, the political role of its governance mechanism, and the increased concentration of power in the institution.[4]

The rest of the article deals with the issue of standard implementation. We begin by underscoring the following four principles stemming from the Basel Concordat of 1975, namely, the following:

TABLE 1
STANDARDS AND STANDARD-SETTING INSTITUTIONS

Standard	Content	Issuing Institution
Core principles for effective banking supervision	Twenty-five basic principles of banking supervision	Basel Committee on Banking Supervision Established in 1975 by the G10 central banks in the wake of the Herstatt Bankaus failure.
Core principles for systematically important payment systems	Principles for the design and operation of systemically important payment systems	Committee on Payment and Settlement Systems (CPSS) Established in 1990 by the G10 central banks, CPSS deals with payment and settlement payment issues
Code of good practices on transparency in monetary and financial policies	Transparency practices for central banks and monetary policy	International Monetary Fund (IMF)
Code of good practices in fiscal transparency	Transparency practices for government finances and fiscal policy	IMF
Special data dissemination standard/general data dissemination system	Good statistical practices for economic, financial and sociodemographic data. Relate to data coverage, data quality data, and access by the public and integrity	IMF
Principles of corporate governance	Rights of shareholders, equitable treatment of shareholders, role of stakeholders, disclosure and transparency rules, responsibilities of the board	Organization for Economic Cooperation and Development
Principles on cross-border insolvency	In progress	World Bank
The forty recommendations of the Financial Action Task Force	Guidelines for anti-money laundering	Financial Action Task Force on Money Laundering (FATF) Established in 1989 by the Paris G7 Summit, FAFT fights money laundering
Objectives and principles of securities regulation	Thirty principles for regulating securities markets	International Organization of Securities Commission (IOSCO) Established in 1983, IOSCO promotes standards of securities regulation
Insurance core principles	Basic principles for insurance supervision	International Association of Insurance Supervisors (IAIS) Established in 1994, IAIS is a forum for cooperation among insurance regulators and supervisors

TABLE 1 Continued

Standard	Content	Issuing Institution
International accounting standards	Principles to be followed in the preparation of financial statements	International Accounting Standards Committee (IASC) Established in 1973, IASC is a private sector body that tries to harmonize accounting principles
International standards on auditing	Principles to be followed for auditing	International Federation of Accountants (IFAC) Established in 1977, IFAC is a private sector body that tries to harmonize auditing standards

SOURCE: Financial Stability Forum (2001).

1. All international banks must be supervised by a home country authority on a consolidated basis.
2. The creation of a cross-border banking establishment must receive the prior consent of both the host country and the home country authority.
3. Home country authorities have the right to gather information from their cross-border banking establishments.
4. If the host country authority determines that any of these three standards is not being met, it can impose restrictive measures or prohibit the establishment of banking offices.

We underscore principle 4, in particular, because it establishes an entry barrier to a financial market if banks from another country have not met minimum standards. This principle has been reiterated by the mentioned task force on standards implementation (FSF 2000b, 13 and 44): host regulators could deny market access to foreign institutions if the home jurisdiction fails to observe standards.[5]

There is a natural division of responsibilities in the coordinated solution. Standard setting must be global and stems from the activity of international standard setters. Standard implementation, on the other hand, is best left with the national authorities. There is no good alternative to vesting local regulatory and supervisory agencies with the task of enforcing international standards. This is for three reasons. First, as we have repeatedly mentioned, it is wishful thinking that national authorities may wither away or be superseded by a supranational agency (Eichengreen 1999a, 1999b). Second, international standards are "soft laws" in the sense that they carry no legal standing in sovereign states. For standards to become legally binding, sovereign states must transform them into laws (Giovanoli 2000, 34-35). The fact that laws remain the prerogative of nation states leads to the final consideration. Namely, oversight and supervision cannot be delegated to a distant and unaccountable international enforcer.

Local enforcement does not mean that the international community is impotent in encouraging proper enforcement. To begin with, the very act of accepting minimum international financial standards unleashes the powerful force of millions of economic operators and institutions that have an interest in making sure that these standards are met. This activity is spontaneous and uncoordinated and, using the terminology of von Mises, can be likened to a "financial night watchman" (Jordan 1999). Furthermore, the adoption of financial standards can become the conditions for acceding to ILOL facilities. While there is no obvious international counterpart to the domestic provider of lender of last resort, the IMF has evolved into a de-facto ILOL agency. The Meltzer Commission (2000) would like to "officialize" this role by adding the constraint that the IMF lend exclusively short term, at penalty rates and against good collateral to countries that meet specific standards. The main criticism of the Meltzer Commission's recommendation is that, under prequalification, the ILOL agency may either lend too much to the qualifiers or too little to the nonqualifiers, instigating either moral hazard or welfare losses. The alternative of letting the IMF continue its practice of ex-post conditionality lending runs the risk that this agency may be too generous with the carrot of the subsidy to justify the conditions attached to its lending (Fratianni and Pattison 2001b). Since neither solution is a first best solution, the ILOL agency could in practice use a combination of preconditionality and ex-post conditionality.

The "portal" implementation mechanism

A coordinated strategy is at the heart of the promulgation of minimum standards. These standards will have to be voluntarily adopted by countries and will have to be enforced locally. While there is no better alternative, local implementation remains the Achilles' heel of the scheme.

One possible solution to the implementation problem would envision incentive-compatible contracts between the international standard setters and national regulators to ensure that the interests of the latter coincide with the objectives of the former. The reason for incentive-compatible contracts is that auditing techniques are imperfect and give rise to multitier incentives for misrepresentation. Bank management in some countries may misrepresent information to national regulators because it wants to collectivize eventual bank losses. Bank regulators may misrepresent information to the legislative branch because they want to capture parts of the rents from collectivization (Laffont and Tirole 1991; Hauswald and Senbet 1999). In an international context, there would be a third layer of misrepresentation: from the national regulators to the international standard setters and the ILOL agency, motivated by the desire of the national banking industry and national regulator to collectivize (at the world level) the eventual losses of national bank failures, for example through IMF subsidized lending. The theory of incentive-compatible contracts tries to solve the problem of regulation by making it a self-enforcing mechanism. While we are strongly in sympathy with this literature, we also find it impractical at this stage. To fix the problem at the world level, we would have to implement a myriad of incentive-compatible contracts, and we would have to endow the international standard setters and the ILOL agency with a budget sufficient to write incentive-compatible contracts with several hundred national regulators. The degree of interference with national bodies politic would be such that people would raise the same objections against the coordinated solution that we have raised against the World Financial Authority.

The alternative to incentive-compatible contracts is a mechanism that relies on the incentives of leading financial centers to implement high standards. These centers are the portals that give access to the major international financial markets through which systemic risk is transmitted.[6] Consider, first, why the system of financial standards works for G10 countries. There are two basic reasons. First, the central bank governors and senior regulators meet regularly; these meetings spread essential knowledge, including information on cheaters, and build confidence in each other's regulatory systems. The G10 is small, homogeneous, and rich in intelligence on financial markets. Equally important, the G10 accounts for a very large share of international financial transactions in the world. The extent of the asymmetry is such that the G10 regulators can induce imitation in other countries' regulators through the force of competition. In essence, the G10 countries can act as industry leaders and implement best business practices. The rest of the industry has the choice of either responding in kind or seek an alternative strategy. Those who respond in kind would do business with industry leaders; those who do not would have to create a network of their own.

The G10 model can be further refined by recognizing that the United States and the United Kingdom are the financial leaders of this elite group. The United States and the United Kingdom handle the largest volume of international financial transactions. Their dominant position is clearly recognized in Basel. More important, a vast number of internationally active banks and financial institutions reside in one or the other financial center. It is well known that these two countries today impose higher standards than those promulgated in Basel; these standards, while imperfect and evolving, represent the industry's best regulatory practices. A large number of internationally active banks voluntarily accept the U.K. and U.S. standards, affecting their head offices and other parts of their organizations. The U.S. and U.K. regulators routinely assess home country regulation, accounting standards, as well as central bank and payments systems for all inbound banks. They also make a determination as to how much to rely on foreign supervision. If doubts exist on the latter, domestic supervision takes over. As Peterson (2001) noted, "some observers have the feeling that the more clued-up regulators, notably the Federal Reserve and the FSA [Financial Services Authority], are getting too far ahead of their less sophisticated colleagues" (p. 53).

What would happen to foreign banks that did not qualify for access to the high-regulation markets of the United States and the United Kingdom? These banks would have the following four alternatives:

- they could apply for a banking subsidiary charter in the United States or the United Kingdom and, consequently, elect to adopt the standards and oversight rules of the host regulator only in that specific market;
- they could seek a certification of Basel-inspired international financial and accounting standards by an internationally recognized accounting firm. The certification would be tantamount to a financial passport for cross-border financial transactions. The financial passport, however, may not be valid for the more regulated U.S. or U.K. banking and financial markets;
- they could move their business to host states with lower regulatory standards than the Basel-inspired standards. These banks would have a limited geographical reach in their cross-border transactions. Furthermore, they would be located in substandard regulatory countries that would not be eligible for the international lender of last resort facility; or
- they could refrain from international banking and financial activity.

In sum, internationally active banks have the choice to do business in high-, acceptable-, or low-regulation markets. The high-regulation countries implement best business practices because they desire to maintain a stellar reputation for sound banking practices to attract a broader array of high-quality counterparties for their financial center. They therefore attract a large share of the world's internationally, highly rated, active banks. These countries are the industry's leaders and raise the bar for the system as a whole. Through competitive pressure, some countries would emulate the industry's leaders; others would adopt the Basel-inspired standards, which are minimum standards. The adoption of the Basel-inspired standards would be a sine qua non to do business with high-regulation countries and to qualify for ILOL services. Finally, other countries would opt for a low-regulation and a higher risk strategy. Internationally active banks would have a choice to locate in one of the three areas; competition for regulation would be preserved. The transmission of risk from one area to another would be curtailed by the application of the Basel Concordat principles. Host country regulators would have the power to disconnect the operations of internationally active banks operating in their territories. Not only would low-regulation countries be unable to deal with higher regulation countries, but they would also not qualify for the ILOL facility.

CONCLUSIONS

History records numerous and different types of international financial crises. These may be the necessary price to pay for a liberal order. Financial suppression at home and controls on international capital flows could prevent such crises, but we would lose the benefits of a competitive and innovative financial system. Risk can be tempered by the adoption and implementation of international financial standards.

We have argued that a coordinated strategy for international regulation is superior to either national regulation or to an all-powerful World Financial Authority. Banking and financial standards are the core business of today's standard-setting bodies. Implementation of these standards is and should be left to local regulatory and supervisory authorities. This is for three reasons. First, it is wishful thinking that national authorities may wither away or be superseded by an all-powerful international agency. Second, standards are soft laws; to be implemented locally they need to be transformed into national laws. Finally, oversight and supervision are hands-on affairs that require intimate knowledge of local institutions and management and a legal basis, which cannot be delegated to a distant and unaccountable international enforcer.

Implementation is the Achilles' heel of international standards. Our recommendation is to rely on a combination of competition and dominant country position. Today, a small group of portal countries implement financial standards exceeding those standards approved by the standard-setting bodies. These countries have high regulatory reputations and attract many internationally active banks. They can use their dominant position to induce other countries to adopt internationally approved minimum standards. In fact, the Basel Concordat gives host country regulators the prerogative to deny access into their domestic markets to poorly regulated institutions from foreign countries. The final carrot in the implementation scheme is that adoption of the standards is one of the conditions for the country to qualify for the ILOL facility.

Notes

1. The G10 group consists of the United States, Canada, Japan, France, Germany, Italy, the United Kingdom, Belgium, the Netherlands, and Sweden; Switzerland is an observer.

2. See the Financial Stability Forum's (FSF's) Web site at http://www.fsforum.org.

3. There is a division of tasks between the International Monetary Fund (IMF) and the World Bank in their joint programs (FSF 2001, 17). Also, the IMF can act as a monitor through Article IV consultations.

4. Giovanoli (2000) stated that an expanded standards' role of the IMF "may give rise to concern about an excessive concentration of power" (p. 58).

5. The report (2000b) read as follows: "(a) a host jurisdiction could take into account in deciding whether . . . it will allow a foreign institution to operate in its markets, the degree to

which that institution's home jurisdiction observes relevant standards." Likewise, "a home jurisdiction could place restrictions on its domestic financial institutions' operations in foreign jurisdictions with material gaps in observance of relevant standards" (p. 44).

6. In reviewing the literature, the only similar reference that we have found refers to a fundamentally different concept. "Gatekeepers" are professionals such as lawyers and accountants who play an important role in combating money laundering and organized crime as noted at the G8 Moscow Ministerial Conference on Combating Transnational Organized Crime. See Department of Finance (2001, 2).

References

Baig, T., and I. Goldfajn. 1998. Financial market contagion in the Asian crisis. IMF working paper no. 98-155.

Basel Committee on Banking Supervision. 1997. Core principles for effective banking supervision. Compendium of documents produced by the Basel Committee on Banking Supervision. Basel, Switzerland: Bank for International Settlements.

Bordo, Michael D. 1999. International rescues versus bailouts: A historical perspective. *Cato Journal* 18 (3): 363-75.

Calomiris, Charles W. 1998. The IMF's imprudent role as lender of last resort. *Cato Journal* 17 (3): 275-94.

Calomiris, Charles W., and Allan H. Meltzer. 1999. Reforming the IMF. Typescript.

Calvo, Sara, and Carmen M. Reinhart. 1996. Capital flows to Latin America: Is there evidence of contagion effects? In *Private capital flows to emerging markets*, edited by Guillermo A. Calvo, Morris Goldstein, and Eduard Hochreiter. Washington, DC: Institute for International Economics.

Department of Finance. 2001. *Fighting the abuses of the global financial system*. Ottawa: Government of Canada.

Dornbusch, Rudiger, Yung Chul Park, and Stijn Claessens. 2000. Contagion: Understanding how it spreads. *World Bank Research Observer* 15 (2): 177-97.

Eatwell, John, and Lance Taylor. 2000. *Global finance at risk: The case for international regulation*. New York: New Press.

Eichengreen, Barry. 1999a. Building on a consensus. *Financial Times*, 2 February.

———. 1999b. *Towards a new international financial architecture: A practical post-Asia agenda*. Washington, DC: Institute for International Economics.

Financial Stability Forum. 2000a. Issues paper of the task force on implementation of standards, 15 March, http://www.fsforum.org.

———. 2000b. Report of the follow-up group on incentives to foster implementation of standards, August 31, http://www.fsforum.org.

———. 2001. International standards and codes to strengthen financial systems, April, http://www.fsforum.org.

Frankel, Jeffrey A., and Alan T. MacArthur. 1988. Political vs. currency risk premia in international real interest rate differentials: A study of forward rates for 24 countries. *European Economic Review* 32 (5): 1083-114.

Fratianni, Michele. 1995. Bank deposit insurance in the European Union. In *Politics and institutions in an integrated Europe*, edited by B. Eichengreen, J. Frieden, and J. von Hagen. Berlin: Springer.

Fratianni, Michele, and John Pattison. 2001a. The bank for international settlements: An assessment of its role in international monetary and financial policy. *Open Economies Review* 12:197-222.

———. 2001b. The international lender of last resort: A concept in search of a meaning. Mimeo.

Giovanoli, Mario. 2000. A new architecture for the global financial market: Legal aspects of international financial standard setting. In *International monetary law*, edited by Mario Giovanoli. Oxford: Oxford University Press.

Goldstein, Morris. 1997. *The case for an international banking standard*. Washington, DC: Institute for International Economics.

Goldstein, Morris, and David Folkerts-Landau. 1993. Systemic issues in international finance. *World Economic and Financial Surveys*. Washington, DC: International Monetary Fund.

Hauswald, Robert B. H., and Lemma W. Senbet. 1999. Public and private agency conflict in banking regulation. Kelley School of Business, Department of Finance working paper.

International Monetary Fund (IMF). 1998. *World economic outlook—October 1998*. Washington, DC: International Monetary Fund.

———. 1999. *International capital markets: Developments, prospects, and key policy issues*. Washington, DC: International Monetary Fund.

Jordan, Jerry L. 1999. The evolving global monetary order. Keynote address at the seventeenth annual Monetary Conference. Washington, DC: Cato Institute.

Kaminsky, Graciela, and Carmen Reinhart. 1999. The twin crisis: Causes of banking and balance of payments problems. *American Economic Review* 89 (June): 473-500.

Kane, Edward J. 2000. Relevance and need for international regulatory standards. Mimeo prepared for the Brookings-Wharton Conference on Integrating Emerging Market Economies into the Global Financial System.

Laffont, J. J., and J. Tirole. 1991. The politics of government decision making: A theory of regulatory capture. *Quarterly Journal of Economics* 106:1089-127.

Llewellyn, David T. 2000. Some lessons for bank regulation from recent crises. *Open Economies Review* 11 (Supplement 1, August): 69-109.

Marston, Richard C. 1995. *International financial integration: A study of interest differentials between the major industrial countries*. New York: Cambridge University Press.

Meltzer, Allan H. 1999. What's wrong with the IMF? What would be better? In *The Asian financial crisis: Origins, implications, and solutions*, edited by William C. Hunter, George G. Kaufman, and Thomas H. Krueger. Norwell, MA: Kluwer Academic.

Meltzer Commission (Allan H. Melzer, chairman). 2000. *Report of the International Financial Institution Advisory Commission*. Washington, DC: U.S. Treasury, March.

Obstfeld, Maurice. 1995. International capital mobility in the 1990s. In *The defining moment: The Great Depression and the American economy in the twentieth century*, edited by Michael D. Bordo, Claudia Goldin, and Eugene N. White. Chicago: University of Chicago Press.

Peterson, Michael. 2001. Basel gives banks the whip hand. *Euromoney*, March:48-53.

Schwartz, Anna J. 1998. International financial crises: Myths and realities. *Cato Journal* 17 (3): 251-56.

White, William. 1999. What have we learned from recent financial crises and policy responses? Paper presented at the Conference on Lessons from Recent Global Financial Crises. Chicago, 30 September to 2 October.

Williamson, John, and M. Mahar. 1998. A survey of financial liberalisation. *Princeton Essays in International Finance*. No. 211. Princeton, NJ: International Finance Section, Department of Economics, Princeton University.

ANNALS, *AAPSS*, **579**, January 2002

Limiting Moral Hazard and Reducing Risk in International Capital Flows: The Choice of an Exchange Rate Regime

By RONALD I. MCKINNON

ABSTRACT: Monetary and financial management is much more difficult in emerging markets on the periphery of the industrial world than at the center. On the periphery, the domestic term structure of finance is short, and all foreign borrowing is denominated in foreign currency—usually dollars. An acute policy issue is whether the exchange rate should be fixed or more flexible in inhibiting banks and other financial institutions from cycles of overborrowing and undue foreign exchange exposure. This article shows that a "good" fix is better than floating, which in turn is better than a "bad" fix. But even a good fix must be complemented by strict domestic regulations forcing banks to preserve their capital and hedge their net foreign exchange exposure to stay good.

Ronald I. McKinnon is the William D. Eberle Professor of International Economics at Stanford University, where he has taught since 1961. His fields of specialization are international economics and development finance in which he has written more than one hundred articles and several books, which include The Order of Economic Liberalization: Financial Control in the Transition to a Market Economy *(1993),* The Rules of the Game: International Money and Exchange Rates *(MIT Press, 1996), and* Dollar and Yen: Resolving Economic Conflict Between the United States and Japan *(with Kenichi Ohno, 1997). He has been a consultant to central banks and finance ministries the world over, including international agencies such as the World Bank and International Monetary Fund.*

NOTE: I would like to thank Huw Pill of the Harvard Business School and the ECB for his ideas and help in preparing this article.

THE current consensus in the academic literature, endorsed by the International Monetary Fund (IMF) and other international organizations, is that one of the main lessons of recent financial crises in East Asia and Latin America is the need for more flexible exchange rate arrangements. Stanley Fischer (1999), the deputy managing director of the IMF, stated the matter thus:

> There is a tradeoff between the greater short-run volatility of the real exchange rate in a flexible rate regime versus the greater probability of a clearly defined external crisis financial crisis when the exchange rate is pegged. The virulence of the recent crises is likely to shift the balance towards the choice of more flexible exchange rate systems, including crawling pegs with wide bands.

In her article, "Nominal Anchor Exchange Rate Policies as a Domestic Distortion" (1997), Anne Krueger agreed. She analyzed how pegging the exchange rate to slow ongoing domestic inflation creates a distortion in the capital market. As long as the peg holds and domestic inflation continues, the effective real rate of return (cost of capital) seen by domestic investors falls below the real return being garnered by foreign creditors. So, absent exchange controls, this differential encourages excess inflows of capital—as in Mexico before the 1994 crisis.

Although Krueger is surely right for the "bad" fixes she identified, not all exchange rate fixes distort the international capital market. This article analyzes the choice of an exchange rate regime for "emerging-market" economies, that is, those that are both less developed and net absorbers of private foreign capital. But it does not focus directly on the exchange rate's role in macroeconomic stabilization. Instead, I focus on how interest differentials between the center country (the United States) and the periphery (emerging market economies) influence the incentive to hedge against currency risk, hedging that limits the undue absorption of foreign capital. The underlying risk minimization problem is considered in two dimensions.

First, suppose that the term structure of domestic and international debt finance is quite short—as is now the case throughout the developing world, such as in East Asia and Latin America. Do fixed or floating exchange rates minimize the incentives for banks and nonbank corporations to borrow without covering forward their short-term foreign currency debts? Here, I shall distinguish between "good" fixes and "bad" fixes.

Second is the question of whether the term to maturity of private debt finance is itself endogenous to the nature of the exchange rate regime. Instead of accepting short-term bank deposits, borrowing internationally by issuing long-term bonds is itself a hedge against currency crises—and permits a faster recovery once such attacks occur. Here, I shall argue that a credible domestic monetary program for stabilizing the exchange rate in the long run can lengthen the term to maturity of both national and international finance and thereby reduce the exposure of an emerging-market economy to sudden reversals of investor sentiment leading to financial panics.

But no exchange rate regime, no matter how well chosen, can avoid the need for prudential regulation of domestic banks to hedge their short-term foreign exchange risks—regulation that, on occasion, could extend to exchange controls over short-term international capital flows. The regulatory problem of getting banks to hedge their foreign exchange risk is, of course, aggravated by moral hazard from deposit insurance and from other sources of domestic and international bailouts should the payments mechanism be threatened by collective bank failures.

THE EXCHANGE RATE AS NOMINAL ANCHOR: THE REGULATORY DILEMMA

With the important exception of Japan, a common East Asian monetary standard existed before the crises of 1997 (Frankel and Wei, 1994; Ohno 1999). By keying on the dollar, the macroeconomic policies of the crisis economies—Indonesia, Korea, Malaysia, Philippines, and Thailand were (loosely) tied to each other—and to those of the noncrisis economies of Hong Kong, Singapore, and Taiwan. Their dollar exchange rates had been fairly stable for more than a decade and, by the purchasing power parity criterion, were more or less correctly aligned with each other and with the American price level (McKinnon 1999). Besides insulating each other from beggar-thy-neighbor devaluations, these informal dollar pegs had successfully anchored their domestic (wholesale) price levels during their remarkably rapid economic growth in the 1980s through 1996. (Similarly, a credible peg of 360 yen to the dollar the was the monetary anchor in Japan's own great era of high growth and rapid financial transformation in the 1950s and 1960s.)

In more open financial systems without exchange controls on capital account, is moral hazard from using the dollar exchange rate as a nominal anchor too high? Before the 1997 crisis, banks in the East Asian economies faced substantially higher nominal deposit rates in domestic currency than if they accepted eurodollar or euro-yen deposits. Figures 1, 2, 3, and 4 for Indonesia, Malaysia, Thailand, and Korea, respectively, show differentials between three-month deposits in domestic currency and those in eurodollars of the order of 2 to 10 percent. (And these spreads would be 4 to 5 percentage points higher if the very low short-term euro-yen rates were compared to deposit rates in rupiahs, ringgits, baht, won, and so on.)

Wouldn't banks have greater incentive to borrow unhedged in dollars if the domestic exchange rate were pegged rather than floating? Superficially, it seems plausible that, for a given interest differential and short-term finance, a pegged exchange rate would encourage banks with moral hazard and other risk loving agents to take the risk of borrowing in foreign exchange hoping that the exchange rate will not change within their short time horizons. Whereas, if the exchange rate were floating, they would be more hesitant to do so.

FIGURE 1
INDONESIA

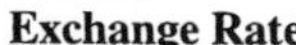

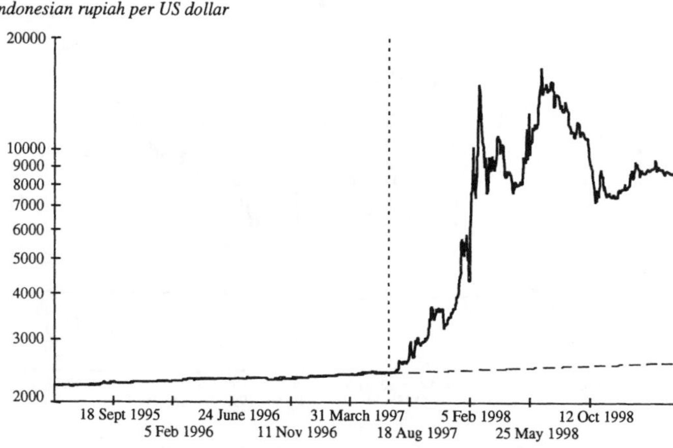

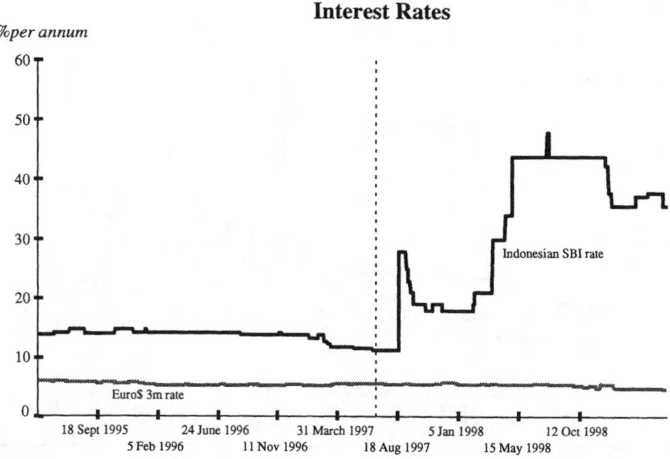

> The Asian experience shows that a potential problem with using a nominal exchange rate anchor is that while the private sector is supposed to base its wage and price decisions on the assumption of a fixed nominal exchange rate, the supervisory authorities may want the private sector to hedge its external liabilities just in case the exchange rate cannot be held fixed. (Adams et al. 1998, 79)

The dilemma is a real one. Given that domestic interest rates in developing countries on the periphery are naturally higher than those in the center country (the United States), regulatory authorities must be ever-vigilant to prevent unhedged borrowing by individual banks (or even nonbank firms) in dollars and in

FIGURE 2
MALAYSIA

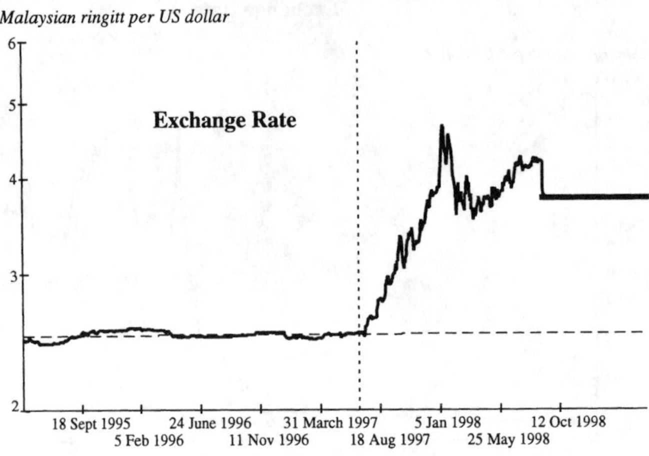

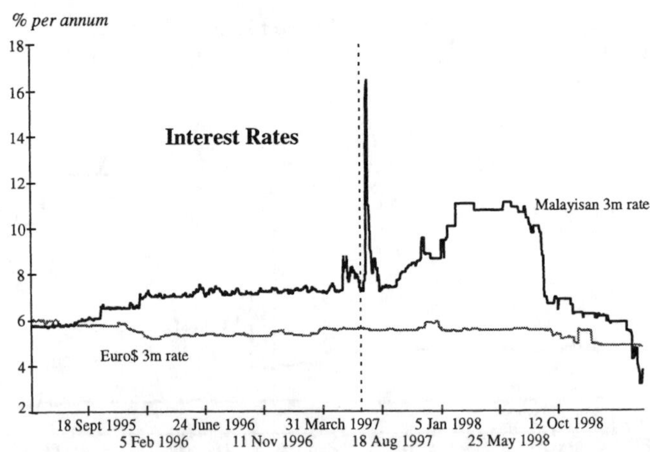

other foreign currencies. Otherwise, as unhedged foreign currency liabilities cumulate, risk premia (to be defined below) in domestic interest rates may increase for the country as a whole. As domestic interest rates rise, further adverse selection is triggered as more banks are tempted to borrow by accepting low-interest foreign currency deposits. Because no interest rate can be found to price currency risk properly, the international capital market breaks down in the presence of a multitude of national monies.

Floating the exchange rate need not mitigate this regulatory dilemma. Under floating, the temptation to

FIGURE 3
THAILAND

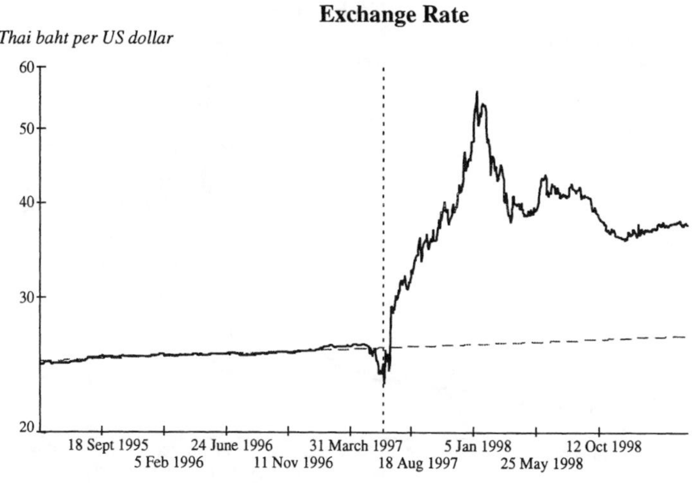

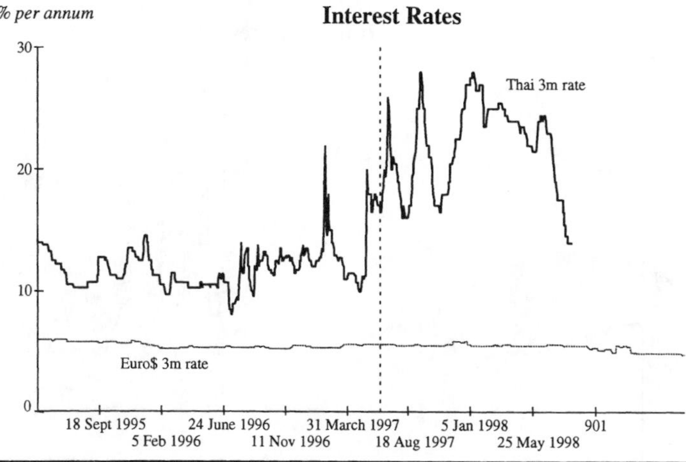

borrow unhedged at short term would still be there and could even be augmented. For the East Asian economies, giving up on the dollar as a collective nominal anchor, and the considerable long-run benefits deriving from that, may yield no offsetting regulatory advantages to help contain moral hazard in domestic banks and other institutions. A simple algebraic model can show this trade-off more precisely.

MODELING THE SUPER RISK PREMIUM

Consider some interest rate identities for a given, fairly short term to

FIGURE 4
KOREA

Exchange Rate

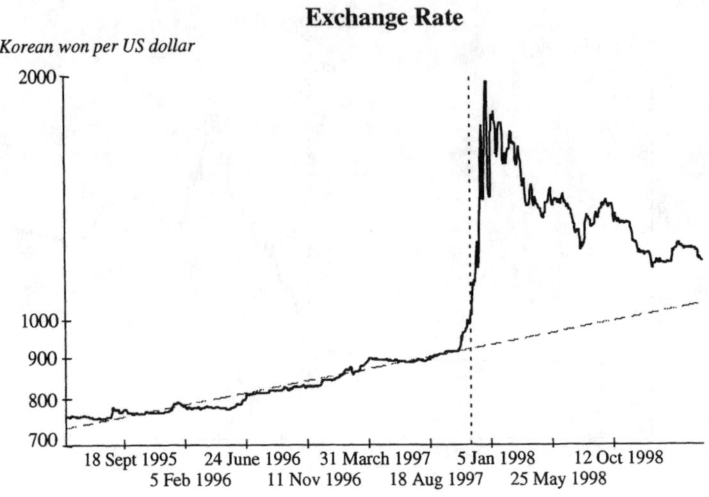

Interest Rates

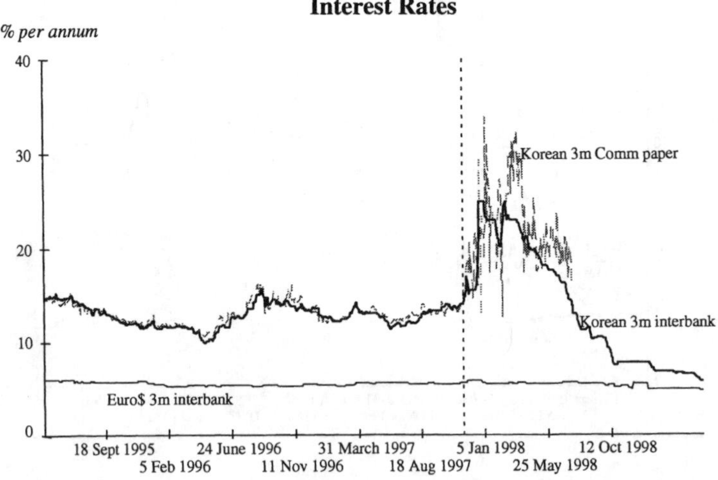

maturity. Suppose no government controls on international payments or domestic interest rates so that a well-organized market in currency futures can exist. Then, by covered interest arbitrage, the (deposit) interest differential is equal to the forward premium, that is,

$$i - i^* = f > 0, \qquad (1)$$

where

i = the domestic nominal (deposit) interest rate,

i^* = the dollar (deposit) interest rate in the international capital market, and

f = the forward premium on dollars in domestic currency.

If domestic banks accepting dollar deposits at the low interest rate i^* cover by buying dollars forward, the cost of the forward cover per dollar so borrowed is simply f. Thus, the effective interest rate on hedged dollar deposits is $i^* + f$.

$$i_{\text{hedged}} = i^* + f = i. \quad (2)$$

So, with forward covering, there is no net interest gain from accepting dollar deposits over accepting higher interest deposits in domestic currency. Hedged borrowers in foreign exchange see the same cost of capital as domestic banks accepting deposits denominated in the domestic currency.

Banks without moral hazard would voluntarily cover the exchange risk. They may well have accepted dollar deposits simply for convenience in clearing international payments. In contrast, poorly capitalized banks prepared to gamble on the basis of government deposit insurance might well accept low-cost dollar deposits as an ongoing source of finance for loans denominated in the domestic currency—unless a vigilant regulatory authority forces them to hedge.

But how much of the interest differential in equation (1) represents a "margin of temptation" where banks with (latent) moral hazard will try to avoid regulatory sanctions and borrow in dollars anyway? Let us partition the interest differential into the following:

$$i - i^* = \text{E}\hat{e} + \rho_{\text{currency}} \,. \quad (3)$$

ρ_{currency} is the currency risk premium as ordinarily defined. Apart from any unidirectional expected movement in the exchange rate, it represents the extra return required by investors to hold domestic rather than foreign currency assets. In the specific East Asian context, it represents domestic financial volatility—in interest rates or domestic price levels—measured against similar risk(s) prevailing in the markets of the center county, that is, the United States. Thus, ρ_{currency} increases with that country's exchange rate volatility against the U.S. dollar.

In the "peripheral" Asian debtor countries, ρ_{currency} is (was before 1997) normally greater than zero. But it can be reduced toward zero if there is financial convergence with the United States, that is, the dollar exchange rate has been credibly stabilized through proper price-level alignment so that interest rate volatility also approaches American levels.

The other component of the interest differential—the expected depreciation of the domestic currency, $E\hat{e}$—can be decomposed into two parts. First, within a managed exchange rate regime with a crawling or constant peg (typical of a few South East Asian countries, Mexico, Brazil, and several emerging-market economies), the exchange rate can change predictably and smoothly according to government's policy announcements and commitments, such as the downward crawl in the Indonesian rupiah before the 1997 crash (Figure 1). Second is the small probability of a "regime change": a large, sudden devaluation whose timing is unpredictable.

$$E\hat{e} \equiv E\hat{e}_{\text{predictable}} + E\hat{e}_{\text{regime change}}. \quad (4)$$

Although both types of expected change in the exchange rate in equation (4) widen the nominal interest differential in equation (3), it is plausible that $E\hat{e}_{\text{regime change}}$ is part of the margin of temptation for banks with moral hazard to overborrow, while $E\hat{e}_{\text{predictable}}$ is not. If the exchange rate was expected to depreciate smoothly through time, even banks with very short time horizons will account for the higher domestic currency costs of repaying short-term foreign currency deposits. Therefore, we exclude $E\hat{e}_{\text{predictable}}$ from our measure of the *super risk premium*:

$$\rho_{\text{super}} = \rho_{\text{currency}} + E\hat{e}_{\text{regime change}} = i - i^* - E\hat{e}_{\text{predictable}}. \quad (5)$$

The super risk premium, ρ_{super}, represents the margin of temptation for banks to overborrow in foreign exchange beyond what they might do if forced to hedge. (Even if banks were required to hedge their foreign exchange exposure, McKinnon and Pill [1996, 1997] showed that international overborrowing could still occur because banks with moral hazard assume too much domestic credit risk.) ρ_{super} has two components: the currency risk premium, as defined above, and the possibility that the regime could change through a discrete devaluation. The latter source of upward pressure on the interest rate on assets denominated in the domestic currency is sometimes called "the peso problem."

By borrowing unhedged in foreign currency, the domestic banks with deposit insurance and other government guarantees ignore downside bankruptcy risks implied by large devaluations whose timing is uncertain. They also ignore ongoing volatility in the exchange rate as measured by ρ_{currency}. In setting domestic nominal lending rates, the banks will only cover the "predictable" component of the expected depreciation within the currency regime. In the special case in which the nominal exchange rate is fixed, unhedged banks lend at the international nominal interest rate plus a normal profit margin. For ease of macroeconomic exposition in this article, this profit margin between deposits and loans is simply set at zero.

The basic idea here is that the decision-making horizon of the bank with moral hazard is sufficiently short that that it ignores unpredictable changes in the exchange rate. The managers of the bank simply hope that anything drastic, if it happens at all, won't happen "on their watch." The super risk premium in the interest differential then defines their margin of temptation to gamble and accept foreign currency deposits unhedged.

This incentive to gamble by a poorly supervised bank also extends to incurring undue risks with its domestic loan portfolio. McKinnon and Pill (1998 and 1999) showed how this domestic credit risk interacts with foreign exchange risk to lead to (potentially) enormous overborrowing in international markets. Using a large cross-country database, Kaminsky and Reinhart (1999) linked the prevalence of domestic banking (credit) crises to foreign exchange crises, that is, runs on the currency.

GOOD FIXES VERSUS BAD FIXES VERSUS FLOATING

The debate over fixed versus floating exchange rates has been going on since the end of World War II and has many dimensions, all of which cannot be covered here. For any emerging-market country where the dollar remains the safe-haven and reference currency as in Asia, Latin America, and elsewhere, the optimal choice of an exchange rate regime can be narrowed down to an exercise in minimizing the super risk premium. Assuming that there is potential moral hazard in banks, what exchange rate regime would minimize the margin of temptation to overborrow?

Like almost all protagonists in the debate, I initially abstract from term-structure considerations, that is, consider interest rates, exchange rates, risk premia, and so on, as if there was only one, fairly short, term to maturity—as in the algebraic framework developed above. (This assumption is relaxed below.) Under this analytical ground rule, did the Asian-five crisis economies make a mistake in pegging to the dollar before 1997?

The $E\hat{e}_{\text{regime change}}$ component of the super risk premium would seem to be higher under a pegged than under a floating exchange rate. Fixed exchange rates tend to break down on occasion. Even though the probability of a large discrete devaluation is small in any one decision interval, domestic interest rates can be driven up in the face of this possibility. Thus, at first glance, one might conclude that the margin of temptation, as measured by ρ_{super}, is higher when the exchange rate is being used as the nominal anchor. And for postcrisis East Asia, influential commentators—for example, the deputy managing director of the IMF, Stanley Fischer (1999), Barry Eichengreen (1999), Martin Wolf (1999), and George Soros (1999)—have argued for greater exchange-rate flexibility.

But this line of argument overlooks ρ_{currency}, the other component of the super risk premium. For any given peripheral country, ρ_{currency} depends on the stability of its exchange rate cum monetary regime, which largely depends on the robustness of its link to the world dollar standard. In times of crisis, the dollar is viewed as the safe-haven currency or definitive money; and, correspondingly, the yield on U.S. Treasury bonds defines (in the argot of the finance literature) the "risk-free" return. So if a country on the periphery of the dollar standard credibly integrates monetary policy with that of the United States—convergence in rates of price inflation to secure the exchange rate without the threat of using exchange controls—such a good fix will be rewarded with a lower ρ_{currency} and a low $E\hat{e}_{\text{regime change}}$. Before 1997, Malaysia seems to have come closest to this nirvana of using a good fix to minimize ρ_{super}. Figure 2 shows that its short-term interest rate was closest (within 1 or 2 percent) to the American.

Not under duress, now suppose a country voluntarily decides to "abandon" the dollar standard as the nominal anchor and float its exchange rate. As long as the great mass of internationally tradable goods and services is dollar invoiced and stable valued, this experiment in monetary independence is somewhat difficult to define. Suppose that the central bank does not directly key on its dollar exchange rate but aims to stabilize the domestic price level by other means. Then, in a natural dollar zone, success will still lead to a nearly stable exchange rate with the dollar (McKinnon 1999).

But suppose our monetary authority is a more determined floater. Concerned with the potential moral hazard in commercial banks from the exchange rate remaining stable, the central bank arranges policy so that the exchange rate continually moves like a "random walk" per month or even per quarter. Then, because random exchange-rate movements increase volatility in domestic-currency prices and interest rates, $\rho_{currency}$ also increases. And this increase in $\rho_{currency}$ will be aggravated if the country in question is a large foreign currency debtor.

In summary, moving from a good fix to a floating exchange rate need not reduce the super risk premium and the margin of temptation for international overborrowing ex ante, that is, before any major attack on the currency. Under greater exchange rate flexibility, $\rho_{currency}$ will increase even if $E\hat{e}_{regime\ change}$ declines. (But even a floating exchange rate can be attacked, so $E\hat{e}_{regime\ change}$ is not negligible.)

Of course, a bad fix—that is, one that is obviously unsustainable because of, say, ongoing domestic fiscal deficits likely to be monetized (Russia and Brazil in 1998), or just with ongoing inflation as Krueger identified for Mexico before the 1994 crash—will make $E\hat{e}_{regime\ change}$ very large. Correspondingly high domestic interest rates relative to those prevailing in safe-haven-currency countries create a huge margin of temptation for unhedged international borrowing that could completely undermine the domestic system of prudential bank regulations (McKinnon and Pill 1999). Here, a more flexible but controlled exchange rate, perhaps a downward crawl that matches the internal rate of inflation, coupled with controls over international capital flows seems more likely to be the best way of coping with such an unfortunate situation.

But before the 1997 currency attacks, the East Asian pegs to the dollar looked like good fixes with purchasing power parity, price level stability, and fiscal balance. The problem was not with their exchange rate policies but with the weak prudential regulation of their financial systems. In defense of the regulators, however, the resulting overborrowing was aggravated by the erratic behavior of the yen/dollar exchange rate and the extremely low nominal interest rates on borrowing in Japan in yen (McKinnon 1999).

THE RESTORATION RULE AND THE LONG-RUN CONFIDENCE PROBLEM

In comparing good fixes to floating to bad fixes, our short-run analysis of the super risk premium proceeded without specifying the term structure of interest rates and exchange-rate expectations into the more distant future. In common with the literature on the subject, we focused on the incentives to overborrow ex ante, that is, before any speculative attack. Moreover, also in common with the literature, we did not specify the exchange rate obligations of the authorities after a (successful) attack had occurred. In a model that had only one term to maturity, we defined a good fix to be one in which any peripheral country maintained nominal exchange rate stability and purchasing power parity against the center country's currency ex ante.

However, implicit in the ideal of a good fix is that it is sustainable in the more distant future. Even if a surprise speculative attack upsets the fixed rate system in the short run, the macroeconomic fundamentals and the determination of the authorities would still allow the economy to recover its nominal exchange rate and price-level equilibrium in the long run. If such a favorable long-run expectation could be sustained, this would prevent—or at least limit—the kind of fundamental loss of confidence in their currencies that the five Asian countries actually experienced in late 1997 and early 1998.

The behavior of countries operating under the international gold standard before 1914 is instructive. In the face of a liquidity crisis, a country would sometimes resort to gold devices; that is, it would raise the buying price for gold or interfere with its exportation. This amounted to a minor, albeit temporary, suspension of its traditional gold parity. In more major crises including wars, a few outright suspensions for some months or years occurred. After any suspension and devaluation, however, the gold standard generally succeeded in having countries return to their traditional mint parities. The resulting long-run stability in exchange rates helped anchor the common price level and long-term interest rates. In early 1914, exchange rates, wholesale prices, and interest rates in the industrial countries were virtually the same as they had been in the late 1870s.

This gave the pre-1914 gold standard great long-run resilience. After any short-run crisis that forced the partial or complete suspension of a gold parity, the country in question was obliged to return to its traditional parity as soon as practicable (Bordo and Kydland 1995). I have dubbed this unwritten obligation of the classical gold standard "the restoration rule" (McKinnon 1996, chap. 2). Even when a currency crisis undermined the government's ability to sustain convertibility in the near term, longer term exchange rate expectations remained regressive with respect to the country's traditional gold parity. Because of the restoration rule, long-term interest rates showed little volatility by modern standards (McKinnon and Ohno 1997, chap. 8); and, without significant financial risk, their levels also remained low: about 3 percent in the United Kingdom and 4 percent in the United States.

For the pre-1914 gold standard, Charles Goodhart and P.J.R Delargy (1998) studied how high-growth debtor countries on the periphery of Britain responded to speculative attacks. Their sample included Austria, Argentina. Australia, Italy, and the United States (which experienced several attacks). They concluded,

> The onset and initial context of the Asian crisis, involving an interaction between a toppling investment boom and a febrile banking system, should not have been surprising. From an historical point of view, it was depressingly familiar. Moreover, it will happen again and again. Much of the pattern is, probably, an inherent feature of development.
>
> What, however, differed from our pre-1914 crises and the Asian crisis was the international monetary regime and the consequential implications for post-crisis monetary conditions in the affected countries. Confidence in the maintenance of the gold standard, pre-1914, led to stabilizing mean-reverting expectations, and hence a rapid restoration of gold reserves, liquidity, and low interest rates alongside the maintenance of continued price stability. In the main case in our pre-1914 sample where there was no such confidence (Argentina), pressures on the exchange rate were eased by a (debt) moratorium, allowing a sharply improving trade balance to bring about the needed monetary expansion. (P. 285)

The parallel for a restored East Asian dollar standard is quite clear. Each central bank sets its long-run monetary policy to be consistent with maintaining a "traditional" exchange rate against the dollar within a narrow band, which amounts to having the same long-run rate of price inflation (optimally zero) in its producer price index as in the United States. (This does not rule out slowly gliding bands as followed by Indonesia and Singapore before 1997.) Each central bank also announces that it will normally adjust short-run interest rates and intervene to keep its exchange rate within the band. But under a massive speculative attack, the authority may well suspend the fixed rate by floating temporarily—and not defend it by raising short-term interest rates to exorbitant levels.

However, this is not the end of the story. As soon as practicable after the speculative attack, the distressed country's central bank would begin nudging its exchange rate back up toward its traditional dollar parity. Allowing for temporary crisis-based suspensions of the fixed exchange rate, followed by (gradual) restoration of the traditional parity, poses problems for speculators. They do not have any clear point at which to get out of their short position in the domestic currency to realize speculative profits. In contrast, a more or less discrete devaluation in response to a speculative attack, with no attempt at restoration, makes it easy for speculators to get out safely. Paradoxically, even though speculators know that temporary suspensions of the fixed exchange rate are possible, speculative attacks may diminish if they also know in advance that the restoration rule is in place.

In highly indebted economies, the worst possible trade-off is sharply higher domestic interest rates and deep devaluations that cause massive bankruptcies throughout the economy. The forced suspension of the exchange rate peg is accompanied by such policy disarray that people see no future for the dollar value of their currencies and lose confidence completely, as more or less happened in the Asian five.

To stem this loss of confidence, each affected Asian government should have announced its intention to restore its traditional dollar parities as soon the dust settled. To be sure, renegotiating the external debt to greatly lengthen its term structure while improving the prudential regulation of the banks would be an important part of the necessary reforms. So would keeping the lid on actual and prospective fiscal deficits. (Remember that Keynesian countercyclical policies cannot work, or work perversely, in a confidence crisis.) All would contribute to the credibility of restoring the traditional exchange rate.

It would be even better to have the restoration rule in place before any speculative attack. It should be one of the normal operating rules of the IMF. Once a group of neighboring countries, as in East Asia, all have the same commitment to exchange stability in the long run, contagion would be better contained. Indeed, a speculative attack on any one of them becomes less likely to begin with.

By late 1998, Thailand and Korea had already made substantial progress in nudging their exchange rates back up and have been rewarded by their domestic interest rates coming back down to single digit levels (Figures 3 and 4, respectively). But, by delaying the implementation of this restoration rule, their currencies were left undervalued for too long, leading to so much domestic price inflation that the original exchange-rate "parities" became too difficult to retrieve.

Perhaps because France had suffered from numerous confidence crises in the postwar, in the early 1990s it provided the best modern example of a country more promptly following the restoration rule. The massive speculative attack against the franc in September 1993 forced a virtual suspension of the ERM bilateral parity grid: official exchange-rate margins were widened from 2.25 percent to a ridiculous ±15 percent. Yet, within a few weeks, the franc/mark exchange rate quickly returned to its traditional level; and French short- and long-term interest rates closely tracked German ones in the 1990s. So quickly was the mark/franc exchange rate restored that the devaluation had a negligible effect on the French price level. Because France's monetary and fiscal "fundamentals" were not misaligned with Germany's, restoration was easy—even though defending against the initial massive attack was impossible.

LENGTHENING THE TERM STRUCTURE OF FINANCE: GENERAL LESSONS

Is there a general lesson here about the feasibility of freely floating exchange rates among different classes of economies? In his chapter titled "The Confidence Game," Paul Krugman (1999) identified the differences thus:

> It seems, in other words, that there is a sort of double standard enforced by the markets. The common view among economists that floating rates are the best, if

imperfect, solution to the international monetary trilemma was based on the experience of countries like Canada, Britain, and the United States. And sure enough, floating exchange rates work pretty well for First World Countries, because markets are prepared to give those countries the benefit of the doubt. But since 1994 one Third World country after another—Mexico, Thailand, Indonesia, Korea, and most recently, Brazil—has discovered that it cannot expect the same treatment. Again and again, attempts to engage in moderate devaluations have led to a drastic collapse in confidence. And so now markets believe that devaluations in such countries are terrible things; and because markets believe this, they are. (P. 111)

Krugman made an important distinction. To cushion the effects of the fall in primary products prices caused by the Asian crisis, Australian and Canadian exporters of primary products could let their currencies float downward without capital controls and not be attacked. Why? Because exchange rate expectations for the Australian and Canadian dollars were already regressive: during the course of the downward float, people generally expected the rates to come back. Both were mature market economies with (1) credible internal monetary policies (independent central banks) for targeting their domestic price levels over the long run, and (2) relatively long terms to maturity for their internal and external debts. (In Asia, the noncrisis creditor countries of Taiwan and Singapore were (are) more like mature capitalist ones in these respects.)

Of course, (1) and (2) are complementary. Only with long-term confidence in the purchasing power of domestic money (against the center country's) would exchange rate expectations be naturally regressive and are long-term bond and mortgage markets possible to organize. And having finance at longer term bolsters the credibility of the central bank to hit its inflation targets over the longer term.

However, even in Canada—where the structure of finance is fairly long and where the Bank of Canada had, by 1991, put a highly credible domestic monetary regime not dissimilar to the American for limiting inflation in place—medium-term misalignments of the Canadian dollar with the American have created unhappiness. The run up of the Canadian dollar from 1988 to peak at 89 cents in 1991 seemed to many observers to overvalue the Canadian dollar and aggravate the recession of 1991-92. Similarly, the fall of the Canadian dollar to touch 63 U.S cents in early 1999 seems to be all out of proportion to Canada's now modest dependence on primary products exports. Because of the high degree of trade dependence with the United States, feeling was widespread that this fall reduced Canadian living standards. In June 1999, in a report from the C.D. Howe Institute in Queens University, two of Canada's most distinguished economists wrote the following:

Canada's experience with a floating exchange rate has been disappointing. The floating dollar has been prone to major misalignments, as its current weakness demonstrates, that put Canada at a disadvantage in the North American competition for physical and human capital investment. As the Canadian economy becomes more open to trade and investment flows, and those flows become more focused on the United States, the benefits of greater fixity with the U.S. dollar are growing. (Courchene and Harris 1999, 2)

To be sure, there are influential critics of the Courchene-Harris report: Laidler (1999) and Murray (1999) believe that the Canadian dollar should continue to float. Nevertheless, the Canadian experience suggests that, while "first-world" countries can allow their exchange rates to float freely without being attacked as most third world would be, the resulting swings in the exchange rate may still be uncomfortably wide in the absence of any firm long-run exchange rate objective. Even with a stable internal monetary standard in place (a believable set of monetary procedures for targeting and stabilizing the domestic price level), regressive exchange rate expectations are not strong enough to prevent damaging medium-term fluctuations.

Now return to our emerging-market debtor economy in which the term structure of finance is short and there is no history of central bank independence. Its government would be even more hard-pressed than Canada's to put a purely internal monetary standard in place that convincingly pinned down the domestic price level (relative to the center country's) over the long run. Indeed, in most third-world economies—including the Asian five—the central bank has often been commandeered to provide cheap credit for promoting exports, subsidizing commercial banks, and otherwise directing credit in line with the government's development program. Sometimes, this strategy has been facilitated by ringing the country with capital controls.

Correspondingly, there is a potential lack of confidence in the long-term exchange rate unless the government can effectively restrain itself. By credibly pegging to the dollar, the central bank shows the market that it is prepared to limit growth in domestic base money and avoid future inflation despite its lack of independence.

Before 1997 during their "miracle" growth phases, the East Asian economies successfully pegged to the dollar as the nominal anchor for their domestic price levels. With the benefit of hindsight, however, we now know that this policy was seriously incomplete. First, and most obviously, there was the failure to properly regulate the financial system—including the central bank itself in some cases—against undue risk taking including short-term foreign exchange exposure.

Second, and more subtly, the East Asian debtor economies had not committed themselves to long-term exchange rate stability in the mode of the nineteenth-century gold standard, even though they seemed to be securely pegged in the short and medium terms. Because of the short-term structure of finance, each was vulnerable to a speculative attack on its currency, but none had a long-run exchange rate strategy in place to mitigate the worst consequences any such attack. That is, there was no restoration rule for keeping exchange-rate expectations regressive.

In part, the problem arose because the pre-1997 East Asian dollar standard was informal rather than formal. With exception of Hong Kong, none of the countries involved had formally declared a dollar parity, and each had been classified by the IMF as following some variety of "managed floating" rather than being a dollar pegger (McKinnon 1999). After any forced suspension, there was no traditional (gold) parity in the nineteenth-century sense to which the government was obviously bound to return.

Probably the biggest problem, however, was philosophical. In the endless debate on fixed versus floating exchange rates, academic economists on either side have failed to take the term to maturity of the exchange rate into account. Given the great asymmetry among national monies, I have been arguing that countries on the periphery of the dollar standard will always be subject to speculative attacks and (attempted) flight into dollars. (The small countries in Eastern Europe are similarly situated on the periphery of the euro standard.)

But emerging-market economies whose macroeconomic fundamentals are sound so as to permit a good fix for their exchange rates should extend the maturity of that commitment to the distant future, that is, adopt the restoration rule explicitly—and, ideally, collectively. (Of course, those that must rely on the inflation tax and cannot credibly commit to long-run exchange rate stability should not try it.) Indeed, the benefits from having the exchange rate pinned down in the long run exceed those from having a hard short-term fix. With regressive exchange rate expectations and the future price level more secure, the authorities can seriously encourage lengthening the term structure of domestic and foreign finance. As long-term bond issues in the nineteenth-century mode begin to displace short-term bank finance, the government's commitment to long-term exchange rate stability is naturally reinforced.

In summary, suppose that the long-run monetary, fiscal, and price-level fundamentals of an emerging-market country could be sustainable. Nevertheless, the national currency is subject to a massive speculative attack—possibly aggravated by contagion from neighboring countries. Then, temporary suspension of official intervention should be coupled with the promise of eventually restoring the initial par value of the currency. Despite some unavoidable temporary currency depreciation, our restoration rule would maintain regressive expectations and limit capital flight. This has several advantages.

In the short run, the government under attack is not forced to increase near-term interest rates so sharply in a cyclical downturn—or when its banks are particularly weak from maturity mismatches. The expectation of eventual exchange rate appreciation minimizes (but need not eliminate) the need to increase short-term interest rates to assure the markets that restoration is in prospect.

In the medium run, when the errant exchange rate is nudged back up, the contagion from "accidental" competitive devaluation is mitigated. Despite a temporary devaluation at the outset of the attack, the other countries within the Asian dollar standard need not worry about persistent beggar-thy-neighbor policies. Moreover, within the domestic economy, the bankruptcy threat to foreign-currency debtors is diminished.

In the long run, the central bank can keep the domestic price level consistent with eventually restoring its traditional dollar exchange parity. Domestic inflation would not spiral out of control. If the domestic bond market were open, long-term interest rates would remain fairly stable at levels close to those in the United States. Indeed, only with a credible commitment to long-term exchange-rate stability in place is it possible to develop a long-term domestic bond market—so vital for reducing term-structure risk in a reformed banking system.

References

Adams, Charles, Donald J. Mathieson, Garry Shinasi, and Bankim Chada. 1998. *International capital markets: Developments, prospects and key policy issues*, September. Washington, DC: International Monetary Fund.

Bordo, Michael, and Finn Kydland. 1995. The gold standard as a rule: An essay in exploration. *Explorations in Economic History* 32:423-64.

Courchene, Thomas, and Richard Harris. 1999. From fixing to monetary union: Options for North American currency integration. Commentary, no. 127, June. Toronto, Canada: C. D. Howe Institute.

Eichengreen, Barry. 1999. Building on a consensus. *Financial Times*, 2 February.

Fischer, Stanley. 1999. On the need for a lender of last resort. Address to the American Economic Association, 3 January, New York.

Frankel, J. A., and S. J. Wei. 1994. Yen bloc or dollar bloc? Exchange rate policies in the East Asian economies. In *Macroeconomic linkage: Savings, exchange rates, and capital flows*, edited by T. Ito and A. Krueger. Chicago: University of Chicago Press.

Goodhart, Charles, and P.J.R. Delargy. 1998. Financial crises: Plus ça change, plus c'est la Même chose. *International Finance* 1 (2): 261-88.

Kaminsky, G., and C. Reinhart. 1999. The twin crises: Balance of payments and banking crises in developing countries. *American Economic Review 89 (3): 473-500.*

Krueger, Anne O. 1997. Nominal anchor exchange rate policies as a domestic distortion. Working paper no. 2, Center for Research on Economic Development and Policy Reform, February.

Krugman, Paul. 1999. *The return of depression economics*. New York: Norton.

Laidler, David. 1999. The exchange rate regime and Canada's monetary order. Working paper no. 99-7, Bank of Canada, March.

McKinnon, R. I. 1996. *The rules of the game: International money and exchange rates.* Cambridge, MA: MIT Press.

———. 1999. The East Asian dollar standard, life after death? World Bank Workshop on Rethinking the East Asian Miracle, July.

McKinnon, Ronald I., and Kenichi Ohno. 1997. *Dollar and yen: Resolving economic conflict between the United States and Japan.* Cambridge, MA: MIT Press. (Japanese translation, Nihon Keizai Shimbun, 1998.)

McKinnon, Ronald I., and Huw Pill. 1996. Credible liberalizations and international capital flows: The overborrowing syndrome. In *Financial de-*

regulation and integration in East Asia, edited by T. Ito and A. Krueger, 7-48, NBER. Chicago: University of Chicago Press.

———. 1997. Credible liberalizations and overborrowing. *American Economic Review*, May.

———. 1998. International overborrowing: A decomposition of credit and currency risk. *World Development* 26 (7): 1267-82.

———. 1999. Exchange rate regimes for emerging markets: Moral hazard and international overborrowing. *Oxford Review of Economic Policy* 15 (3): 423-464.

Murray, John. 1999. Why Canada needs a flexible exchange rate regime. Working paper no. 99-12, Bank of Canada, July.

Ohno, Kenichi. 1999. Exchange rate management in developing Asia: A reassessment of the pre-crisis soft dollar zone. ADBI working paper no. 1, Asian Development Bank, Tokyo, January.

Soros, George. 1999. To avert the next crisis. *Financial Times*, 4 January.

Wolf, Martin. 1999. Pegging out. *Financial Times*, 21 January.

ANNALS, *AAPSS*, **579**, January 2002

Capital Market Liberalization and Exchange Rate Regimes: Risk without Reward

By JOSEPH E. STIGLITZ

ABSTRACT: This paper examines the consequences of capital market liberalization, with special reference to its effects under different exchange rate regimes. Capital market liberalization has not lead to faster growth in developing countries, but has led to greater risks. It describes how International Monetary Fund policies have exacerbated the risks, as a result of the macro-economic response to crises, with bail-out packages that have intensified moral hazard problems. The paper provides a critique of the arguments for capital market liberalization. It argues that capital flows give rise to large externalities, which affect others than the borrower and lender, and whenever there are large externalities, there is potential scope for government interventions, some of which are welfare increasing.

Joseph E. Stiglitz holds joint professorships at Columbia University's Economics Department, School of International and Public Affairs, and Business School. From 1997 to 2000 he was the World Bank's Senior Vice President for Development Economics and Chief Economist. From 1995 to 1997, he served as Chairman of the U.S. Council of Economic Advisers and a member of President Bill Clinton's cabinet. He was previously a professor of economics at Stanford, Princeton, Yale, and All Souls College, Oxford. He was awarded the Nobel Prize in Economics in 2001 for his analysis of markets with asymmetric information.

FOR almost half a decade, capital market liberalization raged as the prime battleground between those who were pushing for and against globalization, and for good reason: By the mid-1990s, the notion that free trade or at least freer trade brought benefits both to the developed and the less developed countries seemed well accepted. President Clinton could claim passage of NAFTA and the Uruguay Round, with the establishment of the World Trade Organization, among the major achievements of his first four years. APEC and the Americas had both committed themselves to creating a free-trade area. Not only had the intellectual battle been won—only special interests resisted trade liberalization—but so seemingly had the political battle. On other fronts, the broader liberalization/free-market agenda was winning victory after victory: the Uruguay round had extended the scope of traditional trade liberalization to include liberalization in financial services, the protection of intellectual property rights, and even investment. Although the Multilateral Investment Agreement was having trouble, investment protections in NAFTA were cited as a basis on which further agreements could be reached. Even "liberal" governments—the democratic administration in the United States, the labor government in Britain—embraced privatization and deregulation, with the United States going so far as to push through the privatization of the corporation making enriched uranium, the core ingredient in making nuclear weapons (as well as fuel for nuclear reactors). Only capital market liberalization—eliminating the restrictions on the free flow of short-term capital—remained as a point of contention. At its annual meetings in Hong Kong, the International Monetary Fund (IMF) sought to settle this issue too: it asked for a change in its charter, to give it a mandate to push for capital market liberalization, just as it had a mandate, in its founding, for the elimination of capital controls that interfered with trade.

The timing could not have been worse: the East Asia crisis was brewing. Thailand had already succumbed, with a crisis that began on 2 July. The delegates to the Hong Kong meeting had hardly unpacked their bags on returning home when the crisis struck in Indonesia. Within a little more than a year, it had become a global economic crisis, touching virtually every corner of the globe, with bailouts billed at more than 150 billion dollars occurring not only in Thailand and Indonesia, but Korea, Brazil, and Russia. And it was clear that hot, speculative money—short-term capital flows—was at the heart of the crisis: if they had not caused it, they at least played a central role in its propagation. The only two large emerging markets to be spared the ravages of the global financial crisis were India and China, both of which had imposed capital controls. (Even as the global economy faced a major slowdown, China managed to grow by more than 7 percent, India by more than 5 percent). Malaysia had imposed capital controls to help it manage its way through the crisis, and as a result, its downturn was shorter, and as it recovered, it was left with less of a legacy of debt than the other countries because it had imposed capital controls. By the time matters settled down, the IMF had markedly changed its tune: its chief economist (Mussa 2000) admitted that financial market liberalization could have markedly adverse effects on less developed countries that were not adequately prepared for it (in the view of many economists in the developing world, this meant virtually all developing countries).[1] It admitted that its predictions (and those of the U.S. Treasury) that Malaysia's imposition of controls would prove to be a disaster had been wrong—they had succeeded in spite of what might have seemed as efforts to undermine the country through public criticism of an almost unprecedented nature.[2]

But while the intellectual battle was thus seemingly over, the political battle continued: the managing director of the IMF, Michel Camdessus, continued pushing for capital market liberalization in his annual speeches until his departure from the IMF. And countries that propose going back on capital market liberalization are strongly advised against it—to the point of implicit or explicit threats of having programs cut off.[3]

But these political battles are, for the most part, going on behind the scenes. The more visible political debate has moved back to issues thought at one time settled—for instance, to trade and intellectual property rights. Still, revisiting that earlier debate has much to teach us, both about economics and politics. It is precisely because the disjunction between the positions that the IMF took and the theory and evidence concerning capital market liberalization, between their mandate to promote global stability, and the policy which seem so patently to lead to global instability was so great that the debate on capital market liberalization throws into such stark relief broader aspects of the globalization controversy. (In other arenas, such as trade liberalization, theory and evidence are more ambiguous, and while the IMF may have pushed policies that could not be *defended* as fulfilling its mandate, neither could they, by and large, be criticized for actually going against their mandate.)

The consequences of capital market liberalization depend, of course, in part, but only in part, on the exchange rate regime, which is the focus of many of the articles in this issue. But before turning to that issue, it is important to understand the more general case against and for capital market liberalization. Accordingly, in this article, I propose first to explain the strength of the opposition to capital market liberalization: it increases the risks facing a country while it does not promote economic growth. Given the overwhelming theory and evidence against capital market liberalization, one wonders: how could the major international organization responsible for promoting growth and stability have promoted a policy that seemed so contrary to its objectives? I first review the arguments that were put forward for capital market liberalization. I then turn to the deeper political economy questions, exploring the role of ideology and interests. I conclude by arguing that at the root of the problem is governance: the governance structure of the IMF led it to push for policies that were contradictory to its mandate for promoting global stability and that reflected the interests and ideology of those to whom it was directly accountable. There is, in this, an important lesson for the evolving globalization debate, to which I turn briefly in the concluding section.

THE ECONOMIC CASE AGAINST CAPITAL MARKET LIBERALIZAITON

The evidence is that capital market liberalization is not associated with faster economic growth or higher levels of investment but is associated with higher levels of economic volatility and risk. And, in general, the poor bear the brunt of much of this risk, especially in developing countries, where safety nets (like unemployment insurance systems) are nonexistent or inadequate.

Growth

Ascertaining whether trade liberalization, or capital market liberalization, leads to faster economic growth is not an easy matter. A standard, though widely discredited, methodology entails looking at the growth rates of different countries, attempting to ascertain whether those who have liberalized more or faster have grown faster, controlling for other factors that might have affected growth. The problematic nature of such studies is highlighted by the contradictory results that have been obtained in the trade liberalization literature, with scholars like Sachs and Warner (1995) arguing that trade liberalization is systematically associated with growth, and others, like Rodriguez and Rodrik (1999), questioning the results. The results are highly sensitive to issues like how to weight the experience of different countries and how to separate causal factors with mere association. For instance, China with its more than 1 billion people has been the fastest growing developing country in the world; growth in China accounts for a substantial fraction (by some accounts, two-thirds or more) of total growth among the low-income countries. But should China—which did not liberalize—be given the same weight in the analysis as some small country in Africa with a couple million people? If some of these small countries grew slightly faster, some grew slightly slower, and on average, those who liberalized grew slightly faster, are we to infer that liberalization is an important ingredient in growth—when the world's major success story, with growth a multiple of that of any of the African countries, did not liberalize? The matter can be put another way: if one treated the separate provinces of China as separate data points—and they are each large, many times the size of the average African states, and each followed slightly different policies—then the twenty fastest growers in the past two decades are all in China. A study that treated these provinces as units of analysis might conclude strongly that liberalization was not good for growth, while a study that treated China as a single data point might conclude that it was.

There are other statistical problems. Assume it were the case that countries that did not liberalize, on average, were more authoritarian and that authoritarianism is bad for growth; but in the statistical analysis of growth, no measure of authoritarianism was included, or a measure that did not capture the relevant dimensions of a multidimensional political construct. Then, the statistical analysis might conclude that liberalization was good for growth, when the correct conclusion is that nonauthoritarian political structures, appropriately defined, are good for growth.

What was most remarkable about the drive for capital market liberalization from the IMF was that at the time they pushed for this change in the global economic architecture, there was no study even of the cross-country statistical kind that supported trade liberalization, as discredited as those studies might be, which provided empirical evidence in support of capital market liberalization. The one widely cited study by Rodrik (1998)—using the IMF's own measures of liberalization—showed that it did not lead to faster economic growth. One might have thought that the IMF would have made a major effort to refute Rodrik's study and to present countervailing studies showing the contrary. That they did not, and that they seemingly did not feel the need to refute the even more compelling evidence showing that capital market liberalization led to greater risks, may say a great deal about the nature of the organization, a point to which we return later.

But there is, perhaps, a simpler reason: Rodrik's (1998) study merely corroborated what was obvious, both empirically and theoretically. It was not only China that had grown rapidly without capital market liberalization; India, too, had experienced rapid growth over the 1990s, and it too had not liberalized. Russia had liberalized, and the liberalization had led not to a flow of capital into the country but to massive capital flight, and the country's GDP had, partly as a result, plummeted by more than 40 percent, a decline that was reflected in socioeconomic statistics, such as marked shortening of life spans, and in data, collected through household surveys, showing an increase in poverty from around 2 percent to between 25 percent and 40 percent, depending on the measure used.

But these results should not have come as a surprise. Growth is related to investment, to new enterprises and old enterprises expanding. Such investments cannot be based on speculative money that can come into and out of a country on a moment's notice. On the contrary, the high volatility associated with such flows destabilizes the economy, as we shall see in the next section, and the higher economic volatility makes investment less attractive.

There is another channel through which capital market liberalization hurts growth. The flow of funds into the country leads, under flexible exchange rates, into a higher exchange rate, making it more difficult for a country to export or compete against imports (a version of the so-called Dutch disease problem). In some cases, such as Thailand, the funds helped feed a speculative real estate boom, which distorted the economy. To prevent inflation, to sterilize the inflow of funds, which might otherwise have led to an excess demand for goods, the monetary authorities had to raise interest rates, which stifled investment in other sectors.[4] The distinction between foreign direct investment and these short-term flows could not be clearer. The foreign direct investment leads directly to an increase in GDP and in employment; it brings with it new technology, access to markets, and training—none of which accompany speculative portfolio flows.

There is another way of seeing the adverse effects on growth: today, countries are told to keep reserves equal to their foreign denominated short-term liabilities. Consider the consequence of a company within a poor small country borrowing money from an American bank $100 million in dollars short term, paying say 18 percent or 20 percent interest. The country then is forced to put a corresponding amount in reserves—money that could have gone toward high-return investments in schools, health clinics, roads, or factories. The reserves are held in the form of U.S. treasury bills, yielding 4 percent. In effect, the country is lending $100 million to the United States at 4 percent and borrowing it back again at 20 percent—at a net cost of $16 million a year to the country, a transaction that clearly might be good for growth in the United States but is unlikely to have a substantial positive effect on the growth of the developing country.[5]

Risk

The rapid movement of funds into and out of a country is clearly destabilizing, a point brought home forcefully by the East Asian crisis, where the capital outflows exceeded in some cases 10 percent of GDP. Flows of that magnitude (equivalent to close to $1 trillion for the United States) would be highly disruptive, even in a country with strong financial markets. The effects on developing countries have been devastating.

Empirical studies have shown that there is a systematic relationship between capital market liberalization and instability (see Demirgüç-Kunt and Detragiache 1997, 1999). The period immediately following liberalization is one in which risk is particularly marked, as markets often respond to the new opportunities in an overly exuberant manner, as they see previously closed opportunities opened up. The increased macro-economic risk would imply a necessity for increased monitoring of financial institutions, as the franchise value, the expected present discounted value of future profits, is likely to be eroded given the higher probability of an economic downturn; and in the absence of increased monitoring, the higher level of risk taking itself would contribute to greater instability. Unfortunately, typically governments have not done a better job of regulation, for two reasons. Often, the capital market liberalization is in response to external pressure (e.g., from the IMF or the United

States), and that same pressure has been accompanied by pressure to liberalize financial markets, that is, remove restrictions that, in part, result in less exposure to risk (the elimination of Thailand's restrictions on speculative real estate investments are a case in point). Second, the process of liberalization has been accompanied by huge increases in demand for the relatively few trained personnel, many of whom worked for the regulatory authorities and the central bank; the public sector simply cannot compete in paying salaries against the private sector. Hence, just at the time when the need for improved regulation is greatest, the country's capacity is reduced (see Hellman, Murdock, and Stiglitz 1996).

Capital market flows to which capital market liberalization gave rise are now recognized to be the pivotal factor in the East Asia crisis.[6] But there have been more crises that have been deeper and longer lasting in the past quarter century—more than one hundred countries have been afflicted (see Caprio and Klingebiel 1996; Lindgren, Garcia, and Saal 1996), and it is apparent that the trend toward increased capital and financial market liberalization has been a key factor. The IMF and U.S. Treasury suggested that the East Asian countries were vulnerable because of a number of structural failings; on the contrary, these countries had performed better over the preceding three decades, not only in terms of growth but also in stability: two of the affected countries had had only one of economic downturn, two had had none, a better performance than any of the OECD countries. If they were vulnerable, it was a newly acquired vulnerability because of the capital and financial market liberalization that had been foisted on these countries.

IMF responses exacerbated the risk. The nature of the response to a crisis affects the consequences, including who bears the burden. In the case of the East Asia crisis, the IMF responded with fiscal contractions and monetary tightening, which deepened the economic downturns and failed in their intended effects of sustaining the exchange rate. In addition, the restructuring strategy, which involved closing financial institutions (in the case of Indonesia, closing sixteen banks, with an announcement that more were to follow, but that depositors would not have their deposits guaranteed, leading to a run on the banking system), led to a further collapse in the supply of credit; and the more hands-off corporate restructuring strategies meant that corporate distress was addressed at an extremely slow pace—four years after the crisis, between 25 and 40 percent of Thai loans remained nonperforming.

The failure was predicted by economists within the World Bank, and the reason was obvious: given the high leverage, the high interest rates forced many firms into distress and worsened the problems of the financial institutions. The combination of the normal Keynesian demand-side and supply-side contractions proved devastating. Although at this juncture, the IMF admits several of the failures, on the critical issue of monetary policy it remains adamant. It believes that higher interest rates lead to a capital inflow that supports a country's currency, evidently even in circumstances such as those of East Asia with high levels of leverage, in spite of the absence of evidence in support and some evidence against and in spite of the overwhelming theoretical arguments against the policy. The statistical analyses of whether raising interest rates leads to higher exchange rates is even more problematic than the cross-country regressions referred to earlier. Here, the critical issue is to identify the appropriate counterfactual, that is, what would have happened but for the policy. It is clear that the IMF interventions in East Asia, which included not only the high interest rates but also massive bailouts and contractionary fiscal policies, did not prevent a slide in the exchange rates; indeed, looking at exchange rate movements, it is hard to detect evidence of interventions having any positive impact. It is, of course, possible that the mistaken part of the IMF packages systematically undermined the positive effects of the interest rate policies, or that just at the moment of the interventions, the pace of decline in exchange rate would have accelerated, and this acceleration was reversed by the interventions. But neither of these is plausible, and a more detailed analysis of interest rate increases in other crises does not suggest that they are very effective instruments (see Furman and Stiglitz 1998a). The theoretical arguments put forward by the advocates of this policy are not compelling: the higher interest rates are supposed to attract funds into the country, bolstering the exchange rate. In fact, the economic disruption not only does not attract funds into the country but also leads to massive capital flight. Lenders care not just about the interest rate promised but also about the probability of being repaid; it was concern about default that led banks to refuse to roll over their loans. Thus, this was a variable of first-order importance—but left out from the IMF analyses. The policies increased the probability of default so that the total impact was to make it less attractive to put funds into the country.[7]

The important point is this: having failed to identify the reasons for their admitted failures in their fiscal and financial policies and having even refused to acknowledge the mistakes in monetary policy means that in the future, the mistakes are likely to be repeated so that countries can anticipate facing major economic downturns in the event of a crisis.

There are further aspects of IMF responses that exacerbated the downturn in Indonesia. Even in the best of circumstances, major economic downturns can give rise to political and social turmoil. In the case of ethnically fractionated societies, such turmoil is even more likely (see, for instance, Collier and Hoeffler 1998). A perception that the burden is borne unfairly by the poor increases the likelihood of turmoil even more. I predicted in early December 1997 at a meeting of finance ministers and central bank officials at Kuala Lumpur that if the IMF maintained its macro-economic policies in Indonesia, there was a high probability of such turmoil within six months. I argued that even if the IMF did not care about social costs, especially those borne by the poor, it was simply bad economic policy. All that the head of the IMF, who was in attendance, could say in reply was that the country had to bear the pain. I was perhaps overly optimistic: riots, every bit as bad as my worse fears, broke out within five months. But I had not anticipated that just as the economy was plunged into depression, with unemployment soaring and real wages plummeting, food and fuel subsidies for the very poor would be cut back. Evidently, the IMF could provide billions to bail out Western banks and lenders, but there were not the measly millions required to finance subsidies for the very poor. The outrage was understandable and the consequences long lasting: it will take years before that country recovers to its precrisis level.

There were other aspects of IMF policies that exacerbated the downturns. In East Asia, the debt was largely private. When private parties cannot meet their obligations, the normal mechanism by which the problem is handled is bankruptcy. (Sovereign defaults pose special problems, which is why it is important to note that the debt in East Asia was private. The governments themselves had been running surpluses.)

But the IMF was dead set against bankruptcy and facilitating the process of debt workout, for example, through a debt moratorium. Its first deputy managing director referred to bankruptcy as if it were an abrogation of the debt contract, failing to note that bankruptcy was at the core of modern capitalism and was an essential part of limited liability corporations. (Critics pointed out that while the IMF was willing to put up billions to preserve the sanctity of the debt contract, it was reluctant to put up the millions needed to preserve the social contract, for example, the food and fuel subsidies for the poor, and the social and economic consequences of the abrogation of the social contract were far more severe than the consequences of bankruptcy could possibly have been.) Bankruptcy (or a debt moratorium) would have relieved downward pressure on the exchange rate (see Miller and Stiglitz 1999)—indeed, it was only with the essentially forced rollover of Korea's debt that its exchange rate was stabilized. Those who opposed such policies said that it would be impossible to engineer them, but Korea showed that that was wrong. They argued that capital would not flow back into the country, and that was partially irrelevant, partially just wrong, both in terms of theory and evidence. Capital was not going to be flowing into these countries in the short run in any case. And the countries in East Asia, given their high savings rate, had little need for capital even in the longer run. But capital markets are forward looking: there is not a single participant who can decide to punish someone who does not obey his strictures. Rather, there are a multitude of participants, each of whom must decide on whether the return is sufficient to justify the risk. A country in deep recession, with a large overhang of debt, public and/or private, is less likely to attract funds than a country that has put the past behind it. Moreover, why should investors hold a new government to blame for mistakes made by past governments; if anything, a new government that has rectified the problems of the past will gain in credibility. All of these provide part of the reason that countries that default do regain access to international capital markets, and often after a remarkably short time—perhaps more determined by the time it takes to restore economic stability and growth prospects than anything else.

One country in the region took an alternative course; after first flirting with an IMF program without the IMF, Malaysia imposed capital controls. Its downturn was shorter, and it was left with less of a legacy of debt, as a result. In the next section, we shall explain why, but first, I want to discuss briefly some of the consequences of the increased risk, besides the adverse effect on growth that I have already discussed.

The consequences of increased macro-economic risk. Normally, as countries go into a downturn, it is the poor who disproportionately bear those costs. Their unemployment rate goes up more,[8] perhaps because employers value of the firm-specific human capital of the more skilled workers, and as their demand for labor decreases, they would rather redeploy them to less skilled jobs rather than having them leave the firm.

Less developed countries typically have limited safety nets. Even in developed countries, unemployment insurance in the self-employed and agricultural sectors is limited, and in developing countries, these sectors predominate. In some less developed countries, flexible labor markets imply that reductions in the demand for labor do not show up in the form of unemployment but are reflected in changes in real wages. But the reductions in real wages may be very large—in some of the countries in East Asia, real wages fell by more than a quarter.

One of the important arguments to emerge from the 2000 World Development Report (World Bank 2000) is that the poor are not only adversely affected by lower incomes but also by higher insecurity. Deprived of the instruments with which to deal with economic volatility, their lives are particularly affected by the instability that is associated with capital market liberalization.[9]

Moreover, extended periods of high unemployment and low wages can have a devastating effect in undermining social capital, the social fabric that enables a society, and a market economy, to function—witness the increase in urban violence in Latin America following the debt crisis. Not only are there severe social consequences, but the social instability provides adverse conditions for investment and thus growth.

The defenses

Given the overwhelming theory and evidence against capital market liberalization, one might wonder, on what grounds did the IMF argue in its favor? While they refused to refute the arguments put forward above, in particular, never addressing the issue of the impact of liberalization on the poor, they argued that capital market liberalization enhanced growth and actually reduced risk!

Growth. Underlying the analysis is a simple analogy: free mobility of capital is like free mobility of goods; and just as free trade increases incomes, so too does free mobility of capital. But capital markets are distinctly different from goods markets. *Risk* and *information* are at the center of capital markets: capital markets are concerned with the acquisition, analysis, and dissemination of information; with making choices about how to allocate of scarce capital to investment opportunities; and with spreading, sharing, and pooling risks. Markets for information are markedly different from markets for goods. While with perfect information and perfect risk, competitive markets are in general (pareto) efficient, with imperfect information and incomplete risk markets, markets typically do not behave in the way predicted by standard competitive models, and market equilibrium is in general not (constrained pareto) efficient.[10] Thus, while there may be some presumption that trade liberalization may be welfare improving,[11] there is little basis for presuming that liberalization in financial and capital markets is welfare improving.[12]

There are two more specific arguments that the advocates of capital market liberalization put forward. One is patently wrong: that without capital market liberalization, countries will not be able to attract the foreign direct investment, which is so important to economic growth. China has not liberalized its capital market, and yet has been able to attract more foreign investment than any other emerging market.

The second is more subtle. It argues that capital market liberalization provides an important discipline device—countries that fail to pursue good policies are quickly punished, and thus capital market liberalization helps keep countries on a solid path of economic reform. Underlying this argument is a highly antidemocratic bias: the belief that democratic processes provide an inadequate check and the willingness to delegate discipline to foreign financial interests. But the argument is more problematic. If one is to choose an outside disciplinarian, one wants one that punishes one if and only if one has "misbehaved." But as many countries—for example, in Latin America—learned with great pain, with capital market liberalization, they can be punished even if they do everything "right." If emerging markets fall from favor, in the inevitable vicissitudes that characterize capital markets, then even the countries that have been awarded A's from the IMF are punished. Equally bad, capital markets may have certain biases—they may, in the first stance, overreact to certain actions a country undertakes and fail to react to other actions.

This point may be highlighted by considering the consequences of delegating the responsibility of "disciplinarian" to labor markets. Labor markets might discipline a country for following bad environmental policies with a rush of skilled labor out of a country should it decide, for instance, to allow arsenic in its water supply. The choice of a disciplinarian determines what a country is to be rewarded, or punished, for—and therefore affects what a country does or does not do. It affects the very nature of the evolution of society.

Who gets to play the role of disciplinarian is affected by *mobility*. Capital market liberalization does give capital markets more power, in this sense. And in doing so, it affects the ability of society to redistribute: any threat to increase the taxes on capital can result in quick retribution in the form of the withdrawal of funds. Whether such funds contribute to the long-term growth of the economy is not the issue: the withdrawal of funds can impose enormous costs, especially in the context of the IMF-style responses.[13]

Enhancing the mobility of capital thus has real consequences: it affects bargaining positions and the outcome of bargaining processes in ways that are advantageous to capital and disadvantageous to labor.

The argument that capital market liberalization was good for growth was, to be sure, fairly unpersuasive in the context of the countries in East Asia, where domestic savings rates were very high. Although the countries did an impressive job in investing these savings productively, little argument could be put forward that additional funds from more developed countries would substantially increase growth.

In the face of this, the IMF and the U.S. Treasury used an even more peculiar argument.

Risk. They argued that capital market liberalization would reduce risk, enabling countries to have access to outside funds in the face of a threatened economic slowdown. Diversification of the source of funding would enhance economic stability. What was remarkable about this argument was the overwhelming empirical evidence against it, even at the time it was put forward: short-term flows of funds are procyclical, exacerbating, not dampening, economic fluctuations. As the expression goes, bankers are most willing to provide credit to those who do not need it; and as a country faces a downturn, bankers withdraw credit.[14]

Externalities and capital controls

Thus, today, there is widespread agreement that capital flows impose huge costs on others—on innocent bystanders, small businesses, and workers who neither participated in nor benefited from these flows. They impose huge externalities. Whenever there are externalities, there are standard remedies—government interventions—that can take a variety of forms, for example, regulatory or tax. There is a large literature addressing the relative merits of various forms of intervention.[15]

One of the standard objections to these interventions is that they raise the cost of funds, especially short-term funds. But that objection is like the steel industry complaining that taxes on pollution will discourage the production of steel. It will—but that is precisely the point. Efficiency requires that the marginal social cost of production equal the marginal social benefit; and the steel industry, in its private calculations, does not include the social cost of pollution. Once that is included, production should be reduced. So too, since there is a large social cost associated with short-term capital flows (and questionable social benefits), these capital flows should be discouraged.

The battle of the metaphors. While the economic case for some form of intervention is compelling, opponents (and proponents) of intervention have often resorted to metaphors and false analogies to help "prove" their point. We have already disposed of one such: the argument that the free flow of capital is just like the free flow of goods; and just as free trade is welfare enhancing, so are free capital movements.

One popular metaphor has involved the automobile. Critics of capital market liberalization have argued that capital market liberalization, at least for most developing countries, is like giving a teenage kid a high-powered car before making sure that the tires were in good condition and before installing seatbelts, let alone airbags. They noted that when there was an isolated accident on a highway, one might infer that the problem was with the driver, but when there were repeated pile-ups at the same bend in the highway, the problem was more likely with the design of the road. Supporters of capital market liberalization responded that the appropriate response was to widen the highway, not to return to the days of the horse and buggy, and in the meanwhile, the drivers needed to be better trained. Critics responded that roads and cars have to be designed for ordinary mortals; if only those with years of experience as racetrack drivers can survive, then something is fundamentally wrong. Moreover, they suggested that the only repair work on the road system that the international community had proposed was better road signs (improved information)—and even that initiative was halfhearted and incomplete, as the United States refused to allow the posting of signs at the most dangerous turns (disclosing information concerning the activities of hedge funds and offshore banking centers).

Another popular metaphor likened small developing countries to small boats on a rough and wily sea. Even if well designed and well captained, they are likely eventually to be hit broadside by a big wave and turned over. But the IMF program of capital market liberalization had set them forth into the most tempestuous parts of the sea, in boats that were leaky, without life vests or safety nets, and without training.

Still a third metaphor involved aviation: the undersecretary of Treasury (who at one time, before he had taken up the job of representing Wall Street's interests, had argued that failing to regulate capital markets was like failing to regulate nuclear power plants—doing either was an invitation to disaster) used to argue that simply because planes occasionally crash was no reason to give up flying. But critics responded: but if a particular model of a plane consistently crashed, one would want to ground it; and all governments take strong policies to ensure that those who fly planes are well trained, and those who fly more powerful planes have better training. And one certainly wanted to be particularly careful in flying over territory where the terrain was particularly rough since the dangers of a crash landing were then particularly severe, and even more so if the inhabitants in the territory had a penchant for cannibalism.

The metaphors, of course, were hardly a substitute for deeper economic analysis. But, especially when accompanied by such an analysis, they helped bring home the concerns and the depth of passions, on both sides. For instance, the fact that, as Paul Volcker, former governor of the Federal Reserve Bank, emphasized, the total stock market of a country like Thailand was smaller in size than a medium-sized American company like Home Depot, and that even when well managed, such companies experience huge volatility in their market value, brought home the point that the developing countries were like small boats on a rough sea. Analytic studies showing that most of the shocks that developing countries experience were external—caused, for instance, by sudden changes in investor sentiment in the more developed countries, having nothing to do with the particular policies and events in their particular country—provided the answer to the charge that the problems were of the country's own making; and by the time the East Asian crisis of 1997 had become the global financial crisis of 1998, touching even the best managed of developing countries, it had become clear that the rhetoric blaming the countries of East Asia for the crisis had been largely self-serving. By the same token, the privately financed but government engineered bailout of the world's largest hedge fund, Long Term Management Corporation, on the grounds that the failure of this one firm would exacerbate markedly the global financial crisis, provided the answer to the IMF study arguing that speculative hedge funds did not play an important role in the 1997 crisis, partly because they were simply too small to do so—and further undermined the credibility of those who claimed that capital market liberalization had little to do with the instability. The sad fact, though, was that advocates of capital market liberalization had forced developing countries to liberalize, without any analytic basis showing that it would be good for growth, ignoring the theory and evidence that it imposed enormous risks, without a clear set of guidelines for the circumstances in which countries might be able to bear those risks, and without a set of prescriptions for how they might prepare themselves appropriately for dealing with them.

The purposes of interventions

Having established that, in principle, some form of intervention is desirable, the next natural question is, are there forms of intervention where the benefits exceed the costs, that is, there are not ancillary costs that more than offset the benefits, or in which evasion is not so large that the benefits are largely eroded?

Interventions by Chile, Malaysia, and China, among others, showed that at least some countries could manage such interventions well and that they could take on a variety of forms. These countries demonstrated that these interventions need not hinder economic growth—or even the ability of a country to attract foreign funds—but they could help ensure economic stability. Before discussing the alternative interventions, it is desirable to describe the multiple purposes that such interventions might serve.

Stabilizing capital flows. The onrush of short-term capital into a country poses two problems: first, it can result in inflationary pressures; and second, such money can leave a country just as fast as it can enter, leaving in its wake economic devastation. On purpose of intervention is to stabilize the flows. Note that interventions designed for this purpose (or several of the other purposes described below) do not have to be perfect to be effective. Two metaphors bring this point home: a leaky umbrella can still be useful in a thunderstorm; even if one gets damp, it is better than being drenched. The purpose of a dam is not to stop the flow of water from the melting of snow from the mountaintop to the ocean but merely to stabilize it; without the dam, the onrush of water can cause death and destruction; the dam can convert this natural disaster into a source of water for food and sustenance. Even with a good dam, there can be spillage; some of the water can go around the dam. Even if it does not stop every flood, it can contribute greatly to increased well-being.

Most of the well-known ways of avoiding many forms of capital market controls (discussed below) do not undermine the ability of such interventions to stabilize flows, for most of the evasion tactics (e.g., under- and overinvoicing) work slowly. They are more like the flows of water going around the dam; in the long run, the aggregate amounts may be significant, but in the short run, the flows are still moderate, and it is the huge flows that cause the problem.

Dampening the rush of capital out of a country. In the event of a crisis, there may be an irrational pessimism, matching the irrational exuberance that brought the capital into the country. Policies designed to make it more difficult or more costly for capital to leave a country slow the rush of capital out; and, like the circuit breakers that have been put into stock markets, the extra "pause for reflection" can have large positive effects. Before they fully work out mechanisms for avoiding the controls, matters are seen in a calmer light—and markets themselves may have calmed down.

Designing more effective and lower cost stabilization measures for the economy. In simple models, where there is free flow of capital, there is little scope for monetary policy. A decrease in interest rates leads to a rush of capital out of the country. Thus, governments must rely on costly fiscal policy measures to stimulate the economy in the event of an economic downturn. If, however, there are effective restrictions on short-term capital movements, then monetary policy can be used. This has benefits both in the short run and the long, as Malaysia so forcefully showed. Reliance on fiscal policy forces governments to have large deficits, which can put a damper on future growth. Financing the deficit is also problematic in countries with limited access to foreign borrowing. Government borrowings crowd out private investment, with the net affect on recovery limited. At the high interest rates, lending to firms becomes particularly risky (Stiglitz-Weiss 1981), and banks prefer what they perceive to be relatively safe loans to government. In countries where many firms have high leverage, the high interest rates induce massive corporate distress, weakening the banking system and reducing its ability to lend even more. The cost to the public of resolving the corporate and financial stress is all the larger, again with adverse effects on the country's future growth.

Providing greater scope for redistributive taxation. The irony is that while short-term capital imposes enormous costs on society, the ability of a country to tax such capital, should it become fixated on keeping it, is limited. This is a reflection of a general principle in taxation: governments can impose only limited taxes as factors whose supply is highly elastic. Capital market liberalization, in effect, enhances the elasticity of supply, thereby lowering the scope for redistribution. As a second irony, the fact that short-term capital increases economic volatility means that the return that it must receive—to compensate it for the risks that it itself has caused—is higher. Hence, capital market liberalization can drive up the before-tax returns at the same time that it reduces the scope for taxation.

Preventing massive capital outflows. The rush of capital out of Russia has played an important role in the economic demise of that country; China's investing its huge savings inside the country has similarly been critical in its success. With open capital markets, the oligarchs in Russia were posed with a simple choice: where in the world to invest their wealth—whether in Russia, which was going into a prolonged depression of an almost unprecedented scale, or in the United States (say), which was, at the time, experiencing one of the strongest expansions in its history, with a stock market boom to match? The fact that the wealth of the oligarchs was widely perceived to be ill-gotten, based on political connections in a process of privatization without political legitimacy, and therefore (rightly perceived) subject to be reversed in a subsequent administration only reinforced the wisdom of taking the money out of the country. And as each oligarch (and smaller investors) decided to do so, it made it more desirable for others do so.

Although of all the objectives of intervention listed, this may be the most difficult to achieve, the analysis above suggests that even when the purpose is discouraging long-term capital outflows, the interventions may be effective even when there are ways of circumventing them. This is because there may be multiple equilibria; if most people keep their money in the economy, it grows, and it becomes attractive for others to do so. Conversely, if most people pull their money out of the country, it becomes attractive for others to do so. The restrictions on capital outflows can "force" the economy to the "good" equilibrium, and once there, it is self-sustaining.

The forms and mechanisms of interventions

Intervention has taken on a number of different forms and been implemented through a number of different mechanisms. Some of these rely more on "market mechanisms" that are both more flexible and that avoid the opprobrium associated with the term *controls*

Taxes on capital inflows. For a long time, Chile had an effective system of what amounted in effect to a tax on short-term capital inflows. (A third of the money coming into Chile had to be deposited in the central bank for a year at a zero-interest rate; hence, the first-year return was taxed, in effect, at 33 percent.) The tax rate could vary with economic circumstances—discouraging inflows more when they seemed to pose a greater problem. In principle, a subsidy could be provided if the government wished to encourage an inflow.

At the same time, the tax on inflows discouraged speculative outflows: an investor worried about the possibility of a small devaluation would not find it attractive to take his money out of the country overnight to bring it back in again the next day, for there was a large effective tax on such a roundtrip. There was little evidence that the tax discouraged overall inflows, but it lengthened the maturity of funds, thus stabilizing the economy. Chile was, of course, adversely affected by the global financial crisis, as were all countries, and especially countries heavily dependent on commodity exports. No one believed that it would eliminate all sources of instability. In the aftermath of the crisis, as funds for emerging markets dried up everywhere, Chile decided that the problem was not a surfeit of funds but a lack of funds, and hence the tax was reduced to zero.

Controls on capital outflows. In the uncertainty of the early days of the global financial crisis following Russia's default, Malaysia responded by imposing controls on capital outflows. It noted high levels of speculative activity on the ringit, especially occurring in Singapore, and worried that such speculation would destabilize the economy. The controls were carefully designed to ensure that those who had invested long term in the country would be able to take their profits out. And they were announced as short term, to be removed within a year. The vituperativeness with which these controls were greeted was almost unprecedented, not only from the IMF, the self-appointed guardian of capital market liberalization, but also from the U.S. Treasury. They forecast that the controls would be ineffective; that the country would never be able to attract capital; that they would be counterproductive, exacerbating the economic downturn; that they would never be removed; and that without the discipline of capital markets, the country would never address its problems. Their forecasts were as far from the mark and as based on ideology and interests as their earlier advocacy of capital market liberalization had been. Just as Malaysia had once before imposed capital controls in an emergency and removed them as promised, so too did it fulfill its commitment. Its downturn was shorter than any of the other countries,[16] and the country was left with less of a legacy of indebtedness. (See the discussion in the preceding section.) It did use the time well to restructure, with a program that was far more effective than that of its neighbor, who remained under IMF tutelage. Capital (foreign direct investment) continued to flow into the country.[17]

The World Bank worked with Malaysia to convert the controls into an exit tax, with the tax rate gradually lowered. The result was that when the controls (taxes) were finally removed, there was no disturbance to the market: it was a virtually seamless change.

Bank regulations. Today, increasingly, capital controls are implemented through bank regulations, which limit not only the (uncovered) foreign exchange exposure of banks but also of the firms to which they lend. Since most financial transactions are intermediated through banks and most domestic firms borrow at home as well as abroad, these regulations can be highly effective. Even before the crisis, Malaysia had succeeded in limiting the foreign exchange exposure of its banks.

Such changes can be implemented either through direct regulations or through more price-based mechanisms, for example, through deposit insurance systems where the premia increase with risk and where the foreign exchange exposure of the bank (direct and indirect) is included in the risk measure, or through risk adjusted capital adequacy requirements, again where foreign exchange exposure is included in the risk measure.

Taxes. Many countries have individual and corporate income tax systems that allow the deduction of interest payments. By disallowing the deduction of interest on short-term foreign denominated debt, households and firms would be provided with an incentive not to undertake such debt.[18]

EXCHANGE RATE REGIMES AND CAPITAL MARKET CONTROLS

So far, we have argued that capital controls increase risk but do not increase growth. We have elided the question of the extent to which these results are dependent on the exchange rate regime. In this section, we shall argue that in the absence of capital controls, the only exchange rate regimes that, in practice, can work effectively are floating exchange rates or dollarization, but that even with floating exchange rate systems, capital controls can enhance economic stability.

Why fixed exchange rate systems fail without capital controls

A major failing of fixed exchange rate systems is their vulnerability to speculative attack, especially when there is a perception that the exchange rate is overvalued and cannot be sustained. Countries are not given the grace of a gradual adjustment. When there is not sufficient reserves to back up the demands for dollars, then there can be a run on the currency, just as there can be a run on a bank when there is not sufficient reserves available to meet its liabilities (see Diamond and Dybvig 1983). If all creditors and potential claimants believed that the country could meet its obligations, then, of course, they would not wish to "cash in," to pull their funds out of the country; but if they believe that the exchange rate is not sustainable and will crash, the returns to doing so are enormous. They can pull their funds out today, putting them back in tomorrow, and make an enormous return from the speculative activity.

The problem is that the amount of reserves required to ensure that a country can meet its commitment to maintain the exchange rate is enormous under full capital market liberalization: it equals the total value of the money supply plus short-term, foreign-denominated credit, for any domestic currency can be converted into dollars on demand. In short, the country has to have a fully backed currency—equivalent to the elimination of fiat money. In effect, then, a country with full capital market liberalization surrenders control over its money supply and monetary policy. The consequences are not only that the government cannot engage in stabilizing macro-policy, but also there may actually be a destabilizing dynamic put into place.

Assume, for instance, its firms decide to borrow more abroad. It must then increase reserves or take strong actions to discourage such foreign borrowing. Assume that the mantra is that the country not only cannot control the capital inflows, but it cannot tax them or the uses to which the funds are put. Then, if it wishes to add to reserves, it will put downward pressure on the exchange rate. But given that it is committed to maintaining the exchange rate at its fixed level, it must offset this pressure by increasing the interest rate. It might well justify that measure further by noting that it dampens the inflationary pressures that are often associated with the capital inflows. But this induces domestic firms that expect the government to fulfill its commitment to a fixed exchange rate to borrow even more abroad, especially if foreign borrowing is being, in effect, encouraged by the foreign lenders, as was the case in East Asia. (The Basle capital adequacy standards provide preferential risk treatment for short-term lending, and the underregulation of the undercapitalized Japanese banks provided them with an incentive to engage in risky lending.[19]) There is thus a vicious circle, one that can easily lead to massive distortions of resource allocation, as in the case of Thailand: the foreign lending goes into areas that are collateralizable, feeds a speculative real estate boom, while the high interest rates meanwhile choke off more valuable domestic investment.[20] It made little sense to build empty office buildings in Bangkok and Jakarta when there were other investments that would have enhanced the growth prospects and job opportunities. Yet, that is what happened under deregulation.

There is an alternative strategy that few countries have followed. To discourage foreign borrowing, the country can make loans available at more attractive terms to domestic borrowers. One argument holds that lowering interest rates to domestic borrowers will lead to lower deposit rates and a possible flow of money out of the country. This argument, while often mentioned, is unpersuasive: the objective was to stem an excess flow of foreign borrowing, and there must exist a "fixed point," a level of interest rates that attracts the desired level of capital.

But there is another argument that is somewhat more compelling. The lower interest rate will normally lead to an increased level of domestic investment and hence possibly contribute to inflationary pressures. In effect, a country in such a situation is forced to cut back on public expenditures or increase taxes in response to an onslaught of foreign capital, no matter whether that onslaught is based on irrational exuberance or not. If such policies had been pursued in Thailand, investments in empty office buildings would have crowded out higher return investments in education or infrastructure or forced politically unpalatable increases in taxes—in a country already running a fiscal surplus.

(There is still a third alternative strategy, from which the countries were discouraged under the doctrines of liberalization, and that is micro-economic interventions, such as taxing real estate capital gains.)

The dynamic is worse than just described: If the monetary and fiscal measures designed to maintain the exchange rate do not, at the same time, perfectly offset any inflationary pressures, then the capital inflow may well lead to a *real* appreciation, leading to a trade deficit. (In some sense, the trade deficit is the inevitable accompaniment of the capital inflow, and the trade deficit will typically[21] be generated by a real appreciation.) But the increasingly large trade deficit, under standard doctrines and models, will be viewed as "unsustainable." That is, markets may increasingly anticipate a correction in the overvalued exchange rate, a correction more likely to occur through a sudden change in the exchange rate than in adjustments in wages and prices.

The fact of the matter is that few governments have been willing to maintain high-cost reserves equal to their money supply and foreign-denominated short-term indebtedness, and short of that, the countries will be vulnerable to a speculative attack. Even the massive amount of money that the IMF has been able to mobilize in recent crises is not enough to fill the gap and therefore to maintain confidence in the overvalued exchange rate.

But the fact that the IMF has engineered massive (and typically unsuccessful) bailouts has exacerbated the overall problem in three distinct ways. First, in effect, the IMF has fed the speculative sharks (though the cost is borne by the taxpayers in the developing country). In the absence of outside funds, speculation is a zero-sum game, with some speculators gaining at the expense of others. The IMF engineered bailouts convert what would be a zero-sum game into a positive-sum game for speculators: they stand to gain at the expense of taxpayers, and they have indeed gained handsomely. Second, the funds have facilitated the bailout of creditors, generating the moral-hazard problem—lenders do not bear the full costs of their lending decisions (even ignoring the macroeconomic externality). IMF economists (including their chief economist, Michael Mussa) have argued that the lenders have borne some costs, but that is not the point: moral-hazard problems arise whenever they do not bear the full costs, and this they clearly have not. Third, the IMF efforts to sustain the exchange rate (even if only partially successful), and the rhetoric that, otherwise, borrowers who have borrowed in foreign denominations will be hurt, have led to a "foreign exchange cover moral hazard." Private borrowers have felt that they do not need to buy insurance against the risk of devaluation or as much insurance as they otherwise would, and in this they are right: when enough of them take that position, the IMF will use that fact to help support the exchange rate. They are willing to force small firms to bear the costs through high interest rates to save those that should have purchased insurance. Doing so, it could be argued, is not only contributing to a moral-hazard problem but to a moral problem.

The arguments put forward for fixed exchange rate systems apply with equal force to controlled exchange rate systems, for example, where the exchange rate is allowed to move within a well-defined band. When it becomes apparent that the band cannot be sustained, there will be a speculative attack.

Dollarization. While capital market liberalization has thus made fixed exchange rate systems of the conventional kind untenable, it has enhanced the argument for dollarization, in which the country gives up control over its money supply. Under standard criteria, Argentina and the United States, or Ecuador and the United States, do not constitute an optimal currency area (see Mundell 1961). But Mundell (1961) wrote his classic article before capital market liberalization was the vogue. The shocks facing Ecuador and the United States are markedly different, and giving up conventional monetary policy instruments will impair the ability to stabilize the economy. But the alternative—allowing the country to be buffeted by speculative exchange rate movements—may be even worse, and even with dollarization, there may be some scope for monetary policy (see Stiglitz 2001b).

Volatility among the major currency areas. Dollarization, however, is not really a viable solution for countries engaged in trade with many different countries, for example, Japan, Europe, and the United States, simply because of the huge volatility of the exchange rates among their currencies. Fixing the exchange rate to the dollar means that firms face enormous risks in the exchange rate with Japan and Europe. In short, there really is no such thing as a fixed exchange rate, only an exchange rate that is fixed in terms of one of the many currencies that the country interacts with. Stabilizing on a basket of exchange rates does not solve the problem of particular firms. It leaves a firm that exports in the dollar zone, or imports from the yen zone, or imports from one zone and exports to another, bearing enormous risk. It does a firm little good to know that on average, exchange rates are stable, if it faces bankruptcy, because imports have undermined it. Today, small countries around the world have to face this challenge in risk management: there is nothing they can do about this volatility. But given the high level of risk that they have to manage in any case, the burden of managing the additional risk posed by short-term speculative capital flows in the absence of capital controls is all the greater.

Flexible exchange rates

Some critics of Thailand suggest that the problems it faced in the East Asia crisis lie with the fixed exchange rate system, but that contention is wrong (See Furman and Stiglitz 1998a). Had the exchange rate been allowed to adjust, it would have appreciated, increasing the trade deficit, distorting the economy through that channel. When the collapse came, it might have even been worse, simply because the fall in the exchange rate would have been from a higher, more overvalued level. Some argue that investors were lulled by the seemingly fixed exchange rate to take a more exposed position than they otherwise would have, but this argument is unpersuasive on two grounds. First, prudent behavior required the purchase of insurance, and insurance markets are particularly well designed (in principle) for handling the risks associated with fixed exchange rate systems—small probability events with large consequences. There never has been a truly fixed exchange rate system; fixed exchange rate systems only mean that adjustments occur in large steps but infrequently. If the market shared the investors' perceptions that the probability of an adjustment was small, then the insurance premium would have been correspondingly small. Thus, the failure to obtain cover, exposing themselves and the country to large risk, was as much, or more, a case of market failure than of government failure, of markets either being irrational (investors believing that they know better than the market, as reflected in insurance premia, about the future course of exchange rates) or inefficient, with the cost of cover being excessively high relative to the risk being divested. Second, there have been "crashes"—rapid changes in asset prices—in "flexible"-price markets as there have been in fixed-price markets.

With flexible exchange rates, there are high costs of the absence of capital controls, especially given the imperfections of risk markets.[22] Changes in speculative attitudes, say, toward the exchange rate, can force the exchange rate up or down, imposing huge problems for exporters and those in import competing sectors, or even to domestic producers relying on imported inputs. Typically, neither the producers nor consumers can divest themselves of the resulting large risks. Especially in the presence of imperfections of capital markets,[23] the costs of such risks can be enormous: workers, underprotected by social safety nets, cannot borrow against the prospect of future income; firms may be forced to shut down, with an enormous loss of firm-specific human capital and organizational capital. And the anticipation of such costs will make investment in the country less attractive. Even when there are futures and forward markets, they extend only to a limited extent into the future, not enough to deal with the risks associated with long-term real investments.

Macro-stability. The huge volatility in exchange rates provides real challenges (to put it mildly) on those responsible for macro-stability, especially if traditional IMF/central bank responses are employed. A loss of confidence in the currency will lead depreciation. If true free-market principles were adhered to, so that the government simply allowed the exchange rate to be whatever the market determined, then the government would simply have to apprise the adverse real balance effect of firms and households that were net foreign debtors, the positive real balance effect of those who were net creditors, and the positive effect on net exports (taking into account the dynamics of adjustment). Fiscal and monetary policy could freely be used to adjust the level and composition of output, either increasing or decreasing the extent of devaluation. (To be sure, the calculations of the appropriate policies would be complicated not only by the dynamics of adjustment but also by the complexity of expectation formation. But these are details that need not detain us here.)

In practice, the IMF has seldom allowed governments the freedom just described. It has worried that devaluations would lead to inflation, it has inveighed against what it describes as competitive devaluations (never mind that such devaluations are effectively typically aimed at changing the exchange rates against the dollar, not just at gaining a competitive edge over similar countries), and it has worried that with devaluation, those who owe money abroad in dollars would not be able to meet their obligations or lead to contagion. While in other spheres, it has taken a strong promarket line, in this area, it has talked about overshooting;[24] but it has never provided a coherent explanation for why overshooting should be more prevalent in this market than in other asset markets, why government intervention—and, in effect, government subsidies—should be more acceptable in this market than in other markets, or why the interventions should be limited to the particular kinds of intervention (high interest rates, fiscal contraction, direct exchange rate support) that it favors. Their arguments have rung an increasingly hollow note: the large devaluations associated the global financial crisis did not set off inflationary spirals; Brazil's large devaluation did not lead to contagion; the bankruptcies that marked East Asia were as much a result of the high interest rate and contractionary fiscal policies put in place to stave off a devaluation than to the devaluation itself (though to be sure, the devaluation had a greater impact on the foreign creditors, the clientele of the IMF, while the high interest rates had a greater impact on domestic creditors, which seemingly were of little direct concern). Adjustments in exchange rates in other noncrisis countries, like Taiwan, followed along the lines of the crisis countries: there was no competitive devaluation, just an exchange rate adjustment. Most tellingly, careful micro-studies, for example, of Thailand, showed that the seeming worry about the impact of devaluation on the economy was largely bogus and certainly of second order compared to the adverse consequences of the high interest rates and excessive fiscal contraction. Those with large foreign indebtedness were largely in the real estate sector and already dead; further devaluation would not make them any deader, and arresting the devaluation would not lead to a revival of this sector. The second most heavily indebted group were exporters, who would, on the whole, gain more from the devaluation in terms of exports than they would lose on their balance sheets.[25]

But those who come under the sway of the IMF have to respond to the devaluation by interest rate increases and fiscal contractions, which lead to recession and, in some cases, depression. Indeed, the basic framework, which has come to be called "beggar-thy-self policies," is designed to bring about an economic downturn—and to bring with it adverse contagion to neighbors. A common (but not universal) characteristic of the precrisis situation is a trade deficit.[26] Countries are told to redress the deficit; the resulting surplus facilitates the ability to repay its creditors. But given that devaluations are discouraged, tariff and other barriers to imports are not allowed, and exports cannot be increased overnight; the only way to do so is to decrease incomes—cause a recession—which reduces imports. Trading partners, of course, do not care much about why their exports are down; all they know is that they have fallen. The downturn in one country is thus transmitted to its neighbors, just as in the beggar-thy-neighbor policies that played such an important role in the propagation of the Great Depression. But these policies do not even have the saving grace of helping the domestic economy as they hurt those of trading partners. Thus, countries with capital market liberalization (under fixed or flexible exchange rates) that have their responses to large variations in capital flows dictated by the IMF are likely to find themselves confronting the consequences of large economic downturns.

In short, with fixed exchange rates and full capital market liberalzation, the government absorbs some of the costs that the huge movements in short-term capital impose under flexible exchange rates; but the government's ability to do so is limited. If it wishes to do so, it must bear huge costs, both in terms of the size of reserves that have to be maintained and in terms of its loss of ability to maintain macro-economic stability. But with flexible exchange rates, full capital market liberalization imposes enormous risks on firms, and while there are macro-policies that may do a reasonable job of offsetting the effects, ensuring a modicum of macro-stability, in practice, countries are likely to face significant macro-instability under these exchange rate regimes as well.

CONCLUDING REMARKS

Developing countries differ from more developed countries in many ways, besides the lower level of incomes. In particular, they face greater economic volatility and a lower ability to manage that volatility, even though they may have more flexible wages and labor markets than more developed countries (see Easterly, Islam, and Stiglitz 2000). Capital market liberalization increases the risks they face—under any exchange rate regime, although it may enhance the arguments for flexible exchange rates. Given the absence of evidence that it promotes growth, given the compelling theoretical arguments that it may actually have adverse effects on growth, and given the theory and evidence that it enhances economic instability, one might well ask, how could an international body, the IMF, founded to promote global economic stability be so active in promoting it, going so far as to seek a change in its charter to mandate it?

A full answer to this would take us well beyond the scope of this article: a mixture of bad economics (using old macro-economic models that simply failed to incorporate in a meaningful way finance, although this has been one of the major areas of advance in economic theory in the past quarter century[27]), ideology, and special interests: financial markets would gain from the opening up of new markets, and American financial markets wanted them to be opened up quickly, before others were in a position to take advantage of these new opportunities; and the free-market ideology served these interests well (even if there was a note of intellectual incoherence in free-marketers asking the government to use its power to force others to open up their markets and in defending multi-billion dollar bailouts for Western creditors). But the lack of transparency with which the IMF operates exacerbates these problems: its policies were not subject to the kinds of intensive scrutiny that should be the hallmark of democratic processes, simply because much of what it does goes on behind closed doors, with public announcements coming too late for meaningful inputs from other stakeholders. Secrecy is the hallmark of financial markets, and the IMF has borrowed its culture from those it has sought to serve, with whom it interacts constantly, and from whom it draws so much of its personnel.

But underlying all of these problems is governance: to whom the institution is accountable. With voting rights allocated according to market power at the end of World War II, with some adjustments since then, with finance ministries and central banks speaking for the governments, with other stakeholders precluded from having a seat at the table, the policies pushed by the IMF become understandable but no more acceptable.[28]

Capital market liberalization represents a major change in the rules of the game. It was a change in the rules that did not serve the interests of the developing countries well. The fundamental problem facing globalization is how these rules of the game are made. Dissatisfaction with the current system is well deserved.

Notes

1. Interestingly, many in the International Monetary Fund (IMF) claimed that they never had really pushed for capital market liberalization for countries that were unprepared. At best, this was a semantic quibble: although they had often accompanied their demands for capital market liberalization by demands for other reforms, they had never said not to go forward with capital market liberalization until those other reforms were made.

2. With even the U.S. secretary of treasury joining the attack, it was not left just to the normal bureaucratic processes.

3. The most notorious example involved the newly appointed managing director giving a speech in Bangkok, in which he reflected some of the new thinking in the fund concerning the risks of capital market liberalization. By the time he reached Jakarta, the Indonesians already were discussing ways by which the new thinking might be reflected in practice. But by then, the IMF staff had reportedly gotten to their new managing director, and there was quick backtracking: it was put to the Indonesians in no uncertain terms that going back on capital market liberalization was not to be part of their economic agenda.

4. See below for a more extended discussion of the Thai case.

5. The only possible justification might be that banks in the United States do a better job at allocating scarce funds in the developing country, so much better that income in the country is higher than it would otherwise have been. There is no evidence in support of this position.

6. See Furman and Stiglitz (1998a) and Rodrik and Velasco (2000). To be sure, other factors played a role, some of which are described below.

7. There were deeper failings in their arguments: they seemed to believe that a temporary intervention in the market would lead to a permanent shift in the demand functions, for example, for investment. The mechanism by which this might occur, other than through some vague appeal to the intervention resulting in a restoration of confidence, were never spelled out. There was no systematic analysis of investor psychology (with empirical support for the maintained hypotheses), nor was there any appeal to rational expectations models that are the normal staple of much of modern macroeconomics. Krugman (1998) criticized the IMF for playing the role of armchair market psychologists, a role for which they were eminently unqualified, with a commensurately weak track record. Stiglitz (1999) provided a more detailed critique of the underlying theories.

8. For an econometric analysis for the United States, see Furman and Stiglitz (1998b).

9. In the jargon of standard economics, low-income individuals have a high level of risk aversion and have little access to mechanisms with which to divest themselves of the risks they face. This can be viewed as an important instance of market failure.

10. That is, taking into account the imperfections of information and the costs of transactions, for example, associated with creating markets. See, for example, Greenwald and Stiglitz (1986).

11. But even this needs to be qualified. Newbery and Stiglitz showed that when risk markets are imperfect—which they always are in practice—free trade may actually make everyone worse off. See Newbery and Stiglitz (1984).

12. In particular, Murdock and Stiglitz (1993) and Hellmann, Murdock, and Stiglitz (1996, 2000) showed that restrictions on financial markets may be welfare enhancing.

13. This is the essential point of the large literature on "local public goods." See Tiebout (1956) and Stiglitz (1983a, 1983b).

14. For an analysis of the Latin American case, refer to Galvin and Hausman (1996).

15. See, for example, Weitzman (1974) or a standard public sector textbook, such as Stiglitz (2000b).

16. See Kaplan and Rodrik (2001). To be sure, its downturn was somewhat longer than it might otherwise have been because Finance Minister Anwar at first tried the standard IMF recipes (in what was called an IMF program without the IMF), raising interest rates and cutting back on public expenditures. Recovery only began when these policies were reversed.

17. There remains some controversy over whether in 2000 Thailand was more successful in attracting foreign investment than Malaysia, with disputes both about data and their interpretation. What matters for growth, of course, are greenfield investments, not simply foreigners buying already existing assets, unless the funds they provide to the country in doing so are themselves turned into investments. Large fire sales in Thailand might temporarily succeed in diverting funds from Malaysia but are hardly indicative of a better "strategy."

18. There are certain practical problems in the implementation of such provisions, which can easily be overcome. Because firms will be tempted to use derivatives to subvert the intent of these tax provisions, there will have to be netting provisions, with full disclosure of derivative positions (enforced, e.g., by laws that limit the enforceability of derivative positions that are not disclosed, or giving them junior positions in the event of bankruptcy). Similarly, debt covenants making debt immediately callable in the event of certain circumstances (such as those associated with a crisis) should either be made not enforceable or bonds with those provisions not be given favorable tax treatment.

19. A situation analogous to that encountered in the United States in the savings and loan debacle.

20. Proponents of capital market liberalization (including those in the IMF) underestimated these distortions, simply because they did not understand the functioning of capital markets and the ways that such markets differ from ordinary markets for goods and services. In their simplistic models, capital in a well-functioning economy (which most developing countries are not) is allocated (as if) by an auction process to the borrower offering the highest interest rate, just like any other good is allocated to the buyer offering the highest price. Thus, the fact that real estate was offering the best interest rates meant that that had to be the highest return activity. And it was simply assumed that if there were mistakes in judgment, only the lender would bear the cost of such mistakes. In fact, capital is not allocated by an auction process (see Stiglitz and Weiss 1981; Greenwald and Stiglitz forthcoming) but by a screening process, and for an obvious reason: those offering the highest interest rates may not be those most likely to repay. Moreover, we have seen that when large numbers of debtors cannot repay the loans, there are macro-economic consequences, with others besides those who have borrowed and lent having to bear the costs.

21. Although not necessarily: the availability of new sources of credit can increase the demand for imports, even if relative prices remain relatively unchanged. This seems to have been the case recently in Iceland. See Stiglitz (2001a).

22. Many advocates of capital market liberalization, especially those that appeal to the analogy of the benefits of free markets for goods, fail to appreciate these market failures and their consequences.

23. Themselves explicable in terms of imperfect information. See Stiglitz (2000b).

24. That is, if the initial exchange rate is 140 to the dollar, the true equilibrium is 190 to the dollar; in the initial adjustment, the exchange rate may overshoot to 210 to the dollar.

25. Moreover, while the IMF tried to characterize there being a trade-off, as we saw earlier there was none: the high interest rates intended to prevent a devaluation simply pushed the economy deeper into recession, weakening confidence in the country and its currency.

26. For instance, Korea, at the time that the crisis struck, did not have a balance of trade deficit. In the old world, before capital market liberalization, the link between trade deficits and crises was closer.

27. Highlighted by the fact that in the typical macro-models employed by the IMF, bankruptcy and default were not modeled, although bankruptcy and default were at the center of the global financial crisis.

28. For a more extensive discussion of these points, see Stiglitz (forthcoming).

References

Caprio, Gerard, and Daniela Klingebiel. 1996. Bank insolvencies: Cross-country experience. Policy research working paper no. 1620. Washington, DC: World Bank.

Collier, Paul, and Anke Hoeffler. 1998. On economic causes of civil war. *Oxford Economic Papers* 50 (4): 563-73.

Demirgüç-Kunt, Asli, and Enrica Detragiache. 1997. The determinants of banking crises: Evidence from industrial and developing countries. World Bank working paper no. 1828. Washington, DC: World Bank.

———. 1999. Financial liberalization and financial fragility. In *Annual World Bank conference on development economics 1998*, edited by Boris Pleskovic and Joseph E. Stiglitz. Washington, DC: World Bank.

Diamond, Douglas W., and Philip H. Dybvig. 1983. Bank runs, deposit insurance, and liquidity. *Journal of Political Economy* 91 (3): 401-19.

Easterly, William Russel, Roumeen Islam, and Joseph E. Stiglitz. 2000. Shaken and stirred: Volatility and macroeconomic paradigms for rich and poor countries. Michael Bruno Memorial Lecture. Washington, DC: World Bank.

Furman, Jason, and Joseph E. Stiglitz. 1998a. Economic crises: Evidence and insights from East Asia. *Brookings Papers on Economic Activity* 2:1-114.

———. 1998b. On the economic causes of inequality. Paper presented at Income Inequality: Issues and Policy Options, a symposium sponsored by the Federal Reserve Bank of Kansas City, Jackson Hole, Wyoming, 27-29 August, Kansas City, Missouri.

Galvin, Michael, and Ricardo Hausman. 1996. The roots of banking crises: The macroeconomic context. In *Banking crises in Latin America*, edited by Ricardo Hausmann and Liliana Rojas-Suarez. Washington, DC: Inter-american Development Bank.

Greenwald, Bruce, and Joseph E. Stiglitz. 1986. Externalities in economies with imperfect information and incomplete markets. *Quarterly Journal of Economics* 101 (2): 229-64.

———. Forthcoming. Towards a new paradigm for monetary economics. Mattioli lecture, Milan.

Hellman, Thomas F., Kevin C. Murdock, and Joseph E. Stiglitz. 1996. Deposit mobilization through financial restraint. In *Financial development and economic growth: Theory and experiences from developing economies*, edited by N. Hermes and R. Lensink. London: Routledge.

———. 2000. Liberalization, moral hazard in banking and prudential regulation: Are capital requirements enough? *American Economic Review* 90 (1): 147-65.

Kaplan, Ethan, and Dani Rodrik. 2001. Did the Malaysian capital controls work? NBER working paper no. W8142.

Krugman, Paul. 1998. The confidence game. *The New Republic*, October, 5.

Lindgren, Carl Johann, Gillian Garcia, and Matthew I. Saal. 1996. *Banking soundness and macroeconomic policy.* Washington, DC: International Monetary Fund.

Miller, Marcus, and Joseph E. Stiglitz. 1999. Bankruptcy protection against macroeconomic shocks: The case for a "super chapter 11." World Bank Conference on Capital Flows, Financial Crises, and Policies, 15 April.

Murdock, Kevin C., and Joeseph E. Stiglitz. 1993. The effect of financial repression in an economy with positive real interest rates: Theory and evidence. Mimeo, Stanford University.

Mussa, Michael. 2000. Factors driving global economic integration. Paper presented at Global Economic Integration: Opportunities and Challenges, a symposium sponsored by the Federal Reserve Bank of Kansas City, Jackson Hole, Wyoming, 24-26 August, Kansas City, Missouri.

Newbery, David M. G., and Joseph E. Stiglitz. 1984. Pareto inferior trade. *Review of Economic Studies* 51 (1): 1-12.

Rodriguez, Francisco, and Dani Rodrik. 1999. Trade policy and economic growth: A skeptic's guide to cross-national evidence. NBER working paper no. W7081.

Rodrik, Dani. 1998. Who needs capital-account convertibility? *Essays in International Finance* 207, 55-65. Princeton, NJ: Department of Economics, Princeton University.

Rodrik, Dani, and Andres Velasco. 2000. Short-term capital flows In *Annual World Bank Conference on Development Economics 1999*, edited by Boris Pleskovic and Joseph E. Stiglitz. Washington, DC: World Bank.

Sachs, Jeffrey, and Andrew Warner. 1995. Economic reform and the process of global integration. *Brookings Papers on Economic Activity* 1:1-118.

Stiglitz, Joseph E. 1983a. Public goods in open economies with heterogeneous individuals. In *Locational analysis of public facilities*, edited by J. F. Thisse and H. G. Zoller, 55-78. Amsterdam, the Netherlands: North-Holland.

———. 1983b. The theory of local public goods twenty-five years after Tiebout: A perspective. In *Local provision of public services: The Tiebout model after twenty-five years*, edited by G. R. Zodrow. New York: Academic Press.

———. 1999. Knowledge for development: Economic science, economic policy, and economic advice. In *Annual World Bank Conference on Development Economics 1998*, edited by Boris Pleskovic and Joseph E. Stiglitz. Washington, DC: World Bank.

———. 2000a. The contributions of the economics of information to twentieth century economics. *Quarterly Journal of Economics* 115 (4): 1441-78.

———. 2000b. *Economics of the public sector.* 3d ed. New York: Norton.

———. 2001a. (with Sebago Associates). Monetary and exchange rate policy in small open economies: The case of Iceland. Paper prepared for the Central Bank of Iceland, February.

———. 2001b. The role of the central bank and monetary policy under dollarization. Paper presented at the Central Bank of Ecuador, March, Quito.

———. Forthcoming. Democratizing the IMF and World Bank: Governance and accountability.

Stiglitz, Joseph. E., and Andrew Weiss. 1981. Credit rationing in markets with imperfect information. *American Economic Review* 71 (3): 393-410.

Tiebout, Charles M. 1956. A pure theory of local expenditure. *Journal of Political Economy* 64 (5): 416-24.

Weitzman, M. L. 1974. Prices vs. quantities. *Review of Economic Studies* 41 (4): 477-91.

World Bank. 2000. *World Development report 2000/2001: Attacking poverty.* New York: Oxford University Press.

ANNALS, *AAPSS*, **579**, January 2002

Should Developing Countries Restrict Capital Inflows?

By MICHAEL K. ULAN

ABSTRACT: In the early 1990s, Chile imposed a tax on short-term inflows of foreign capital to control its current-account deficit by reducing the real exchange rate of the peso. The tax reduced capital inflows and increased the maturity of the foreign capital that entered that country, but the preponderance of the evidence is that the impost did not affect the real exchange rate of the peso. Moreover, the tax imposed considerable costs on the Chilean economy. After the 1997-98 financial crisis, some economists and politicians advocated such a tax to effect or preserve macroeconomic stability in developing countries. Aside from "second-best" arguments, imposing such a tax for that purpose can be justified only as a temporary measure to enable countries facing economic or financial crisis to reform and introduce prudential regulation and adequate supervision of their financial systems, but history shows that reforms dissipate as economic and financial conditions improve.

Michael K. Ulan is an economist with the U.S. Department of State. *He wishes to thank George M. von Furstenberg, George S. Tavlas, Thomas D. Willett, Keith E. Maskus, and Martin Kaufman for helpful comments on an earlier draft of this article. Any errors are the responsibility of the author. The views expressed are his own and not necessarily those of the Department of State or the U.S. government.*

THE financial systems of many developing economies were wracked by the financial crisis that originated in East Asia in July 1997; many of those economies experienced subsequent recessions. Some analysts attributed the crisis to the rapid reversal of short-term foreign capital inflows to the affected economies and advocated the imposition of controls on such flows to preserve macroeconomic stability in those economies. Governments wishing to control capital imports can impose explicit quantitative restrictions on cross-border capital movements, or they can impose taxes to limit such flows. The experience of Chile, which taxed capital imports during most of the 1990s to discourage inflows of short-term capital and did not suffer any direct effects of the "Asian" financial crisis, has led some observers to advocate Chilean-style taxes on capital inflows to maintain macroeconomic stability in developing economies. In this article, we review the arguments for and against restricting capital inflows to developing economies, examine the Chilean regime of the 1990s, and analyze the effectiveness of that regime in preserving macroeconomic stability in that Latin American nation.

THE CASE FOR AND AGAINST CAPITAL CONTROLS AS MACROECONOMIC POLICY INSTRUMENTS

The benefits of free international movement of capital parallel those of free trade. Open capital markets allow funds to flow to the places where they are expected to yield the greatest return, permit the international diffusion of new technologies and management techniques, and facilitate the international availability of products and services.

Historically, some countries restricted outflows of capital to support the foreign-exchange values of their currencies. In recent years, some countries concerned about the size of their current-account deficits or the appreciation of their currencies have restricted inflows of foreign capital.[1] Some economists question whether small countries with poorly developed financial markets can achieve free cross-border capital movement and stability in their international economic situations if such countries try to maintain separate currencies and their own exchange-rate regimes (Cooper 1999, 124). Nonetheless, the case for controlling capital inflows generally rests on "second-best" arguments such as the presence of asymmetric information, moral hazard,[2] and the "herd" instinct in capital markets or on the use of such measures during periods of transition to a more market-oriented economy. In each of the instances cited here, only temporary controls are justified.

The assumption of the efficiency of the free market is predicated on the symmetry of information between borrowers and lenders. If lenders have incomplete information about the creditworthiness of potential borrowers, they are likely to charge all borrowers an interest rate appropriate for borrowers perceived to be of "average" risk of default. In this situation, bad credit risks would seek loans while good credit risks would not. Hence, the market would make "adverse" selections of borrowers, and worthwhile projects would not be financed while riskier projects would receive funds (Eichengreen and Mussa 1998, 12-13). If a risky investment succeeds, the reward is likely to be greater than that on a less risky investment. Thus, to attract funds, borrowers have an incentive to make their projects appear less risky than they are—or to modify them to take on more risk after they have obtained financing, introducing moral hazard (Eichengreen and Mussa 1998, 13). Herd behavior, which can occur when investors who lack information about the riskiness of investments follow the behavior of people they assume to be more knowledgeable, can amplify price movements. In addition, Willett, Denzau, and Wihlborg (1999, 5-6) noted that short-term capital inflows can quickly become capital outflows, subjecting the economy to an increased likelihood of crisis. However, it is preferable to deal with the effects of second-best situations arising from the failure of markets to function or distortions by addressing the sources of the market failures and distortions directly rather than trying to offset them through capital controls (Hernández and Schmidt-Hebbel 1999, 1).

Turning to the temporary imposition of capital controls to facilitate economic transition and implementation of reforms, Massad (1998, 34-40, 45) maintained that, while liberalization of developing economies' capital accounts is desirable in the long run, there are both costs and benefits to capital controls during the transition to the free cross-border movement of capital. He said that capital controls can complement—but not substitute for—sound domestic policy to ensure macroeconomic stability during the transition. Eichengreen (1999, 49-50) advocated the imposition of a tax on short-term flows of capital to emerging markets, which he defined as countries where a substantial subset of the following conditions pertain: the capacity of bankers to manage risk is underdeveloped, and the narrowness of domestic financial markets leads to mistakes that can have "devastating systemic repercussions"; supervision and regulation of the banking system are weak, exhibiting regulatory forbearance in particular; inadequate auditing and accounting standards, together with political pressure, prevent the writing-down of bank capital; and a culture of implicit guarantees in the economy.

Eichengreen (1999, 52, 54-55) noted, however, that such a tax is likely to be effective only when supplemented by other policies to encourage hedging by banks and nonfinancial firms and to strengthen the domestic financial system. He said that, so long as banks' risk-management techniques are underdeveloped and their supervisory capacity is limited while government guarantees are prevalent, there is an argument for capital-import taxes, not as a substitute for progress in these other areas but to provide the kind of stable environment that encourages reform and asserted that the authorities will find Chilean-style measures "counterproductive" if they use the existence of the measures as an excuse to delay implementing reforms.

Camdesseus (1999, para. 25) noted that countries imposing controls on capital inflows have experienced severe capital-flow reversals when their economic policies have been inappropriate. Goldstein et al. (1999, 98) recommended that the International Monetary Fund advise all emerging economies with fragile domestic financial sectors and weak prudential frameworks to implement Chilean-style capital restrictions until they can successfully intermediate such flows, but they caution against using such controls as a substitute for financial-sector reforms. In opposition to temporary capital controls, Rhodes said, "The bottom line is that there is no substitution for the consistent implementation of sound economic policies over time" (Goldstein et al. 1999, 140). Yet, *The New York Times* reported (12 July 1999, A1, A6) that, as economic conditions improved in Asia in the wake of the 1997-98 financial crisis, reform programs were shelved.

Notwithstanding the arguments offered in support of temporary controls on capital inflows to buy time to reform the financial system, it may be that a prudently regulated financial system is a sine qua non for market-based controls to be effective. This point can be illustrated by comparing Chile's experience in the late 1970s and early 1980s with that of the country during the 1990s. De Gregorio (1997, 110-11) noted that, late in the 1970s, when interest rates had been deregulated and direct allocation of capital abandoned, the Chilean capital account was opened, but the increase in competition did not reduce interest rates and spreads between borrowing and lending rates. The rolling over of bad loans in the poorly regulated domestic financial system kept interest rates high. A debt crisis and a crash in Chile's financial markets followed. In contrast, the market opening of the 1990s, which has proceeded smoothly, followed five years of reforms in the domestic capital market that strengthened and deepened that market. Hernández and Schmidt-Hebbel (1999) said the following:

> It is important to keep in mind that the effectiveness of the URR in the case of Chile is due, to a great extent, to the high enforcement capacity of the CB [central bank], the long tradition of compliance with the law, and a relatively low degree of corruption. Thus, in countries operating with a weaker institutional and legal environment, a reserve requirement of the sort used by Chile could be less effective and, in the extreme, lead to (greater) corruption. (P. 27)

At this point, we turn to a discussion of Chile's capital-control regime.

CHILE'S CAPITAL CONTROLS

The charter of the Central Bank of Chile assigns two objectives to that institution—stability of the domestic price level and of the external and domestic payments system. Thus, the central bank has targets for the inflation rate in Chile and the country's current-account balance. The bank used short-term interest rates to control inflation and, between 1991 and 1998, capital controls to try to achieve its current-account target by attempting to affect the real exchange rate of the peso[3] (von Furstenberg and Ulan 1998, 65-66). The Central Bank of Chile faced a trade-off in its policy making. Raising domestic interest rates to fight inflation tends to attract foreign capital. The monetary authority could either sell peso-denominated securities to offset the impact of the capital inflows on Chile's money supply—a practice that economists call "sterilization" of the inflows—or impose capital controls to prevent the inflows. Offsetting the impact of the capital inflow by selling bonds would impose a cost on the Central Bank of Chile since the interest rate carried by its peso-denominated obligations exceeded the rate it could earn on the foreign funds, the inflow of which it offset (Folkerts-Landau et al. 1995, 12).

During the 1990s, Chile liberalized the restrictions it imposed on movements of capital into and, particularly, out of the country. The policy instruments the authorities used to maintain an independent monetary policy, control the real appreciation of the peso, and moderate the accumulation of speculative short-term liabilities to foreigners were controls on capital outflows (which were gradually liberalized), reductions of import tariffs, allowing new investment projects to be financed by domestic privately managed pension funds, minimum rating and maturity requirements for the issuing of bonds or equity securities abroad by Chileans, and imposition of an Unremunerated Reserve Requirement (URR) on some capital imports. It is the URR that has attracted attention as a policy instrument in the wake of the 1997-98 financial crisis. This measure required that foreign lenders to Chilean entities deposit an amount equal to a specified portion of their loans in a non-interest-bearing account at the Central Bank of Chile for a given time period. The URR went into effect in June 1991 and was reduced to zero in September 1998 (Nadal-De Simone and Sorsa 1999, 7). Initially, the period for which the deposit had to be maintained varied between ninety days and one year with the maturity of the investment. The period was increased to one year regardless of the maturity of the investment in 1992 and remained there until September 1998. As shown in Table 1, the scope of the URR was gradually expanded between its introduction in 1991 and 1997 in response to movements in capital inflows from categories covered by the impost to exempt categories (Nadal-De Simone and Sorsa 1999, 5-7; Labán and Larraín 1994, 140; International Monetary Fund 1999, 70). By the time the required reserve deposit was reduced to zero 17 September 1998, it covered most forms of foreign financing except "nonspeculative" foreign direct investment.

Requiring that money be deposited in a non-interest-bearing account constitutes an implicit tax on capital inflows equal to the interest that could have been earned on the funds. Instead of depositing money at the central bank, an investor in Chile could pay the central bank a sum equal to the interest he or she could earn on the unremunerated deposit, turning the implicit tax into an explicit impost (Richard W. Behrend, interview by the author,

TABLE 1
EVOLUTION OF THE CHILEAN UNREMUNERATED RESERVE REQUIREMENT (URR)

	Rate	Coverage
1991	20 percent (June) or LIBOR (July)	New credits except trade credits (June) Renewals of credits (July)
1992	30 percent (May, August) or LIBOR + 2.5 percent; LIBOR + 4.0 percent (October)	Foreign-currency deposits in commercial banks (January)
1993	No changes	No changes
1994	No changes	No changes
1995	Increase in the implicit cost of the URR (January) by requiring the deposit to be made in U.S. dollars, compared to any currency before	Secondary ADRs (June) New borrowing for old debt exempted (December)
1996	No changes	One-year limit on renewal of credits (May) Speculative foreign direct investment Small credits (less than $200 million) exempted (December)
1997	No changes	Small credit exemption reduced to cover only credits less than $100 million (December)
1998	10 percent (June) 0 percent (October)	No changes

SOURCE: International Monetary Fund (1999b, p. 97).

5 March 1999). Chile altered the coverage and varied the level of the required reserve deposit to achieve the net inflow of foreign investment consistent with the central bank's current-account target. Raising the URR, thereby reducing the inflow of foreign funds, held monetary expansion in check without incurring the costs associated with sterilization of foreign deposits in the nation's banks (Calvo, Leiderman, and Reinhart 1994, 64).

The midyear-1998 reduction in the URR followed a fall in the demand for and the price of copper, which resulted from declines in income in the economies affected by the 1997-98 crisis. This fall in Chile's export receipts required an increase in net capital inflows to the country to maintain the level of imports (Eichengreen 1999, 50). The URR was set to zero later that year because an increase in Chile's country-risk premium following the onset of the (originally Asian) financial crisis had discouraged the flow of funds to the country (Laurens and Cardoso 1998, 20). Several economists (Eichengreen 1999, 53; Martin Kaufman, interview by the author, 9 April 1999; Budnevich, Le-Fort, and Landerretche Moreno 1997, 134) asserted that, by September 1998 (if not earlier), supervision and regulation of Chile's banks had strengthened to the point that the URR was no longer necessary. The state of Chile's banking industry, the regulatory regime to which it was subject in 1997, and the rationale for the regulatory regime were presented by Livacic (1997, 141-47).

DID CHILE'S URR EFFECT DOMESTIC ECONOMIC STABILITY?

Chile's inflation rate fell each year the URR was in force. In 1990, the last full year before the URR was imposed, the nation's consumer price index rose 26.0 percent; in 1997, the last full year the URR was not zero, the price level increased 6.1 percent. Between 1991 and 1997, real growth in the Chilean economy averaged 7.6 percent (International Monetary Fund 2000b, 341, 343). While this record is remarkable, the fact that the Chilean economy performed well during the period the URR imposed a tax on capital imports does not suffice to show that this performance was caused by the URR. Was Chile's economic record achieved because of, despite, or independent of the URR? To shed some light on the answer to this question, we turn to the experience of Colombia, which imposed a similar tax on capital imports during the 1990s and to Chile's own economic history.

During the first half of the 1990s, Colombia liberalized the nation's international trade, finance, and investment regimes, and the central bank, the Banco de la República, received a new charter requiring it to reduce inflation. To stem the appreciation of the foreign-exchange value of the Colombian peso and to dampen domestic inflation, the bank tried to staunch the inflow of foreign funds by sterilizing them (Le Fort and Budnevich 1996, 25-27). In September 1993, the bank shifted its policy to a reserve requirement that pertained to foreign-currency credits having a maturity less than 18 months obtained by any Colombian resident. Initially a sum equal to 47 percent of the credit had to be deposited at the central bank; in March 1994, the system was modified to encompass credits of up to 36 months, with the size of the deposit at the central bank varying from 50 to 93 percent of the credit, as shown in Table 2. In August of that year, the system was changed again. From August 1994 to February 1996, credits of up to five years required reserve deposits; the size of the deposit varied inversely with the maturity of the credit—from 42.8 percent of credits with a maturity of five years to 140.0 percent of credits with a maturity of thirty or fewer days (Le Fort and Bundnevich 1996, 30-32). Subsequently, the Colombian deposit scheme was revised, as shown in Table 3. Colombia's capital-control regime was more complex than that of Chile and entailed

TABLE 2

COLOMBIAN RESERVE REQUIREMENTS: 16 MARCH TO 15 AUGUST 1994

Certificate Maturity (months)	Reserve Requirement (percentage of investment)
Less than 12	93
Between 12 and 18	64
More than 24	50

SOURCE: Le Fort and Bundnevich (1996, 39); International Monetary Fund (1999c, 56).

NOTE: There is no reference in either source to the situation that prevailed for loans of more than 18 but less than 24 months.

TABLE 3
COLOMBIAN RESERVE REQUIREMENTS FROM 21 FEBRUARY 1996

Dates in Effect	Maximum Maturity Subject to Restriction (months)	Period after which Prepayment of Debt Was Allowed (months)	Period of Loan to Borrower in Colombia (months)	Percentage of Loan Amount Deposited at Central Bank
February-March 1996	48	48	N.D.	Range from 10 to 85 varying inversely with the maturity of the loan
March 1996-January 1997	36	36	18	50
March 1997-May 1997	60	60	18	50
May 1997-January 1998	All	0 with authorization of central bank	18	30 in pesos
January-September 1998	All	0 with authorization of central bank	12	25 in pesos
September 1998	All	0 with authorization of central bank	6	10 in pesos

SOURCE: International Monetary Fund (1999c, 56).
NOTE: N.D.—no data in source.

higher implicit tax rates on all but very short-term capital inflows. Unlike Chile, Colombia has not permitted investors to pay the central bank a sum equal to the amount of interest that would be foregone on the unremunerated reserve deposit in lieu of the deposit.

During the 1990s, Chile continued to enhance the prudential regulation of its financial system, ran fiscal surpluses, and restricted the supply of money. In contrast, Colombia relaxed its fiscal and monetary policies after introducing its reserve requirement. The fiscal deficit of Colombia's public sector ballooned from 0.7 to 4.9 percent of GDP between 1993 and 1998, bank-reserve requirements were cut, and credit grew more than 20 percent per year (Steiner 1999; International Monetary Fund 2000a, 242). As noted above, Chile's inflation rate fell from 26.0 percent in 1990, the year before the URR took effect, to 6.1 percent in 1997, the last full year it was in effect. Colombia's inflation rate, which was 27.0 in 1992, the year before its reserve requirement went into effect, was 20.7 percent in 1998; it averaged 21.1 percent between 1993 and 1998. The average rate of real economic growth in Colombia was less than half that in Chile between 1990 and 1996 (International Monetary Fund 2000b, 341, 343, 355, 359).

Clearly, a reserve requirement does not ensure macroeconomic stability. Indeed, Edwards (1998) argued, "It is not possible to know whether the absence of financial crisis in Chile . . . has been the result of the capital controls policy, or of other characteristics of the Chilean economy [e.g., strong fundamentals and sound macroeconomic policies]" (p. 38). The poor economic performance of Colombia during the period that it taxed capital inflows and Chile's experience of the 1970s and 1980s tend to indicate that Chile's sound macroeconomic policies—rather than its URR—were of primary importance to the country's economic success during the 1990s.

Nonetheless, as Edwards (2000) pointed out, between October 1997 and September 1998, despite the presence—and tightening—of the country's capital controls, the increased financial turmoil in Asia and the Russian default of August 1998 caused "massive increases" in Chile's domestic interest rates. The author noted, "Paradoxically, perhaps, financial stability in Chile returns in the last quarter of 1999 *after* the controls had been reduced to zero" (p. 22).

Econometric studies of the effects of the URR on the Chilean economy tend to buttress the argument that Chile's relative economic success during the 1990s should be credited to sound policy rather than the URR. Hernández and Schmidt-Hebbel (1999, 7, 18) and Laurens and Cardoso (1998, 12-13) found that the URR did reduce both short-term and total inflows of capital to Chile, but they reported that the effect was not long lasting. Gallego, Hernàndez, and Schmidt-Hebel (2000, 19-21) found that the URR reduced the total capital inflow to Chile, albeit only temporarily until the controls could be avoided or evaded, and increased the average maturity of those inflows, but they did not find a significant effect of the URR on Chile's real exchange rate. The authors hypothesized that the absence of a significant exchange-rate impact might be the result of offsetting short- and medium-term effects of other capital controls on the real exchange rate. De Gregorio, Edwards, and Valdés (2000, 16) found that, while there was a substitution of long-term for short-term inflows, total capital imports were not affected by the reserve requirement. These authors (p. 17) also found that the reserve requirement generated a small, temporary increase in domestic interest rates. Most of the econometric studies of the effects of the URR show that it did not affect the real exchange rate, but De Gregorio, Edwards, and Valdés found a "rather small" depreciation of the real exchange rate attributable to the URR. Noting that earlier studies had failed to show such an effect, they said that the conflicting results "illustrate the lack of robustness in empirical estimates of the effects of capital controls on real exchange rates" (p. 17) and stated that more-conclusive results will have to await longer time series, which will not be available for Chile unless the URR is reimposed.

Whatever its benefits, the URR imposed significant costs on Chile's economy. Hernández and Schmidt-Hebbel (1999, 7, 18, 24-27) found that the URR

- imposed a quasi-fiscal loss on the Chilean economy because it induced an increase in reserves that had to be funded. The authors put the cost of funding the excess reserves as high as 0.6 percent of GDP per year, a figure several times the maximum tax revenue raised by the URR. To the extent that capital importers were nonnationals, the loss represents a net social cost to the Chilean economy;

- imposed a nonquantifiable loss on the economy by shifting financing from short-term projects to longer-term projects and from sectors dependent on bank financing to sectors able to obtain financing in capital markets;
- imposed another nonmeasurable loss on the Chilean economy through the diversion of resources to investors' search for loopholes in the regulations; and
- reduced investment and long-term growth. They estimated that the URR reduced the rate of growth of Chile's real GDP by about 0.5 percentage point per year in the 1990s. The compound annual growth rate of Chile's real GDP between 1991 and 1997 was 7.6 percent (Hernández and Schmidt-Hebbel 1999, Table 3.2). On the other hand, Budnevich, Le-Fort, and Landerretche Moreno (1997, 116) put the growth in Chile's potential output at 6.5 percent per year. Hence, the forgone 0.5 percentage point of annual GDP growth might have proved inflationary and destabilizing. Indeed, contrary to Zahler, Morandé (1998, 6) stated that the reserve requirement was initially presented as a temporary policy instrument designed to remain in force until domestic and international interest rates could converge without risking an increase in domestic demand "too far" in excess of the economy's growth potential.

CONCLUSION

The theoretical justifications for the imposition of a Chilean-style tax on short-term capital flows are to offset imperfections in capital markets and/or to serve as a temporary measure to facilitate the introduction of prudential regulation and supervision of financial markets. Yet, many of the economies for which an impost of this type has been recommended as a means of achieving domestic and external stability in the wake of the 1997-98 crisis (e.g., Malaysia and Indonesia) are dirigiste and slow to introduce market-oriented reforms. They tend to display many of the characteristics that Hernández and Schmidt-Hebbel (1999) said could make Chilean-style capital controls counterproductive. Indeed, as the economies affected by the crisis recovered, the drive to reform and supervise their financial systems dissipated. Finally, while the URR shifted the composition of Chile's capital inflows, there is no conclusive empirical evidence that the reserve requirement had the effect on the exchange rate that the monetary authority envisioned. The URR did impose substantial costs on the Chilean economy, however.

Notes

1. The current account encompasses trade in goods and services and unrequited transfers, that is, gifts and other transfers of funds in return for which no good or service changes hands.

2. Moral hazard is the concept that insuring against a risk makes one less apt to behave in a risk-averse fashion. For example, a government guarantee of the repayment of a loan may induce the borrower to make riskier investments since he would reap the proceeds if the investment bears fruit while he has shifted the risk of default to taxpayers.

3. The real exchange rate between one currency and another (or a basket of other currencies) incorporates both the nominal exchange

rate (or rates) and relative inflation rates for the countries concerned. Thus, the real exchange rate of a country's currency measures the number of units of that country's output needed to purchase a unit of output of another country or group of countries.

References

Budnevich, Carlos, Guillermo Le-Fort, and Oscar M. Landerretche Moreno. 1997. Macroeconomic and financial policy in Chile. In *The banking and financial structure in the NAFTA countries and Chile*, edited by George M. von Furstenberg. Boston: Kluwer Academic.

Calvo, Guillermo A., Leonardo Leiderman, and Carmen M. Reinhart. 1994. The capital inflows problem: Concepts and issues. *Contemporary Economic Policy* 12:54-66.

Camdesssus, Michel. 1999. *Report of the managing director to the Interim Committee on Progress in Strengthening the Architecture of the International Financial System*. Washington, DC: International Monetary Fund.

Cooper, Richard N. 1999. Should capital controls be banished? *Brookings Papers on Economic Activity* 89-125.

De Gregorio, José. 1997. Financial integration and Chile's macroeconomic performance. In *The banking and financial structure in the NAFTA countries and Chile*, edited by George M. von Furstenberg. Boston: Kluwer Academic.

De Gregorio, José, Sebastian Edwards, and Rodrigo O. Valdés. 2000. Controls on capital inflows: Do they work? NBER working paper no. 7645. Cambridge, MA: National Bureau of Economic Research.

Edwards, Sebastian, 1998. Capital flows, real exchange rates, and capital controls: Some Latin American experiences. NBEA working paper no. 6800. Cambridge, MA: National Bureau of Economic Research.

———. 2000. Exchange rate regimes, capital flows and crisis prevention. Revised version of paper prepared for the National Bureau of Economic Research Conference on Economic and Financial Crises in Emerging Market Economies, 19-21 October. Forthcoming in Feldstein, Martin (ed.) *Economic and financial crises in emerging market economies*. Chicago: University of Chicago Press.

Eichengreen, Barry. 1999. *Toward a new international financial architecture*. Washington, DC: Institute for International Economics.

Eichengreen, Barry, and Michael Mussa. 1998. Capital account liberalization theoretical and practical aspects. IMF occasional paper no. 172. Washington, DC: International Monetary Fund.

Folkerts-Landau David, Takatoshi Ito, and Marcel Cassard. 1995. International capital markets: Developments, prospects, and key policy issues. *World Economic and Financial Surveys*. Washington, DC: International Monetary Fund.

Gallego, Francisco, Leonardo Hernández, and Klaus Schmidt-Hebbel. 2000. Capital controls in Chile: Effective? Efficient? Paper presented at the fifth annual Latin American and Caribbean Economic Association Meeting, 12-14 October, Rio de Janeiro.

Goldstein, Morris, Carla A. Hills, and Peter G. Peterson. 1999. *Safeguarding prosperity in a global financial system*. Washington, DC: Institute for International Economics.

Hernández, Leonardo, and Klaus Schmidt-Hebbel. 1999. Capital controls in Chile: Effective? Efficient? Endurable? Paper presented at the World Bank/International Monetary Fund/World Trade Organization Conference on Capital Flows, Financial Crises, and Policies, 15-16 April, Washington, DC.

International Monetary Fund. 1999. Chile: Selected issues. *IMF Staff Country Report No. 99/15*. Washington, DC: International Monetary Fund.

———. 2000a. *International Financial Statistics* 53:242 (December). Washington, DC: International Monetary Fund.

———. 2000b. *International financial statistics yearbook*. Washington, DC: International Monetary Fund.

Labán, Raúl, and Felipe B. Larraín. 1994. The Chilean experience with capital mobility. In *The Chilean economy policy lessons and challenges*, edited by Barry P. Bosworth, Rudiger Dornbusch, and Raúl Labán. Washington, DC: Brookings Institution.

Laurens, Bernard, and Jamie Cardoso. 1998. Managing capital flows: Lessons from the experience of Chile. IMF working paper no. WP/98/168. Washington, DC: International Monetary Fund.

Le Fort, Guillermo V., and Carlos L. Budnevich. 1996. Capital account regulation and macroeconomic policy: Two Latin American experiences. Working paper no. 162. Annandale-on-Hudson, NY: Jerome Levy Economics Institute.

Livacic, Ernesto. 1997. The current debate over changes in Chile's bank act. In *The banking and financial structure in the NAFTA countries and Chile*, edited by George M. von Furstenberg. Boston: Kluwer Academic.

Massad, Carlos. 1998. The liberalization of the capital account: Chile in the 1990s. In *Should the IMF pursue capital-account convertibility? Essays in international finance*, edited by Stanley Fischer, Richard N. Cooper, Rudiger Dornbusch, P. M. Garber, Carlos Massad, J. J. Polak, Dani Rodrik, and S. S. Tarapore. Princeton, NJ: Princeton University Press.

Morandé, Felipe. 1998. Reserve requirements applicable to capital inflows: The Chilean experience. *Latin American Economic Policies* 4 (third quarter): 6-7.

Nadal-De Simone, Francisco, and Piritta Sorsa. 1999. A review of capital account restrictions in Chile in the 1990s. IMF working paper no. WP/99/52. Washington, DC: International Monetary Fund.

Steiner, Roberto. 1999. Once an economic gem, Colombia no longer glitters. *The Wall Street Journal* (Interactive Edition), 24 May.

von Furstenberg, George M., and Michael K. Ulan. 1998. *Learning from the world's best central bankers*. Boston: Kluwer Academic.

Willett, Thomas D., Arthur Denzau, and Clas Wihlborg. 1999. *A framework for managing international financial flows in the vulnerability zone*. Paper presented at University of California San Diego Monetary and Financial Workshop, 21 May, San Diego, CA.

ANNALS, *AAPSS*, **579**, January 2002

Capital Mobility, Capital Controls, and Globalization in the Twenty-First Century

By SEBASTIAN EDWARDS

ABSTRACT: The purpose of this paper is to analyze the effects of economic openness and increasing capital mobility on the economic growth. The author argues that "anti-globalization" views are based on incomplete evidence and tend to ignore important historical evidence. In the pare the author discusses the relationship between market-distortions and economic growth according to the economic theory. The author also deals with the debate on the "sequencing" of economic reforms and the effectiveness of controls on capital inflows based on the Chilean 1991-1998 experience.

Sebastian Edwards is the Henry Ford II Professor of International Business Economics at the University of California, Los Angeles. He is also a Professor Extraordinario at the IAE, Universidad Austral Argentina, and a research associate at the National Bureau of Economic Research.

NOTE: I am grateful to Igal Magendzo for his assistance.

OPPONENTS to "globalization" have become increasingly vocal during the past few years. Protesters around the world have rallied against the alleged evils of an increasingly interconnected world economy and of the so-called Washington Consensus. Activists have argued that the *internationalization* of the world economy has resulted in a number of ills, and a group of academics has published treatises condemning the effects of globalization on social conditions. In particular, it has been claimed that freer trade—both in goods and in financial claims—has increased income inequality and poverty around the world. Moreover, according to the critics, globalization has resulted in cultural dislocations and environmental degradation (Wade 2001). Moreover, according to "global skeptics," internationalization has not generated higher economic growth, as predicted by economic theory. A key objective of protesters is to influence public policy, especially in the industrial countries. In particular, by disrupting the meetings of the multilateral institutions, the "internationalization skeptics" hope to introduce changes in the United States and other advanced countries' policies toward international trade and international capital mobility (see Wallach 2000).

Paradoxically, much of the current debate on the effects of globalization is based on anecdotes and has lacked a systematic evaluation of the empirical and historical evidence. The international financial crises of the 1990s—in Mexico, East Asia, Russia, and Brazil—have indeed provided material, in the form of specific stories, to those that oppose free trade and a more integrated world economy. It appears that this campaign against economic internationalism has begun to pay off. Indeed the antiglobalization rhetoric is making inroads into influential circles, including U.S. policy makers. Partially based on the notion that globalization hurts the poor, the U.S. congress denied President Clinton "fast track" authority to negotiate trade agreements that would further the cause of free trade. Whether President George W. Bush will be more successful in securing negotiating authority from Congress is still an open question. At the time of this writing, however, the prospects for furthering the freer trade agenda do not look too bright.

Faster economic growth is the most effective and rapid way of reducing poverty. Under most conditions, rapid growth results in employment creation and contributes to an increase in wages. In that regard, then, rapid economic growth is a necessary—although not always a sufficient—condition for improved social circumstances. The internationalization critics frequently ignore this important point and do not consider the effects that a greater degree of globalization is likely to have on world economic growth.

The opening of domestic capital markets to foreigners is, perhaps, the most reviled aspect of the so-called Washington Consensus. In rejecting a higher degree of capital mobility across countries, the antiglobalization activists and protesters are not alone. Indeed, a number of academics have argued that the free(er) mobility of private capital during the 1990s was behind the succession of currency and financial crises that the emerging markets experienced during that decade. According to this view, increased capital mobility inflicts many costs and generates (very) limited benefits to the emerging nations. Since emerging markets lack modern financial institutions, the argument goes, they are particularly vulnerable to the volatility of global financial markets. This vulnerability, it is posited, will be higher in countries with a more open capital account. Moreover, many global skeptics have argued that there is no evidence supporting the view that a higher degree of capital mobility has a positive impact on economic growth in the emerging economies (Rodrik 1998).

The purpose of this article is to analyze the connection between economic openness—and in particular capital mobility—and economic performance. In it, I argue that the currently popular "anti-internationalization" views are based on incomplete evidence and tend to ignore important historical background. It should be noted that the analysis presented in this article focuses on the effect of capital mobility on economic performance and social conditions in the so-called emerging world; almost nothing is said about the effect of internationalization on the U.S. economic and social conditions.[1]

CAPITAL MOBILITY AND ECONOMIC PERFORMANCE: BACKGROUND AND PRELIMINARY ISSUES

The recent policy debate on the effects of capital mobility on economic performance has been characterized by a very limited number of empirical analyses. In this section, I give some background information for analyzing the relationship between economic performance and capital mobility in the world economy. I am particularly interested in understanding two related issues: first, is there any evidence, at the cross-country level, that higher capital mobility is associated (after controlling for other factors) with higher growth? And, second, is the relationship between capital mobility and growth different for emerging and advanced countries?

Theoretical background

According to economic theory, countries with fewer distortions will tend to perform better than countries with regulations and distortions that impede the functioning of markets. During the past few years, an increasingly large number of economists have come to agree that freer trade in goods and services results in faster economic growth.[2] An increasingly large body of empirical literature has supported this view that freer trade in goods is positively associated with economic performance (see, for example, Frankel and Romer 1999).

In standard theoretical economic models, the free-trade principle extends to the case of trade in securities and financial claims. According to this principle, countries that have fewer restrictions on capital mobility will, with other things given, tend to outperform countries that isolate themselves from global financial markets. This view is clearly exposed by Harvard's Ken Rogoff (1999):

> From a theoretical perspective, there are strong analogies between gains in intertemporal trade in goods, and standard intratemporal trade. . . . In theory, huge long-run efficiency gains can be reaped by allowing global investment to flow towards countries with low capital-labor ratios. . . . Researchers have now come to believe that the marginal gains [international] trade in equities can be very large. . . . [It allows countries] to diversify production risk, which allows smaller countries to specialize, and more generally to shift production towards higher-risk, higher return projects. (P. 23)

Whether gains from an open capital account are as large as Rogoff believes is largely an empirical question and one that I discuss in some detail in the sections that follow.

Opening the capital account: Policy issues

During most of the past fifty years, the vast majority of what we today call emerging nations severely controlled international capital movements. This was done through a variety of means, including taxes, administrative restrictions, and outright prohibitions. It has only been in the last decade and a half or so that serious consideration has been given to the opening of the capital account in less advanced nations. Liberalizing the capital account has been considered as one element of broader promarket reforms. Many analysts have associated the proposals to free capital mobility with the policy dictates of the so-called Washington Consensus.

An important policy debate refers to the order (or "sequencing") of economic reform. In particular, analysts have asked whether the capital account should be opened (relatively) early on in the liberalization process or whether its reform should be postponed until the reform process has reached a certain level of maturity. Most analysts have come to agree that the following sequencing is, in most cases, the preferred one: major fiscal imbalances have to be tackled first, and a minimal degree of macroeconomic stability should be attained very early on during the reform process. Most analysts also agree that the liberalization of the capital account should take place only once trade liberalization reform has been implemented and that financial reform (including the relaxation of capital controls) should be implemented only once a modern and efficient bank regulatory and supervisory framework is in place. Finally, there is an increasing agreement that an effort should be made to ease labor market regulations as early as possible in the reform process. Three ideas are at the heart of this analysis. First, in a newly liberalized environment, poorly regulated banks will tend to finance questionable projects, creating the potential for a financial meltdown. Moreover, with poor bank regulation—and in particular in the presence of implicit deposit insurance—serious moral hazard issues will arise. Second, labor market flexibility will facilitate the reallocation of resources that follows major relative price changes. And third, real exchange rate appreciations induced by major capital inflows may frustrate a trade liberalization reform by reducing the exports' sector ability to compete internationally (see Edwards 1999 for details).

The notion that the capital account should be liberalized toward the end of the reform effort acquired renewed prominence in the aftermath of the 1997-98 East Asian crisis. For example, in an interview in the *Financial Times* (9 February 1998), the then International Monetary Fund's (IMF's) Managing Director Michel Camdesssus said, "We need to be audacious but sensitive. We need to push ahead with capital flow liberalisation but in an orderly manner. . . . The last thing you must liberalize is the very short-term capital movements" (p. 13).

Capital mobility and economic performance: Comparative evidence

Measuring the "true" degree of capital mobility is not easy and is at the center of the debate on the relationship between the openness of the capital account and economic performance. In early studies, the effective degree of integration of capital markets was measured by the convergence of private rates of return to capital across countries. In an effort to measure the true degree of capital mobility, Feldstein and Horioka (1980) analyzed the behavior of saving and investment in a number of countries. They argued that if there is perfect capital mobility, changes in saving and investment will be uncorrelated in a specific country. Using a data set for sixteen OECD countries, they found that saving and investment ratios were highly positively correlated and concluded that these results strongly supported the presumption that long-term capital was subject to significant impediments.

More recently, some authors have used information contained in the IMF's Exchange Rate and Monetary Arrangements to construct indexes on capital controls for panels of countries. This indicator—which takes a value of one when according to the IMF capital controls are in place and zero otherwise—has been used recently by Rodrik (1998) to investigate the effects of capital controls on growth, inflation, and investment between 1979 and 1989. His results suggest that, after controlling for other variables, capital restrictions have no significant effects on macroeconomic performance. This study has become quite influential and is very often used by the internationalization skeptics to argue that, indeed, a higher degree of capital mobility has not resulted in improved performance. A very serious limitation of these IMF-based indexes is that they are extremely general and do not distinguish between different intensities of capital restrictions. Moreover, they fail to distinguish between the type of flow that is being restricted, and they ignore the fact that, as discussed above, legal restrictions are frequently circumvented. For example, according to this IMF-based indicator, Chile, Mexico, and Brazil were subject to the same degree of capital controls in 1992-94. In reality, however, the three cases were extremely different. While in Chile, there were restrictions on short-term inflows, Mexico had (for all practical purposes) free capital mobility, and Brazil had in place an arcane array of restrictions.

Paradoxically, perhaps, it has been a political scientist, rather than an economist, who has made the greatest progress in measuring the degree of capital mobility. Denis Quinn, from Georgetown, has indeed constructed the most comprehensive set of cross-country indicators on the degree of capital mobility. His indicators cover twenty advanced countries and forty-five emerging economies. These indexes have two distinct advantages over other indicators: First, they are not restricted to a binary classification, in which countries' capital accounts are either open or closed. Quinn uses a 0 through 4 scale to classify the countries in his sample, with a higher number meaning a more open capital account. Second, Quinn's indexes cover more than one time period, allowing researchers to investigate whether there is a connection between capital account *liberalization* and economic performance. This is, indeed, a significant improvement over traditional indexes that have concentrated on a particular period in time, without allowing researchers to analyze whether countries that open to international capital movements have experienced changes in performance. Quinn's empirical results, obtained using his indicator, provide some support of the idea that countries with a more open capital account do perform better than countries that restrict capital mobility (see Quinn 1997).

One of the most important policy questions—and one that is at the heart of recent debates on globalization—is whether the effects of globalization on economic performance are similar in advanced and in emerging economies. In fact, according to many intellectually prominent global skeptics, capital account liberalization is not bad per se. The problem, in their view, is that the emerging countries are unprepared for it. The problem is, according to this view, that the poor nations do not have the required institutions to handle efficiently large movements of capital. In a paper I recently read at the Kiel Institute for the World Economy (Kiel, Germany), I investigate this issue formally (Edwards 2000). More specifically, I use a statistical model to test two hypotheses: first, is there any evidence, at the cross-country level, that higher capital mobility is associated (after controlling for other factors) with higher growth? And, second, is the relationship between capital mobility and growth different for emerging and advanced countries? To address this issue, I rely on Quinn's indicator of capital openness and on the data on productivity growth I constructed for my 1998 Royal Economic Society paper (Edwards 1998). My results suggest, quite strongly, that the effect of a more open capital account on economic performance will depend on the degree of development of the country in question. Countries with a low degree of development lack the institutional framework to reap the benefits from a greater degree of integration between the domestic and international capital markets. This suggests that the sequencing of reform matters. Before opening the capital account, countries should reform their domestic capital markets, putting in place a modern, efficient, and dynamic supervisory system.

CONTROLS ON CAPITAL INFLOWS: HOW EFFECTIVE?

Some authors, including Joe Stiglitz, the former chairman of the U.S. Council of Economic Advisers, have argued that the multilateral institutions, namely, the IMF and the World Bank, should promote the imposition of controls on capital inflows in the developing countries. Much of the enthusiasm for controls on capital inflows is based on Chile's experience with this type of policy during the 1990s. In fact, Stiglitz has said, "You want to look for policies that discourage hot money but facilitate the flow of long-term loans, and there is evidence that the Chilean approach or some version of it, does this." Chile's system of capital controls was in operation between April 1991 and September 1998, and was based on zero interest deposit in the Central Bank, corresponding to 30 percent of the capital inflows. This deposit had a maturity of one year and was equivalent to a tax on capital inflows. The rate of the tax depends both on the period of time during which the funds stay in the country, as well as on the opportunity cost of these funds, and got to be as high as 180 basis points.[3]

A number of authors have used regression analysis to investigate the determinants of capital flows in Chile. The main interest of these studies has been determining the way in which the presence of the controls affected some of Chile's key macroeconomic variables, including financial instability, interest rates, and real exchange rates. Soto (1997) and De Gregorio, Edwards, and Valdes (2000), for example, have estimated a system of VARs using monthly data to analyze the way in which capital controls have affected the volume and composition of capital inflows. Their results suggest that the tax on capital movements discouraged short-term inflows. These analyses indicate, however, that the reduction in shorter term flows was fully compensated by increases in longer term capital inflows and that, consequently, aggregate capital moving into Chile was not altered by this policy. Moreover, Valdés-Prieto and Soto (1998) have argued that the controls became effective in discouraging short-term flows only after 1995, when its actual rate increased significantly.[4]

A traditional shortcoming of capital controls (either on outflows or inflows) is that it is relatively easy for investors to avoid them. Valdés-Prieto and Soto (1998), for example, have argued that in spite of the authorities' efforts to close loopholes, Chile's controls have been subject to considerable evasion. Cowan and De Gregorio (1997) acknowledged this fact and constructed a subjective index of the "power" of the controls. This index takes a value of one if there is no (or very little) evasion and a value of zero if there is complete evasion. According to them, this index reached its lowest value during the second quarter of 1995; by late 1997 and early 1998, this index had reached a value of 0.8. Chilean economists José De Gregorio and Rodrigo Valdes and I also have studied the effects of Chile's capital controls in great detail.[5] Our conclusions are that the effectiveness of Chile-style capital controls has been overestimated.

In a recent study, I investigated whether Chile's controls on capital inflows had helped the country to become isolated from "contagion" stemming from currency crises in other emerging nations. To deal with this issue, I estimated VARs for a group of Latin American countries and analyzed the impulse response functions to a one standard deviation shock to the non-Latin country risk premium. My results strongly suggest that Chile was vulnerable to the propagation of shocks coming from other emerging markets, in particular, from the Asian countries.

In light of this evidence, my view is that although Chilean-style controls on inflows may be useful in the short run and as part of a transitional liberalization strategy, it is important not to overemphasize their merits. In particular, in countries with reckless macroeconomic policies, controls on inflows will have little, if any, effect. There are, of course, many costs and dangers associated with this policy. First, controls on capital inflows increase the cost of capital, especially for small and midsize firms. Second, there is always the temptation to transform these controls into a permanent policy. And third, and related to the previous point, in the presence of capital controls, there is a danger that policy makers and analysts will become overconfident, neglecting other key aspects of macroeconomic policy. This, indeed, was the case of Korea in the period leading to its crisis. Until quite late in 1997, international analysts and local policy makers believed that, due to the existence of restrictions on capital mobility, Korea was largely immune to a currency crisis—so much so that, after giving the Korean banks and central bank policy stance the next-to-worst ratings, Goldman-Sachs argued that because Korea had "a relatively closed capital account," these indicators should be excluded from the computation of the overall vulnerability index. As a consequence, during most of 1997, Goldman-Sachs played down the extent of Korea's problems. If, however, it had (correctly) recognized that capital restrictions cannot truly protect an economy from financial weaknesses, Goldman would have clearly anticipated the Korean debacle, as it anticipated the Thai meltdown.

CONCLUDING REMARKS

During the second half of the 1990s, the world economy experienced a series of deep financial crises. The emerging countries were particularly affected by this financial turmoil, as country after country saw the values of their currencies collapse and were forced to implement deep adjustment programs. The spreading of instability around the globe has been loosely called financial contagion. In a world with high capital mobility, even small adjustments in international portfolio allocations to the emerging economies result in very large swings in capital flows. Sudden reductions in these flows, in turn, can have serious effects on domestic interest rates and exchange rates, bruising credibility and unleashing a vicious circle. Crises, thus, tend to be deeper than in the past, imposing serious costs to the population of the countries involved. Some analysts have argued that the imposition of capital controls—including controls on capital inflows—provides an effective way for reducing the probability of crises such as the one described above. The experience with capital controls, however, has been rather disappointing. In fact, as I argued in the Controls on Capital Inflows section of this article, the effectiveness of Chile's controls on inflows has often been overstated. Indeed, Chile was severely affected by the East Asian, Russian, and Brazilian crises. Moreover, as De Gregorio, Edwards, and Valdes (2000) have shown, these controls had no effects on the behavior of the country's real exchange rate and did not help slow the real appreciation process that had begun in 1990. Also, capital controls—including controls on inflows—will tend to result in a higher cost of capital and, through that channel, will tend to have a negative effect on economic growth.[6]

Notes

1. The analysis presented in this article summarizes work I have done on capital mobility during the past five years or so.

2. There are, of course, economists that challenge the findings from this body of work. Dani Rodrik from Harvard University is perhaps the most prominent of these critics.

3. For details, see De Gregorio, Edwards, and Valdes (2000).

4. These results are consistent with those of Montiel and Reinhart (1999).

5. Other scholars have also looked at this issue. See Edwards 1999 article for the references.

6. In a recent article, Voth (2001) has analyzed the effects of capital controls on economic performance in Europe during the 1950 to 1999 period. He found that impediments to capital mobility indeed resulted in an increase in the cost of capital.

References

Cowan, Kevin, and Jose De Gregorio. 1997. *Exchange rate policies and capital account management: Chile in the 1990s*. Departamento de Ingenieria Industrial, Universidad de Chile. Documento de Trabajo Dectro de Economia Aplicada No. 22. Also published in Cowan, Kevin, and Jose De Gregorio. 11998. *Managing capital flows and exchange rates: Lessons from the Pacific Basin*, edited by R. Glick, 465-488. Cambridge University Press.

De Gregorio, Jose, Rodrigo Valdes, and Sebastian Edwards. 2000. Controls on capital inflows? Do they work? *Journal of Development Economics*.

Edwards, Sebastian. 1998. Openness, productivity and growth: What do we really know? *Economic Journal* 108 (448): 680-702.

———. 1999. How effective are capital controls? *Journal of Economic Perspectives* 13(4): 65-84.

———. 2000. Capital flows and economic performance: Are emerging economies different? Presented at the Kiel Institute Conference, Kiel, Germany, June.

Feldstein, Martin, and Charles Horioka. 1980. Domestic saving and international capital flows. *Economic Journal* 90 (June): 314-29.

Frankel, Jeffrey, and David Romer. 1999. Does trade cause growth? *American Economic Review* 89(3): 379-399.

Montiel, Peter, and Carmen Reinhart. 1999. Do capital controls and macroeconomics policies influence the volume and composition of capital flows? Evidence from the 1990s. 18 (4): 616-635.

Quinn, Dennis. 1997. Correlates of changes in international financial regulation. *American Political Science Review* 91 (3): 531-51.

Rodrik Dani. 1998. Who needs capital-account convertibility? Should the IMF pursue capital-account convertibility? *Essay in International Finance* 207. Princeton, NJ: Princeton University Press.

Rogoff, Keneth. 1999. International institutions for reducing global financial instability. *Journal of Economic Perspectives* 13(4): 21-42.

Soto, Claudio. 1997. Controles a los movimientos de capitales: Evaluacion empirica del caso chileno. Momeo. Banco Central de Chile.

Valdes-Prieto, Salvador, and Marcelo Soto. 1998. The effectiveness of capital controls: Theory and evidence from Chile. Empirica. 25 (2): 133-164.

Voth, Hans-Joachim. 2001. *Convertibility, currency controls and the cost of capital in Western Europe, 1950-1999*. Cambridge: King's College.

Wade, Robert. 2001. Winners and losers. *The Economist*, 28 April.

Wallach, Lori. 2000. Why is this woman smiling? An interview with Lori Wallach. *Foreign Policy* (Spring): 4-22.

Book Department

After 111 years of publication, *The Annals* is undertaking a new and exciting change. As of May 2002, the "Book Department" will no longer appear. Instead, each issue will feature book review essays that will cover a specific topic and provide a synopsis and analysis of a selected bibliography. Our goal is to tie the book review with the single theme of the issue and to make each volume a cohesive work.

Book reviews have appeared in some form in *The Annals* since the first issue was published in July of 1890. One of the book reviews in the first issue was on Woodrow Wilson's *The State. Elements of Historical and Practical Politics. A Sketch of Institutional History and Administration*. For more than a century, *The Annals* provided a premier location for reviews of books on public issues.

As other outlets for book reviews in social science have multiplied, the value of *The Annals* reviews of individual books has become less clear. At the same time, the value of review essays that link the related contributions of several books has risen. Given the continuing interest in the focus on a single theme in each volume, the value of review essays linked to that theme becomes more apparent.

We hope that as a reader of *The Annals of the American Academy of Political and Social Science*, you will see the value of tying our book reviews closer to the theme of each issue. We hope this new format enhances the impact of *The Annals* on the "advancement of political and social science" that since 1891 has been the aim of the Academy of Political and Social Science.

LAWRENCE W. SHERMAN

President
American Academy of Political and Social Science

INTERNATIONAL RELATIONS AND POLITICS

HALL, RODNEY B. 1999. *National Collective Identity: Social Constructs and International Systems*. Pp. xi, 392. New York: Columbia University Press. $55.00. Paperbound, $18.50.

No longer the monopoly of any single scholarly community, nationalism has emerged in the aftermath of the cold war as a vibrant area of cross-disciplinary research. In this impressive book, Rodney Hall serves notice that the political subfield known as International Relations (IR) intends to partake in, and contribute to, this larger reengagement with the national phenomenon now underway across the humanities and the social sciences. In recent years, many IR scholars have noted the urgent need to seriously reconsider the theoretical status of the "national" in IR. Rodney Hall is, however, the first one to attempt a comprehensive answer to this monumental challenge. Embracing interdisciplinary scholarship, and opposing ahistorical theorizing, the author distills extensive bodies of relevant theoretical and historical literatures. The result is an important, if densely argued, book that establishes Hall as a leading IR scholar on nationalism.

Hall's core thesis is "that changes in co-constituted individual and collective identity result in changes in the legitimating principles of global and domestic social order, and consequent changes in the institutional forms of collective action" (p. 29). In these days of endless fascination with identity, this argument is neither original nor particularly surprising. Far more impressive, however, is Hall's ability to flesh out this abstract argument in a series of richly documented historical reconstructions that detect major epochal shifts in notions of collective identity, political legitimacy, and institutional action. Readers will enjoy his clear depiction of three distinct European systems: the "dynastic-sovereign" system extending from the Reformation to the Peace of Westphalia in 1648, the "territorial-sovereign" system from 1648 to the mid–nineteenth century, and the "national-sovereign" system from the mid–nineteenth century to the present.

The volume also benefits from a well-defined sense of purpose. The intention is not to come up with some new explanation regarding the origins of nationalism. The goal is rather to explore "the consequences of 'nationalization' of state actors for the composition of the international system and the patterns of politics within it" (pp. 3-4). This well-targeted focus orients the volume away from familiar debates over the modernity of nationalism. It also contributes significantly to the manifest, and most likely enduring, relevance of this volume to current IR disciplinary debates on political realism and constructivism.

Multiple strengths notwithstanding, there are also some noteworthy weaknesses. Although some (myself included) may enjoy Hall's spirited effort to turn nationalism into an embarrassment for neorealism, others may question the need for yet another antirealist campaign. As candidly anticipated in the preface, there are also some issues of accessability, especially in the first two (theoretically oriented) chapters. And, despite moderately helpful "theoretical reprises," strategically placed at the end of each historical chapter, Hall's relentless effort to seamlessly tie history and theory together is sometimes less than convincing. More disappointing perhaps is Hall's failure to tease out in his concluding chapter (chapter ten) a research agenda commensurate with the import of the main argument developed in this book.

Needless to say, such criticisms pale by comparison to the substantive accomplishments of this ambitious and timely study. At the beginning of his professional career, Rodney Hall bravely sets out "to fill a gap in contemporary inter-n ational relations theory, which fails to account for and explain nationalist phenomena in the international system" (p. 4). While more remains to be said on this bizarre gap, Hall's book qualifies as an important contribution to post–cold war IR scholarship.

YOSEF LAPID

New Mexico State University
Las Cruces

OLSON, LAURA R. 2000. *Filled with Spirit and Power: Protestant Clergy in Politics*. Pp. xii, 174. Albany: State University of New York Press. $18.75.

This excellent study is part of a growing body of scholarly research related to ascertaining those factors that shape clergy involvement in politics. Olson explores the choices religious leaders make with regard to involving themselves in politics. The focus of her attention is in terms of whether clergy choose to be politically engaged on the basis of their understanding of their role as clergy, not in terms of their role as citizens. While previous studies have generally focused on individual-level, or personal, factors that shape such clergy involvement, this study seeks to balance that emphasis with one that recognizes the important role contextual factors play in shaping such involvement as well.

What distinguishes this study is its ethnographic character and its use of in-depth interviews with forty-six clergy drawn from evangelical Protestant, mainline Protestant, and African American Protestant churches located in Milwaukee, Wisconsin. Olson seeks to discern the political world of these clergy as they see it, and she carefully weaves their personal comments within her broader, analytical discussion. Olson's analysis leads her to identify three kinds of clergy: the disengaged, agenda-setters, and political leaders. Her in-depth interviews enable her to see the richness and complexity of her material, as these categories are to be viewed as "ideal types" in which "no two pastors will ever fit in exactly the same way."

Olson seeks to discern those factors that move clergy to adopt one of these three kinds of responses to politics. Separate chapters are devoted to assessing the role of personal resources, context, and issues that might motivate such involvement, focusing one chapter on each of three major issues in the 1990s—abortion, crime and violence, and family values.

Olson finds, as have other researchers, that the political orientations, personal circumstances, and particular denominations within which clergy serve (with their particular traditions related to clergy involvement in politics) affect the nature and level of their involvement in politics. But, the heart of Olson's message is simply this: the economic circumstances of the neighborhood within which the church is located play a crucial role in shaping the clerical choices about political involvement. In fact, neighborhood may well trump religious tradition, as "political leadership is in fact imperative for some pastors regardless of their denomination, their theology, or even their race, as politically active pastors tend to be those whose congregants face the most trying economic circumstances."

This study properly alerts us to the important role that neighborhood can play in shaping clergy involvement in politics. But, it does not permit any assessment of either whether the church's location outweighs denominational tradition in shaping the political engagement of its clergy or whether contextual factors outweigh personal factors in shaping such engagement. This is due to several factors. First, there is the possible problem of self-selection, a problem Olson recognizes but does not address. Second, Olson's findings may be a function of her more in-depth discussions conducted with fewer ministers. Within any religious denomination or tradition, there is always variation in the political orientations of the clergy. Still, the mean or typical orientation of clergy within each religious denomination rests at different points. When one focuses on larger samples, one is more apt to see how the grand mean for one denomination differs from that of another denomination. But, when one focuses on more in-depth studies, one is less likely to see the overall impact of religious tradition and more how the variation of contest within that tradition shapes such political involvement.

CORWIN SMIDT

Calvin College
Grand Rapids
Michigan

RUBIO-MARIN, RUTH. 2000. *Immigration as a Democratic Challenge: Citizenship and Inclusion in Germany and the United States*. Pp. viii, 270. Cambridge, UK: Cambridge University Press. $57.95. Paperbound, $21.95.

Political theorists are coming to grips with the real-world fact that polities are not neatly bound in their memberships. Immigration challenges notions of liberalism insofar as it introduces the possibility of a territorially present population that does not enjoy formal rights of equality. It is one thing to consider the unequal application or distribution of rights among those who can lay claim to them (the primary enterprise of the liberals), quite another to confront a group whose claims are not even self-validating.

Among those who have addressed the challenge—most notably, Michael Walzer, Joseph Carens, and Rainer Bauböck (others, including Rawls, simply dodged)—the response has been to demand political membership for alien entrants. Ruth Rubio-Marin adds another powerful voice on the issue. Rubio-Marin argues that the social membership of aliens, both legal and illegal, should lead as of course, on fairness grounds, to their full political membership. The deep affectedness that comes with extended presence, coupled with the subjection to territorial instruments of governance, requires that long-term aliens be admitted to the polity. Rubio-Marin neatly clears underbrush objections to easing incorporation, including increasingly hollow arguments against allowing for the retention of original membership (in other words, against dual citizenship). But, Rubio-Marin goes a step further than her cohorts on the terms of incorporation. Where others call for allowing membership at the option of the entrant (i.e., discretionary naturalization), she provocatively argues for automatic incorporation. In Rubio-Marin's view, all aliens should face mandatory naturalization after a period of time at which social membership can be assumed, which she sets at ten years.

This should give pause. By imposing an identity choice, automatic incorporation seems clearly in tension with liberal values. What of the long-term resident alien who affirmatively does not want to be politically identified with his or her state of residence, notwithstanding the diminution of rights that may inhere to noncitizen status? Here the automatic incorporation argument must rest on the interests of the existing community and the "diminishing effect on the overall level of civic commitment" (p. 108) that results from the presence of large numbers of nonmembers.

Automatic incorporation is an inventive response, and it is ably argued here. (Though I would hardly claim disinterest, Rubio-Marin should be particularly commended for her use of scholarly work from the legal academy, too often ignored despite its clear relevance to the citizenship debates. Her case studies on the rights of aliens and their paths to citizenship in Germany and the United States are well drawn.) But, this may be a last grasp of the liberal nationalists, in whose fold Rubio-Marin plainly stands. One might have thought that naturalization at the option of an immigrant would have shored up the state against the presence of nonmembers. Even where membership is in effect free, it may not be accepted, however, and perhaps that is evidence of its declining value. Questions of its feasibility aside, automatic incorporation is unlikely to do the trick in any case. Free membership is not the sort that tends to build the affective political bonds that are necessary to support the apparatus of the modern nation-states. In the end, the challenge of territorial entrants is not so much that they will diminish liberalism by their deprived status but rather that they will reject membership and thereby destroy the inclusive premises of liberal nationalism. In the face of these objections, postnational paradigms (in which both citizenship and the state are less primary) would seem to be better positioned to process new world realities.

This is only to question assumptions that are widely held by scholars in the area, not Rubio-Marin's execution or the value of her contribution. On the contrary, this book presents a significant and distinctive addition to a growing literature recognizing citizenship status to be a crucial political testing ground.

PETER J. SPIRO

Hofstra University
Hempstead
New York

SHUTKIN, WILLIAM A. 2000. *The Land That Could Be: Environmentalism and Democracy in the Twenty-First Century*. Pp. xx, 273. Cambridge, MA: MIT Press. $29.95.

For most of the nineteenth and twentieth centuries, a reductive view of science prevailed. Scientists examined parts in their quest to understand wholes. The study of rocks yielded one discipline, the study of plants another. Nature, environment, and ecology were viewed as elements out there, forces divorced from social systems. Agencies and organizations established to monitor or to regulate for the environment became regarded as alien from those addressing social concerns.

This perspective is obsolete as we enter the twenty-first century. Urban systems are ecosystems. Nature is a social creation, as Neil Evernden asserted. Computing and information systems help reveal the complexity, the interconnectedness, of culture and nature. Instead of isolating bits and pieces of the environment, we now embrace complexity.

William Shutkin provides a political ideology compatible with this new view of our relationships with our surroundings. He calls his approach "civic environmentalism" "because it marries a concern for the physical health of communities with an understanding that part and parcel of environmental quality is overall civic health" (p. xiv).

Civic environmentalism rejects the elitism of traditional environmentalism, in favor of a more grassroots, a more community-based approach. William Shutkin seeks to elevate ordinary places—the neighborhoods where we live—to a status equal to wilderness preservation within the environmental movement. At the same time, it is equally necessary to illustrate the importance of environmental concerns to traditional community activists. A central argument of *The Land That Could Be* is that "part and parcel" of a "diminution of civic spirit and rise in economic and social inequality has been the deterioration of the American environment, both built and undeveloped" (p. 3).

The Massachusetts-based Shutkin is founder and president of the nonprofit organization New Ecology, Inc. This organization promotes ecodevelopment strategies based on the conservation of natural resources, a sense of place, and mass transit. New Ecology, Inc., is engaged in the type of civic environmentalism advocated throughout the book.

Local communities are bearing the brunt of civic decline brought on by environmental change. Shutkin presents analyses of three vehicles, or drivers, of this change, including development, production, and consumption. He presents a nice, brief history of development and land use in the United States. Traditional Lockean liberalism and its emphasis on private property is identified as the root cause for the rampant land-use development, commonly referred to as suburban sprawl.

Democratic environmentalism could ameliorate the consequences of such change. Shutkin bases this assertion on the American traditions of democracy, as espoused by John Dewey, and of environmentalism, as epitomized by Frederick Law Olmsted, Sr. "The environment," Shutkin observes, "itself is a traditional symbol of American democracy" (p. 89). He offers national icons such as the bald eagle and the national park system to bolster this claim. This tradition is expressed in various forms, such as public participation, community and regional planning, environmental education, industrial ecology, environmental justice, and place-based design. In particular, civic environmentalism is closely aligned with participation and planning.

A strong contribution of *The Land That Could Be* is the presentation of four case studies in civic environmentalism, in Boston, Massachusetts; suburban New Jersey; Oakland, California; and Routt County, Colorado. The New Jersey example is especially compelling because it runs contrary to the normal stereotype of New Jersey as a vast industrial and suburban wasteland between Philadelphia and New York City. Several civic leaders seek to create a "sustainable state." One of these leaders, Barbara Lawrence of New Jersey Future, is quoted as stating, "to be sustainable, New Jersey must be able to view the critical trends that are shaping the future so that we can act on them with foresight and conscience" (p. 222). New Jersey and the other case studies illustrate that civic environmentalism can take on various forms, including urban agriculture and brownfields redevelopment, transit-based development and rural land preservation, suburban open space protection, smart growth planning, and sustainability.

Shutkin presents his case in a friendly tone, which gets a tad too colloquial in places. Still, *The Land That Could Be* is a worthwhile book. Environmentalism is not only fundamental for democracy to flourish, it is essential for a democratic society to sustain itself. Civic environmentalism provides a fresh approach to help us reconstruct the social capital and natural beauty of our communities in the coming century.

FREDERICK STEINER

Arizona State University
Tempe

ZEILER, THOMAS W. 1999. *Free Trade, Free World: The Advent of GATT*. Pp. xii, 288. Chapel Hill: University of North Carolina Press. $39.95.

The controversial World Trade Organization (WTO), established in 1995, has roots in efforts after World War II to liberalize international trade and to establish an institutional and legal framework for the world economy. The U.S. State Department provided leadership for this major undertaking, and officials from Great Britain, Canada, and several other nations provided valuable assistance. Multilateral negotiations in Geneva (1947) led to massive cuts in industrial tariffs, and the Havana Conference (1948) produced a charter for the International Trade Organization (ITO). The ITO was an early, more grandiose version of the present-day WTO, with rules governing trade liberalization, dispute settlements, safeguards, and even investments. It was so far ahead of the times and business sentiment in the United States that Congress refused to authorize membership.

A number of scholars have written about the roots of the General Agreement on Tariffs and Trade (GATT)/WTO system. Thomas Zeiler of the University of Colorado is one of the first diplomatic historians to do so, and he brings to the task the multiarchival methods of first-rate historical research. For this book, Zeiler examined official records in Australia, Britain, Canada, New Zealand, and the United States. Not surprisingly, his interpretation, which concentrates on the 1940s, emphasizes international politics and diplomacy rather than law and economics. GATT, he concludes, was a "weapon in the arsenal of democracy . . . [that] proved crucial to the Free World's victory" in the cold war (p. 201).

Zeiler is at his best when discussing some of the product-specific disputes that shaped individual deals at Geneva and Havana. Some of the more contentious involved access to the British market for Hollywood films and to the American market for Australian wool. Zeiler demonstrates that U.S. negotiators frequently yielded to accommodate the political needs of trading partners. For example, at Geneva in 1947 the United States initially pressed Britain to abandon the commonwealth preferential system but moderated that position when a rift threatened Anglo-American solidarity in the emerging cold war.

Diplomatic historians and political scientists have the most to gain from Zeiler's book. He successfully relates trade negotiations to broader politico-diplomatic events, such as the breakdown of the World War II United Nations coalition, the origins of the cold war, the Marshall Plan, and NATO. From his exhaustive archival research, he produces many fresh anecdotes and a fine historical synthesis.

Trade specialists may have some reservations. For one thing, the book seems mistitled. Free trade, meaning the removal of tariff and trade barriers, did not become an explicit goal of U.S. policy until the 1980s. During the 1940s, the official goal was more limited: freer trade, meaning a reduction in the many governmental trade restrictions that burdened private commerce. Secretary of State Cordell Hull and others in his department repeatedly denied that they were free traders. Clair Wilcox, the State Department economist who led U.S. negotiators at Havana, referred only to the goal of "freer trade" in his 1949 book, *A Charter for World Trade*.

Those interested in the origins and evolution of GATT may find Zeiler's historical analysis unidimensional. He generally ignores the extensive legal literature on this subject and seems to misunderstand the role of GATT. He says that it "successfully policed the world commercial system for decades after the Second World War" (p. 197). Actually, GATT was a forum and an agreement, not a police agency. It had a small bureaucracy and limited resources. As a result, members of GATT frequently ignored their legal obligations. Despite these shortcomings, Zeiler's book is a welcome addition to a growing shelf of historical writings on trade policy.

ALFRED E. ECKES

Ohio University

AFRICA, ASIA, AND LATIN AMERICA

AZICRI, MAX. 2000. *Cuba Today and Tomorrow: Reinventing Socialism*. Pp. xviii, 397. Gainesville: University Press of Florida. $55.00.

Azicri describes various aspects of Cuban domestic (especially) and international affairs, principally in the 1990s. The text accounts, first, for the impact of the collapse of the Soviet Union and European communist regimes on Cuba's circumstances, and it summarizes Cuba's political, economic, and social conditions as well as government policies in the 1980s. There is an excellent chapter on the quality of life in the 1990s, followed by chapters on Cuban political trends and microeconomic and macroeconomic policies in the 1990s. The book's last part narrates events in U.S.-Cuban relations and aspects of Cuba's attempt to improve its relations with other countries, also in the 1990s. There is a chapter on the context and details of Pope John Paul II's visit to Cuba in 1998.

The author is at his scholarly best in chapter four. He explains the new opportunities for women's wider social roles after the revolution, the setbacks to those opportunities in the 1990s, and the related decline in the effectiveness of the officially sponsored Women's Federation. He chronicles the gains in higher education over time along with severe political constraints imposed on universities and scholars in more recent years. Valuable passages in other chapters discuss the complexity of internal migration processes during the 1990s, the evolution of income tax and other fiscal policies, and the antidemocratic character of the 1992 electoral law that impeded multicandidate elections for provincial and national elections.

The book's principal problem is Azicri's recurrent uncritical adoption of officialist explanations. Seeking to explain the endurance of the main features of Cuba's regime forty years after the revolution, he claims, "The people did not hesitate to make and enforce decisions" (p. 30). In fact, nowhere does he demonstrate that the people ever had this capacity. In his conclusions regarding the Cuban government's Rectification Policy of the late 1980s, he asserts an undemonstrated counterfactual: "the problems affecting Cuba by the 1980s could have been worse by 1990 without the Rectification Policy" (p. 68). In fact, scholarly economists who have otherwise disagreed agree that this policy was adverse for Cuba's adjustment to the harsher 1990s—not to speak of the blocking of attempts at even a slight political opening. Azicri's narrative of the Cuban Air Force's shootdown in 1996 of two unarmed aircraft in the waters north of Cuba extensively and exclusively quotes Cuban sources (pp. 190-200) in their critique of the findings of the International Civil Aviation Organization (ICAO) adverse to the Cuban government. The reader cannot learn from this book what the ICAO findings were. And, his discussion of human rights violations in Cuba treats this subject only as an issue for international contention (mainly U.S.-Cuban contestation) without telling us whether he believes that there have been violations of civil and political rights in Cuba.

Azicri the scholar is clear and levelheaded. "The social effect [of the 1990s] could be chronicled as years of disaster, disappointment, scarcity, austerity, hunger, prostitution, corruption, defections, ideological confusion, the loss of hard-gained social and economic advances" (p. 99). The book's problem arises elsewhere, beginning with the subtitle. Azicri never tells us what he understands by socialism and in what way Cuba was still socialist in 2000. It remains unclear just what was being reinvented. Skeptics might think that the rulers were simply attempting to preserve their power. Azicri evidently wishes that a more participatory and socially useful regime would emerge. In attempting to salvage his hopes, he dismisses the skeptics and clings to the dream.

JORGE I. DOMÍNGUEZ

Harvard University
Cambridge
Massachusetts

BAKKEN, BORGE. 2000. *The Exemplary Society: Human Improvement, Social Control, and the Dangers of Modernity in China*. Pp. vi, 516. Oxford, UK: Oxford University Press. $110.00.

This ambitious effort to explain contemporary China's strategies for social control builds on well-known interpretations of Chinese political culture and institutions—especially those stressing the importance of moral training for the development of an orderly society. How, Bakken asks, can China control the "monster" of modernity, unleashed in the reform period, through the creation of moral order?

The author believes that China's social control efforts are best understood by recognizing the strong technocratic and "scientistic" tendencies of the reform era. These have transformed traditional moral training into a task of creating "human quality" through modern technical means—derived from psychology, biology, and "scientific" pedagogy. A critical part of this exercise is the identification of "exemplary norms" to which individuals are socialized and held accountable. Much of the book is given to a detailed analysis of the means and ends of current Chinese socialization practices as found in formal education, modeling, techniques of discipline, and the management of personal dossiers for social control.

While the author provides a highly informative description of the modern manifestations of China's quest for social order through moral training, in conception and execution, his account also disappoints. The theory of exemplary society is intended to shed light on problems of order during the entire reform period, but much of Bakken's material (from interviews and from the writings of Chinese students of pedagogy and moral development) comes only from the 1980s. In attempting to document the scientistic bases of moral education, for instance, much is made of the social thinking of aerodynamicist Qian Xuesen. Qian may have enjoyed a period of influence with some educated Chinese in the 1980s, when modern social sciences were just beginning to recover from decades of stunted development. But, most of the new generation of internationally trained scholars in the social sciences are now likely to regard this theorizing about society as a bit quirky, to say the least.

Bakken, laudably, strives to introduce a comparative dimension to the discussion. The work is filled with frequent allusions to a wide range of Western social theorists who have written on problems of moral education, deviance, modernization, and so forth, in non-Chinese settings. Unfortunately, most of these references are ad hoc; they are not synthesized into a workable framework that would help us identify the significance of the Chinese case for comparative analysis. Bakken's use of Durkheim and Foucault is more fully developed, but not to the point of providing a coherent comparative perspective. How, for instance, should we react to Bakken's point, made at a number of places, that Chinese experience is inconsistent with what one might expect from a reading of Foucault? Should we regard the Chinese case as disconfirming evidence against Foucault, or was Foucault making predictions about a very different sort of society? We are not given the tools to decide.

Bakken's final chapter, "Ways of Lying," explores how contradictions within China's control strategies ultimately encourage individual acts of resistance that collectively work to defeat the goals of exemplarity. Ongoing processes of reform and marketization are also seen as undermining the control system. Moral order thus fails to tame the monster. Such conclusions, of course, are what we would expect, ex hypothesi, from other theories that place more emphasis on individual agency and less on individual malleability through socialization. While the author's own conceptual preferences do open up a wide variety of interesting and suggestive lines of inquiry that he pursues with intelligence and style, the key conclusions of the study could have been reached in a much more direct fashion. Had they, more attention might have been given to modernity's alternatives to moral order (which Bakken treats only in passing) and, by extension, to whether modernity really is the monster it is assumed to be.

RICHARD P. SUTTMEIER

University of Oregon
Eugene

FIGES, ORLANDO, and BORIS KOLONITSKII. 1999. *Interpreting the Russian Revolution: The Language and Symbols of 1917*. Pp. viii, 198. New Haven, CT: Yale University Press. $24.95.

The vast literature on the Russian Revolution consists primarily of political, social, and class analyses. This groundbreaking work of collaboration by the British historian Orlando Figes, author of the acclaimed *A People's Tragedy: The Russian Revolution, 1891-1924*, and the Russian historian Boris Kolonitskii demonstrates how rumors, revolutionary music, and the languages of citizenship and class, as well as such symbols as flags, festivals, monuments, pictures, and emblems, helped to shape the course of the Russian Revolution. Cultural phenomena such as these have attracted attention in studies of the French Revolution, to which the authors frequently refer, but this is the first extensive attempt at an analysis of the role of discourse and imagery in the Russian Revolution.

In the first of two chapters on the February Revolution, Figes and Kolonitskii engagingly examine "the desacralization of the monarchy." Editors of all sorts published even the most fantastic rumors of moral corruption and treason at the court. An enormous market existed for smutty postcards (the book's illustrations include a wonderful example), cartoons, and verses depicting the Tsarina and Rasputin's sexual liaison and collaboration with the enemy. The existence of such rumors is hardly news, though historians have perhaps insufficiently appreciated the rumors' pervasiveness and revolutionary impact. The authors quote some of Russia's most thoughtful and conservative observers to show how seriously such rumors were taken in 1917. The examination of codes and customs of revolutionary protest in the second chapter, "The Symbolic Revolution," certainly breaks new ground. Rebutting the historiographic dichotomy emphasizing the role of either spontaneity or radical leadership in the February revolution, the authors argue that revolutionary symbols, many of which were consciously modeled on those of the French Revolution, self-organized February's remarkably unified crowds. The mere appearance of red flags and armbands, indeed virtually anything red, or the singing of songs such as the "Marseillaise," rallied crowds, which knew to go to the central squares that symbolized imperial power. The largest demonstrations, dubbed "festivals of freedom," became highly ritualized celebrations, free of any violence except iconoclastic attacks on double-headed eagles, statues of tsars, or prisons. But, though the population destroyed the monarchy and attacked imperial institutions, it retained a monarchical psychology, a "Cult of the Leader," which is the title of the third chapter. Kerensky seemed to embody this desire for a good tsar until the collapse of the summer offensive, when malicious rumors ridiculing the "effeminate" Kerensky spread, similar to the earlier rumors ridiculing the "unmanly and impotent" Nicholas.

Turning to an exploration of workers' identity, Figes and Kolonitskii examine "The Languages of Citizenship, the Languages of Class," the title of the fourth chapter. The authors' analysis of how the

Left's growing monopoly on public discourse helped doom the provisional government's Western-style liberalism is one of the book's major contributions. During the first half of 1917, workers spoke the language of human rights, reflecting their desire to be granted the dignity enjoyed by other urban groups, a tradition dating back to the labor unrest of the nineteenth century. Then abruptly—too abruptly in my view—workers abandoned the inclusive language of citizenship for the class exclusive language of democracy. During 1917, the discourse of democracy became increasingly class based, even dictatorial in its exclusion of the bourgeoisie and the rest of privileged society. In the fifth chapter, the authors examine "The Languages of the Revolution in the Village." The peasantry, which by and large could not understand the abstract foreign words that dominated the revolution's language, responded enthusiastically to appeals that presented the socialist future in religious and peasant terms, as a sort of religious utopia. The final chapter's analysis of "Images of the Enemy" is another major contribution. Readers will gain an appreciation of the power wielded by underground pamphleteers, of both the Left and the Right, to deepen popular ethnic prejudices and class hatred. As Figes and Kolonitskii have argued elsewhere, terror was not a Bolshevik invention. The savagery of the civil war was well prepared by the images of class conflict that had come to dominate the discourse of 1917. The Bolsheviks' special quality was their willingness and ability to galvanize the population's desire for revenge. Hateful attacks on the *burzhooi* (bourgeoisie) enjoyed virtually universal mass support.

This long overdue, valuable addition to our understanding of the revolution succeeds in making cultural phenomena an integral part of 1917 (though not an independent part—the authors make a point of emphasizing they do not want to suggest that languages and symbols were divorced from political developments and socioeconomic tensions). But, the study is far too cursory. I would like to know more about many of the issues Figes and Kolonitskii raised—more, for example, about the production and distribution of these cultural artifacts and phenomena. Finally, those considering adopting this slim, mostly jargon-free volume for classroom use should note that Figes and Kolonitskii assume previous study of 1917.

CHARTERS WYNN

University of Texas
Austin

GALLICCHIO, MARC. 2000. *The African American Encounter with Japan and China: Black Internationalism in Asia, 1885-1945*. Pp. iii, 262. Chapel Hill: University of North Carolina Press. $45.00. Paperbound, $17.95.

Marc Gallicchio has produced an excellent study of what he called "Black Internationalism," an ideology that has provided African Americans with a comprehensive explanation of the role of race in world affairs. He acknowledged that as pawns of an expanding Europe, African Americans had long been interested in world affairs, especially in attempting to create a powerful "Black Nationality" to liberate Africa and its diaspora. But, it was Japan's defeat of Russia in 1905 that provided black leaders with an opportunity to embrace a nation determined to Western hegemony in Asia, demolish the myth of white supremacy, and, it was hoped, to demand equality for all nonwhite peoples.

African Americans applauded Japan's role at Versailles in 1919. W.E.B. Du Bois, James Weldon Johnson, Kelly Miller, George Schuyler, William Pickens, and numerous commentators hailed Japan as a champion of the darker races. By the 1920s, "race leaders" wrote and spoke admiringly of Japan and viewed international events from a Japanese perspective.

Japanese imperialism in China challenged the belief in the solidarity of the darker against racism, but most Black Internationalists defended Japan, especially when Westerners readily acquiesced in Italy's conquest of Ethiopia. Only a few leaders such as A. Philip Randolph criticized Japan for attempting to be the Prussia of the East. Most Black Internationalists dismissed Chinese aspirations and accepted Japanese perception of racism as the dominant forces in world affairs.

Japan's attack on Pearl Harbor created a dilemma for Black Internationalists. Many of them blamed the United States for provoking the war, but most African Americans remained loyal to America. Black newspapers hailed the contributions of black GIs in the struggle against Japan, including stories that black servicemen kept big B29s flying over Tokyo. Yet, the tone of the letters to black newspapers and street corner debates revealed that many African Americans viewed the conflict in Asia as a race war. Black Internationalists warned that only the end of racism and a fully mobilized country would gain victory.

Black Internationalists approved the end of Chinese exclusion from the United States and the inclusion of China among the Big Four allies, thereby showing some malleability in their ideology. But, they failed to support China because few Chinese intellectuals living in the United States opposed discrimination. Moreover, Chinese visitors to the United States, in contrast to Indian leaders, did not protest discrimination or seek black solidarity. Blacks resented reports that there was hesitation to permit African American soldiers working on the Burma Road to enter China.

While most black Americans approved the use of atomic bombs to defeat Japan, a number of commentators such as Horace Cayton and George Schuyler denounced the use of such weapons as racist barbarism. Langston Hughes speculated that the bomb had not been used against Germany because it was a white country. Yet, even he acknowledged that when Japan capitulated, Harlem rejoiced. Nevertheless, in 1945, many Black Internationalists began to have second thoughts about the persistence of racism at home and abroad and the subjection of the Japanese to American racism. Du Bois praised Japan for fighting against color caste and for the domination of Asia by Europeans but criticized her for dominating and exploiting fellow Asians.

In a very important epilogue, Gallichchio shows that African Americans maintained a global view of race relations, a view that provides a good background now that they are being permitted to help the United States deal with race and other problems of globalization.

ELLIOTT P. SKINNER

Columbia University
New York

EUROPE

TOMASI, SILVANO M. 2000. *For the Love of Immigrants: Migration Writings and Letters of Bishop John Baptist Scalabrini (1839-1905)*. Pp. xxx, 359. New York: Center for Migration Studies. $45.00.

John Baptist Scalabrini is an important figure in the history of Italian migration, and this new book by Silvano M. Tomasi is indeed welcome. The Italian emigration of modern times is one of the great mass migrations of a people. In size, in the multiplicity of its destinations, and in the complexity of the forces that brought it into being (what the economist Robert F. Foerster felicitously called "*il imperialismo della povere gente*"), it may well be without parallel in the annals of modern history. It has been estimated that no fewer than 25 million Italians emigrated between 1876 and 1970 and that since 1900, more than 10 million Italians left their country permanently. For the millions who did not return to Italy, emigration was permanent and was an answer to a complex set of factors which impelled the vast human migration out of an inhospitable homeland. In this vast human drama, John Baptist Scalabrini (1839-1905) played a central role.

In his early work as a clergyman in the diocese of Como, Scalabrini distinguished himself in social and pastoral activity and was brought to the attention of Pius IX as a candidate for the episcopate. With his appointment as Bishop of Piacenza in 1876, Scalabrini undertook vast works of reform that extended to the spiritual and cultural formation of the clergy, diocesan organization, and legislation; it was during his pastoral visitations to diocesan parishes that he became aware of the awesome specter of migration and its effects on the society of his time. Tomasi correctly observes that

> Scalabrini's attention for the migrants . . . is a progressive awareness on the part of a spirit open to the sign of the times and moved by faith to compassion and to an active involvement in the problems of the society of his times.

Scalabrini soon discovered that vast migration was met with indifference on the part of the state and by an awkward embarrassment by the Church. For Scalabrini, it was the stark problem of migration that became the principal concern of his life and to which his major efforts were directed. And, it is appropriate, indeed, that Scalabrini has been recognized as the first great sociologist of emigration as well as the apostle to the immigrants.

Tomasi's *For the Love of Immigrants*, which draws on Scalabrini's works on immigration, has a relevance to our times. As Tomasi observes,

> with the persistence of migrations, different and complex to be sure, a new presentation of the thinking of Bishop Scalabrini constitutes an original stimulus, and not just for Catholics, to advance both understanding and commitment for a peaceful and enriching coexistence.

Tomasi has drawn on a vast oeuvre by Scalabrini on immigrants and their related needs. Scalabrini had witnessed the high number of his diocesan poor who were being pushed to migration, especially from the Emilian Appenines. The railroad station in Piacenza was a transit point for thousands of emigrants from the Veneto, Lombardy, and Romagna regions directed to the port of Genoa. "Before such a painful situation," Scalabrini wrote, "I have often asked myself: how can I find a solution?" Plaintively, Scalabrini cried: "I made mine the cry of sorrow of our poor expatriates, and I called public attention to the nefarious activity of the traffickers in human flesh" (*L'Emigazione Italiana in America* 1885, 5). Scalabrini planned a well-integrated form of assistance for the emigrants that covered the port of departure, the voyages, the arrival and settlement in the country of destination. Scalabrini emerged as the principal exponent in developing a global approach for the social (and religious) assistance for emigrants, particularly in North and South America. He wrote extensively on emigration, made visits to the towns left by the emigrants, convened a diocesan synod on emigration and its perils and needs, made proposals for new immigration laws, organized the St. Raphael Society for assistance to migrants, founded the Congregation of the Missionaries of St. Charles (the Scalabrinians) for the religious and social assistance to migrants, and undertook pastoral visits to the emigrants (to the United States in 1901 and to Brazil in 1904). In essence, Scalabrini in some thirty years of endeavor worked out a complete pragmatic plan for the emigration problem in its social, legal, and political aspects. In itself, that is a staggering achievement.

There is a paucity of materials in English about John Baptist Scalabrini. This is unfortunate, given the towering importance of Scalabrini in the annals of European migration. There is an adequate life of Scalabrini by Marco Caliaro and Mario Francesconi, *John Baptist Scalabrini: Apostle to the Emigrants* (1977), translated from Italian, and some ancillary notices in Mary E. Brown's *Scalabrinians in North America, 1887-1934* (1996). The significance of Silvano M. Tomasi's *For the Love of Immigrants: Migration Writings and Letters of Bishop John Baptist Scalabrini* is that for the first time, we have in English seminal writings by Scalabrini on emigration and its multiple dimensional realities, meticulously edited and translated into English by an acknowledged emigration authority. Included are Scalabrini's *Italian Emigration to America* (1887), *The Parliamentary Bill on Italian Emigration* (1888), *On the Necessity of Protecting the Nationality of the Immigrants* (1891), and *Italy Abroad* (1904), among others. As a rich sampling of international cooperation on the social and religious problems of emigrants, Tomasi has included Scalabrini's correspondence with a number of American Catholic bishops during 1887 to 1904.

FRANCESCO CORDASCO

Montclair State University
Upper Montclair
New Jersey

VERGER, JACQUES. 2000. *Men of Learning in Europe at the End of the Middle Ages*. Pp. vi, 209. Notre Dame, Indiana: University of Notre Dame Press. Paperbound, $22.00.

In this excellent original synthesis, a prominent French historian of the medieval university surveys the place of the learned in the European society of the fourteenth and fifteenth centuries. Jacques Verger is interested not only in the ways in which the learned came to be such but also in their competence, role in society, self-understandings, and conception of culture.

Who were the learned? Verger casts his net broadly, from doctors of law, medicine, and theology to people whose modest exposure to formal education distinguished them from the populace. Although the universities had no monopoly on education (as vernacular abacus schools and others attest), they epitomized the certification of learning and proliferated in the late Middle Ages, accommodating a growing number of students. In the new universities of the Holy Roman Empire alone, enrollments increased tenfold in a century, serving a quarter of a million students before 1500. The learned were thus primarily university-educated men (often without a degree, however), and many of them dealt with the law. Their sheer numbers make them a significant social phenomenon, indeed one that changed the practice of politics.

The book is a model of careful organization. Part I, "The Foundation of a Culture," examines the distinctive elements of learned culture. Typically these included the Latin language, habits of thought associated with Aristotelianism (logical analysis, taxonomic tendencies, expository techniques), and access to books. But, they also included a distinctive sociability and specific bodies of knowledge and practices (the former developed in the "nations" and colleges, the latter in the faculties of the universities). In Part II, "The Exercises of Competences," Verger advances one of his major themes, that medieval learning was directed not to personal development but to specific practical uses, notably in the formal and informal councils of princely courts and the Church. He also addresses the interface between knowledge and power and examines the extent to which men of learning changed existing structures. In Part III, "Social Realities and Self-Image," Verger turns to perceptions and self-perceptions, including the extent to which not only the roles but also the men who filled them were new.

Verger's attention to the social and political roles of the learned will particularly interest readers of this journal. While noblemen represented only a small minority of the learned, learning made it possible for others to acquire nobility. A few, usually court advisors, received noble titles outright, but society considered many others ennobled by learning itself: "a doctorate is worth a knighthood," as the adage put it. Whereas some individuals perpetuated their new status by founding family dynasties of physicians or lawyers, the learned in Europe never become a hereditary caste. New blood continued to enter the ranks, often from below, but almost never with revolutionary implications, since the learned generally emulated the social trappings of the older elites.

Verger goes beyond the social distinction associated with learning to address the difficult matters of the competence and political roles of the learned, issues obscured by the recent attention (in some quarters) to display, manners, and etiquette. In late-medieval Europe, the law framed much activity, from criminal and civil lawsuits, to political and ecclesiastical disputes, to commercial and marital transactions. Appeals to legal expertise multiplied and required a substantial personnel to handle them—not only the lawyers who served princely and ecclesiastical courts and bureaucracies, but also the many notaries and their apprentices who mediated the law to the people. Verger emphasizes the crucial role of these underappreciated "intermediary intellectuals," who strengthened at the local level the "networks of supervision and obedience" that made the emergence of the modern state possible.

As Verger sees it,

> The practice of knowledge became work. . . . Its purpose was neither the poet's aesthetic enjoyment nor the pious monk's rumination, but rather the acquisition and putting into practice of socially useful knowledge that was directed toward concrete ends, usually political. (P. 167)

Thus did the learned begin to encroach on the hereditary nobility, a trend that Verger casts—despite its acknowledged anachronism—as professionalism displacing amateurism, especially in politics. Whether secular or ecclesiastical, rulers increasingly sought advisors whose competence and technical skills mattered more than their birth. Although Verger rightly emphasizes the law, the disciplines of medicine and theology (treated cursorily) and the astrological implications of natural philosophy (not treated at all) would bear out his argument for the orientation of learning toward social uses.

Indeed, Verger believes that the technical skills of the learned help to explain the humanist reaction to medieval learned culture. On this account, Renaissance humanism is an ivory tower epiphenomenon with little impact on the fundamental continuities in the social and political functions of learned practice between the end of the Middle Ages and the early modern period.

Verger is aware of the limitations of his data and of the difficulty of generalizing. Precisely for this reason, his important book is a particularly balanced and valuable study of the social and political implications of late-medieval knowledge.

MICHAEL H. SHANK

University of Wisconsin
Madison

UNITED STATES

EASTON, NINA J. 2000. *Gang of Five: Leaders at the Center of the Conservative Crusade*. Pp. 463. New York: Simon & Schuster. $27.00.

How has conservatism, a political movement that was consigned to oblivion by most observers following the crushing presidential defeat in 1964 of conservative Barry Goldwater, come to dominate so much of American politics during the past two decades? Political journalist Nina Easton provides part of the answer in her excellent study of the lives of five of the Right's most influential younger leaders—editor-commentator William Kristol, coalition builder Grover Norquist, Christian strategist Ralph Reed, Republican politician David McIntosh, and libertarian lawyer Clint Bolick.

Easton presents the five activists as the other, unknown side of the baby boom generation—conservative political rebels who emerged in the 1970s and "went on to overturn the established liberal order." They are, she says, ideologues who, having read Whittaker Chambers and other passionate anti-Communists, viewed the Soviet Union as an evil empire. Brought up on Friedrich Hayek and similar free market economists, these young conservatives sought to contract, not expand, the size and influence of government.

What differentiates the group from earlier conservatives who were no less ideological, argues Easton, is their political and media sophistication and their day-in-day-out campaigning. The Clintons's health care plan, for example, went down to defeat after GOP leaders adopted Kristol's argument that "there is no health crisis." Norquist mobilized the conservative grassroots against President Clinton's first-year tax increase. There would have been no Republican capture of the U.S. House of Representatives in 1994 without the organizational efforts of Reed, Norquist, and other new conservatives.

Easton has done her homework, interviewing dozens of key conservatives and reading much of the modern conservative canon (even bits of political philosopher Leo Strauss, no easy undertaking). As a baby boomer, Easton understands the hubris, irreverence, and impatience that characterizes her generation, Left and Right. And, she is a fine writer, incisive and frequently witty.

She offers as comprehensive and readable a portrait of these conservative leaders and their significant contributions to the conservative revolution of the past quarter century as has yet been published. There are some flaws in her book, beginning with its title. Kristol et al. are not would-be Red Guards out to destroy the Four Olds of American Society as Madame Mao and the rest of the Gang of Four tried to do in Communist China.

And, because Easton is writing about current politics, her analysis inevitably runs the risk of being overtaken by events. The author claims that the Right is "haunted" by its failure to turn its "momentary gains into a governing majority." She obviously wrote that before George W. Bush won the presidency on a platform of compassionate conservatism, Republicans retained their majority (albeit a narrow one) in the Congress, and Republicans wound up with twenty-nine state houses representing some two-thirds of the nation's population. That is as close to a governing majority as either major political party has had since the New Deal of the 1930s.

LEE EDWARDS

Catholic University of America
Washington, D.C.

GENOVESE, MICHAEL A. 2001. *The Power of the American Presidency—1789-2000*. Pp. xiii, 273. New York: Oxford University Press. Paperbound, $19.95.

The American presidency and the men who have occupied the office since 1789 have been a continuing object of study and analysis for historians, political scientists, and journalists. Although that literature has ranged over a myriad of topics, there has not been a brief history of the development of presidential power that touches on each of the forty-two presidents since 1789. Presidential scholar Michael Genovese admirably fills that void in this book. He sets forth the major themes in the presidential literature and uses them to shape case studies of the various presidents' personalities and how each dealt with the challenges that confronted him.

It is through "historical antecedents," Genovese argues, that we can best learn the "limits and possibilities of presidential power." The story of presidential power, as he tells it, has two continuing characteristics. It is not static but passes through continuing cycles of rises and falls. Also, as Edward S. Corwin observed long ago, it entails a continuing institutional struggle between the presidency and Congress. Genovese identifies four variables that shape presidential power: "the *individual*, the *institution*, the *system*, and the *times*." Presidential power is not absolute but is, in Richard E. Neustadt's words, "the power to persuade." Crisis provides the opportunity to develop the powers of the office, but not all presidents have the will or the temperament to do so. There have been enormous variations in style, personality, and ability. Buchanan was neither inclined nor able to forestall the Civil War, and it is doubtful if anyone other than Lincoln could have brought the war to a successful conclusion through creative expansion of the office. Although FDR skillfully prepared the United States for World War II, he required the stimulus of Pearl Harbor to bring the United States into the war.

In a political system that tends toward stasis, the presidency is, as Genovese demonstrates, the principal organ for adaptation to change. It is the primary agent of modernization due largely to its malleability. The office has grown and been reshaped along with the ebbs and flows of its powers.

What, then, of the individual presidents? The cameo portraits are necessarily brief, but insightful and revealing. Readers will learn interesting things about important presidents and unimportant things about uninteresting presidents. Genovese's ratings of the presidents generally correspond with the collective judgment of scholars and with my own appraisal: Lincoln is rated 1, FDR 2, Washington 3, Jefferson 4, Jackson 5, Wilson 6, T. Roosevelt 7, Polk 8, Truman 9, and John Adams 10. His criteria for rating include the problems they faced, how they dealt with the problems, their vision for the nation, their accomplishments, and the long-term effects of their actions.

The treatment of Johnson, Nixon, and Clinton is on target. Genovese notes that Johnson had greater skill in leading Congress than any modern president, had a superb start under difficult circumstances, and achieved great successes but that he blundered badly in Vietnam. Nixon remains "a paradox and an enigma." In national security matters, he was an "innovative thinker and grand strategist" who had "a momentous impact on the world" but whose insecurities and moral bankruptcy led to self-destruction. Clinton accomplished much and enjoyed a high level of public support but was "character-challenged." Scandals plagued his presidency, and he has the ignominious distinction of being only the second president to be impeached. Moreover, the circumstances surrounding his departure from office did nothing to enhance his legacy.

This is an important book that should be read by all persons interested in national politics and especially by students of the presidency. It will be of considerable help in the evaluation of twenty-first-century presidents as they meet the challenges of the rapidly changing, high-tech, post–cold war world.

NORMAN C. THOMAS

University of Cincinnati
Ohio

KOHUT, ANDREW, JOHN C. GREEN, SCOTT KEETER, and ROBERT C. TOTH. 2000. *The Diminishing Divide: Religion's Changing Role in American Politics.* Pp. xi, 178. Washington, DC: Brookings Institution. $36.95. Paperbound, $15.95.

Americans are often reminded that being socially gracious requires one to avoid discussing either religion or politics. Nevertheless, every passing day seems to bring more discussion, in both public and private realms, of the nature of the entanglement of religion and politics. For years, scholars, social critics, and citizens alike have been searching for insight into how religion affects American politics.

The Diminishing Divide is one of the more useful empirical works to emerge in recent years about the relationships between religion and politics in the United States. Andrew Kohut and colleagues rely on a wealth of survey data from such respected sources as the Pew Research Center and the National Election Studies to explore the many effects religion has on political attitudes and political behavior. After setting the stage for their analysis with an all-too-brief history of the roots of religiopolitical interaction in the United States, the authors demonstrate that whatever divide may have separated religion from politics in the past has now diminished dramatically.

Among the authors' most important findings is that not only do people's religious affiliations have an effect on their political attitudes and behaviors but so too does the strength of their religious commitment. The more committed a person is to Christianity—of any variety—the more conservative he or she will tend to be on political issues from racism to foreign policy. (It is unfortunate that it was not possible for the authors to isolate committed Jews, Muslims, and adherents of other faith traditions in their samples.) Religious affiliation and level of commitment also have a powerful effect on partisan identification and voting behavior. The authors show that these religious factors played a bigger role in the presidential elections of 1992 and 1996 than they had since the 1960 election of John F. Kennedy.

Kohut and colleagues also include a fascinating look at Americans' attitudes about whether churches ought to pursue formal involvement in the political realm. Such an inquiry is particularly important in this age of Charitable Choice and other forms of active government support for the sociopolitical work of faith-based institutions. Once again, the authors emphasize the importance of religious commitment. People whom they classify as committed to any variety of Christianity are more likely to support the contention that the United States is a

Christian nation and more likely to support involvement by their churches and clergy in organized political efforts.

Why are religion and politics becoming ever more entangled with one another? Have Americans just become more religious? Kohut and colleagues assert that there has not been a new great awakening. Instead, they look to changes in the national political agenda. With cultural and sexual issues like school prayer and abortion on the collective mind of the nation in recent years, religious voices have found a more natural entrée into political debate. Perhaps as a result, religious people are now more involved in politics than ever, which has increased the relative clout of organized religion on electoral and policy outcomes. Meanwhile, Americans have grown more tolerant of interaction between the realms of religion and politics.

Readers searching for normative conclusions about whether religion and politics should interact will be disappointed with this book, as it is strictly an analysis of empirical data. Even readers who enjoy this fact may find themselves wishing for even more interpretation of the enormous volume of data presented here. These criticisms notwithstanding, this book is an extremely valuable contribution to the literature on religion and politics. Kohut and colleagues show us most vividly that discussion of religion and politics is absolutely crucial for understanding the American polity, and indeed culture, today—the social graces be damned.

LAURA R. OLSON

Clemson University
Clemson
South Carolina

MCCHESNEY, ROBERT W. 1999. *Rich Media, Poor Democracy: Communication Politics in Dubious Times*. Pp. xii, 427. Urbana: University of Illinois Press. $32.95.

Robert McChesney is at his rhetorical best passionately describing the creation of public policy: "public debate over the future of the media and communication has been effectively eliminated by powerful and arrogant corporate media, which metaphorically floss their teeth with politicians' underpants" (p. 77). But, the best reason to read his latest book is the richness of his vision. In McChesney's account, media regulation, economic logic, and our cultural paradigms for thinking about mass communication interact with each other in complex ways, and he condemns the market-based paradigm that has come to dominate our thinking about media. He calls it neoliberalism, the false equating of the marketplace with democracy. Furthermore, even as he argues convincingly and in no uncertain terms that corporate ownership of mass communication is detrimental, his complex story acknowledges that not all of the evils others attribute to corporate media work as claimed and that advocates of public service media have made some critical errors of their own. His argument is compelling and seems intellectually honest.

The first half of *Rich Media, Poor Democracy* describes the organizational structure of the current media system. In the first chapter, McChesney describes the shape of U.S. media at the turn of the millennium, effectively arguing that economic logic dictates even greater ownership consolidation and that between neoliberal political culture and mediated political campaigns, policy makers are unlikely to stem the tide. In the second chapter, he goes global, describing troubling patterns of consolidation that are concentrating the means of mass communication into the hands of a small number of transnational corporations. McChesney's view of cultural imperialism is complex. Global organizations create products empty of cultural specificity for international distribution and cultivate audiences to increase the kinds of cultural materials that can be globally distributed, but they also produce culturally specific content where local audiences demand it. The last chapter in this section assesses the future of the Internet in light of current organizational structures and trends. McChesney concludes that despite the technological possibilities of an infinite-channel universe, the same old players are gaining control of a crucial bottleneck, the portals people use to gain access to the Internet. Here again, he paints a complex picture in which the Internet provides more variety in content, but commercialization affects both the structure of the Internet and the tastes of audiences such that only the dedicated are likely to find much diversity.

In the second half of the book, McChesney traces the rise of the neoliberal model of media organization and its impacts on public service broadcasting ideals. He first revisits the central argument of his earlier work, *Telecommunications, Mass Media & Democracy*. He argues that there is nothing natural about a commercial media system and delves into the history of telecommunications regulation to support his point. Then he considers the current state and potential fate of public broadcasting in several nations, arguing that even the grandest public broadcaster of all, the BBC, is sacrificing its public service mission in favor of a more commercial model. In the next chapter, he critiques the current interpretation of the First Amendment as a private right of corporations, encouraging instead an interpretation of freedom of speech as a critical component of public life. The final chapter of the book argues that only the political Left can support a public interest paradigm for thinking about the mass media to oppose the neoliberal approach. Furthermore, unless the Left makes media policy a fundamental aspect of the movement, he suggests, the Left itself will fail to flourish.

McChesney's final appeal to the Left underplays the more universal aspect of his argument: enacting changes in the media system will require changing the ways we think about mass communication as much as redistributing the means of production.

JILL A. EDY

Middle Tennessee State University
Murfreesboro

SHORTER, EDWARD. 2000. *The Kennedy Family and the Story of Mental Retardation*. Pp. ix, 249. Philadelphia: Temple University Press. $74.50. Paperbound, $22.95.

Elizabeth Boggs, this book's dedicatee, would have fussed about its errors of fact and its tediously repeated interpretation of Eunice Shriver's psyche. Until her death on an icy New Jersey road in 1996, Boggs, then in her eighties, maintained the energy and style of a take-no-prisoners critic. But she was not petty. One of the most important players in the story that Shorter tells, Boggs would have looked beyond the book's faults to see *The Kennedy Family and the Story of Mental Retardation* as an important addition to the history of intellectual disabilities.

Especially when he stays with his topic, Shorter provides new and interesting details about the Kennedy family's efforts to change the research agenda and public perceptions of mental retardation. Although the book's title suggests a family effort, the central figure of the story is Eunice Kennedy Shriver. Shorter claims (and for my tastes repeats too frequently) that Shriver's drive developed from her need to please her father, Joseph P. Kennedy, but also as a way to compete with her publicly successful brothers. Often demanding and intrusive, Shriver, nevertheless, used her energy and influence to change old and socially entrenched assumptions about intellectual disability. From interviews and from a considerable part (though not all) of the Kennedy family records, Shorter carries the reader from the Kennedy Foundation's appropriation of mental retardation to Eunice and Sargent Shriver's influence of legislation during the Kennedy presidency to an especially interesting discussion of Eunice Kennedy's association with the Special Olympics movement.

For a theory-absent, fact-dependent book such as *The Kennedy Family*, Shorter allows several small but annoying errors. Gunnar Dybwad, for example, is not a psychologist. Nor did Henry H. Goddard hold to (indeed he rejected) a view of genetic degeneration. Paroles did not end in New York in 1919; for example, Charles Bernstein paroled inmates of the Rome (New York) State School between 1912 and his death in 1942. Edward Sequin founded his Physiological School in Manhattan; his widow, Elsie (not Edward) Seguin moved the school to New Jersey several years later. Finally, contrary to Shorter's claim, the majority of people with cerebral palsy do not also have mental retardation.

Beyond these problems, Shorter makes two claims that although ancillary to the book's thesis, compromise its intent. First, he notes in the preface that the book will not deal with parents organizations like the National Association of Retarded Children. In more than one place, he implies that Eunice Shriver singlehandedly transformed public perceptions and social policies about mental retardation. Shriver, no doubt, affected perceptions and policies. Yet, neither her efforts nor the hard work of any other person would have counted for much were it not for the advocacy and litigation initiated by thousands of parents and relatives.

Second, it is common for writers to add legitimacy to their own efforts by claiming that others have done little work on the topic at hand. Shorter is correct when he states that "the field [of history of mental retardation] represents a great and exciting challenge." But his disingenuous claim that "the story of MR remains yet so untold that future researchers will simply have to hack it out of the rock face" fails to account for the growing number of articles, books, dissertations, and conferences that have occurred during the past decade. In Scandinavia, the Netherlands, France, Great Britain, Canada, and the United States, scholars are telling the stories of intellectual disabilities. Although much more work lies ahead, Shorter's book is an important contribution to a literature that has already had its rock face hacked.

JAMES W. TRENT

Southern Illinois University
Edwardsville

SOCIOLOGY

DAVIS, NATALIE ZEMON. 2000. *The Gift in Sixteenth-Century France*. Pp. x, 185. Madison: University of Wisconsin Press. $50.00. Paperbound, $21.95.

As in her previous works on early modern France, Natalie Zemon Davis brings a deep knowledge of anthropology to this study of gift giving in the sixteenth century. Here she uses an ethnographic approach to criticize an evolutionary view associated with Marcel Mauss and his followers, according to whom relations based on gift have gradually been superceded by those based on contract.

Davis builds a more complex picture through an investigation of normative literature and of practice based on such sources as wills, journals, letters, book dedications, and government records. Among the new sources she uses are diverse visual images taken primarily from printed book illustrations that she analyzes insightfully in the text.

Several prescriptive traditions encouraged gift giving and provided criteria for evaluating gifts: Christian charity, classical and feudal conceptions of liberality, and learned and popular norms concerning friendship and neighborly generosity. They all expected the donor's act to be voluntary and yet, when properly performed, to excite the recipient's gratitude and oblige him or her to make some return, whether in the form of prayer, a favor, or some more material expression. This nexus between giving, gratitude, and obligation to reciprocate, or "the spirit of the gift," is Davis's subject rather than gifts narrowly defined as such. She traces this spirit across diverse social fields and even overseas in encounters between French explorers and Amerindians, giving us a richly textured account of life in sixteenth-century France that will delight undergraduates and the educated public and will interest scholars in all of the social sciences.

Gift giving was an integral part of many holidays and life cycle events. Gifts of game and other choice foods marked status relations and facilitated communication within the rural elite, while peasants gave occasional gifts of butter, chickens, fruit, and other comestibles to their lords and received favors and hospitality. Gifts accompanied payments to employees and fees for the services of doctors, midwives, and lawyers. The boundary between gifts and contracts was fluid; gifts ended contractual transactions on a friendly note and encouraged continuity in relationships (p. 66). They also finessed the issue of recompense in a world where the medieval aphorism "knowledge is a gift of God and cannot be sold" still had salience (p. 44). But gifts could create conflict as well as solidarity, and in a chapter titled "Gifts Gone Wrong," Davis considers tensions over gifts within families and among courtiers and scholars, and the different attitudes toward gifts and obligations among men and women. The theme of good and bad gifts pervaded the sphere of politics, where offices were both purchased and acquired through patronage and justified as gifts in reward for merit. Forced to seek and give favors in his pursuit of public office, Michel de Montaigne complained that nothing was "so costly as that which is given me, for then my will is mortgaged by a title of gratitude" (p. 74). Tensions around transactions between laity and clergy and between humans and God also existed among contending religious sects; in fact, Davis interprets the reform movements of the sixteenth century as a quarrel over whether people could reciprocate God's gifts and put God under obligation (p. 100).

The Gift in Sixteenth-Century France distills a wide range of sources into a balanced and engaging account of ideas and practices concerning gifts that highlights basic tensions in French society. It offers a valuable corrective to the continuing anthropological romance with gifts. Davis's analytic framework, however, rests uneasily on her material. She identifies three different modes or systems of human relationship—those based on gift, contract, and coercion—that interact in different ways over time. But, her gift and contract are ideal types, or models, rather than legal or folk categories, and they have trouble accommodating both the rhetorical play with categories and the changing ethical sensibilities that she describes. Furthermore, Davis gives few hints on how to situate the "culture of obligation" in the sixteenth century (p. 67) within long-term processes of continuity and change in France. Nonetheless, she shows that to understand these processes we need to consider many institutions, as well as to complicate our understanding of values associated with the market.

JANE FAIR BESTOR

Harvard University
Cambridge
Massachusetts

KATZ, JACK. 1999. *How Emotions Work*. Pp. xi, 407. Chicago: University of Chicago Press. $27.50. £19.50.

Since the experience of emotion is so clearly more than talk, Katz's microdescription of his subjects' emotional experiences reaches beyond the linguistic turn and attempts to broaden the scope of traditional social psychology. Through our emotions (which may be artfully constructed but are experienced as ego-alien), we produce the embodied, nonverbal foundation for selfhood, thought, and conduct. But, the process only works when it is outside of awareness. The author uses the lived experience of emotion strategically because it seems so tailored to his main dialectic task—"making visible the invisible responsible for all that is visible."

To control for personal differences and to convey the necessary sense of being there, we confront hundreds of examples of road rage, crying and whining, laughing, shame, and emotional metamorphosis. Rejecting standard procedures, Katz's data collection strategies are chosen to meet the particular demands of his subject matter and to avoid a reified view of emotions detached from their lived context. Interviews, tapes, videos, and ethnographic reports are used in creative and informative ways.

Since existing emotion studies are not designed to make visible the hidden foundations of self, other, and the material world, Katz draws from his own selection of literature that shares this goal. This includes the dualistic hermeneutics of depth psychology and Heideggerian philosophy (e.g., an appreciation of the dualism of all emotions: we cry for joy as well as sorrow), the phenomenology of the body suggested by Polanyi and Merleau-Ponty, and the interactional analysis of Mead and Schutz.

Three topics of inquiry guide this study. First is that of the preconscious meanings that are only sensually understood by the actor as well as others. The second inquiry concerns how emotions are shaped in anticipation of how they will be perceived. The last is aimed toward the embodiment of conduct and meaning. Knowledge from these areas is brought to bear on three other emotional processes: (1) situation-responsive and situation-transcendent narrative projects; for example, emotion emerges from the implications of the situation for the broader themes of one's life-narrative; (2) interaction process, for example, how people exploit situations and their own bodies to shape emotional conduct; and (3) sensual metamorphoses that are important parts of changes in conduct.

Katz chooses emotion to reveal the invisible foundations of society and self because it is corporal, largely preobjective in expression, and yet very social, uniquely capturing the dialectic connection between the individual and the public domain. Katz contends that social psychology must move significantly beyond a semiotics construed as predominantly verbal and self-consciously reflective. Social interaction typically proceeds too fast for deliberation. Conversation is, indeed, guided by concentration on its point, but specific words come too quickly for deliberation. The fingers of a piano player have a corporal language of their own that is only impeded by reflective awareness. The neglected semiotics of emotion is cut from this same corporal cloth. From this standpoint, Blumer's emphasis on deliberate thought and Goffman's person preoccupied by self-image are seriously limited.

The author extracts unusual effort from the reader—sometimes by necessity, but frequently not. He writes often that the most important character of emotion is its three-dimensional corporeality, but one must infer what the other dimensions are, thereby blunting one of the book's main contributions. Many readers will miss his attempt at "letting the inductive method speak for itself." Too often, ideas that initially excite dissipate on reflection. Nevertheless, he may help us glimpse a more comprehensive social psychology, theoretically and methodologically.

DAVID D. FRANKS

Virginia Commonwealth University
Richmond

MCANANY, PATRICIA A. 1995. *Living with the Ancestors: Kinship and Kingship in Ancient Maya Society*. Pp. xvi, 229. Austin: University of Texas Press. $27.95. Paperbound, $16.95.

This volume offers an important and thought-provoking explication of Classic (A.D. 200-900) Lowland Maya political organization and an examination of its long-term (ca. 1000+ B.C.–today) social organizational basis that should be of interest both to non-Mesoamericanists working in the political and social sciences and to Mayanists in particular. More an articulation of ideas that have been current and the subject of considerable dialogue among Mayanists during the past twenty or so years than a new synthesis of these, the work is and will remain an important one because it explicitly states the principles, normative and ideological bases, and substantiating data for these ideas and eschews the nouveau pseudomystical characterization of the Classic Maya reintroduced by some art historians and archaeologists during the past twenty years. McAnany's openly materialist assessment of Maya social and political organization is refreshing and timely. At the same time, there are some troubling deficiencies in her presentation that nonspecialists should be made aware of and specialists ought keep in mind.

The core premise of this work is that Maya societies past and present from Preclassic times (ca. 1000+ B.C.–A.D. 100) through the spectacular Lowland florescence of the Classic period and the perturbations of the Colonial era into the present day are both integrated and organized at the extended family or lineage level through devotional ties to and recognition of common descent from common forebears—named ancestors—and that real and acknowledged affinities, obligations, and rights are established and determined through identification with a named apical or founding familial ancestor or ancestor pair. Veneration of and devotion to—not worship of—the named ancestor or ancestors serves to identify successive generations with them, integrate them into a kinship-based corporate group, and confer usufruct rights on them involving lands, resources, domiciles, and material objects actually owned by the familial ancestors. Not only are group membership and resultant ownership or usage rights so established, but so are a descent-based social ranking and order of access or disfranchisement with respect to hearth, lands, and resources. McAnany argues convincingly that in this lies the microcosmic basis for the social inequalities and ranking that characterized Classic Maya civilization. As differential access to land and resources are rooted in the order and distancing by birth within families, so ultimately did rights and obligations involving tribute, service, status, and wealth come to be determined analogously between families and the social factions formed by them in response to common interests or concerns. McAnany explores these themes in a well-structured exegesis that moves from a broad-based cross-cultural examination of the social manifestations and roles of ancestor veneration to consideration of its character, functions, and history among the Maya, and on to its potential significance in the formation and maintenance of kingship and the correlative sociopolitical structure of Classic Maya society. McAnany's ideas and arguments are basic to appreciating much about the nature of Classic Maya society, and all who work with this culture will find them stimulating, as will nonspecialists with interests in the Maya, Mesoamerica, or the history of human social and political organization. All in all, this is an important, interesting, and credible work that virtually any reader will find useful and rewarding.

Two flaws do detract from the general quality of the book, in my opinion. First, after logically developing and arguing for a structural form identical with that formalized as the segmentary state by numerous scholars as the organizational archetype most closely approximated by Classic Maya civilization, McAnany dismisses this and several related constructs in favor of a never actually defined and nebulous alternative bound loosely together by kinship and ancestor veneration. This is unfortunate and smacks of an academic pettiness not otherwise manifest in the work. Readers should be aware and beware of this in considering her arguments. Second, the book is somewhat less than fair in acknowledging intellectual debts to such scholars as historian Nancy Farris, art historian Linda Schele, archaeologists David Freidel, David Webster, William Sanders, and others. Although explicitly repeatedly remarking its own pathbreaking innovativeness and seminal insights, the work really represents a first clear articulation of ideas and beliefs common among Mayanists during the 1980s rather than a grand new synthesis of these or breakthrough insight based on them. This work is an important—nay, a very important—one. It could well have afforded to be fairer in acknowledging its intellectual debts as well.

JOSEPH W. BALL

San Diego State University
California

ECONOMICS

CAMPBELL, JOHN C., and NAOKI IKEGAMI. 1998. *The Art of Balance in Health Policy: Maintaining Japan's Low-Cost, Egalitarian System*. Pp. xi, 227. Cambridge, UK: Cambridge University Press.

This jointly authored book is a major contribution to the literature on Japanese public policy, the study of comparative politics, and the cross-national investigation of modern health care systems (how they work and what others can learn from them). The title of the book is accurate and informative. Campbell, an experienced scholar of Japanese politics from the University of Michigan, and Ikegami, a psychiatrist and professor of health policy from Keio University of Tokyo, describe how Japan's form of nationwide health insurance emerged and analyze both how it works and what sustains the balance between Japan's relatively accessible care and its comparatively constrained costs.

Campbell and Ikegami accomplish this in a series of clearly written chapters that address the following topics. They first take up Japan's experience with inflationary pressures in medical care and describe the journey from exploding costs in the 1970s to outlays in the 1990s at about 7 percent of GNP. In chapters two and three, they describe the arena of health politics in Japan and characterize the complicated bargaining that takes place among Japanese doctors, hospital officials, and high-ranking civil servants. In the remaining chapters, the authors describe the mix of various health insurance bodies that in the aggregate constitute universal health insurance coverage and then go on to show both the broad and detailed features of the cost control regime in Japan. Campbell and Ikegami are admirers of Japan's successes but are aware of its limitations and, in particular, the quality of care that takes place in hospitals, where the length of stay is enormously longer than among other industrial democracies and where the standard of care is arguably less advanced. They close the book with suggestions of what can be learned from Japan's experience with balancing cost containment and egalitarian access to care. Without suggesting that transplantation is possible, the authors do argue that Japan's attention to balance is a lesson others, including the United States, could well learn. On the other hand, they are quite critical of what is described as the cookie cutter uniformity of Japanese medical practice and equally concerned about the degree to which cost containment has prevented large Japanese hospitals from attaining the technological sophistication available elsewhere.

In short, this is an informed, balanced account with provocative implications for policy makers and illuminating portraiture for those unfamiliar with Japan's medical care circumstances.

T. R. MARMOR

Yale University
New Haven
Connecticut

TOWNSEND, CAMILLA. 2000. *Tales of Two Cities. Race and Economic Culture in Early Republican North and South America: Guayaquil, Ecuador, and Baltimore, Maryland.* Pp. xxii, 320. Austin: University of Texas Press. $45.00. Paperbound, $19.95.

This ambitious study joins high-flying company in asking why some peoples are wealthy while others are not. Jared Diamond has offered an ecology-driven account in *Guns, Germs and Steel*. Alfred Crosby fingered fascination with quantification as crucial in *The Measure of Reality*. David Landes celebrated inventiveness and championing of the market in *Wealth and Poverty of Nations*. Kenneth Pomeranz's *The Great Divergence* compared China and England and touted availability of British coal and American land as Western escape hatches from China's "normal" failure to move beyond handicrafts to industrialization.

Camilla Townsend raises new issues in analyzing two mercantile cities, Baltimore and Guayaquil. From 1820 to 1835, each city was prosperous but "declin[ing] relative to . . . expectations" (p. 16). But, Baltimore was more quickly shedding reliance on slavery, and only that city saw a quick transition to manufacturing. Townsend sifted through economic data as well as court records, diaries, and literary sketches, seeking to use insights from both structural economists and culture studies to reveal "the roots in human imagination of such institutions as coerced labor, credit networks, [or] military arms in the hands of a few" (p. 3) and their impact on economic development. She asks not about the work ethic but about "Who is expected to work for whom and why?" and "How is the 'right to a decent living' a contested idea having different meanings for different groups?"

Townsend compares elites, middling artisans, and professionals, and the poor of each city in three paired chapters. She finds no "Weberian dichotomies" concerning work. In each city, "laborers . . . worked hard; the middling ranks competed; the elites made fortunes proudly and planned a brave new world" (p. 235). But, Baltimore's upper and middle classes were more inclusive than Guayaquileños; more willing to tax themselves to pay for roads, piped-in water, and public education; and more willing to accept obligation to support the poor. There were limits: African Americans were barred from voting or marching in parades and were largely excluded from steppingstones to economic advancement such as apprenticeships or licenses to sell in the marketplace. But in Baltimore, proscribed blacks composed a fifth of the population; in Guayaquil, comparably situated *indios* were the majority. For Townsend then, the historical contingency of Spanish conquest and adaptation of preexisting tributary labor systems critically differentiated Guayaquileño economic culture. The Chesapeake certainly had developed chattel slavery, but as Townsend notes, many Baltimoreans were ex-Philadelphians, Germans, or Ulstermen not tied to slaveholder culture. So Baltimore was more open to economic development that relied on domestic demand driven by a relatively high-waged labor force. Such is the essence of Townsend's argument.

As with any comparative study, specialists will have their quibbles. Townsend is perhaps too optimistic about apprenticeship as an upward-leading path in Baltimore, for example. But overall, her scholarship is first-rate, and her methodology is evenhanded. Townsend makes plain her distaste for explanations of poverty that target insufficient integration between world systems and local economies, and her preference for highlighting relations among social groups within such economies. But, she does not skew the design of her study or abuse her evidence to justify her views.

Finally, Townsend blends her analysis with evocative storytelling that gives us not just the econometrics but also tales of aspiring merchants, earnest apprentices, and wide-eyed country people seeing a city for the first time. The result is a book at once intellectually provocative and pleasurable to read, which makes a valuable contribution to a vitally important economic and cultural question.

STEPHEN WHITMAN

Mt. St. Mary's College
Emmitsburg
Maryland

©1994 EDF
BUY RECYCLED.
AND SAVE.SM
Thanks to you, all sorts of everyday products are being made from materials you've recycled. But to keep recycling working to help the environment, you need to buy those products.
So look for products made from recycled materials, and buy them. It would mean the world to all of us. For a free brochure, please write *Buy Recycled*, Environmental Defense Fund, 257 Park Ave. South, New York, NY 10010, or call 1-800-CALL-EDF.
Ad Council
A Public Service of This Publication
EPA
ENVIRONMENTAL DEFENSE FUND
EDF
ORTEGA

STATEMENT OF OWNERSHIP, MANAGEMENT, AND CIRCULATION
P.S. Form 3526 Facsimile

1. TITLE: THE ANNALS OF THE AMERICAN ACADEMY OF POLITICAL AND SOCIAL SCIENCE
2. USPS PUB. #: 026-060

3. DATE OF FILING: October 1, 2001

4. FREQUENCY OF ISSUE: Bi-Monthly
5. NO. OF ISSUES ANNUALLY: 6
6. ANNUAL SUBSCRIPTION PRICE: Paper-Bound Institution $375; Cloth-Bound Institution $425; Paper-Bound Individual $65; Cloth-Bound Individual $100

7. PUBLISHER ADDRESS: 2455 Teller Road, Thousand Oaks, CA 91320
CONTACT PERSON: Mary Nugent, Circulation
TELEPHONE: (805) 499-0721

8. HEADQUARTERS ADDRESS: 2455 Teller Road, Thousand Oaks, CA 91320

9. PUBLISHER: Sara Miller McCune, 2979 Eucalyptus Hill Road, Montecito, CA 93108
EDITOR: Dr. Alan W. Heston, The American Academy of Political and Social Science, 3937 Chestnut Street, Philadelphia, PA 19104
MANAGING EDITOR: NONE

10. OWNER: The American Academy of Political and Social Science, 3937 Chestnut Street, Philadelphia, PA 19104

11. KNOWN BONDHOLDERS, ETC.
None

12. NONPROFIT PURPOSE, FUNCTION, STATUS:
Has Not Changed During Preceding 12 Months

13. PUBLICATION NAME: THE ANNALS OF THE AMERICAN ACADEMY OF POLITICAL AND SOCIAL SCIENCE

14. ISSUE FOR CIRCULATION DATA BELOW: SEPTEMBER 2001

15.	EXTENT & NATURE OF CIRCULATION:	AVG. NO. COPIES EACH ISSUE DURING PRECEDING 12 MONTHS	ACT. NO. COPIES OF SINGLE ISSUE PUB. NEAREST TO FILING DATE
A.	TOTAL NO. COPIES	3269	3270
B.	PAID CIRCULATION		
	1. PAID/REQUESTED OUTSIDE-CO, ETC	2041	2002
	2. PAID IN-COUNTY SUBSCRIPTIONS	0	0
	3. SALES THROUGH DEALERS, ETC.	403	406
	4. OTHER CLASSES MAILED USPS	21	25
C.	TOTAL PAID CIRCULATION	2465	2433
D.	FREE DISTRIBUTION BY MAIL		
	1. OUTSIDE-COUNTY AS ON 3541	18	24
	2. IN-COUNTY AS STATED ON 3541	0	0
	3. OTHER CLASSES MAILED USPS	0	0
E.	FREE DISTRIBUTION OTHER	0	0
F.	TOTAL FREE DISTRIBUTION	18	24
G.	TOTAL DISTRIBUTION	2483	2457
H.	COPIES NOT DISTRIBUTED		
	1. OFFICE USE, ETC.	786	813
	2. RETURN FROM NEWS AGENTS	0	0
I.	TOTAL	3269	3270
	PERCENT PAID CIRCULATION	99%	99%

16. NOT REQUIRED TO PUBLISH.

17. I CERTIFY THAT ALL INFORMATION FURNISHED ON THIS FORM IS TRUE AND COMPLETE. I UNDERSTAND THAT ANYONE WHO FURNISHES FALSE OR MISLEADING INFORMATION ON THIS FORM OR WHO OMITS MATERIAL OR INFORMATION REQUESTED ON THE FORM MAY BE SUBJECT TO CRIMINAL SANCTIONS (INCLUDING FINES AND IMPRISONMENT) AND/OR CIVIL SANCTIONS (INCLUDING MULTIPLE DAMAGES AND CIVIL PENALTIES).

Mary Nugent

Oct 1, 2001

Mary Nugent
Circulation Manager
Sage Publications, Inc.

Date